P9-DEO-886

Two Thumbs Up for  SCREENING SCRIPTURE

"This colorful collection contains some of the smartest writing on Bible and film that I have seen. Two thumbs up!"
  —Stephen D. Moore, author of *God's Gym* and *God's Beauty Parlor*

"The lively essays comprising *Screening Scripture* claim that certain films quote or translate the Christian scriptures in a different medium, interpreting and presenting biblical insights in vivid images. The essays use contemporary film, cultural criticism, and psychoanalytic theory to exhibit the profound, subtle, and skillful way the films discussed refer to scripture. The book represents the next stage of sophisticated studies of religion and film."
  —Margaret Miles, author of *Seeing and Believing: Religion and Values in the Movies*

"Scholars interested in religion and film—and the number, happily, seems to be expanding exponentially by the year—will find *Screening Scripture* a challenging invitation to a multi-faceted dialogue, where 'magic dwells.' Setting themselves apart from either the possessors of or searchers for universal truths, and thus supporting pluralism and a postmodern worldview, Aichele, Walsh, and their contributors propose four-way conversations between scriptural texts, films, critics and readers that seek, in the editors' words, 'to creative livable human space.' The diverse and rich selection of texts ranges from Genesis to Revelation, and *David and Bathsheba* to *End of Days*."
  —John R. May, Alumni Professor of English and Religious Studies at Louisiana State University, and the author of *Nourishing Faith Through Fiction*

"*Screening Scripture* provides a provocative viewing of how contemporary culture can re-awaken and re-interpret ancient scripture. From Arnold Schwarzenegger to St. Paul; *Midnight Cowboy* to the book of Ruth; *Sling Blade* to Jesus, this series of essays instigates an examination of the relationship between culture and religion. *Screening Scripture* boldly challenges the reader to view scripture through the interpretive lens of individual authors and of contemporary films."
  —Conrad Ostwalt, co-editor of *Screening the Sacred*

SCREENING SCRIPTURE

Intertextual Connections Between Scripture and Film

EDITED BY

GEORGE AICHELE AND RICHARD WALSH

TRINITY PRESS INTERNATIONAL
HARRISBURG, PENNSYLVANIA

Trinity Press International, P.O. Box 1321, Harrisburg, PA 17105

Trinity Press International is a division of The Morehouse Group.

Design: Corey Kent

Library of Congress Cataloging-in-Publication Data

Screening scripture : intertextual connections between scripture and film / edited by George Aichele and Richard Walsh.
    p. cm.
Includes bibliographical references and index.
    ISBN 1-56338-354-3 (alk. paper)
    1. Motion pictures—Religious aspects. I. Aichele, George. II. Walsh, Richard G.
    PN1995.5 .S35 2002
    791.43'682—dc21

                                                                2001008555

Printed in the United States of America

02 03 04 05 06 07   10 9 8 7 6 5 4 3 2 1

CONTENTS

103066

INTRODUCTION
Scripture as Precursor
George Aichele and Richard Walsh

The word "precursor" is indispensable to the vocabulary of criticism, but one must try to purify it from any connotation of polemic or rivalry. The fact is that each writer *creates* his precursors. His work modifies our conception of the past, as it will modify the future.[1]

MOVIES AND THE BIBLE

Readings from outside of the accredited guilds of biblical scholarship, including positions not identified with traditional Christianity or Judaism, or with any religious position, have offered rich insights into biblical texts. In addition, the claims of established methods of expert scholarly criticism to objective neutrality in the reading of the Bible have been shown to be ideological screens concealing theological interests of the scholars involved. All readers read from concrete social and material locations, and no reader has privileged access to some site of authoritative, univocal meaning, such as the mind of the text's author, the social context of the text's production, or even "what really happened." There is no proper or correct *exegesis* of any text. All readings are eisegeses,

---

1. Jorge Luis Borges, *Selected Non-Fictions*, ed. Eliot Weinberger, trans. Esther Allen (New York: Penguin, 1999), 365.

biased expressions of one ideology or another, and the conflict of readings is often a conflict of ideologies.[2]

With the advent of semiotically and ideologically critical approaches to biblical interpretation, increased awareness of the limitlessness of semiosis has opened the prospect of an indefinite range of readings of the Bible. New understanding of the mechanisms of myth and ideology result when biblical texts are brought into play with each other and with non-biblical texts, and with the inevitable and continual demands for cultural and historical recycling of the Scriptures. Texts that include language, themes, and images from the Bible appear in countless books, as well as in a wide variety of artistic works, including movies. Even popular commercial films of the type produced in Hollywood generate such rewritings. Given the mass production and mass orientation of these highly conventionalized movies—huge production costs require enormous ticket sales—one does not expect especially valuable insights from them. Nevertheless, sometimes we are pleasantly surprised.

The following essays both pursue and employ such serendipity. They "screen" scripture in a twofold sense. First, their authors read recent popular movies (for the most part) as rewriting the Scriptures in a different medium. In one way or another—and more or less explicitly—these movies actually "project" biblical texts on to the silver screen. Second, both the contributors to this book and the movies "screen" scripture in the sense of filtering the texts. They repeat the Scripture in a highly nuanced way. The movies themselves are not scriptures, but they project Scripture in a "new light," in terms of culture as well as in terms of medium. They "quote" the biblical text, translate it to a different narrative context, and give it the concreteness that cinema always does to written text. Some of these movies attempt to "reproduce" a biblical story (such as that of Moses, David, or Jesus) as such. Many others refer directly or indirectly to biblical texts in a fragmentary way and as part of some larger, nonbiblical story. Still other movies employ characters or themes based upon biblical prototypes (such as the various Christ-figure movies), and they rewrite those prototypes for a new culture.

In each case, the movie in question does not merely transfer the written, biblical text into the new medium without otherwise affecting it. The screening of Scripture is an act of translation; like every act of translation, it is profoundly ideological. As in the translation of any text,

---

2. See further George Aichele and Gary A. Phillips, "Exegesis, Eisegesis, Intergesis," *Semeia* 69/70 (1995): 7–18.

the movies transform the biblical materials in question, rewriting and recontextualizing them. Even the "same words" have different meaning in the new medium, just as they do in any new linguistic or cultural context.[3] Each of these cinematic texts offers a rewriting of the Bible that in turn implies a reading or interpretation of the biblical text. In other words, these contemporary rewritings of the Bible produce commentaries on the biblical stories and on the culture that produces and consumes both the Scripture and the movies.

The contributors to this book reject the notion that movies such as these simply restate Scripture or fail to do so properly. We do not expect moviemakers to be biblical scholars, but we do entertain the possibility that cinematic artistry may contribute to biblical scholarship. As a result, and unlike most books that bring together Scripture and film, *Screening Scripture* does not privilege the scriptural side of the conversation. The essays included here avoid that style or tone that asserts Scripture (or the biblical scholars' understanding of it) is right and that the film in question is wrong if it should differ on some particular issue, theme, character, plot, or story. Such a tone presumes, as we do not, that there is only one true understanding of the text. Instead, we seek to create a conversation between particular movies and particular scriptures. This endeavor requires "thick description" of both partners to the conversation, but we do not propose a definitive or final interpretation of either one. We want to bring the selected movies and biblical texts into a genuine exchange that will open up illuminating connections between them. We hope that these conversations will open new insights into ancient Scriptures while providing cross-cultural illumination of popular film and contemporary culture.

The result is not unlike the situation described in Jorge Luis Borges's story, "Kafka and His Precursors."[4] Borges remarks that although he began his study of Franz Kafka's precursors with assumptions about Kafka's uniqueness, he eventually "felt I could recognize his voice, or his habits, in the texts of various literatures and various ages."[5] Indeed, it is not clear whether Kafka had in fact read all of these precursors, such as

---

3. Borges's famous story (*Ficciones*, ed. Anthony Kerrigan [New York: Grove, 1962], 45–55) about Pierre Menard's "miraculous" word-for-word repetition of Cervantes nicely illustrates that the same words have different meanings in different times.

4. Borges, *Non-Fictions*, 363–65. Robert Funk used this story as the *leitmotiv* of an interesting book on *Jesus as Precursor* (Philadelphia: Fortress, 1975) of various literary figures, including Kafka.

5. Borges, *Non-Fictions*, 363.

Han Yu or Lord Dunsany; in any case, it is unimportant whether he did or not. The precursors are not necessarily sources of Kafka's writing. Indeed, the likenesses between these "heterogenous" pieces only become apparent when Borges reads them as though they were precursors of Kafka. The later texts provoke transformed readings of the earlier ones; they become precursors after the fact. As Larry Kreitzer has suggested in several books on the Bible and popular film, the "hermeneutical flow" is "reversed." If Borges, Kafka, or any writer "creates his precursors,"[6] they change future readings of the precursor texts—that is, these earlier texts must henceforth be read in the light of the successor texts. Likewise, each of the essays in this book testifies that its author has read a biblical text profoundly changed—rendered a precursor—by the movie's translation of that text. However, each of these readings is in turn embedded in the intertextual particularities that form it. The scripture in question may well be the movie's precursor only for the essayist and for those who read through the essayist's particular succession of precursors.

"IN COMPARISON A MAGIC DWELLS"[7]

Previous scholars have offered theoretical justifications for pairing biblical texts and film by claiming that both Scripture and film operate in mythic and ritualistic ways, or that they share religious functions or settings, or that they deal with important existential questions, or that they transmit important values, or that they resolve cultural tensions, or that they provide escape. Others aver that both Scripture and film are cultural artifacts or ideological tools and that proper analysis reveals much about the cultures or ideologies that produced these disparate entities. Still others observe that Scripture and film, although distinct as media, share certain common discourse and content features. After all, Scripture began as oral tradition while film represents the new orality of electronic media. Further, both biblical texts and films are "popular" products.

The essays in this book share no single theoretical justification for their existence. Some of them announce only their authors' personal interest in the texts involved. For these scholars, this means only that they enjoy the movies and scriptures that they have chosen to discuss. Other essays are more theoretically explicit: they reflect a variety of

---

6. Ibid., 365.
7. See Jonathan Z. Smith, *Imagining Religion: From Babylon to Jonestown* (Chicago: University of Chicago Press, 1982), 19–35.

deliberate literary- or culture-critical designs. However, here too subjective interest plays an important role. None of the contributors claims "pure knowledge" or "immaculate perception"[8] of the cinematic and biblical texts involved. They do not hide behind one true method, nor do they make surreptitious claims to universality. Instead, they deal with the historic, the concrete, and the particular. In the concrete, historical particularity of their readings of these texts, these essays bring specific movies and scriptural passages into conversation.

Previous examinations of Scripture and film have let pass almost unnoticed this particularity and, by so doing, have often hidden the third member of such conversations—namely, the scholar making the comparison. Such obfuscation may be rhetorically useful to those with aspirations to universal truths, but it is unacceptable to those seeking to understand particular conversations. For that aim, "screenings" of Scriptures, films, and even of the scholar-critics themselves are far more productive. After all, it is that often reticent, third member of the conversation who actually voices and indeed dominates the conversation. The "real" (material) justification for any connection between Scripture and film is the scholar whose specific experience and interpretative reading alone supplies the connection. Various scholars have recently begun to concentrate on the intertextual quality of texts; they have demonstrated that any reading of a text includes and interprets myriad other texts.[9] Any text, especially any reading of texts, cinematic or written, is an intertext. Furthermore, conjunctions of Scripture and film dramatically demonstrate that the scholar him- or herself also takes the form of an intertext. The strange collages of Scripture and film that appear in this book make sense because they belong to particular intertexts that inform speaking, reading scholars. There is no question of one such intertext being better or more correct than another, although some intertexts will inevitably be more interesting—more provocative—than others. Yet even this conclusion can only be reached by yet another reader and another reading.

This focus on the actual conversation, rather than on theory or Scripture or film as primary, suggests that the theoretical underpinning of this volume, insofar as there is one, is supplied by the minimal conviction

---

8. See Friedrich Nietzsche, *Thus Spake Zarathustra: A Book for Everyone and No One*, trans. R. J. Hollingdale (New York: Penguin, 1969), 144–47.

9. For example, Aichele and Phillips, "Exegesis," and indeed the entire contents of *Semeia* 69/70.

that the scholar, as well as the Scripture and film, is an intertextual construct. The focus on particular perspectives, rather than on universalizing theory, arises from an approval of pluralism and, hence, the general adoption of a postmodern worldview. The tone of this postmodern hermeneutic is wonderfully described by Jonathan Z. Smith's comment that "in comparison a magic dwells":[10]

> In the case of the study of religion, as in any disciplined inquiry, comparison, in its strongest form, brings differences together within the space of the scholar's mind for the scholar's own intellectual reasons. It is the scholar who makes their cohabitation— their "sameness"—possible, not "natural" affinities or processes of history. . . .
>
> That is to say, the statement of comparison is never dyadic, but always triadic; there is always an implicit "more than", and there is always a "with respect to". In the case of an academic comparison, the "with respect to" is most frequently the scholar's interest, be this expressed in a question, a theory, or a model— recalling, in the case of the latter, that a model is useful precisely when it is different from that to which it is being applied.[11]

That there are differences and incongruities between scholar, movie, and biblical text is precisely the point that makes the essays possible and interesting. As Wilhelm Dilthey observed, "Interpretation would be impossible if [past] expressions of life were completely strange. It would be unnecessary if nothing strange were in them. It lies, therefore, between these two extremes."[12]

Furthermore, although it may not be immediately clear, the contributors to this book are at work on something and in a way that Smith would consider "religious" or "mythic." For some time, Smith, in conscious disagreement with Mircea Eliade's view that religion arises from and creates experiences of sacred order, has been elaborating a view of religion rooted in the recognition of incongruity.[13] Where Eliade sees myth, for example, as a symbolic discourse about a cosmogony, Smith

---

10. Smith, *Imagining*, 19–35.
11. Jonathan Z. Smith, *Drudgery Divine: On the Comparison of Early Christianities and the Religions of Late Antiquity* (Chicago: University of Chicago Press, 1990), 51.
12. Quoted in Jonathan Z. Smith, *Map Is not Territory: Studies in the History of Religion* (Leiden: Brill, 1978), 242.
13. For a concise summary of Eliade's position, see his *The Sacred and the Profane: The Nature of Religion*, trans. Willard R. Trask (New York: Harcourt Brace & World, 1959). For

sees myth as a legal-exegetical discourse more like theodicy than cos-mogony.[14] Accordingly, for Smith, religion is one way that human beings construct worlds of meaning, a conscious quest "within the bounds of the human, historical condition, for the power to manipulate and negotiate ones [sic] 'situation' so as to have 'space' in which to meaningfully dwell."[15]

The following essays are "religious" in this Smithian sense. As they read cinematic and biblical texts, the contributors attempt to create livable human space. They do not attempt to inhabit orders transcendently delivered. They do not gesture at the traditionally transcendent (or sacred) so much as they delight in postmodern play or seek fantastic serendipities offering temporary respites from paramount cultural reali-ties.[16] If this is transcendence at all, it is the transcendence by way of "difference" that postmodern pluralism, with its multiple intersections of perspectives, offers—not some ideal rising above the fray of the his-torical and the particular. If this is to engage in mythology, it is never-theless not a myth that disguises cultural constructs as the "natural" or the "true."[17] Rather, these essays revel in something like the recent, witty insight of Bruce Lincoln that "scholarship is myth with footnotes."[18] That is to say, they differ from myth in pointing out the lineaments by which they are constructed and by calling others—you who read our texts—like ancient wisdom, "to try and see for themselves." In short, these essays are invitations to consider, to differ, and to converse. They succeed to the extent that they screen Scripture in new lights as they open up new conversations with new precursors.

THE ESSAYS, THE MOVIES, AND THE SCRIPTURES

The essays in this book represent a wide range of critical and hermeneu-tical approaches, both to the Bible and to films, and they refer to a wide range of biblical texts and movies. They also display varying interests in

---

Smith's, see his essay "Map is not Territory" in *Map*, 289–309. In a recent public lecture, Smith has now connected this insight with Borges's delightful short piece imagining cartographers making a map that is useless because it is the same size as the territory mapped. See Jorge Luis Borges, *Dreamtigers*, trans. Mildred Boyer and Harold Morland (Austin: University of Texas Press, 1964), 90.

14. Smith, *Map*, 299-300.

15. Ibid., 291.

16. Compare Stanley Cohen and Laurie Taylor, *Escape Attempts: The Theory and Practice of Resistance to Everyday Life*, 2nd ed. (London: Routledge, 1992).

17. For a critique of myth on this point, see Roland Barthes, *Mythologies*, trans. Annette Lavers (New York: Hill & Wang, 1972).

18. Bruce Lincoln, *Theorizing Myth: Narrative, Ideology, and Scholarship* (Chicago: University of Chicago Press, 1999), 209.

differences of nuance and performance on the part of the chosen cinematic and scriptural conversation partners. None of the essayists denies
that biblical texts and the cinema are strikingly disparate entities.
Scripture and film depend on different media, arise from different cultural
contexts, and have distinct social functions. Nonetheless, Scripture and
film interact with each other. They resonate in various ways and on various levels. This book explores and plays with some of those interactions.

The opening two essays focus on cinematic rewritings of the book of
Revelation. In "On Finding a Non-American Revelation," Richard Walsh
juxtaposes *End of Days* and the Book of Revelation. Popular American
interpretations of Revelation emphasize calculations of the end, sectarian
religion, and fantasies of revenge. Using *End of Days* as a lens, Walsh
reads Revelation alternatively and emphasizes the realized eschatology
of sectarian worship, a sectarian community rather than lone individuals,
and a renewed focus on Revelation's slain lamb. His alternative encourages
the abandonment of the use of Revelation as a simplistic endorsement
of either sadistic revenge or masochistic martyrdom. Tina Pippin juxtaposes various vampire films with the Book of Revelation in "Of Gods and
Demons: Blood Sacrifice and Eternal Life in *Dracula* and the Apocalypse
of John." Her reading investigates the similarity between the Dracula
tradition and the apocalyptic tradition—both in terms of "marks" and
boundaries and in terms of the life that comes through "drinking blood."
She finds the Other—demonized or desired—and sacrificial imagery so
intimately linked that "our Draculas" tell us as much about ourselves as
do our heroes or our gods.

The next three articles focus on socio-cultural dimensions of cinematic citations of Scripture. Neal McCrillis compares various biblical
passages (notably Genesis 3 and Job 41) with *The Giant Behemoth* and
other radiation-induced monster films from the 1950s. His combination
highlights similar treatments of the blessings and dangers of "unlimited"
power. In particular, he demonstrates how filmmakers have used various
biblical concepts, like the fall and behemoth, to value and situate modern
science and nuclear technology. In "Alienation, Sex, and an Unsatisfactory
Ending: Themes and Features of Stories Old and New," Ralph J Brabban
conjoins *Midnight Cowboy* and the Book of Ruth. Ignoring explicit references to Jesus and his teaching in the film, Brabban connects the film
more creatively with Ruth. His analysis reveals a similar treatment of
sex, alienation, and sadness in both sources and results in an ambiguously "sexual" reading of Ruth. Jennifer Rohrer-Walsh combines *The
Prince of Egypt*, Exodus 1–20, and various children's genres—notably

coming of age stories—in "Coming-of-Age in *The Prince of Egypt.*" While her analysis demonstrates common "coming of age" elements in both stories, she finds them different modulations of the genre. What Exodus 1–20 treats as Israel's coming of age, Stephen Spielberg's film treats as an individual's (Moses) coming-of-age. Rohrer-Walsh traces the variances to different cultural locations and to differing purposes.

Transformations of reality, both metaphysical and psychoanalytic, dominate the next two essays. In "Sitcom Mythology," George Aichele draws on Benjamin, Calvino, and Tolkien to explore the rewriting of the biblical stories of Eden and the Flood in *Pleasantville.* Transfers and exchanges between various "levels of reality" in the movie center around and eventually collapse due to an inversion of the film's biblical precursors. In a trajectory that runs from *Total Recall* and the fiction of Philip K. Dick through the theories of Lacan, Ronald Boer arrives at a reading of Paul's writings as psychotic. In "Non-Sense: *Total Recall,* Paul, and the Possibility of Psychosis," Boer compares Paul's "religious," visionary experiences with those of modern psychotics like Daniel Schreber and Philip Dick. For Boer, Paul is a psychotic; more importantly, the very possibility of psychosis in subsequent Western culture is grounded in the religious language of Paul.

The following two articles focus on matters of gender and sexuality in relation to texts from the Hebrew Bible. In "Gazing at Impotence in Henry King's *David and Bathsheba,*" Julie Kelso connects the story of David and Bathsheba with Henry King's 1951 film of the same name. The combination allows Kelso to point to certain male-in-crisis patterns in the Bible—particularly David's identity crisis vis-à-vis his divine election—and the film that allow female protagonists increased presence and control. She challenges perceptions that the fixed, monolithic, male gaze is the ideal position from which to view the film. In fact, in the film, Bathsheba's gaze helps identify David. In "Why Girls Cry," Erin Runions reads Ezekiel 16 and Kimberly Pierce's film, *Boys Don't Cry,* alongside Judith Butler's argument in *The Psychic Life of Power* that gender is the function of melancholia produced by ungrieved homosexual cathexis. Both film and text depict disturbing, extended, and perhaps titillating sexual violence as punishment for improperly performed gender and as the result of overblown male jealousies over heterosexual love objects. Runions finds similar themes of male jealousy and sexual violence as a punishment for sexual crimes in both, but her reading also reveals that Ezekiel 16 is less predictable and thus provides a way into a more nuanced critique of the film and of the text.

The final four contributions address aspects of the narrative figure of Jesus. In "Meeting Patch Again for the First Time," Jeffrey Staley critically conjoins *Patch Adams* and the Gospel of Mark and thereby highlights the dangers involved in transgressing purity boundaries even for compassionate purposes. Staley's comparison leads to a critique, not of the film or of the Gospel, but of Marcus Borg's compassionate Jesus who challenges purity with impunity. Carl Dyke compares *The Life of Brian* with traditional readings of the Gospels in "Learning from *The Life of Brian*: Saviors for Seminars." While he finds the Monty Python film a richly imaginative reconstruction of the historical life world of Jesus and the Gospels, Dyke's focus is on various readings of and uses of *The Life of Brian* for Christian, confrontational, and ultimately "counterhegemonic" purposes. Taking an autobiographical approach, he demonstrates the difficulty of deviating successfully from a culture still dominated by Christianity and accordingly demonstrates as well the potentially conservative effect of *The Life of Brian*.

In "The Characterization of Martin Riggs in *Lethal Weapon 1*," Fred Burnett connects *Lethal Weapon* with the New Testament's portrayal of Jesus Christ to depict elements in the ideology and mythology of Western hero/savior figures. Reading through the lens of Martin Riggs, Burnett discovers that a "death wish," or a coming to terms with nihilism, is a common element in Camus' absurd hero, Nietzsche's *Übermensch*, and in the Gospel's Jesus. In "Paradoxical Protagonists: *Sling Blade*'s Karl and Jesus Christ," Mark Roncace compares *Sling Blade* and Matthew 25:31–46. In the movie's discomforting hero, Karl, Roncace sees a paradoxical figure, both victim and avenger. While many critics like to restrict their Christ-image to one side of that paradox, Roncace presses home the point that the New Testament includes images of Jesus Christ as both victim and avenger. In fact, Roncace finds both in the parable of the sheep and the goats by identifying Jesus Christ with both the "least"—that is, the victims—and the judge of that story.

1. ON FINDING A NON-AMERICAN REVELATION
End of Days and the Book of Revelation
Richard Walsh

Despite the prevailing opinion, the Branch Davidians were well integrated into the American myth. William Miller and David Koresh after him drew directly from the Puritan style of biblical interpretation. They believed the Bible not only explained history but revealed many things about the future, including when Christ would return. This sect of the Seventh-Day Adventists had not sought to modernize its parent denomination, but to restore it to the past: to a time when people lived out their Bible, when prophets received revelations, explained the mysteries of God, and anticipated the return of Christ with great expectation.[1]

AN AMERICAN REVELATION

The Puritans and the Branch Davidians so vigorously sought to restore the past that they elided all historical distinctions between a chosen scriptural past and their present. To do so, they employed a typological reading strategy:

---

1. David Saul, "Children of the American Myth: David Koresh, the Branch Davidians, and the American Bible," *The Bible and the American Myth: A Symposium on the Bible and Constructions of Meaning*, ed. Vincent L. Wimbush (Macon, Ga.: Mercer University Press, 1997), 151.

> In this conception, an occurrence on earth signifies not only itself
> but at the same time another, which it predicts or confirms, with-
> out prejudice to the power of its concrete reality here and now.
> The connection between occurrences is not regarded as primarily
> a chronological or causal development but as a oneness within
> the divine plan, of which all occurrences are parts and reflections.
> Their direct earthly connection is of secondary importance, and
> often their interpretation can altogether dispense with any
> knowledge of it.[2]

Typology enabled them to forego their historical peculiarities and to live
in an eternal divine present that does not distinguish past, present, and
future. Thus, the Puritans interpreted the move from Europe to America
as a new exodus establishing a new Israel. Martin Luther King Jr. read
the status of blacks in the American South as another Egyptian captivity
and accordingly asserted, "Let my people go." The Branch Davidians
and others have seen themselves as the suffering, soon-to-be-delivered
martyrs of Revelation.

Such interpretations construe the Bible as an oracle[3] for which history is relatively unimportant.[4] The present—not past—text provides
divine insight into the present and future. Revelation figures prominently in such divination for the obvious reason that its content, more
than any other biblical book, deals with the future.

Apocalyptic seers from Daniel to Joachim of Fiore have used visions
and texts to calculate the end—using typology to read forward as well as
backward in light of the eternal divine present—but recent American
interpretations of Revelation have reemphasized this use of Revelation.
In the 1970s (and on into the 1980s), Hal Lindsey, for example, pre-
dicted the imminent end by pairing a reading of Revelation and other
"prophecies" with his observation that it had been roughly a generation
since the founding of the modern state of Israel.[5] More recently, the
"turn" of the millenium (although calculated incorrectly) generated

---

2. Erich Auerbach, *Mimesis: The Representation of Reality in Western Literature*, trans.
Willard R. Trask (Princeton: Princeton University Press, 1968), 555.

3. Compare Burton L. Mack, *Who Wrote the New Testament? The Making of the Christian
Myth* (San Francisco: Polebridge, 1995), 293–300.

4. Compare Northrop Frye, *The Great Code* (New York: Harcourt Brace Jovanovich, 1982),
78–83; Michael Drosnin, *The Bible Code* (New York: Simon & Schuster, 1997).

5. Hal Lindsey, *The Late Great Planet Earth* (Grand Rapids: Zondervan, 1970).

another even more popular spate of end-of-days calculations (e.g., in the movies *End of Days* and *Left Behind*).[6]

Revelation is deeply embedded in American culture for another reason, as well. One can use Revelation to harmonize tensions in the American myth. In such a reading, Revelation functions as a "myth" in Lévi-Straussian terms. It becomes a means to harmonize binary oppositions in the culture.[7] Thus, Americans often use Revelation to deal with the dissonance created when the American sense of cultural uniqueness and superiority—for example, the Puritan mandate to make their colony "a city set on a hill"—meets the inevitable frustrations of history—for example, the effect of Vietnam.

Two different readings of Revelation—an imperialist and a sectarian variant—struggle with this dissonance. Robert Jewett has dubbed the imperialist reading "the Captain America Complex":

> Jesus' message was interpreted by posterity in the light of Deuteronomy, of Daniel, and, worst of all, of Revelation . . . throughout much of the course of the American experience in particular, it was the book of Revelation that placed its stamp upon the whole Bible. . . . the book of Revelation provided the mythic framework for the mission of the nation. The materials were there ready and waiting for the development of the Captain America Complex.[8]

"Captain America" reprises the Puritans' "city set on a hill." According to Jewett, Revelation so read provides America with a triumphal, militant national self-understanding. Typologically, America becomes Revelation's militant messiah, the rider on the white horse. Such readings endorse the American empire's "innocent" use of force against various others.

---

6. Movies calculating the end do not, of course, have to interpret Revelation. Despite their wealth and power, Americans are insecure about the future in light of uncertainties about modernization, about mechanization and computers, about nuclear weapons, and about ecology. The calculable end provides catharsis for fears by naming and localizing the anxieties faced and by imagining successful denouements. Compare Bernard Brandon Scott, *Hollywood Dreams and Biblical Stories* (Minneapolis: Fortress, 1994), 193–217; Conrad E. Ostwalt Jr., "Hollywood and Armageddon: Apocalyptic Themes in Recent Cinematic Presentation," *Screening the Sacred: Religion, Myth, and Ideology in Popular American Film*, ed. Joel W. Martin and Conrad E. Ostwalt Jr. (Boulder, Colo.: Westview, 1995), 55–63.

7. See Claude Lévi-Strauss, *The Naked Man*, trans. John and Doreen Weightman (New York: Harper & Row, 1981), 625–91. Compare Bernard Brandon Scott, *Hollywood Dreams*, for an application of Lévi-Strauss's understanding of myth to Hollywood movies.

8. Robert Jewett, *The Captain America Complex*, 2nd ed. (Santa Fe: Bear, 1984), 22, 24.

This triumphant "Captain America" appears repeatedly in various popular media. According to Jewett and Lawrence, this hero story occurs so often that it deserves to be considered the American mono-myth: "A community in a harmonious paradise is threatened by evil: normal institutions fail to contend with this threat: a selfless superhero emerges to renounce temptations and carry out the redemptive task: aided by fate, his decisive victory restores the community to its paradisal condition: the superhero then recedes into obscurity."[9]

Movies like *Shane* (as well as *Cool-Hand Luke, One Flew Over the Cuckoo's Nest,* and *The Matrix*) incarnate this monomyth. While this monomyth resembles Joseph Campbell's more famous monomyth, it also differs importantly from it: "A hero ventures forth from the world of common day into a region of supernatural wonder: fabulous forces are there encountered and a decisive victory is won: the hero comes back from this mysterious adventure with the power to bestow boons on his fellow man."[10] Campbell parses tales about social initiations in which the community (at the tale's beginning and end) remains stable. The hero—one undergoing a lifecycle transformation—ventures off, changes, and returns to the community. By contrast, Jewett and Lawrence deal with changeable communities saved through the violence of "visiting" heroes.

Critics often refer to these heroic, violent strangers as "Christ-figures."[11] If so, they are filtered through Revelation's triumphal warrior. They bear little resemblance to the crucified Jesus of the canonical Gospels (although the Jesus of John is a "visiting stranger," as is the Jesus of Thomas). The "Captain Americas" and Revelation's warrior impose suf-fering; they do not suffer.

Americans not in imperial power or seeing themselves as unjust vic-tims read Revelation differently. Their sectarian variant does not justify a present, imperialist self-identity. Instead, it provides a compensatory fantasy dealing with frustrations by externalizing evil. Nefarious, mysteri-ous forces, not the embattled sect, are responsible for lost Eden. Fortunately, God will soon provide these evil forces their comeuppance, and the sect will arrive at the Eden that is their God-given right.

---

9. Robert Jewett and John Shelton Lawrence, *The American Monomyth* (Garden City: Anchor Press, 1977), xx.

10. Joseph Campbell, *The Hero with a Thousand Faces* (Princeton: Princeton University Press, 1972), 30.

11. Compare Lloyd Baugh, *Imaging the Divine: Jesus and Christ-Figures in Film* (Kansas City: Sheed & Ward, 1997), 157–71.

Recent millennial groups like the Branch Davidians are not the only ones who read Revelation in such a way. The sectarian variant occurs almost as often as some American group sees itself as the pure elect in a sea of corruption. Examples include the producers and consumers of the nineteenth-century pre-millennial Bible conferences, the dispensationalism popularized in the American heartland by the *Scofield Bible*, the extraordinarily popular *Late Great Planet Earth*, and the *Left Behind* series of novels (the first in the series is now a movie in its own right).

Even imperialistic "Captain Americas" have strong tendencies toward this sectarian reading. After all, American identity was forged in revolution[12] and in notions of the separation of church and state. For Americans, then, there can be no "church," no state-founded and supported religious institution. Rather, there can be only sects, although Americans refer to well-established sects as denominations and to those they question as cults.

Individualism further exacerbates this American sectarianism. According to Bellah et al., Americans so emphasize individualism that they lack a language to articulate social responsibilities.[13] Similarly, Bloom sees American religion as an intensely personal, virtually Gnostic, religion of the self:

> The American finds God in herself or himself, but only after finding the freedom to know God by experiencing a total inward solitude. . . . In perfect solitude, the American spirit learns again its absolute isolation as a spark of God floating in a sea of space. . . .
>
> Salvation, for the American, cannot come through the community or the congregation, but is a one-on-one act of confrontation.[14]

Individuals are the ultimate sects. Historically and mythically, then, the American empire is in its own self-understanding, no matter how paradoxical it may sound, a sectarian empire. Accordingly, the American

---

12. Compare James Oliver Robertson, *American Myth, American Reality* (New York: Hill & Wang, 1980); Bruce Babbington and Peter William Evans, *Biblical Epics: Sacred Narrative in Hollywood Cinema* (Manchester & New York: Manchester University Press, 1993).

13. Robert N Bellah et al., *Habits of the Heart: Individualism and Commitment in American Life* (Berkeley: University of California Press, 1985).

14. Harold Bloom, *American Religion: The Emergence of the Post-Christian Nation* (New York: Simon & Schuster, 1992), 32. While Bloom, 260–65, realizes crucial differences between ancient Gnosticism and American religion, his comparison highlights the American religious focus on the self and on salvific knowledge. American religion does not, like ancient Gnosticism, eschew the world or the body; nor is it an elitist movement.

Jesus is the ultimate loner—without father or mother—standing alone against inevitably "corporate" forces of corruption. This is the Christ for both sectarian groups and for "Captain America" imperialists.[15]

Embedded in American culture, Revelation has acquired a dominant popular reading stretching from the Puritans through popular religion and media to the Branch Davidians. Three themes dominate this American reading of Revelation: (1) the calculable end; (2) sectarianism; and (3) fantasies of innocent revenge. The question is whether one can read Revelation in another, less American way.[16] This essay proposes such a reading by placing Revelation in dialogue with the recent Hollywood apocalypse, *End of Days*.

READING *END OF DAYS*

End of Days is a 1999 Peter Hyams film in which Satan escapes from hell on the eve of the millennium to inaugurate a demonic kingdom upon earth. To do so, he takes over a human body (Gabriel Byrne) to impregnate his bride-elect, Christine (Robin Tunney), and thereby sire the antichrist. The Vatican, with advance knowledge of this dilemma through occult scriptures and astrology, divides into two competing groups: one led by the Pope, which struggles to find and protect Christine from Satan; and one led by a renegade cardinal, which decides to protect humanity from Satan by assassinating Christine. Jericho Cane (Arnold Schwarzenegger), a suicidal, washed-out ex-cop, overcomes his own demons to play Christine's messiah. A wisecracking buddy (Kevin Pollock) and reluctant mentor (Rod Steiger) assist him.

The movie's characters are the standard Hollywood adventure cast: hero, buddy, damsel in distress, villain (with numerous powerful associates), and older mentor figure. These characters develop along ethical paths similar to those in the Hollywood classic *The Wizard of Oz*.

---

15. Even the non-apocalyptic Jesus of some recent American scholars is a counter-cultural figure. See Marcus Borg, *Jesus: A New Vision* (San Francisco: Harper & Row, 1985); Burton L. Mack, *A Myth of Innocence: Mark and Christian Origins* (Philadelphia: Fortress, 1988); and John Dominic Crossan, *The Historical Jesus: The Life of a Mediterranean Peasant* (San Francisco: HarperSanFrancisco, 1991). This scholarly reconstruction of Jesus, replacing somewhat the apocalyptic Jesus who had dominated scholarship since Schweitzer, is, if anything, an even more American figure, because he is more sectarian than the apocalyptic Jesus.

16. The academy has often dissented from this popular, typological reading through its use of historical criticism, a method that locates the context for Revelation's meaning in the past, rather than in an American present. Such a hermeneutic is closer to science's historical causation than to typology's teleological thrust. Compare Frye, *Code*, 78–83.

Christine learns courage and Bobby learns loyalty. The central development, however, is Jericho's move from anger to faith.

The undeveloped character is Satan, who is little more than a "horny adolescent." This weak depiction does little justice to the banality (contrast *Apt Pupil; Heart of Darkness; Dogma*), seductiveness (contrast *Indecent Proposal; The Devil's Advocate; A Simple Plan*), and monstrousness (contrast *Alien; Independence Day*) of evil. Other movies (noted in the parentheses above) illustrate these themes better. Not surprisingly, then, one critic responds to the depiction of Satan here by saying, "Come back, John Milton; all is forgiven."[17]

Generically, the movie is late and derivative. If it is typical Schwarzenegger action fare—and Schwarzenegger reportedly wished to make a big-budget, big-action film to announce his return from heart surgery—it is hardly first-flight Schwarzenegger. *Conan the Barbarian, Terminator, Total Recall,* and *True Lies* are arguably better action films.[18] If it is religious horror, it does not compare favorably with *Dracula, The Exorcist,* or *Stigmata*. If it is a Satan-siring-a-baby film, it does not advance beyond *Rosemary's Baby* or *The Omen*. If it is a religiously conceived end-of-days film, *The Seventh Sign* has been there before.

In fact, the movie cadges together elements from various previous movies of disparate genres. Steve Schneider, for example, describes it as *Rosemary's Baby* with heavy artillery.[19] The amalgam leaves many viewers confused or amused. What seems an action movie suddenly turns intensely religious. Jericho Cane ceases to be an action hero and converts to a prayerful believer. So transformed, Jericho moves away from the typical American Christ-figure of the monomyth toward the less familiar, violence-eschewing Jesus of the Gospels and of some Hollywood Jesus movies (e.g., *The King of Kings, King of Kings, The Greatest Story Ever Told*). Unlike those Jesuses, however, Jericho does not rise again, an absence that intensifies his characterization as victim. Jericho is not the triumphant hero of action movies.

---

17. Steve Schneider, "Full Devil Jackass" [cited 13 November 13, 2000]; from http://orlandoweekly.com/movies/review.asp?movie=521.This page is no longer available.

18. Few critics found the movie successful as a big-screen action film. Peter Hyams has directed numerous films: *End of Days* (1999); *The Relic* (1997); *Sudden Death* (1995); *Timecop* (1994); *Stay Tuned* (1992); *Narrow Margin* (1990); *The Presidio* (1988); *Amazing Stories—Book Three* (1987); *Running Scared* (1986); 2010: *The Year We Make Contact* (1984); *The Star Chamber* (1983); *Outland* (1981); *Hanover Street* (1979); *Capricorn One* (1978); *Busting* (1974); and *Our Time* (1974). Despite a move toward "horror" in the two most recent films, the defining characteristic of most is the typically (sectarian) American paranoia pitting the individual against some corrupt evil group.

19. "Full Devil Jackass."

Neither is *End of Days* a clear example of Hollywood apocalyptic. As Ostwalt notes, Hollywood apocalypses differ from ancient apocalypses by replacing a supernatural apocalypse with a catastrophe initiated and potentially avoided by humans.[20] In *End of Days*, the catastrophe is supernaturally engendered (though demonic, rather than divine), but the salvation is mundane. While Jericho's faith resolves the plot religiously, Jericho is merely human, no matter how heroic. He is not the supernatural messiah of ancient apocalyptic.

This pattern—supernatural dilemma and heroic human resolution—is more typical of Hollywood's religious horror films. Obvious examples include *Rosemary's Baby, The Exorcist, The Omen, The Seventh Sign,* and *Stigmata.* In each case (with the possible exception of the last), concerted, heroic (often religiously advised) human action overcomes supernatural evil. A central theme of *End of Days*—the human struggle with supernatural evil—locates the movie within this genre. The action and the apocalyptic motifs are less central and confuse both audiences and critical readings of the movie.

Until recently,[21] most Hollywood treatments of the supernatural have dealt with the demonic. According to John May, the Hollywood tendency to depict the supernatural in terms of evil, rather than in terms of the benevolent Western God, is consistent with the American cultural and artistic tradition:

> The reason why Hollywood . . . never asks the God question "in so many words" . . . the way some outstanding European directors like Fellini, Bergman, Buñuel, and Rohmer have is surely this: It is more in the American cultural tradition (formed by Hawthorne, Melville, and Twain) to raise the "demonic"question, and this is precisely what American cinema at its recent best has been doing—subverting the facile optimism of the American dream by revealing the evil within us and our institutions.[22]

---

20. "Hollywood and Armageddon," 55-63. Compare B. B. Scott, *Hollywood Dreams,* 193–217.

21. Since May's article, some movies—e.g., *Powder; Grand Canyon; Michael*—have portrayed a non-demonic supernatural. Each depicts the supernatural vaguely enough to be at home both in recent religious pluralism and for the popular religion of most eras.

22. John R May, "The Demonic in American Cinema," *Religion in Film,* ed. John R. May and Michael Bird (Knoxville: University of Tennessee Press, 1981), 80–81. The sacred is not easily portrayed in film. One might trace the failure to portray Jesus adequately in film at least partially to this difficulty.

May isolates three different depictions of the demonic in the American cultural tradition: (1) as externalized persona (e.g., *The Exorcist*; *The Omen*; and *Jaws*); (2) as secular confidence man, seen metaphorically as an end-time loosing of Satan (e.g., Melville, *The Confidence-Man*; Twain, *The Mysterious Stranger*; *The Godfather*; *Mean Streets*; *Easy Rider*; *Midnight Cowboy*; and *Doctor Strangelove*); and (3) as internalized evil, the evil within each human heart (Flannery O'Connor's works; *The Rain People*; *Alice's Restaurant*; *Shampoo*; and *Scarecrow*). May sees the last two depictions as sophisticated artistically and theologically because they suggest that evil transcends human culpability and resolution.[23]

End of Days presents an actual end-time loosing of Satan that blends May's depictions one and two. Nevertheless, despite this externalization of evil, the movie devotes most of its time to a presentation and refutation of depiction three. Jericho conquers the demons within, his anger. Much of the movie's dialogue sketches this transformation, which comes about through the influence of Jericho's priest mentor (Steiger), the negative example of Satan and his anger against God, and Jericho's contemplation of the church's religious iconography.[24]

Jericho's temptation is the movie's crucial dialogue scene. Surprising Jericho in his apartment, Satan offers to restore Jericho's murdered wife and child if Jericho will betray Christine's location. When Jericho rejects Satan's proffered "dream" family, Satan reminds Jericho of the "painfulness" of reality by replaying the murder of his wife and child. Claiming that God failed to support Jericho in his hour of need, Satan flatteringly compares Jericho to himself, for both have left God out of anger. Satan contends that God's reputation depends on "that overblown press kit they call the Bible"[25] and offers Jericho a ground-floor position in the new end-of-days management. When Jericho resists these temptations, Satan turns first to force and then to guile to discover Christine's hiding place.

Thereafter, Jericho's anger provides the movie's leitmotiv. Taking Christine from the church, Satan has Jericho crucified but not killed, so that Jericho will give in to his anger and see Satan's triumph. When

---

23. Ibid., 81–100.

24. Clearly, this development is the film's thematic core and primary "intellectual" concern. Karen Butler ("In *End of Days*, Satan Thwarted by Faith, Not Guns" [cited 13 November 2000]; available from http://www.apbnews.com/media/celebnews/1999/11/24/end1124_01.html?s=daily) notes that Schwarzenegger has opined that on the eve of the millennium "he was compelled to do a film in which he wasn't playing a perfect hero who would 'kick some butt over here and wipe up the enemy. That worked in the 1980s and the early 1990s. That doesn't work any more.'"

25. Quotations from the film are my own transcription.

Jericho recovers, he arms himself and enters Satan's temple-theater undeterred because Satan's henchmen recognize the anger in Jericho's heart. Inside, Jericho resorts to violence to rescue Christine and take her to the church. Violence and anger get the duo to the church on time.

In the climax, however, Jericho abandons his anger. In the last ten minutes of the millennium, Satan, as a monstrous, ghostly dragon, pursues the duo into the church. Contemplating the church's religious iconography depicting Michael with his sword (cf. Revelation 12:7) and Christ crucified, Jericho eschews guns for prayer. Undeterred, Satan destroys the church and takes over Jericho's body. Throwing Christine onto the altar, Satan-Jericho taunts Christ crucified by telling him that he died for nothing. Jericho looks back and forth between Michael's sword and Christ crucified as Christine begs Jericho to resist Satan. Finally, Jericho throws himself on the sword, Satan is sucked back into hell, and Jericho dies smilingly with a vision of his wife and daughter.

Roughly the last half of the movie, then, deals with Jericho's transformation. Other movies have sketched the move away from an external to an internal depiction of evil more convincingly. For example, the first release (*Star Wars*) of the original *Star Wars* trilogy externalizes evil in the empire and in Darth Vader. By the third release, *The Return of the Jedi*, however, Luke learns that he cannot defeat evil through violence. Instead, à la Jung, he must embrace the evil within himself to conquer. While three films trace the development more easily than one, *Seven* demonstrates that one can make this move in one film. Artistically, *End of Days* is simply not up to *Seven*'s standards. It is not merely that *Seven* has better acting and directing (which it does), or that it has a better text to build upon (which it does; Dante rather than Revelation), but that it treats evil more effectively. Both the external monstrous evil (the character played by Kevin Spacey) and the internal evil (the capitulation to anger by the character played by Brad Pitt) are more realistic and more thoughtful than their counterparts in *End of Days*.

The comparatively shallow treatment of evil in *End of Days* is a corollary of its heavy-handed symbolism. For example, Jericho Cane's initials and the name Christine for the damsel in distress are too blatant. Allusions to certain famous passages in the book of Revelation are equally obvious:

> When the thousand years are ended, Satan will be released from his prison and will come out to deceive the nations at the four corners

of the earth, Gog and Magog, in order to gather them for battle. (Revelation 20:7–8)[26]

A great portent appeared in heaven: a woman clothed with the sun, with the moon under her feet, and on her head a crown of twelve stars. She was pregnant and was crying out in birth pangs, in the agony of giving birth. Then another portent appeared in heaven: a great red dragon, with seven heads and ten horns, and seven diadems on his heads. His tail swept down a third of the stars of heaven and threw them to the earth. Then the dragon stood before the woman who was about to bear a child, so that he might devour her child as soon as it was born. And she gave birth to a son, a male child, who is to rule all the nations with a rod of iron. But her child was snatched away and taken to God. . . . And war broke out in heaven; Michael and his angels fought against the dragon. The dragon and his angels . . . were defeated, and there was no longer any place for them in heaven. The great dragon was thrown down, that ancient serpent, who is called the Devil and Satan, the deceiver of the whole world. (Revelation 12:1–9)

The first passage provides the film's setting—the end-time release of Satan. The second provides the plot—Satan's pursuit of a woman. In keeping with Hollywood conventions, the film transforms this setting and plot in two important ways. First, the primary characters are mortals, not heavenly portents. Even Satan assumes human form for the movie's plot. Second, the movie's Satan does not plan a war on heaven nor seek to destroy the heavenly woman's child. Instead, he seeks to beget a child through the pursued damsel in distress. The result is an erotic, inverted (or demonic) reading of Revelation 12.

The sexual aspect and the damsel in distress add the romantic element that Hollywood favors. This "sexual" notion of evil may reflect, as well, the influence of Puritan and Victorian ethics on American morality. To be "bad" in America means to act out sexually; mere violence is never enough. By contrast, sex does not enter into the Gospel depiction of Jesus' temptation (cf. Matthew 4:1–11; Luke 4:1–13). In Milton's version of this temptation, a demonic council suggests sexual temptations,

---

26. All biblical quotations are from the New Revised Standard Version.

but Satan favors temptations "with manlier objects . . . such as have more show/Of worth, of honour, glory, and popular praise/Rocks whereon greatest men have oftest wreck'd . . ."[27] For Hollywood, however, sex is essential.

While the movie makes no blatant reference to it, another passage from Revelation provides important clues to the movie's deeper action:

> Then I saw between the throne and the four living creatures and among the elders a Lamb standing as if it had been slaughtered, having seven horns and seven eyes, which are the seven spirits of God sent out into all the earth. He went and took the scroll from the right hand of the one who was seated on the throne. When he had taken the scroll, the four living creatures and the twenty-four elders fell before the Lamb, each holding a harp and golden bowls full of incense, which are the prayers of the saints. They sing a new song: "You are worthy to take the scroll and to open its seals, for you were slaughtered and by your blood you ransomed for God saints from every tribe and language and people and nation; you have made them to be a kingdom and priests serving our God, and they will reign on earth." (Revelation 5:6–10)

In Revelation's opening heavenly throne vision (Revelation 4–5), God holds a sealed scroll that only the "lamb" is "worthy" to open. The lamb is worthy to open the scroll of divine judgments (Revelation 6:1–8:5) because he, too, has been a victim. Thereafter, this lamb gives way to a more conventional military figure, a sword-bearing warrior on a white horse (Revelation 19:11–16). Of course, the lamb does return in the wake of the warrior in Revelation 21–22.

Here again, *End of Days* inverts Revelation. While Revelation moves from suffering to (redemptive) violence, the movie moves from violence (guns) to faith. This transformation occurs not at Jericho's rather gratuitous crucifixion scene (more heavy-handed symbolism), but when Jericho eschews guns and his demonic anger for prayerful faith. He makes this move by turning from the armed Michael to the crucified Christ, to an alignment with Revelation's lamb rather than with Revelation's warrior. That is, *End of Days* takes the focus off the rider on the white horse (or armed Michael) and recalls the suffering lamb that

---

27. John Milton, *Paradise Lost and Paradise Regained* (New York: Signet Classic, 1982), 2.225–28.

is Revelation's generative core. In this regard, *End of Days* improves Revelation because it refuses to externalize evil to the extent that Revelation does.

Placing *End of Days* alongside Revelation, then, exposes the anger and resentment at the heart of Revelation. Revelation never manages to reflect at length on internal evil (though see Revelation 2–3) because it identifies its producers and consumers as righteous martyrs like the suffering lamb. Apparently, Revelation's ancient Christian author could not seriously imagine the lamb having an internal struggle with personal demons.[28]

Other inversions of Revelation by *End of Days* are less salutary. Revelation envisions the present evil age divinely interrupted and replaced by a new divine age and kingdom. By contrast, *End of Days* envisions a demonic interruption, ruining an American present and ushering in a kingdom of evil. *End of Days* is comfortable with the American present and wishes to preserve it against a monstrous foe (a pattern reminiscent of Cold War horror and science fiction movies). Jericho's death is not the apocalyptic-engendering death of the hero of Mark or of the martyr heroes (including the lamb) of Revelation. Jericho's death restores normal life. This death is far more like the deaths of various ancient fertility gods that restored the new, fertile year, than the deaths of the righteous martyrs of apocalyptic. Appropriately, then, *End of Days* ends with a new year's celebration.

AN AMERICAN REVELATION?

These reflections note the American cultural location of *End of Days*. The movie provides an American reading of Revelation. To what extent, then, does *End of Days* emphasize the calculable end, sectarian religion, and fantasy of revenge characteristic of popular American readings of Revelation?

The movie clearly plays upon calculations of the end. The movie's opening provides deep background (from twenty years earlier) for its primary action. That background calculates the end of days by conflating astrological abnormalities (the eye-of-God sign in heaven) and ancient Scriptures (an interpretation of Revelation 20:7). Roughly the first half of the movie is a supernatural mystery as Jericho struggles to

---

28. The public reception of Scorsese's *Last Temptation of Christ* indicates that modern audiences also lack such imaginative powers.

uncover this esoteric knowledge. He finally penetrates these secrets through several encounters with references to Revelation 20:7, a priest's homily on the symbols of Revelation, and his temptation encounter with Satan. The movie intensifies the dramatic tension of the calculable end by repeatedly emblazoning the countdown to the millennium on the screen (cf. the omnipresent clock in *High Noon*).

Ultimately, however, the movie is less interested in divination than in capitalizing on millennial fears. Released in late 1999, the movie filled a time-sensitive market niche in the popular frenzy associated with the millenium, popularly (and incorrectly) understood to begin with the advent of the year 2000. In discourse, if not story, the movie seized the day in a mercenary and opportunistic fashion.

Despite its capitalist designs, *End of Days* has a surprisingly complicated view of religion and the religious.[29] On the negative side, the movie opens with a montage of various broken religious symbols that give way to various elements used in satanic rituals. Further, Satan repeatedly destroys churches that never quite provide sanctuary. On the positive side, and apparently with deliberate irony, the theater is the real "house" of Satan. Most importantly, deliverance ultimately comes in a church with the hero's thoughtful contemplation of crucial Christian symbols. In sum, the Christian symbols bend but do not break. Literally and metaphorically, the movie seeks refuge in the church.

Similarly, there are bad and good religious individuals. The renegade assassin-priests are the noteworthy "bad guys." The seer-priest, the mentor-priest (Steiger), and the Pope are the "good guys." Despite a positive portrayal of the Pope, the conflict within the Vatican reveals that in this movie, as in ancient apocalyptic, what you see is not what you get. The truly religious are "hidden." *End of Days* becomes even more (American) sectarian when it opts for the oft-repeated Hollywood pattern of the lone, good individual who stands against mysterious and nefarious groups.

Despite this familiar American pattern, *End of Days* is less committed to fantasies of revenge than are most popular American readings of Revelation. *End of Days* externalizes evil far less than does Revelation. While it acknowledges the monstrous (the ghost-dragon) and the seductive (the Wall Street banker played by Gabriel Byrne) aspects of evil, it devotes most of its attention to Jericho's internal demons.

---

29. *End of Days* demonstrates that Michael Medved's claim (*Hollywood vs. America* [New York: HarperPerennial, 1991]) that Hollywood almost always presents the religious in a nefarious light is overstated.

While May locates this internal struggle with evil at the center of the American artistic tradition,[30] he never explains why this is the tradition. The answer lies in part in the centrality of individualism in American myth and culture. The myth expressed artistically individualizes both good (the individual) and evil (personal, psychological struggles). When the myth is not expressed so artistically or consistently (and myths do not need to be), evil can lie outside in some corrupt group (most of popular cinema). *End of Days* simply moves back and forth across these mythic possibilities.

Its focus on the internal struggle, however, foregoes fantasies of vengeance. Jericho is a suffering victim, not an avenging victor. He is a Gospel Jesus, not a Revelation or "Captain America" Christ-figure. Nonetheless, he is an American Jesus because his suffering preserves a threatened good order, rather than ending (or signifying the end) of some wicked age. Jericho's death does what the devil incarnate says Jesus' sacrifice accomplished. It buys humans more time. The devil is not defeated, only restrained. In such a worldview, there is no real opportunity for violent revenge.[31]

REVISITING REVELATION

Apocalypses, the classic examples of which biblical scholars date in a fairly specific time period from the second century B.C.E. to the second century C.E.,[32] reflect the demise of natural, traditional religions in the face of world empires (primarily Hellenistic or Roman). The new empires destroyed the old, familiar boundaries of various small kingdoms and the natural religions that were part of the warp and woof of those kingdoms' social-political orders. For the old political-religious arrangements and their adherents, the crisis was intense. Unless they adapted to the new larger empires, they faced falling behind the success curve. If they continued to play by the rules of now lost orders, they faced potential suffering for their nostalgia.[33]

---

30. May, "Demonic," 80–81.

31. *End of Days* is also a typically American film in its romantic element, as noted above.

32. Most biblical scholars admit that examples exist outside this particular timeframe. For a typology of modern sectarian movements, see Bryan Wilson, *Magic and the Millennium* (New York: Harper & Row, 1972).

33. Compare Richard Walsh, *Reading the Bible: An Introduction* (Notre Dame: Cross Cultural, 1997), 318–20. The summary above describes Jewish apocalypses better than it does Christian, because the Roman Empire was in place before Christianity. Nevertheless, it also

Confronting this problem, apocalyptic seers create new identities for minority dissenters. Their apocalypses urge their believers to hold on to the past even though that commitment now means suffering (or at least alienation from the social pathways to success) rather than reward. The new identity the apocalypses offer, then, is sectarian, a sense of its adherents as the suffering righteous in the midst of a larger evil empire.

The seer's apocalypse creates this new identity through a vision report: (1) of a seer's trip to heaven and a description of what he saw there; or (2) of a prediction of the upcoming end of history or of the end, at least, of the present evil empire and its replacement by a new age ruled by God and his saints. The apocalyptic sect, of course, is in tune with this larger transcendent identity, while culture at large is not.

Daniel (7–12) and Revelation are examples of the historical type (although Revelation's seer has "heavenly" transports as well). Revelation's historical apocalypse is the centerpiece of a narrative with three "surrounding" narrative levels:

- Narrative level one: letters offering the words of the risen Christ to seven churches (Revelation 1-3; 22:6–21)
- Narrative level two: visions of the worship of God and the lamb in heaven and in the new heaven and earth (Revelation 4–5; 21:1–22:5)
- Narrative level three: the reading of the Lamb's sealed scroll and the reading of the books of works and life (Revelation 6:1–11:19; 20:11–15)
- Narrative level four: the apocalypse proper (Revelation 12:1–20:10): a conflict between divine and demonic forces in which dragon-beasts oppose a heavenly woman and her children (Revelation 12–14) and in which a heavenly bride finally replaces a great whore (Revelation 17–18; 21) in a grand "final" conflict (Revelation 19:11-20:10).[34]

---

applies to Christian apocalypses for two significant reasons: (1) Generally, Christian apocalypses are revisions of earlier Jewish apocalypses. In fact, until recently, most scholars claimed that Christianity grew out of apocalyptic Judaism (and that Jesus was an apocalyptic seer). (2) Christians never admitted they were newcomers. They always claimed to be the true descendents of some ancient group. In their understanding, then, "before Rome, they are." For a slightly different cultural situating of Christian apocalyptic, see Burton Mack, *A Myth of Innocence*; *The Lost Gospel: The Book of Q and Christian Origins* (San Francisco: HarperSanFrancisco, 1993); and *Who Wrote the New Testament?* He argues throughout these works that openness to the world antedates apocalyptic in both Jesus communities and early christianities. In his reconstruction, these groups became apocalyptic only when their mission to the world was frustrated.

34. Compare Walsh, *Reading*, 486–88.

The apocalypse proper transfers to the future the plot and characters of a common ancient Near Eastern creation-through-combat myth. In the *Enuma Elish*, for example, Marduk, the chief god of the Babylonian pantheon, defeats Tiamat, an older deity now conceived as a monstrous dragon. Marduk's victory over Tiamat made possible the social and cosmic order of the Babylonian empire. A festival enacted the myth each year, thereby creating the order of each new Babylonian year. Apocalyptic and *End of Days* transpose this conflict to the future. Apocalyptic does so because the present is now experienced as so radically evil that old rituals no longer deal with it sufficiently. Now, nothing less than a new battle and a new creation (new age) are required. The apocalyptic vision provides this future in advance.

The surrounding narratives framing this centerpiece have two functions. First, levels two and three emphasize the divine sovereignty so blatantly that by the time the reader arrives at the apocalyptic conflict, it no longer seems a legitimate conflict. It is a matter already decided by the divine sovereign (level two) and is more a judgment (level three) than a battle. Second, levels one and two connect the apocalyptic vision with heavenly (level two) and sectarian (level one) worship. Level one, in particular, grounds Revelation's vision of the future in the present worship realities of the actual churches mentioned in Revelation 2–3. In short, Revelation is to be read in their worship.[35] In this worship, these apocalyptic sectarians experienced imaginatively the heavenly and future sovereignty and averred that that sovereignty would someday be a larger and public reality. The present experience is certainly as important, if not more important, than the future imagination. At the very least, the worship provides the material and realistic context for the apocalyptic seer's gothic, otherworldly visions.

In fact, worship becomes a kind of pressure chamber by which the sectarian community moves from the reality of the evil, bestial empire to the equally real experience of the sovereignty of God and the lamb. In brief, Revelation is what Geertz says religion generally is, "a system of symbols which acts to establish powerful, pervasive, and long-lasting moods and motivations in men by formulating conceptions of a general order of existence and clothing these conceptions with such an aura of factuality that the moods and motivations seem uniquely realistic."[36] For

---

35. Worship figures prominently in the plot of Revelation (e.g., Revelation 6:9–11; 7:9–17; 11:15–19; 14:1–5; 15:2–8; 16:5–7; 19:1–8) as well as in the external frame.

36. Clifford Geertz, *The Interpretation of Cultures* (New York: Basic Books. 1973), 90. His italics and enumeration omitted.

Geertz, the alternative reality of religion's myth and ritual becomes for worshipers a "really real" that overwrites their commonsense reality.[37] Although Revelation's "really real" would have little immediate impact upon earthly empires (it would go largely unnoticed by the empire), it would completely reconfigure that sovereignty for the sectarian worshipers as both bestial (and/or demonic) and temporary.

A NON-AMERICAN REVELATION?

Like the characters in *End of Days*, Revelation's characters are ethical stereotypes. Its depiction of Satan, while not that of a horny adolescent, is still rather weak. In particular, Revelation belittles evil's seductive and internal aspects. Further, from the comfortable distance of modernity, its attempt to present evil as monstrous is more cartoonish and grotesque than frightening. Like *End of Days*, Revelation's genre is mixed and derivative. In fact, some scholars consider Revelation a Christian adaptation of an earlier Jewish apocalypse. Whether or not that is the case, Revelation clearly reworks older texts like Exodus, Jeremiah, and Daniel as well as the ancient conflict creation myth. Finally, its symbolism is so heavy-handed that one can still decipher much of it after almost two thousand years.

Is Revelation, however, simply what the popular American reading says? Can one find an alternative to the calculable end, sectarianism, and violent revenge fantasies?

Remembering Revelation's ritual context helps avoid calculations of the end. Used in sectarian worship, Revelation provides a present experience of the divine sovereignty envisioned as ultimately victorious by the apocalypse. This experience provides an alternative reality to that of the evil empire and, thereby, makes the actual arrival of the apocalyptic end much less pressing. In worship, Revelation's ostensibly futurist eschatology is already "realized."[38]

In Eliade's understanding of religion, myths are cosmogonies; they are stories about the founding hierophanies of particular religions. Enacted in ritual, they allow the worshiper to live within the founding time (*in illo tempore*) or in what amounts to an eternal present.[39] As

---

37. Ibid., 109–23.

38. C. H. Dodd (*The Parables of the Kingdom*, rev. ed. [New York: Scribner's, 1961]) made "realized" eschatology famous by arguing that Jesus' parables were originally about the present experience of the kingdom, rather than a future, apocalyptic kingdom.

39. Mircea Eliade, *The Sacred and the Profane: The Nature of Religion*, trans. Willard R. Trask (New York: Harcourt Brace & World, 1959), 68–113.

Revelation projects the ancient Near Eastern creation myth to the future, its ritual enactment anticipates a cosmogony to come, rather than reflecting on a past hierophany. Nonetheless, when ritual enacts Revelation, the worshiper already lives *in illo tempore*. The worshiper does not wait for, but already lives with, the experience of the future divine sovereignty.

That the evil empire continues to reign matters less than a modern (American) reader might think. After all, worship has always changed the world less than it has the worshiper's attitude to the world. In its worship content, then, Revelation did not play on millennial fears in order to gain adherents or capital—as does *End of Days*—nor did it raise illusory hopes—as does the popular American reading of Revelation—rather, it provided a communal solace.

This "realized" view of Revelation's apocalyptic vision is the "truth" that historical-critical readings of Revelation—the interpretation of the symbols of Revelation in light of dissident sectarian communities' experiences of the Roman Empire near the end of the first century C.E.—struggle to depict. Unfortunately, such interpretations have always foundered on the paradox that the symbols made sense in that ancient context but that the end had not come. What the Enlightenment-inspired historical criticism overlooks is Revelation's worship context. In the sectarian community's worship, the end had already come. As a result, the community did not expect the end as ardently and specifically as historical critics (and Americans) have assumed.

A sectarian reading of Revelation is more difficult to avoid than the calculable end. Ancient apocalyptic groups were sectarians dissenting from larger cultural definitions of reality. In fact, apocalyptic often seems little more than reactionary propaganda envisioning the restoration of the displaced natural religions of small kingdoms. One may choose, however, to maximize or minimize the alienation of these groups. For Mack, frustration with the world creates apocalyptic sects voyeuristically consigning the world to hell.[40] By contrast, for Hanson, apocalyptic represents a group's temporary, tactical retreat from the world for the purpose of future "prophetic" engagement with the world.[41] For Hanson, only that prophetic return renders apocalyptic a redeemable social vision. In Hanson's view, apocalyptic groups may

---

40. Mack, *Myth of Innocence*, 331.
41. P. D. Hanson, "Apocalypticism" *The Interpreter's Dictionary of the Bible: Supplementary Volume*, ed. Keith Crim et al. (Nashville: Abingdon, 1976), 33–34.

have real change, rather than a mere exchange of the name of the group in power, in view.

Recent work by the sociologists Cohen and Taylor corroborates Hanson's optimistic but temporizing view. Cohen and Taylor have studied various "escape attempts" from paramount reality only to note their inherent fragility: "We would start by describing a particular method by which people would try to dissociate themselves from the world. Such identity work was always *against* paramount reality. We would then immediately puncture the notion of an alternative reality by showing its inner frailty, its vulnerability to being co-opted, packaged, invaded, exploited by the very forces which it tried to evade."[42] Despite the ephemerality of these escapes, Cohen and Taylor aver that these utopian flights and visions are necessary to human living.[43] Like Hanson, then, they do not condemn escape.

Cohen and Taylor are describing *individual* escapes from dominant reality. They see these attempted but failed escapes as the modern form of being human.[44] By contrast, ancient sectarian escapes were communal. Cohen and Taylor's escaping individuals and the common Hollywood story of the lone hero versus some mysterious, corrupt group—so faithfully enacted by *End of Days*—are more sectarian than these ancient worshipers. Accordingly, the movie's audience does not emulate Jericho's martyrdom. By contrast, Revelation's slain lamb is joined by (largely anticipated) martyrs (Revelation 6:9–11; 12:11; 17:1–19:10) and received by worshipers who identify the lamb as their mythic role model. Finally, worship is a far more communal experience than are movies or videocassettes.

Ironically, while *End of Days* reprises Revelation's apocalypse proper, it reminds us of worship more dramatically than does Revelation and its popular American reading. After all, Jericho's struggle with anger comes to a dramatic conclusion in a church. There, Jericho discovers sacrificial faith through the contemplation of religious symbols—the crucified Christ and the armed Michael. Paired with Revelation, *End of Days* reminds one that a worship frame contains Revelation's dramatic apocalypse both textually and contextually.

While attention to Revelation's worship context may avoid calculations of the end and minimize sectarian notions of religion, the fantasy

---

42. Stanley Cohen and Laurie Taylor, *Escape Attempts: The Theory and Practice of Resistance to Everyday Life*, 2nd ed. (London: Routledge, 1992), 14–15.

43. Ibid., 27.

44. Ibid., 30–45, 223–32.

of innocent revenge is far more difficult to avoid. Except for Revelation 2–3, Revelation externalizes evil and, thereby, misses completely evil's seductiveness and banality. When Revelation conceives evil monstrously, it falls victim to Nietzsche's dictum: "Whoever fights monsters should see to it that in the process he does not become a monster. And when you look long into an abyss, the abyss also looks into you."[45] Revelation becomes monstrous itself. It forgets that evil has a very human and familiar face, because it is one's own. In her report on Eichmann's trial in Jerusalem, Hannah Arendt remarks on a similar thoughtlessness:

> Eichmann was not Iago and not Macbeth, and nothing would have been farther from his mind than to determine with Richard III "to prove a villain." Except for an extraordinary diligence in looking out for his personal advancement, he had no motives at all. . . . He merely, to put the matter colloquially, never realized what he was doing. . . . He was not stupid. It was sheer thoughtlessness . . .[46]

Despite its baroque symbolism, Revelation, like Eichmann, suffers from a pitiful and dangerous lack of imagination when it comes to evil. Failing to see evil's human face leads Revelation far too close to a fantasy of revenge incarnating a voyeuristic damnation of the world. Thus, while Revelation starts with a slain lamb, it ultimately returns a warrior:

> Revelation's conquering Lamb significantly rewrites the ancient combat myth. Nevertheless, the eventual and climactic advent of the rider on the white horse (19:11–21) undoes this irony. A warrior, not a Lamb, ultimately wins. The return of the warrior means that Revelation does not subvert the apocalyptic combat myth to the extent that Paul and Mark do. Both of them invert apocalypticism by recognizing the cross itself as the ultimate divine act ushering in the new age. By contrast, for Revelation, it is the warrior who turns the ages.[47]

---

45. Friedrich Nietzsche, *Beyond Good and Evil: Prelude to a Philosophy of the Future*, trans. Walter Kaufmann (New York: Vantage, 1966), 89.

46. Hannah Arendt, *Eichmann in Jerusalem: A Report on the Banality of Evil*, rev. ed. (New York: Penguin, 1965), 287.

47. Walsh, *Reading*, 495. Jewett (*Captain America*, 23) makes the point more dramatically by contending that the warrior motif has actually transposed the idea of the lamb from an image for redemptive self-sacrifice (e.g., in Isaiah 53; John 1:29) to one of ferocious redemptive wrath from which all must hide (Revelation 6:16).

It is extremely hard, if not impossible, to absolve Revelation (and much of Hollywood cinema) of the charge of minimizing evil by externalizing it. Even here, however, attention to the worship context may help one avoid the sadistic voyeurism to which the externalization of evil ultimately leads. While Revelation, like Eichmann, could profit from more (sympathetic) imagination, the surrounding worship narrative (Revelation 4–5; 21:1–22:5)—almost universally ignored in the popular American reading of Revelation—does finally enclose the warrior (the apocalyptic centerpiece). Perhaps that enclosure leads away from Mack's voyeuristic to Hanson's temporizing apocalypticism.

Despite its "boilerplate" character, *End of Days* is helpful here. Its focus on Jericho's struggle with his anger and his ultimate refusal to become monstrous (i.e., satanic) offers a more robust imagination than does Revelation. The movie encourages one to turn away from Revelation's warrior or to consider such a figure merely a temporary, imaginative respite. It and Revelation, read as its precursor, refocus attention on the lamb.

A flight from sadism, however, does not necessarily lead to either masochistic martyrdom or to an idealistic pacifism. Mythically speaking, masochistic martyrdom is as unrealistic, simplistic, and dangerous as the sadistic fantasy of innocent revenge. Although some critics have lampooned the movie's inability to forego violence and others have chastised Revelation on similar grounds,[48] Revelation and *End of Days* have both warrior-heroes and victim-heroes for good mythic reasons. Both Revelation and *End of Days* create a mythic harmony out of the tension between violence enacted and violence suffered. Their struggles for a "realistic" position between a glorification of violence and a call to pacifism resemble more carefully crafted movies like *Shane, High Noon, Witness, Seven,* and *Falling Down.* While Revelation and *End of Days* do not attain the artistic level of these movies or others, they do struggle with the human relationship to violence.

Idealists and ideologues like to cut the Gordian knots of mythic harmonies. Here, they would prefer the simplicities of imperialism, voyeuristic sadism, or masochism. Of course, they do not thereby avoid historical particularity. Accordingly, readings emphasizing one side or another of this mythic tension—that is, violence versus others or versus

---

48. Compare Jewett, *Captain America*; Mack, *Myth of Innocence*; and Walsh, *Reading*, 500–502.

self—reflect particular cultural situations. The popular reading of Revelation as a celebration of innocent revenge responds to frustrations in American culture related to the end of the "Protestant kingdom" in the late nineteenth century (with Catholic immigration and modernity's arrival) and related, more recently, to the Cold War, Vietnam, and postmodernity. Readings emphasizing the other mythic pole (the slain lamb) may reflect deep-seated Christian masochism, idealist pacifism, liberal guilt over empire and its guns, fears about escalating violence, or simply a deconstructive and cynical stance vis-à-vis the popular American myth reflected in popular readings of Revelation.

While less precise ideologically, it would be more human and humane to remember the mythic struggle with violence—if not the particular answers and "art"—of Revelation and *End of Days*. Certainly, these works—at least read together—contain suggestions about dealing with frustrations that the popular American reading of Revelation and American myth in general find difficulty in accepting. Perhaps, if *End of Days* renders Revelation its precursor, it may help one to deal with frustrations more healthily, to "imagine Sisyphus happy," and to give up "the divine fable that amuses and blinds" for the human "terrestrial face, gesture and drama in which are summed up a difficult wisdom and an ephemeral passion."[49]

---

49. Albert Camus, *The Myth of Sisyphus and Other Essays*, trans. Justin O'Brien (New York: Vintage International, 1991), 117–18, 123.

2. OF GODS AND DEMONS
Blood Sacrifice and Eternal Life in *Dracula* and the Apocalypse of John

Tina Pippin

INTRODUCTION: THE MARK OF THE BEAST

Perhaps the most frequently returning demon to haunt the twentieth century was the vampire Dracula. He arose out of uncertain (medieval?) origins and gained momentum in the haunted Victorian landscape of Bram Stoker's world. Since Stoker's 1897 novel there have been legions of "Draculas" stalking fiction and film. All these Draculas function in more or less successful ways as embodiments of multiple horrors that are either real or imagined—of changing gender roles and sexualities, of modernization, of imperialism, of wars, of the threat of the annihilation of Western societies, and ultimately, of the earth. Dracula plays on an apocalyptic stage, and I will discuss some of his film appearances as they relate to the Apocalypse of John (Revelation). Dracula and other vampires leave their beastly marks on popular culture and consciousness in ways similar to the Apocalypse of John. I want to follow the trails of blood to both castles/temples of doom—Transylvanian and heavenly— and see what these visions of eternity offer. Entrance into both realms requires blood sacrifice and the marks of ownership. And like Dracula, the return of Christ in the "second coming" haunts the Christian millennial mind.

But there is supposed to be a big difference between Dracula and God; Dracula is from the order of the Dracul or Dragon, and thus represents the beasts of Satan, the ancient serpent. The marks they give their minions are also different; the traditional two puncture wounds on

24

the neck to create fellow vampires, and the "X" (or tau) on the forehead
for God's chosen: "Go through the city, through Jerusalem, and put a
mark on the foreheads of those who sign and groan over all the abominations that are committed in it" (see Ezekiel 9:4).[1] The latter mark is
reminiscent of the final Exodus plague: the lamb's blood on the
door/tent posts wards off the evil wilderness demon, God (see Exodus
12:21–27). In the Apocalypse one angel instructs four other angels: "Do
not damage the earth or the sea or the trees, until we have marked the
servants of our God with a seal on their foreheads" (Apocalypse 7:3).
Those with this special mark ". . . will see his [God's] face, and his name
will be on their foreheads" (Apocalypse 22:4). Because of the allegiance
of the elect, they will be granted everlasting life; "death will be no more"
(Apocalypse 21:4). The evil beasts also mark people; for example, the
Beast of the Earth enforces worship of the Beast of the Sea. "Also it
causes all, both small and great, both rich and poor, both free and slave,
to be marked on the right hand or the forehead, so that no one can buy
or sell who does not have the mark, that is, the name of the beast or the
number of its name" (i.e., the infamous number 666; Apocalypse
[Revelation] 13:16–17). The market economy relies on beast/emperor
worship to build its empire. And of course there is the bloodthirsty, primary symbol of the empire, the whore of Babylon: "[A]nd on her forehead was written a name, a mystery: 'Babylon the great, mother of
whores and of earth's abominations.' And I saw that the woman was
drunk with the blood of the saints and the blood of the witness to Jesus"
(Apocalypse 17:5–6). The whore is the ultimate vampire, sipping chalices
full of saints' blood. Like the traditional Dracula, she does not drink
wine but prefers a stronger drink.

Which mark is one to accept or avoid—the various brands on the
forehead or hand, or the punctures on the neck? All are inscriptions, and
the victim has been claimed by some demonic power if marked by the
Beast or a vampire. The imprint of name (666) or of teeth both drain the
soul and lead to eternal damnation. One mark will deter the various
plagues; another will increase them. Vampires are certainly a plague or
threat of plague, as are apocalyptic frogs or locusts or even the larger-
than-life reptilian, multiheaded beasts. With their link to eternal suffering
and damnation, vampires have much in common with the hell-
mouthed beasts of the artistic traditions of the Apocalypse, but the

---

1. All biblical citations are from the New Revised Standard Version.

plagues initiated by human forms are perhaps more frightening. The imperialist domination represented by the whore of Babylon in the Apocalypse of John and by the antichrist in millennialist interpretations provide more political context for fear and horror. The twentieth-century vampires represented a variety of modern plagues: for example, anti-Semitism (F. W. Murnau's 1922 film, *Nosferatu: eine Symphonie des Grauens*; Carl Dreyer's 1931 film, *Vampyr*) or Nazism (Werner Herzog's 1979 film, *Nosferatu*). As Nina Auerbach observes, "[T]he rapidity with which our Draculas become dated tells us only that every age embraces the vampire it needs."[2] Every age needs an apocalypse (or multiple apocalypses) and a multitude of creatures to populate it. In the United States, the "vampires" (those that drain the "blood" or life from its upstanding citizens) shift and vary. Immigrants, homosexuals, AIDS, Iraq, liberals, West Nile virus, feminists, the poor, union organizers, to name a few, all threaten to drain traditional values and standards of living. Having the mark of the beastly vampire can mean infection or solidarity with a dangerous group. It is all about blood and blood ties. Although there are people who believe in vampires or think they themselves are vampires, there are far more fundamentalist Christians who believe in an imminent apocalypse and rapture/tribulation period headed by the antichrist. The need for boundaries—and for the demons that cross them—is eternal. And these demons have to leave their mark, so to speak, for there to be a mythic trace to explore and fear. But God marks true believers, too, pursuing them with the choices of eternal life or damnation.

THE UN-USUAL SUSPECTS

The simple equation is that evil is evil and good is good. The famous Draculas, Max Schreck and Klaus Kinski (as Nosferatu/Count Orlock, and Willem Dafoe as Max Schreck/Count Orlock), Bela Lugosi, Christopher Lee, and Frank Langella, are each differently evil. These Draculas are the undead who live forever, until of course they are staked in the heart with the appropriate wood. They live on blood, mostly human blood, so they are constantly feeding on society. The Draculas arising from Stoker's novel live in their times of some distant past, the

---

2. Nina Auerbach, *Our Vampires, Our Selves* (Chicago: University of Chicago Press, 1995), 145. See also her comment on 117: "Perhaps, in twentieth-century America, monsters are shadows, not symbols, of crises; or perhaps we live in a continuing crisis—fanned by rabid journalism and seemingly incessant change—that sometimes takes the shape of vampires."

present, and the future. Exotic and/or erotic as they might be, these revenants have definite ties with the demonic.

The name "Dracula" has been traced from the root "dracul" to mean "child of the dragon" or "devil"—with a feminine "a" ending.[3] Scholars dispute the linking of Stoker's Dracula with Vlad the Impaler of the fifteenth century; the warrior Vlad impaled his victims with bloodthirsty wrath, but may not have been a true vampire.[4] The origins and history of the more general term "vampire" are numerous: from the Turkish word for witch (*uber*) to the Greek verb to drink (*pi*) to the Serbian-Croatian word for to blow (*pirati*).[5] As for Dracula as reptile/lizard: "The peculiar 'lizard fashion' with which Dracula scales the castle walls . . . and the fact that Harker first meets the vampire on St. George's Day . . . indicate that the battle against Dracula is an archetypal fight with the dragon."[6] Vampires are a specific subcategory of the more general term for the undead, "revenant." Paul Barber defines vampire/revenant as "any dead human being who, in folklore, is believed to return to life in corporeal form."[7] Barber collected a large amount of data on the revenant; revenants are likely to be associated with plague: "Murder victims, suicides, and victims of plague tend to become revenants. Indeed, revenants cause plagues.[8] They were often unpopular people even before their deaths";[9] their bodies do not decompose; they can be killed with a stake. According to *The Encyclopedia of Fantasy*, revenants are ghosts (and definitely not zombies) who "retain an identity and purpose— possibly vengeance."[10] Evil comes in all-too-human but not quite human enough form in the vampire. Jules Zanger relates that in *Nosferatu* the Count Orlock is bat-like, reptilian, and thus a true monstrous presence:

---

3. Ibid., 133.

4. See the arguments made by Elizabeth Miller, ed., Dracula's Homepage [cited 31 July 2001]; available from *http://www.ucs.mun.ca/~emiller/*; and her *Dracula: The Shade and the Shadow* (Essex, U.K.: Desert Island Books, 1998).

5. Katharina M. Wilson, "The History of the Word *Vampire*," *The Vampire: A Casebook*, ed. Alan Dundes (Madison: University of Wisconsin Press, 1998), 4.

6. Valdine Clemens, *The Return of the Repressed: Gothic Horror from The Castle: Otranto to Alien* (Albany: State University of New York Press, 1999), 171.

7. Paul Barber, "Forensic Pathology and the European Vampire," *The Vampire: A Casebook*, 112.

8. James B. Twitchell also points out the connection of vampires and plagues, linking it to Christianity: "The rise of Christianity, ironically, did as much to nurture the vampire as the plague would later do, for the Catholic Church found in the story of this fiend a most propitious analogy to describe the intricate workings of evil" (*Dreadful Pleasures: An Anatomy of Modern Horror* [New York: Oxford University Press, 1985], 106).

9. Barber, "Forensic Pathology," 113.

10. Mike Ashley, "Revenants," *The Encyclopedia of Fantasy*, ed. John Clute and John Grant (New York: St. Martin's Griffin, 1997), 810.

"The solitary Dracula could, like the Old Testament God, only relate to humans and only within a very narrow range of interlocking emotions: in Dracula's case, hunger, hate, bitterness, contempt."[11]

Murnau's unauthorized 1922 version of Stoker's *Dracula* presented a rat- and bat-like Count who brings a plague-infested ship to infect northern Germany. Klaus Kinski carried on Murnau's interpretation of the vampire in Herzog's 1979 film. Most recently, in *The Shadow of the Vampire*, Willem Dafoe played the actor Max Schreck who played Count Orlock of the 1922 film. The convention here is that Schreck was so convincing on screen because he was really a vampire who made an agreement with Murnau to act in the movie if he could "have" the lead actress at the end. The trouble is that Schreck starts killing off some of the crew, frustrating Murnau, who has to keep finding replacements. One contention is that film offers eternal life, Hollywood devours its own, and stars devour everything around them, but more importantly, that these shadow-less shadow creatures continue to haunt across centuries. Dafoe's Schreck speaks a little, but there is no talking with the vampire in the silent film. In his review of *Nosferatu* Roger Ebert observes: "Human speech dissipates the shadows and makes a room seem normal. Those things that live only at night do not need to talk, for their victims are asleep, waiting."[12] Subsequent Counts took Bela Lugosi's lead and became smooth talking, albeit mysterious and eccentric, aristocrats. Ebert writes of the 1931 *Dracula*: "[S]omehow Count Dracula was more fearsome when you could hear him—not an inhuman monster, but a human one, whose painfully articulated sentences mocked the conventions of drawing room society."[13] The main vampire of my childhood, Barnabas Collins of the television soap opera *Dark Shadows*, wielded power and control like any other corporate mogul on the soaps, but with a particularly evil twist. Blood was not merely spilled, but ingested, too; enemies and friends alike were drawn into the demon's lair.

It is difficult to know exactly how to defeat a vampire. Rules constantly change to fit the drama of each particular literary or dramatic work.[14] Crosses are not always effectual vampire repellents; in *The Fearless*

---

11. Jules Zanger, "Metaphor into Metonymy: The Vampire Next Door," *Blood Read*, ed. Joan Gordon and Veronica Hollinger (Philadelphia: University of Pennsylvania Press, 1997), 22.

12. Roger Ebert, "Nosferatu" [cited 31 July 2001]; from http://www.suntimes.com/ebert/ebert_reviews/1999/01/feratu1118.htm [review available through www.IMDB.com].

13. Roger Ebert, "Dracula" [cited 31 July 2001]; from http://www.suntimes.com/ebert/ebert_reviews/1999/01/dracula1001.htm [review available through www.IMDB.com].

14. David Glover notes, "[T]he vampire continues to reproduce itself in a seemingly endless series of copies, always resourcefully different from previous incarnations, often revising the

Vampire Killers the Jewish vampire reacts to a cross a young woman puts in his face with: "Boy, have you got the wrong vampire." Lloyd Worley explores the "protestant work ethic" of Anne Rice's vampires, who live as heretics in a Roman Catholic New Orleans. Crosses, church spaces,[15] and consecrated hosts do not work on them either. "[The vampire] Lestat's callous invulnerability to the holy made readers very uneasy. . . . The problem these vampires have is that they have rejected the objective power of God, but they have not developed an internal expression of faith and repentance."[16]

Vampires cannot exist without God's curse. Alan Dundes quotes Montague Summers: "For the hauntings of a Vampire, three things are necessary: the Vampire, the Devil, and the Permission of Almighty God." Summers is not sure whether it is the devil who energizes the corpse or whether the deceased reappears by himself through "some dispensation of Divine Providence."[17] In Coppola's version, Vlad curses God and the church and is damned to grieve his lost love for all eternity. As in the prologue of the Book of Job, God and Satan seem to be in cahoots in some way, making deals behind the scenes and bartering human life.

Many scholars note this difference between vampires and Satan, the avenging angel. Cynthia Freeland argues that monsters in the horror genre are complex and interesting and the evils they represent are as important as the evil of the ultimate religious representative, Satan. "Do [horror films] afford us ways of meditating on death, the limitations of the flesh, and our tiny place in the cosmos or on ways to create values once religion has lost its grip? I think so. . . ."[18] She argues with Fred Alford about the uniqueness and power of the vampire stories. Alford sees no suitable replacement to head evil: "Satan tempts your soul, corrupting you from inside out, exploiting your pride against your will. The

---

rules of the game in order to secure a new lease on life, without ever finally being laid to rest. This protean durability of the Undead is undoubtedly what confers true immortality upon them and it is also what qualifies their incessant returns as *myths*, those potent cultural stories we listen to again and again and never tire of retelling" (*Vampires, Mummies, and Liberals: Bram Stoker and the Politics of Popular Fiction* [Durham, N.C.: Duke University Press, 1996], 139).

15. "The church building itself was believed to be consecrated ground and to constitute a sacred and timeless space, 'haunted,' in a sense, by the holy spirit" (Clemens, *The Return of the Repressed*, 20).

16. Lloyd Worley, "Anne Rice's Protestant Vampires," *The Blood Is the Life: Vampires in Literature*, ed. Leonard G. Heldreth and Mary Pharr (Bowling Green, Ohio: Bowling Green State University Popular Press, 1999), 85-86.

17. Alan Dundes, "The Vampire," *The Vampire: A Casebook*, ed. Alan Dundes (Madison: University of Wisconsin Press, 1998), 162.

18. Cynthia A. Freeland, *The Naked and the Undead: Evil and the Appeal of Horror* (Boulder, Colo.: Westview, 2000), 2.

vampire just wants to suck your blood; about your soul he knows and cares nothing. . . . Evil is no longer a force in the world, no longer about temptation of the soul. Instead, evil has lodged in the body, and has become weakness."[19] Freeland further acknowledges the existential nature of vampires: "Vampires pose a deep metaphysical puzzle about how to create new structures for meaning and value within the time scale of godless eternity. Like Nietzsche's Zarathustra, some vampires seek to create new ethical norms in a vacuum where traditional science and religion have lost their grip."[20] She notes that in Coppola's film, *Bram Stoker's Dracula*, "[T]he final death scene of Vlad/Dracula here takes on Luciferian dimensions that would no doubt have appalled Stoker. . . . As [Vlad/Dracula] waits for Mina to release him, in somewhat shocking parody or allusion to Christ's last words, Dracula complains first that God has forsaken him and then says, 'It is finished.'"[21] Coppola's Vlad/Dracula is a sympathetic figure, cursed to roam the earth mourning for his beloved wife. David Glover quotes from a Coppola interview in the *Village Voice*: "I made a big point that when Dracula dies he just becomes a man, I found that very Christ-like somehow. There are those figures in our lives, and maybe that's what Christ really means, who are the ones that must die or the ones who must court evil, they do it for us. In the end, it's the sacrificial role Christ plays—he who must die."[22] This depiction of Dracula is far removed from Stoker's rodent-vampire. Stoker drew the vampire as a hopeless romantic for whom "Love Never Dies" (the movie's slogan). I do not see Dracula as a Satan replacement due to Satan's (or the antichrist's) starring role in apocalyptic narrative. One monster could never cover all human fears; there have to be greater and lesser demons and manifestations of the demonic. And against Alford I would argue that evil is still a force in the world. Dracula invades not only the human body but 1897 London.

Dracula as the most famous vampire has been seen as a type of antichrist figure. Zanger states, "Dracula, for Stoker and for Stoker's readers, is the Anti-Christ," evidenced by Stoker's use of He/Him for Dracula.[23] Then Zanger follows the vampire trajectory from Stoker: "My

---

19. Fred C. Alford, *What Evil Means to Us* (Ithaca, N.Y.: Cornell University Press, 1997), 95, cited in Freeland, *Naked and Undead*, 123.
20. Freeland, *Naked and Undead*, 124.
21. Ibid., 142.
22. Glover, *Vampires, Mummies, and Liberals*, 187 n. 17.
23. "The Vampire Next Door," 18. In his historical book on the antichrist tradition, Bernard McGinn fails to recognize the wider cultural manifestations of the antichrist; he completely

premise in what follows is that the construction and popularity of the 'new' vampire represent a demoticizing of the metaphoric vampire from Anti-Christ, from magical, metaphysical 'other,' toward the metonymic vampire as social deviant (from Count Dracula to Ted Bundy), eroding in that process of transformation many of the qualities that generated its original appeal."[24] Still, Draculas live on in various guises and styles.

The Draculas raise the issues of good and evil that Eve discovered from the serpent in the garden of Eden. This knowledge turns out not to be so simply defined by a deity who both loves and condemns creation. In his study of evil, philosopher Jean Baudrillard shows how "the theorem of the accursed share" operates. The "accursed share" is represented by radical Otherness or difference, the threat of disruption and terror from something outside. Baudrillard relates, "The uninterrupted production of positivity has a terrifying consequence. Whereas negativity engenders crisis and critique, hyperbolic positivity for its part engenders catastrophe, for it is incapable of distilling crisis and criticism in homeopathic doses."[25] Vampires are part of this "accursed share"; they are inevitable manifestations of needing to put a human face (and to supply human consorts) to evil. And Stoker's Dracula and his minions are expressions of nineteenth-century imperialism, sexual "deviations," and the Industrial Revolution. All the positivity of the British Empire, spreading influence and "civilized culture" over the world, was headed toward apocalypse. Of course, Draculas immigrated (by the hundreds) to the United States in the twentieth century, and at the turn of the millennium return to replay their filmic origins (in *Shadow of the Vampire*). The vampire-demon-serpent-whore that seduces in Genesis and in the Apocalypse of John is always a possibility, and possible in the realm of desire and death (or undeath). Baudrillard argues:

> The principle of Evil is not a moral principle but rather a principle of instability and vertigo, a principle of complexity and foreignness, a principle of seduction, a principle of incompatibility, antagonism and irreducibility. It is not a death principle—far from it. It is a vital principle of disjunction. Since the Garden of

ignores the vampire tradition and notes a decline in antichrist mythologies since the Enlightenment (*Anti-Christ: Two Thousand Years of the Human Fascination with Evil* [San Francisco: HarperSanFrancisco, 1994]).

24. "The Vampire Next Door," 17.

25. Jean Baudrillard, *The Transparency of Evil: Essays on Extreme Phenomena*, trans. James Benedict (London/New York: Verso, 1993), 106.

Eden, which Evil's advent closed to us, Evil has been the principle of knowledge. But if indeed we were chased from the Garden for the sin of knowledge, we may as well draw the maximum benefit from it. Trying to redeem the accursed share of the principle of Evil can result only in the establishment of new artificial paradises, those of the consensus, which for their part do indeed embody a true death principle.[26]

Thus, paradise and hell, creation and apocalypse are linked. There are too many ruptures in the garden already—forbidden trees, snakes, conversations, thoughts, actions—all part of the paradisiacal structure. And there are ruptures in the apocalyptic new Jerusalem/the new paradise as well—the abyss,[27] the too-confining walls, the sameness (of the 144,000), the "uninterrupted production of positivity." Is paradise then all "good"? Are these Draculas trying to tell us something about the power of the cross, the host, and Christian symbolism and presence? Is heaven possible without blood sacrifice, the genocide of billions of Others and of the earth?

"I Want to Drink Your Blood" and Other Perversions

The vampire world is clearly apocalyptic; there is the nagging fear that Dracula has infected just enough people to cause the complete downfall of humanity. Although Dracula never completely prevails, vampires have still invaded the full apocalyptic imagination. For example, in the 1964 film *The Last Man on Earth*, Vincent Price plays a scientist who is the sole human survivor of a worldwide vampire plague. For a while he is able to escape the vampire hoards, but they eventually destroy him. The Draculas are always reappearing, but in film there is no final apocalypse because in Stoker's novel England is set right again and the heroes destroy Dracula.[28] In an episode of television's *Buffy the Vampire Slayer*,

---

26. Ibid., 107. Another French philosopher, Georges Bataille, makes a case for a "hyper-morality" arising from any investigation of evil in literature: "A rigorous morality results from complicity in the knowledge of Evil, which is the basis of intense communication" (*Literature and Evil*, trans. Alastair Hamilton [London/New York: Marion Boyars, 1985], ix). Veronica Hollinger says that we are never given much of the internal life/thoughts of God/the monsters: "It is also worth noting that, however threatening Stoker's vampire is, it serves a crucial function in his novel: in its role as evil Other, it necessarily guarantees the *presence* of the Good" ("Fantasies of Absences: The Postmodern Vampire," *Blood Read*, ed. Joan Gordon and Veronica Hollinger [Philadelphia: University of Pennsylvania Press, 1997], 202).

27. See my argument on the abyss as a tear in the text, *Apocalyptic Bodies: The Biblical End of the World in Text and Image* (London/New York: Routledge, 1999), chap. 5.

28. Kim Newman begins her novel, *Anno Dracula* (New York: Carroll & Graf, 1983) where Stoker's ended; the British Empire is ultimately threatened when Dracula's followers increase and he captures Queen Victoria.

Dracula (a modern Bela Lugosi type) returns as the King of the Undead and seduces Buffy. She breaks out of his hypnotic spell and fights him. After Buffy stabs him with a stake, he tries to return in the form of fog. Buffy quips, "You think I don't watch your movies? You always come back."[29] Then she stabs him again; when the fog tries to return, she warns him she is standing right there. So Dracula leaves, but as Buffy observed, he always returns eventually.

If the vampire world is apocalyptic, is the apocalyptic world vampiric? Christian symbols can frequently ward off vampires. And the vampiric whore of Babylon, the only demonic character who is portrayed as drinking blood, is utterly and brutally destroyed and cannibalized. She represents empire (among other things)—the imperial feeding frenzy. "Cannibalism is a radical form of hospitality," states Baudrillard.[30] Ten kings and the beast devour the whore (Apocalypse 17:16) before the kings and some others are cannibalized by the birds of "midheaven" (19:17–18): ". . . the flesh of kings, the flesh of captains, the flesh of the mighty, the flesh of horses and their riders—flesh of all, both free and slave, both small and great." Excessive hospitality reigns: "And the rest were killed by the sword of the rider on the horse, the sword that came from his mouth; and all the birds were gorged with their flesh" (19:21). In this reversal of the wedding feast of the bride and the lamb (19:6–10), the evil feast and are in turn feasted upon. While there is the drinking of blood and the eating of flesh, the Apocalypse of John does not have vampires as they evolved in the nineteenth century and beyond. But the traces are there; the strange attractors of the chaotic whirl of evil, empire, and more.

There are also similarities in the narrative desire for and refusal of seductive forces. The domain of the vampire and other revenants is usually seen as the demonic inverse of the heavenly realm of the resurrected believers. In a sort of hell on earth, Dracula and his minions are damned to a bloodthirsty immortality and roam the earth at night until they perish in some complex series of death rituals applied to them by a vampire slayer. The saved of heaven exist for eternity in a state of peaceful bliss. Jesus was nailed to a stake/cross,[31] and believers drink his "blood" and

---

29. Quotations from television and movies are my own transcription.

30. *Transparency of Evil*, 144.

31. According to John F. Crossan, "In historical and linguistic terms, there is not much distance between the cross and the stake" ("The Stake That Spoke: Vlad Dracula and a Medieval 'Gospel' of Violence," *Dracula: The Shade and the Shadow*, ed. Elizabeth Miller [Essex, U.K.: Desert Island Books, 1998], 181). Vlad the Impaler used the stake/cross and other Christian symbols as parody: "A close examination of the 'Dracole Waida' woodcut (Strasbourg 1500)

eat his "flesh" in the eucharistic feast. The "good news" is that those who "feed" on Jesus will be granted eternal life.[32] "Cannibalism is a radical form of hospitality"—in this case glorious, eternal hospitality. In the Apocalypse of John they (i.e., the feeders) will join the heavenly revenant class, living out eternity bound to a covenantal city, the new Jerusalem. Dracula, like Jesus, is creating a "new order of beings."[33] What vampires and Christian revenants share is immortality, the status of being forever undead gained through the drinking of (natural or supernatural) blood and even more—the eating of flesh. Only the vampires experience the immortality as bondage.

The themes of life and death are central in the Apocalypse and in the stories of the Draculas. Jesus gives life through his blood; vampires suck the life-force out of their victims. Apocalyptic fire sucks the world dry; living water comes through Jesus (John 4) and in heaven.[34] Vampires are the ancient Greek lamias, demonic females who seduce men, who often

---

reveals that the Impaler appears to be imparting a priestly blessing in a gruesome parody of the Eucharist. . . . The presence of a plate and cup (paten and chalice) strengthens the image of a perverted Last Supper. Keeping in mind the crucifixion piety of the late Middle Ages, these images may be interpreted as deliberate parodies of the Gospels, twisting the nationalistic fanaticism of the tyrant into a hellish evil while at the same time presenting him as a necessary evil, Christendom's last hope against the Turk" (ibid., 184).

32. "In Revelation, it is not the enemy's blood that must be removed to achieve purity, but a sharing in the Lamb's blood itself which generates purity" (Wes Howard-Brook and Anthony Gwyther, *Unveiling Empire: Reading Revelation Then and Now* (Maryknoll, N.Y.: Orbis Books, 1999], 210).

33. Franco Moretti, "A Capital *Dracula,*" *Dracula,* ed. Nina Auerbach and David J. Skal, (New York: Norton, 1997), 433. Christopher Gist Raible shows how Dracula inverts Christian theology and then lures his victims into his heresy: "There are Draculas all around us. Their seductive heresies are tempting" ("Dracula: Christian Heretic," *Dracula: The Vampire and the Critics,* ed. Margaret L. Carter [Ann Arbor, Mich.: UMI Research Press, 1988], 105). James Twitchell adds, "The vampire myth explained the most difficult concept—the Eucharist. It explained the doctrine of transubstantiation in reverse. . . . What the medieval church found in the vampire legend was not just an apt mythologem for evil, but an elaborate allegory for the transubstantiation in reverse. . . . For just as the devil-vampire drank the blood and then captured the spirit of a sinner, so too could the penitent drink the blood, eat the body, and possess the divinity of Christ" (*Dreadful Pleasures,* 108).

34. Dundes's Freudian read from his field of folklore studies tells us that the dead are dry and thirsty; in heaven there is another drink of choice: "We know very well from our own Judeo-Christian eschatological cosmology that heaven, the promised land after death, offers 'milk and honey,' an old-fashioned form of sweetened milk offered to infants. The idiom of 'a land flowing with milk and honey' as a metaphor for abundance occurs no fewer than twenty-one times in the Bible. . . . And what are we to make of the phrase 'and the hills shall flow with milk' (Joel 3:18)? The only hills that flow with milk are maternal breasts. So the idea of a blissful death involving a regression to a postnatal paradise including lots of milk and honey is seemingly consonant with Judeo-Christian worldview" ("The Vampire," 169). Medieval mystics often envisioned breastfeeding on Jesus; milk, blood, semen collude here.

appear in their nightmares (as succubae), and then drink their blood. Sometimes they appear in the form of serpents.[35] The most famous lamia, the Babylonian night demon Lilith, is often cited as the ancestor of vampires.[36] This femme fatale or queen of the vampires must be kept powerless by amulets and by patriarchal creation and apocalyptic myths in which God overpowers the serpent (e.g., Genesis 2–3; Apocalypse 12:7–9; 20:7–10). In the film *Lifeforce* space vampires invade Earth through the leadership of a queen vampire, who has deposited a bit of her life-force into an astronaut from Earth and plans on retrieving it, along with the entire life-force of everyone on Earth. Her spaceship travels the universe sucking out the life-force of planets and totally destroying them. The queen vampire is a shape-shifter and can inhabit a variety of different host bodies. Men find this tricky femme fatale from outer space irresistible. As Dracula (and Nosferatu) creates the erotic demon vampire women who seduce Jonathan Harker, the image of woman as monster with supernatural powers to draw the life-force (blood, semen) out of men takes a particularly misogynistic bent. Harker is especially drawn to/by the vampire women's red lips, another serpent mouth (Tiamat?) and abyss/hell mouth, in which the vagina dentata fears are played out.

But is this beast/vampire so clearly female? Are not also fantasies of repressed homoeroticism represented by the vampiric mouth?[37] The femme fatale is surely a usual suspect and one of the forces bringing and maintaining evil in the world. But the gender lines are blurred. For instance, is the whore of Babylon a female-male? Or a male-female—as

---

35. Brian Stableford, "Lamias," *The Encyclopedia of Fantasy*, ed. John Clute and John Grant (New York: St. Martin's Griffin, 1997), 557. Carol Senf names other cultural manifestations of women who seduce and/or drink blood: Bruxsa (Portugal), Langsuir (Malaysia), baobham sith (Scotland), and Mara (Danish), and notes that "[M]ost exhibit at least one of the three characteristics associated with women vampires in literature: bloodsucking, rebellious behaviour, and overt eroticism" ("Daughters of Lilith: Women Vampires in Popular Literature," *The Blood Is the Life: Vampires in Literature*, ed. Leonard G. Heldreth and Mary Pharr [Bowling Green, Ohio: Bowling Green State University Popular Press, 1999], 200).

36. Brian Stableford, "Lilith," *The Encyclopedia of Fantasy*, ed. John Clute and John Grant (New York: St. Martin's Griffin, 1997), 581. See also Richard Davenport-Hines, *Gothic: Four Hundred Years of Excess Horror*, Evil and Ruin (New York, North Point, 1998), 232. There is an interesting lesbian vampire film called *The Mark of Lilith*; in it a South Asian female is orientalized and exoticized.

37. Franco Moretti speaks of the return of the (Freudian concept of the) repressed in vampire literature: "The lesson these books wish to impart is that one need not fear one's own repressions, the splitting of one's own psyche. No, one should be afraid of the monster, of something material, something external. . . . Madness is nothing in comparison with the vampire. Madness does not present a problem. Or rather: madness in itself, does not exist: it is the vampire, the monster, the potion that creates it" ("A Capital Dracula," 442).

Catherine Keller describes, "imperial patriarchy in drag"?[38] From Eden,[39] the gender of "evil" has been both clear and not clear. The same goes for the gender of "good." As for vampires, both male and female penetrate with sharp teeth from an inviting, feminine, blood-dripping mouth. And in the Apocalypse, the Son of Man penetrates the enemy with the "sharp, two-edged sword" in his mouth (1:16). Why carry one's (phallic-shaped) weapon in one's mouth? Despite the sword the Son of Man is able to speak: "Do not be afraid; I am the first and the last, and the living one. I was dead, and see, I am alive forever and ever; and I have the keys of Death and of Hades" (1:17–18). On this topic of desire for the teeth/sword, Christopher Craft summarizes: "A swooning desire for an overwhelming penetration and an intense aversion to the demonic potency empowered to gratify that desire compose the fundamental motivating action and emotion in *Dracula*."[40] The sexualized women in the Apocalypse have to be destroyed (the Jezebel and the whore).[41] The sexualized woman character in *Dracula*, Lucy, who breaks the Victorian gender norms, has to be staked and destroyed.[42] Craft explains:

> Dualities require demarcations, inexorable and ineradicable lines of separation, but Dracula, as a border being who abrogates demarcations, makes such distinctions impossible. He is *nosferatu*,

---

38. Catherine Keller, *Apocalypse Now and Then: A Feminist Guide to the End of the World* (Boston: Beacon, 1996), 77. See Christopher Craft, "'Kiss Me with Those Red Lips': Gender and Inversion in Bram Stoker's *Dracula*," *Dracula*, 453, on Stoker's repressed homoeroticism in *Dracula*: "His sexualized women are men too."

39. On vampire hunger Mary Pharr notes: "Ironically, the hunger of the hoards links them instead to Adam and Eve, humanity's metaphorical parents, whose indulgence in 'forbidden food' for 'secret knowledge' led not to immortality but to expulsion and suffering beyond anything they could have imagined beforehand" ("Vampiric Appetite in *I Am Legend*, *Salem's Lot*, and *The Hunger*," *The Blood Is the Life: Vampires in Literature*, ed. Leonard G. Heldreth and Mary Pharr [Bowling Green, Ohio: Bowling Green State University Popular Press, 1999], 94).

40. "Kiss Me," 445. Craft goes on to say: "Everywhere in this text such desire seeks a strangely deflected heterosexual distribution; only through women may men touch" (ibid., 448).

41. Bram Dijkstra shows how in the early twentieth century "twisted 'erotic' fantasies of gynecide had opened the door to the realities of genocide" (*Evil Sisters: The Threat of Female Sexuality in Twentieth-Century Culture* (New York: Henry Holt, 1996), 4). Vampires are everywhere. The beast has infected millions. In Swinburne's poem "Laus Veneris" of 1866 the ancient vampire is the goddess Venus. Men turn from Christ to her: "Even men whose lips were once 'Stained with blood fallen from the feet of God' now 'grow sad with kissing Christ'" (ibid., 267).

42. Craft further comments on the role of the women in Stoker's *Dracula*: "If, as Van Helsing admits, God's women provide the essential mediation ('the light can be here on earth') between the divine but distant patriarch and his earthly sons, then God's intention may be distorted by its potentially changeable vehicle. If woman-as-signifier wanders, then Van Helsing's whole cosmology, with its founding dualisms and supporting texts, collapses" ("Kiss Me," 451).

neither dead nor alive but somehow both, mobile frequenter of the grave and boudoir, easeful communicant of exclusive realms, and as such he toys with the separation of the living and the dead, a distinction critical to physician, lawyer, and priest alike."[43]

And this distinction is also critical to theologians and biblical scholars. If we could just go back to the time when beasts were beasts, Satan was Satan, and God was God. The apocalypse fantasies are clearly laid out from Daniel through the Apocalypse of John to their hyper-translation in current rapture/tribulation novels and films. The biblical end of the world gives such comfort and hope; men are men and women are women, and all is right with the universe. Or is it? In these near-future visions there are no Draculas (or offspring) or biblical satanic beasts to toy around with the dualities of male/female or living/dead, perverting the civilized world. The Draculas tamper with the notion of an ordered Victorian universe in Stoker's 1897 England. And they continue to crash through repressed emotions even in a new millennium. The Apocalypse crashes in with macho fervor; a male holy-warrior class united forever with the sword-wielding deity. Beware of the kiss of peace. "We know vampires are stalking the earth. We also know there's a God, too," a priest in John Carpenter's slasher film *Vampires* declares. James Woods's vampire slayer character replies, "We just don't understand him."

VAMPIRES 'R US

"More than our heroes or pundits, our Draculas tell us who we were," says Nina Auerbach.[44] The Draculas from Stoker through twentieth-century film have told us about racism, anti-Semitism, the rise of Nazism, imperialism, and plagues (in particular, AIDS). Our Draculas signify our private and public terrors, our secret hates and irrational inventories of

---

43. Ibid., 449. See also Moretti, "A Capital *Dracula*," 444: "The conscious mind can rest easy: all that remains of the original fear is a word, 'Dracula': That splendid and inexplicable feminine name. . . . The vampire is turned into a man by mass culture, which has to promote spontaneous certainties and cannot let itself plumb the unconscious too deeply. . . . Serious certainties and terror support each other."

44. *Our Vampires, Our Selves*, 112. Veronica Hollinger comments on the thin line between the monstrous and the human: "For this is one of the functions of our monsters: to help us construct our own humanity, to provide guidelines against which we can define ourselves . . . the roles played out by this figure [the vampire] shift as our desires and anxieties adapt to particular cultural/political moments" ("Introduction: The Shape of Vampires," *Blood Read*, 5).

anything that is different. Of course, the "-isms" and fears are not only past tense, and the repressed hate and projections continue.

In the portrayal of Dracula, Stoker captured an image of the dangerous foreigner. Like various mythic figures of accursed wanderers, Dracula (as most other vampires since) has no soul. The "wandering Jew" stories are seen as a backdrop for Stoker's aristocratic vampire. Bram Dijkstra reveals how the focus shifted from novel to first film: "In [Stoker's] *Dracula* the erotic depredations of the Semitic vampire still took precedence. In *Nosferatu* the *economic* eroticism of the vampire took center stage."[45] Glover sees Dracula as "a tormented racialized Other."[46] But since Dracula lives on the "edge" of Christendom, he can also represent the Turkish/Muslim threat, as in Coppola's retelling at the beginning of his film of Vlad/Dracula's fighting the Muslims in 1462. Transylvania has become a mythic place of many monsters in contemporary Halloween culture, but geographically it is remote and rural, strategically located for placing the Other.

Since "location is everything," many scholars have theorized that Stoker's Dracula, moving from Eastern Europe to England, embodies a "reverse colonization." At the height of empire, England had penetrated much of the world. Stephen Arata speculates: "Vampires are generated by racial enervation and the decline of empire, not vice versa. They are produced, in other words, by the very conditions characterizing late-Victorian Britain."[47] But (in Stoker and Murnau, not in Coppola) Dracula's goal is the British women, especially Mina. Arata provides insight: "If in this novel blood stands for race, then women quite literally become the vehicles of racial propagation. The struggle between the two camps is thus on one level a struggle over access to women's bodies, and Dracula's biological colonization of women becomes a horrific parody

---

45. *Evil Sisters*, 427. Dijkstra has much to say about the anti-Semitic shadowing of the vampire: "It's an old story: the Jew's gynersensual erotic degeneracy creates the effeminacy that causes him to hunt for blood" (ibid., 431). "The monster of Nazism still roams among us—for the fictions of gender dualism that permitted it to gain power still darken our lives" (ibid., 444).

46. *Vampires, Mummies, and Liberals*, 21. "What is finally at stake in *Dracula* is the continuing possibility of racial glory, and consequently questions of birth and reproduction are always close at hand"(ibid., 98).

47. Stephen D. Arata, "The Occidental Tourist: *Dracula* and the Anxiety of Reverse Colonization," *Dracula*, 465. Glover adds that this reverse colonization goes further: "Dracula imperils not simply his victims' personal identities, but also their cultural, political, and racial selves. In *Dracula* vampirism designates a kind of colonization of the body" (*Vampires, Mummies, and Liberals*, 21). Zanger considers Dracula as "an inverted Crusader" ("The Vampire Next Door," 23).

of the sanctioned exploitation practiced by the Western male characters."[48] So Dracula becomes a parody of British imperialism, with all its sexism, religious superiority, and economic exploitation. As Max Schreck/Count Orlock says to Murnau in *Shadow of the Vampire*, "You and I are not so different."

Both colonization and the threat of reverse colonization are apocalyptic, depending on your position. I want to argue that the Christian Apocalypse can be read as other than a victory of good over evil, of God over the threat of the reverse colonization of earth and heaven. Or is it that the colonizer, represented by the whore of Babylon and various beasts, is being defeated and then colonized by God? The whore and the kings are certainly aristocrats, reveling in their excessive wealth until the end. But God is also an aristocrat, encased in the heavenly throne room, surrounded by adoring musicians and worshipers. God, too, colonizes bodies; in an admittedly literal reading, the intaking of communion wine and bread has a price. Even further, in the future utopia, the new Jerusalem, there is wealth almost beyond excess. Dracula's aristocratic settings are in real need of renovation. God provides the ultimate luxury. "Vampires provide a metaphor for capital accumulation";[49] so too does the Apocalypse serve as a model for otherworldly social mobility.

Moretti (from Marx) confirms that capitalism is vampiric. In an example closer to home, I am reminded of Canadian First Nation spiritual beings, the We(e)ndigoes, who are vampiric, cannibalistic creatures of the northern regions. Ojibway scholar Basil Johnson shows how these creatures arose out of fear of the frozen winters and scarcity of food, but also in response to European colonization and genocide. One can become Wendigo by being greedy or selfish, by the abuses of another human being. "Going Wendigo" has to do with indulging in excesses and with going insane, even to the point of eating relatives. Like the beasts of the Apocalypse, these creatures do not speak. And like the medieval renditions of the hell mouth, Wendigoes eat up their victims. One must be very watchful not to succumb to this northern ghost-demon, or to

---

48. Arata, "The Occidental Tourist," 468. Michael Dennison notes that Harker arrives at Dracula's castle on the Eve of St. George's Day, seen by the locals as a time when evil reigns. "St. George is reported to have destroyed a woman-eating dragon (and Dracula means son of a dragon)." "Also, St. George is patron saint of England, and Harker and his companions do no less than save England from reverse colonization by Transylvanian vampirism" (*Vampirism: Literary Tropes of Decadence and Entropy* (New York: Peter Lang, 2001), 89).

49. Davenport-Hines, *Gothic*, 262.

become one. Margaret Atwood observes: "[T]he Wendigo is a psychic fragment. . . ."[50] I wonder if all the apocalyptic monsters—the demonic beasts, along with the Son of Man, warrior angels, God—are not "psychic fragments" in various ways. The vampiric excess and destruction leave one terrorized. The Christian believer has to drink blood (of Christ/the Lamb) in order to gain access to the heavenly excess. The alternative is eternity in the profusion of hell. That begs the question: who are the real vampires?

There are many variations on the ancient Wendigo stories, but Johnson makes a link to the present. He states, "Actually, the Wendigoes did not die out or disappear; they have only been assimilated and reincarnated as corporations, conglomerates, and multinationals."[51] The vampire is really living large in the modern world—designer clothes, luxury cars, multiple homes—all at the expense of land and nature and traditional cultures. Perhaps the plague-bearer (the Nosferatu) has millions of offspring, only now they have evolved, like the filmic Draculas, into romantic and corporate heroes. The invisible hand (of capitalism) has become one more shape-shifting form of the vampire.

CONCLUSION: THE THIRST FOR RIGHTEOUSNESS

With the turn of the new millennium I half imagined that vampires might begin to die out, or at least lose some visibility. But no, they are gaining momentum, like the apocalyptic rapture books and films. To be one of the undead, either cursed (in hell, or roaming the earth as a vampire) or blessed (in heaven as an angelic believer), seems to come in waves of both fear and desire in these fictional fantasies. Stoker's reptilian figure has staying power in whatever form he morphs. So does Jesus. Vampires are starting to make sense. But with James Woods's character in *Vampires*, I still do not understand God. After watching a multitude of vampire movies and reading way too much apocalyptic literature and theology, I am beginning to think the Draculas in particular have something important to tell us about apocalyptic fear and desire.

At the time of this writing, I am embarking with others on a "living-wage campaign" both in the city where I live and at the college where I teach. In investigating the huge economic inequities that exist in our

---

50. Margaret Atwood, *Strange Things: The Malevolent North in Canadian Literature* (Oxford: Clarendon, 1995), 73.

51. Basil Johnson, *The Manitous: The Spiritual World of the Ojibway* (New York: HarperCollinsPublishers, 1995), 235.

society, I am learning more about systemic classism. Writer Barbara Ehrenreich spent a year working low-wage jobs in various cities in the United States. What she discovered was how impossible it was to live on one low-wage job; in most locations she had to work two jobs—without health care, adequate or safe housing, or the ability to put any of her income into savings. While working in Maine, she walked across the street one night to attend a Christian tent revival. The preaching was centered on eschatological hope, the promise of Jesus' second coming, and the heavenly rewards for belief. Ehrenreich's thoughts went elsewhere:

> It would be nice if someone would read this sad-eyed crowd the Sermon on the Mount, accompanied by a rousing commentary on income inequality and the need for a hike in the minimum wage. But Jesus makes his appearance here only as a corpse; the living man, the wine-guzzling vagrant and precocious socialist, is never once mentioned, nor anything he ever had to say. Christ crucified rules, and it may be that the true business of modern Christianity is to crucify him again and again so that he can never get a word out of his mouth. I would like to stay around for the speaking in tongues, should it occur, but the mosquitoes, worked into a frenzy by all this talk of His blood, are launching a full-scale attack. I get up to leave, timing my exit for when the preacher's metronomic head movements have him looking the other way, and walk out to search for my car, half expecting to find Jesus out there in the dark, gagged and tethered to a tent pole.[52]

Ehrenreich envisions the impaled, silent Jesus, but there is also the apocalyptic, triumphant, almost-silent Jesus. I want the Jesus of the Apocalypse of John to preach for economic justice and human rights. When the Virgin Mary was appearing in Conyers, Georgia, in the 1990s, she continually expounded on sin and repentance and the end time. She never once called for an increase in the Georgia minimum wage (which until recently was $3.25 an hour). The vampires are definitely on the loose again, but the demon hunters do not know whom to stake. Such a vision of apocalyptic hope is in itself draining the life-force out of the soul of justice. Obviously, there is a difference between hungering and thirsting for righteousness—or for the righteous. The Draculas desire the latter. But does God desire both?

---

52. Barbara Ehrenreich, *Nickel and Dimed: On (Not) Getting by in America* (New York: Metropolitan, 2001), 68–69.

3. ATOMIC ANXIETY IN COLD WAR BRITAIN
Science, Sin, and Uncertainty in Nuclear Monster Films
Neal R. McCrillis

With the Cold War now definitely ended, interest in the subject has broadened geographically and topically from the nearly exclusive focus on U.S.-Soviet diplomacy. In fact, the long dominant approach, Alan Dobson writes in a recent essay, relied upon "an over-simplified paradigm which offers an analysis based on a bipolar zero-sum security conflict between contending and irreconcilable socio-political economic systems led by two superpowers accompanied by their attendant acolytes."[1] Consequently, we have begun to rethink Britain's position during the late 1940s and 1950s and to give greater consideration to the culture that characterized Britain during the immediate postwar period.

As the most popular entertainment medium of its day, film provides a rich insight into attitudes during the Cold War that gripped the West for decades after the Second World War. Recent works such as Stephen Whitfield's *The Culture of the Cold War* (1996) and Joyce Evans's *Celluloid Mushroom Clouds* (1998) explore and attempt to explain the nature of Cold War culture.[2] On the other hand, very little work has been done on

---

1. Alan P. Dobson, "Anglo-American Relations and the Cold War," *Deconstructing and Reconstructing the Cold War*, ed. Alan P. Dobson (Aldershot: Ashgate, 1999), 70.

2. Other works include Nora Sayre, *Running Time: Films of the Cold War* (New York: The Dial Press, 1982); Michael Strada, and Harold Troper, *Friend or Foe? Russians in American Film and Foreign Policy, 1933–1991* (Lanham, Md.: Scarecrow, 1997); and Steven Mintz and Randy Roberts, eds., *Hollywood's America: United States History Through Its Films* (St. James, N.Y.: Brandywine Press, 1993). For a Cold War filmography, see Mick Broderick, *Nuclear Movies: A Critical Analysis and Filmography of International Feature Films Dealing with Experimentation, Aliens, Terrorism, Holocaust and Other Disaster Scenarios, 1914–1989* (Jefferson, N.C.: McFarland, 1991).

Britain, particularly on British cinema during the immediate postwar years.[3] Yet Britain had the second highest output of Cold War films and one of the highest rates of cinema attendance in the world. In 1946 the British public made 1.635 billion visits to the cinema, or thirty-three visits per person per year. Even in 1960, after television had made massive inroads into attendance, the British public made 515 million visits to the cinema each year. Roughly a third of the films seen were British: well over a hundred films per year. And Britain was the second largest producer of Cold War genre films, accounting for 12 percent of the world's total output.[4] A number of these were science fiction films—couched in Christian notions of human imperfection and sin—that demonstrate the level of British skepticism about Cold War truths and nuclear weaponry.

During the period from 1946 to 1960, Cold War tensions reached their peak and then gradually and episodically eased, leading, belatedly, to détente.[5] In America the cinematic cold war began in 1948 with the release of films such as *The Iron Curtain*. The United States government had already proclaimed the Truman Doctrine and was investigating Communist activity in Hollywood. In October 1947 a Gallup poll found 76 percent of Americans agreed with the statement, "Russia is trying to build herself up to be the ruling power of the world."[6] Responding to the new environment, Hollywood began producing overtly anti-Communist films, such as *Red Menace* (1949), as well as developing more subtle anti-Communist science fiction pictures. Within a short period, however, the American public became increasingly concerned about its government's nuclear testing. By 1956 the United States had carried out twenty-three nuclear tests at the Bikini Atoll, including the infamous "Bravo Test" (1954), which severely injured hundreds of inhabitants of Rongelap Island and Japanese fishermen on the *Fukuryu Maru*. Between 1951 and 1963 the United States also conducted one

---

3. The authoritative *British Cinema Source Book* by Elaine Burrows, Janet Moat, David Sharp, and Linda Wood (London: British Film Institute, 1995) lists books on each film era. Counting publications covering each decade, there are eighteen works on the 1920s and ten publications on the 1960s. For the 1950s, however, the *Source Book* lists only two works, one of which is a fifteen-page pamphlet. For the second half of the 1940s the situation is better, with seven works listed. However, none of these works is concerned with Cold War films or culture.

4. John Caughie and Kevin Rockett, *The Companion to British and Irish Cinema* (London: British Film Institute and Cassell, 1996); and Broderick, *Nuclear Movies*, xviii.

5. Although the U-2 affair of 1960 demonstrated the Cold War was not over, the late 1950s witnessed the first easing of tensions with the Geneva Summit (1955), the nuclear test ban talks (1957), and the Nixon-Khrushchev exchanges (1959).

6. Joyce A Evans, *Celluloid Mushroom Clouds: Hollywood and the Atomic Bomb* (Boulder, Colo.: Westview, 1998), 59.

hundred above-ground nuclear tests in the Nevada desert. Scientists such as Linus Pauling and Leo Azilard, presidential candidate Adlai Stevenson, and leaders of the National Committee for a Sane Nuclear Policy (SANE) criticized such testing. Finally, in 1959 the government began warning Americans about strontium 90, which was found in increasing concentrations in milk due to radioactive fallout.

The British government and people were also concerned about the Communist threat and the dangers of nuclear weapons. As early as February 1946 British observers were appalled to watch the Soviets forcibly merge the SPD and KPD in their zone of Germany. This was quickly followed by the formation of a Foreign Office committee to investigate the Soviet threat.[7] During 1946 one of the first spies was discovered passing nuclear secrets to the Soviets. Dr. Alan Nunn May, a British scientist, had worked in the Canadian Chalk River Plant. In 1948, two years before the United States, the United Kingdom adopted new civil defense measures in response to the perceived Soviet threat.[8] During the same year, the British government purged Communists from the civil service; the following year the Trades Union Congress withdrew from the Communist-led World Federation of Trade Unions.

Yet the British response to the Soviet threat also differed from that of the United States. Although one critic thought he "smelled communism" in the Italian film *The Bicycle Thief* (1947), in Britain there was nothing comparable to the American anti-Communist scare. In 1950 the famous British director and producer Basil Wright openly ridiculed "the anti-Communist psychosis" which characterized the American and Canadian film world.[9] In addition, British officials were increasingly uneasy about the Anglo-American "special relationship." The McMahon Act of August 1946 ended atomic cooperation between the United States and Britain; soon after, the British government began development of its own nuclear weapons.

---

7. In 1948 this committee was supplanted by the covert Information Research Department, which prepared materials on Communist activities around the world.

8. Actually, British civil defense measures were suspended but never repealed after WWII. The legislation of 1948 modified civil defense to take into account the expected effects of nuclear attack. See Royal Daniel Sloan, "The Politics of Civil Defense: Great Britain and the United States" (Ph.D. diss., University of Chicago, 1958).

9. Richard Winnington, "Bicycle Thieves," *Sight and Sound* 19 (1950): 26; and Basil Wright, "Flesh, Fowl or . . . ?" *Sight and Sound* 19 (1950): 43. On the response to America's Cold War hysteria, see Robert Mayer, "Hollywood Report," *Sight and Sound* 17 (1948): 32–34; Karel Reisz, "Hollywood's Anti-Red Boomerang," *Sight and Sound* 22 (1953): 132–37, 148; and John Cutts and Penelope Houston, "Blacklisted," *Sight and Sound* 27 (1957): 15–19, 53.

There were other indications of Anglo-American tensions. In a March 1947 letter, one Foreign Office official complained that further financial assistance from the United States "will be made dependent on our accepting 'US Administrators', one of whom will sit in the little room next to Uncle Ernie's [Foreign Secretary Ernest Bevin] where we sometimes have tea." A few years later Anthony Eden, foreign secretary in the new Conservative government, criticized U.S. leadership and its "rampant posturing." He remarked to his private secretary that the Soviets and Americans were like "two unwieldy prehistoric monsters floundering about in the mud."[10] British leaders sometimes found their country's interests jeopardized by America's overriding focus on Soviet expansionism. Only repeated threats by the British government forced the United States in 1954 to ease the trade embargo against the Soviet Union.[11] During the 1955 war games conducted by NATO shortly after the United States had adopted a strategic policy based on massive nuclear retaliation, over three hundred imaginary H-bombs were dropped in the European theater.[12] At the same time, Britain's humiliating setback during the 1956 Suez Crisis undermined British pretensions. The 1957 "White Paper on Defence" offered a simple but brutal assessment: "It must be frankly recognized that [t]here [sic] is at present no means of providing adequate protection for the people of this country against the consequences of an attack with nuclear weapons."[13]

Some British observers rightly concluded that the country would be fatally vulnerable during a world war. In the television play *Offshore Island*, produced in 1959 but written in 1954, Margharnita Laski follows a family that has survived atomic warfare. An American reconnaissance squad discovers the "C.P.s" (contaminated persons) and seeks to sterilize them and ship them to an American concentration camp. Afterward the Americans and Soviets jointly destroy the uncontaminated valley with a tactical nuclear weapon. Superpower harmony and preservation of American genetic stock takes precedence over British lives. The

---

10. Gladwyn Jebb to Pierson Dixon, 13 March 1947, quoted in Sean Greenwood, *Britain and the Cold War, 1945–1991* (Houndmills, Basingstoke: Macmillan Press, 2000), 42; and E. Shuckburgh, *Descent to Suez: Diaries 1951–56*, 24 November 1952, quoted in Greenwood, Britain and the Cold War, 106.

11. Dobson, "Anglo-American," 82–83.

12. Spencer R Weart, *Nuclear Fear: A History of Images* (Cambridge, Mass.: Harvard University Press, 1988), 216.

13. William P.Synder, *The Politics of British Defense Policy* (Ohio State University Press, 1964), 2.

geneticist J. B. S. Haldane, who left for India in 1957, expressed similar anti-American sentiments. On July 25, 1956, Haldane told *The Times* that he was leaving Britain because "I want to live in a free country where there are no foreign troops based all over the place."[14]

The British were profoundly uneasy about American foreign policy, especially as it related to nuclear weaponry. Polls during the late 1950s regularly found that one-third to one-fifth of the British public supported unilateral British disarmament. These polls demonstrated the widespread concern about superpower domination and nuclear weapons that found its most memorable expression through the Campaign for Nuclear Disarmament (CND), launched in 1958. There was a pervasive pessimism in Britain. In a 1953 article that appeared in the film magazine *Sight and Sound,* critic and historian Penelope Houston argued that the popularity of science fiction films demonstrated an increasing sense of vulnerability. "Human agency now counts for little," she wrote, "and the rocket, the atomic weapon, the electronic gadget, the cybernetics brain machine . . . have taken charge." David Fisher, another *Sight and Sound* contributor, argued this sense of human helplessness explains the British public's affection for the cartoon character Mr. Magoo. According to Fisher, Mr. Magoo "represents for us the man who would be responsible and serious in a world that seems insane; he is a creation of the 'fifties', the age of anxiety; his situation reflects our own."[15] This characteristic British response to the Cold War explains why Cold War comedy proved more popular in Britain than in America.[16]

British films were reflective of a less-pronounced anti-Communism, of a sense of distance from the near hysteria of the American Red scare. Especially during the second half of the 1950s, British films suggest a skepticism toward Cold War "truths." British films also reveal tensions between British and American views of the Cold War. There were, for instance, relatively few British films castigating "the Communist menace" or glorifying the military machine in the manner of the American

---

14. Quoted in Sloan, "The Politics of Civil Defense," 78.

15. Penelope Houston, "Glimpses of the Moon," *Sight and Sound* 23 (1953): 188; and David Fisher, "Two Premieres: Disney & U.P.A.," *Sight and Sound* 23 (1953): 41.

16. Notable British Cold War comedies include *Mr. Drake's Duck* (1951), *Our Man in Havana* (1959), and *The Mouse That Roared* (1959). See also Neal R. McCrillis, "British Comedy Films during the Cold War: Signs of Discord in the Anglo-American Special Relationship (1945–1960)" (paper presented at the Southern Conference of British Studies and Southern Historical Association, Louisville, Ky., 11 November 2000).

film *Strategic Air Command* (1955). In fact, the British film *Seven Days to Noon* (1950) suggests an apprehensive attitude toward nuclear weapons. In this Boulting brothers' film the main character, a professor angered by unrestricted nuclear research, steals an atomic bomb and threatens to destroy London if government research is not halted.[17] Typically, however, the British public seemed to respond to the Soviet nuclear threat with apprehension or even despair rather than with protest or aggression.[18]

During the 1950s the British public (like their American and Japanese counterparts) flocked to see radiation-induced monster films, a flourishing new science fiction genre. The popularity of nuclear monster movies began with the American film *The Thing from Another World* (1951) and continued largely unabated for a decade and a half. Typically these films were very inexpensive, costing about $100,000, one-tenth the budget of a Hollywood feature. When *The Beast from 20,000 Fathoms* (1953) was released in America, its box-office success guaranteed many imitators. For several years, audiences, particularly younger moviegoers, rushed to see a whole array of monster films such as *Them!* (1954). These popular 1950s films were overtly nonpolitical but provided audiences with a means of addressing their concerns about nuclear weapons while profiting movie studios. Joyce Evans argues that American films in this genre shared a "fear of transmutation" sparked by worries about Communism.[19] Such worries were deeply imbedded in American Cold War culture and its fear of Communist subversion.

This essay focuses on two Cold War British films from the nuclear-monster genre. *Behemoth the Sea Monster* (1958) and *The Quatermass Xperiment* (1955) expressed many of the same concerns about human fallibility and technology as American films. Yet, these British films were demonstrably different. In contrast to their American counterparts, these British films suggest a less pronounced anti-Communism, a sense of distance from the paranoia in America. The films also articulate a different national sensibility by contrasting American and British characters. In both films, an American scientist is the main protagonist. He represents the ambiguous nature of modern science with its supremacy of reason and knowledge over morality and humanity. These British films also express a pervasive unease about science's tampering with the

---

17. The American film *The Day the Earth Stood Still* (1951) addresses somewhat similar concerns about nuclear weaponry.
18. Sloan, "The Politics of Civil Defense," 207.
19. Evans, *Celluloid*, 117.

natural order. Frequently these concerns are expressed in Judeo-Christian terms and through biblical references.

One of the more persistent themes of Western thought is the struggle between our thirst for knowledge to control nature and our awareness of the human potential to misuse these powers. This theme is central to the Jewish tradition of the Leviathan, a she-dragon who embodies all evil, including sin and egotism. The myth can be traced back to ancient Mesopotamia.[20] In the second-century story *The Golden Ass*, the Roman writer Apuleius tells the story of Lucius, whose quest for magical powers leads to disaster. Misusing a spell, Lucius is metamorphosed into an ass, the slave of his animal passions and whims. He is freed only after accepting the goddess Isis and "bend[ing his] neck to the yoke of this ministry."[21] Although central to the Western understanding of human beings and the nature of evil, these ideas were suppressed after the Enlightenment.

Only after the incredible destruction of the First World War did Western literature and thought return to the old ideas. Postwar poetry and fiction questioned the very viability of human beings, given their war-making capacity. W. B. Yeats offered a frightening vision of a new cycle of human history in "The Second Coming" (1921):[22]

> Surely some revelation is at hand;
> Surely the Second Coming is at hand.
> The Second Coming! Hardly are those words out
> When a vast image out of *Spiritus Mundi*
> Troubles my sight: somewhere in the sands of the desert
> A shape with lion body and the head of a man,
> A gaze blank and pitiless as the sun,
> Is moving its slow thighs, while all about it
> Reel shadows of the indignant desert birds.
> The darkness drops again; but now I know
> That twenty centuries of stony sleep
> Were vexed to nightmare by a rocking cradle,
> And what rough beast, its hour come round at last,
> Slouches towards Bethlehem to be born?

---

20. Arthur Cotterell, *A Dictionary of World Mythology* (New York: Putnam, 1979), 37–38.

21. Apuleius, *The Golden Ass*, trans. Jack Lindsay (Bloomington: Indiana University Press, 1960), 244.

22. Available from http://well.com/user/eob/poetry/The_Second_Coming.

Yeats's unique personal vision bears the stamp of traditional Western concepts of sin and retribution. He also alludes to a half-human, half-animal creature that may be Yeats's postwar definition of human nature. Like the Leviathan of Jewish tradition, this monster will turn against us who have wreaked havoc and transgressed the nature order. Similarly, the series of expressionist drawings, "The War, as I Saw It," carried by *Simplicissimus* magazine during 1920, conveyed the same despairing tone and fear that humans would destroy themselves. The film *Things to Come* (1936), based on H. G. Wells's novel, also depicted the destruction of a future world war, although it suggested humankind would survive to create a better world in the distant future.

During the Cold War, concerns about human fallibility and sin were exacerbated by worries about the devastating nature of nuclear technology. There was profound unease about the consequences of this quantum leap in human power, given our flawed and fallible nature. Beginning with the first nuclear test, commentators were drawn to biblical allusions—creative, destructive, apocalyptic—in their search to understand the dilemma posed by nuclear power. Observing the Trinity Test, the first atomic bomb explosion, journalist William Laurence lapsed into a mystical frame of mind, freely resorting to religious phraseology:

> Up it went, a great ball of fire about a mile in diameter, changing colors as it kept shooting upward, from deep purple to orange, expanding, growing bigger, rising as it expanded, an elemental force freed from its bonds after being chained for billions of years. For a fleeting instant the color was unearthly green, such as one sees only in the corona of the sun during a total eclipse. It was as though the earth had opened and the skies had split. One felt as though one were present at the moment of creation when God said: "Let there be light."
>
> To another observer . . . the spectacle was "the nearest thing to doomsday that one could possibly imagine. I am sure," he said, "that at the end of the world-in the last millisecond of the earth's existence-the last man will see what we have just seen."[23]

Even the normally phlegmatic military commander of the Manhattan Project thought the nuclear explosion "warned of doomsday and made

---

23. William L. Laurence, *Dawn Over Zero: The Story of the Atomic Bomb* (New York: Knopf, 1956), 10.

us feel that we puny things were blasphemous to dare tamper with the forces heretofore reserved to the Almighty."[24] What would be the retribution for such a violation of the natural order? Such questions and worries were often channeled through Cold War films. In contrast to American films such as *The Thing* (1951) and *Them!* (1954), British films in the nuclear monster genre largely ignored Communist subversion while focusing on the threat posed by "the false promises of science."[25]

In Britain the director of *The Beast from 20,000 Fathoms* (1953), Eugene Lourie, made *Behemoth the Sea Monster* (1958) at Eros Films. The film, now rarely seen or discussed, was an inexpensive "B" movie, although passably acted and—for the time—containing reasonably good special effects and animation sequences. Eugene Lourie was an art director brought into directing by the famous French director Jean Renoir. The film offers insights into Cold War British attitudes, particularly concerns about nuclear weapons. *Behemoth the Sea Monster*, like a number of other films of its day, invoked biblical warnings about the development, testing, and use of nuclear weapons. The film opens with a shot of a stormy sea and a voice intoning "And the Lord said, 'Behold now the behemoth'" (Job 40:15).[26] This is followed by stock footage of the Bikini Atoll H-bomb test explosion and scientists in protective gear carrying Geiger counters. "And afterwards," says American scientist Steve Karnes, "these mysterious figures, faces masked with lead. They are ourselves, men, kings of the earth, trying to measure the extent of the destruction they themselves have created."

The camera pulls back to a lecture hall where Steve Karnes is delivering a paper to a gathering of British scientists. He explains that there have been approximately 143 nuclear tests to date and that each one of them has released hundreds of tons of radioactive material into the air and water. Yet, we know that humans should not be exposed to more than one millionth of a gram of radiation. Moreover, he explains, we have disposed of nuclear waste in lead containers that are disintegrating in the sea and building up horrific levels of radioactivity among sea life

---

24. Ibid., 194. See also Weart, *Nuclear Fear*, 184.

25. Marcia Landy, *British Genres: Cinema and Society, 1930–1960* (Princeton: Princeton University Press, 1991), 395. In *The Thing* (1951) a man-eating carrot attacks an Antarctic science station and tramples an overly inquisitive scientist. *Them!* featured giant ants, which mutated after the Trinity Test in 1945 and threatened Los Angeles from their sewer lair. The plots of both films feature incomprehensible and alien outsiders that threaten to destroy all life. There is an obvious parallel to American fears of Communism.

26. Quotations from the film *Behemoth* are my own transcription.

as it works its way up the food chain. We have created a "biological chain reaction, a geometrical progressive of deadly menace." "For all we know," he ends, "what we have started may have already matured. And who can tell when this, this, whatever it is, will rise to the surface and strike back at us."

The technological menace spawned from international Cold War tensions is contrasted with the unhurried, idyllic life of the Cornish village of Looe. A young woman and her father have brought in their day's catch using techniques unchanged from the previous century. It is here, in remote traditional England with its friendly village pub, that Karnes's prediction comes to fruition. A rabid-like dinosaur, brought from the ocean depths by nuclear testing and now emitting a highly lethal level of radiation, kills a fisherman and then other innocent civilians along the coast. When Karnes and his British colleague Professor Bickford investigate, they find a surviving fisherman with ulcers, burns, and spotting on his skin. In case the audience has not connected these symptoms to historical experience, Karnes notes, "The same symptoms as Hiroshima." Later in the film, a boy who encounters the behemoth falls into a crouched position and is immediately turned to charred remains. The film thereby makes a visual link to photographs of the Hiroshima victims.

In contrast to *Them!* and a number of other American films, the threats posed in *Behemoth the Sea Monster* are, in the main, concretely physical and scientific, rather than subversive and cultural. Following as it did on the heels of the Suez Crisis of 1956, the film conveys a foreboding sense of the nuclear threat and contains a contradictory attitude toward modernity as represented by science. When informed of the monstrous reptile's existence, the director of the natural history museum, Dr. Sampson, excitedly decides to investigate. His fascination seems a little perverse. He has waited all his life to see a dinosaur and seems to regret the need to eliminate such a wonderful specimen. He volunteers to fly over the area where the serpent is believed to be to take photographs. After sighting the monster, Sampson, the helicopter, and its pilot are vaporized by the behemoth's radiation. Given the eccentric nature of the Sampson character, the film reinforces the genre's portrayal of academic scientists as "obstructionists or troublesome idealists."[27]

The film's main character and protagonist, however, is also a scientist, although a "practical" marine biologist. American Steve Karnes initially

---

27. Sayre, *Running Time*, 198.

alienates British colleagues with his somewhat forceful manner. The chairman of the royal commission, Professor Bickford, haughtily dismisses Karnes's claim that he is sitting on his "tail" and seems bemused by Karnes's familiarity ("You chaps are great ones for shaking hands."). But unlike the American scientist in *The Quatermass Xperiment*, Karnes is willing to defer to British authority and collaborate with it. The result is a gradually increasing respect between British leaders and the American scientist. In the end, Karnes works with British scientists to devise a radium-tipped torpedo, which he fires at the behemoth from a mini-submarine in the Thames River. This scientific solution ends the immediate threat. But as the two scientists return to their automobile, a radio announcer reads a report from America about "mountains of dead fish washing ashore along the coast from Maine to Florida." The danger remains.

Behemoth the Sea Monster suggests that technological and scientific progress, as epitomized by nuclear weaponry, represents a grave threat for Cold War Britain. The opening of the film makes this point clearly. At the funeral of a fisherman killed by the monster, a minister reads from the Book of Job. The minister combines passages from chapters 40 and 41, referring to both Leviathan and Behemoth. Although there is no consensus on the literal meaning of the Old Testament references,[28] in Hebrew legend the Behemoth is a powerful creature who will come forth during a climactic battle between good and evil. In the film, the minister quotes from Job: "Out of his mouth go burning lamps, and sparks of fire leap out. Out of his nostrils goeth smoke, as out of a seething pot or cauldron. His breath kindleth coals, and a flame goeth out of his mouth. . . . He maketh the deep to boil like a pot: he maketh the sea like a pot of ointment."[29] In other passages from Job not quoted by the minister, the sea monster appears to be God's wrath upon the unfaithful and egotistical: "Upon earth there is not his like, who is made without fear. He beholdeth all high things: he is a king over all the children of pride" (Job 41:34).[30] Through the biblical references the film links its concerns about nuclear weapons to an older tradition of worrying about human power and pride.

---

28. The behemoth is a marsh creature, sometimes thought to be a hippopotamus. Leviathan, on the other hand, is generally regarded as a sea monster, possibly a crocodile or whale, who is also identified as a manifestation of God's power (Job 41:10). The film combines references to the two creatures.

29. The minister's eulogy combines Job 41:19–21 and 31.

30. Biblical quotations are from the *King James Version*.

In 1955 Sir James Carrera produced the highly successful film *The Quatermass Xperiment*. His company, Hammer Films, was later to become synonymous with the revival of horror films.[31] Critics have noted that Hammer Films became notorious for exploiting every opportunity to increase audience interest, in the case of *The Quatermass Xperiment* using a salaciously suggestive "X" in the title. Like *Behemoth the Sea Monster, The Quatermass Xperiment* opens with a foreboding musical score. Against a nighttime sky broken by a church steeple, stereotypical celluloid lovers giggle and embrace as they run into a field. Suddenly the quiet night air is filled with a whining noise, and the couple flees to a nearby farmhouse. Then a remarkably phallic rocket buries itself deep into the ground where the couple had been kissing. The combination of sex and violence so characteristic of later Hammer Films is already apparent in this early movie.

The protagonist, American researcher Dr. Quatermass, has sent the first rocket into space and now awaits news of the fate of his crew. Later we discover that two of the crewmembers have been turned into an unidentifiable gel. Meanwhile a third, Victor Caroon, is suffering from a serious ailment, possibly "rocket radiation."[32] Caroon is unable to communicate, and his skin appears scarred like that of a victim of radiation burns. His bone structure has also been altered. Dr. Quatermass speculates that Caroon has been affected by some kind of celestial energy organism "with the ability to destroy, and possess, and multiply . . . at will."

The brilliant but aggressive and egotistical Dr. Quatermass personifies science. At one point a Ministry of Defense official, Mr. Blake, criticizes Quatermass for sending up the spaceship without official approval. The scientist dismisses the charge. "If the whole world waited for official sanction, it would be standing still. You took too long; I made my own decision. . . . Every experiment is a gamble." Furthermore, he adds, the astronauts in the spacecraft will be heroes, and the Ministry of Defense will not be able to stop them. "You mean I can't stop *you* now," says Blake. The film also suggests scientific inquiry precludes normal human pursuits. Quatermass has no female relationships or friendships of any kind. The only female character he addresses in the film is the wife of one of the

---

31. Beginning with *The Curse of Frankenstein* (1957), Hammer produced a succession of profitable horror films. Costing only £65,000, *The Curse of Frankenstein* grossed £2 million, half of which came from America.

32. Quotations from the film *Quatermass* are my own transcription.

astronauts, Judith Caroon. At one point he dismisses her concerns about Victor, telling her: "There's no room for personal feelings in science, Judith. Some of us have a mission. You should be very proud to have a husband who's willing to risk his life for the betterment of the whole world." Judith responds, "What world? Your world! The world of Quatermass!"

The scientist's antagonist is Inspector Lomax from the London Metropolitan Police. Although they eventually work together to destroy the monster, Lomax and Quatermass work within radically different ethical frameworks. Lomax's self-effacing, practical manner is contrasted with the rigid rationality and aggression of Quatermass. The audience is introduced to the middle-aged Lomax after he has received his paycheck and is preparing to take his wife out for their weekly lunch date. At a later point in the film, Lomax has to leave his wife on Sunday just as they are preparing for tea. His domesticity is a contrast to the sexless and apparently single life of Quatermass. Lomax is an old-fashioned Englishman with simple religious values. When Quatermass storms into his office, Lomax quietly asks him to sit; he does not want to be rude by sitting down while Quatermass remains standing. He explains that he is "a plain simple Bible man" with a "routine mind," and that he will investigate the disappearance of two astronauts as a murder case. He vainly asks for Quatermass's help. "Now look, Sir," he says pointedly, "nobody ever wins a cold war. One of us had better come over to the other side." The American scientist, on the other hand, places the search for knowledge above moral values and social mores. He is willing to sacrifice everything for the pursuit of scientific knowledge. He even refuses Lomax access to the dying Caroon, because "There's only one investigation likely to serve us any good purpose in this situation, Inspector. That's a scientific one."

The film does not resolve the conflict between Christian humanism and the seemingly amoral search for scientific knowledge. After escaping from the hospital and unsuccessfully attempting to commit suicide, Caroon continues his metamorphosis, first developing a bloated, cactus-like hand. Eventually he is transformed into a monstrous amoeba organism that can climb walls and hatches offspring from nodules in its skin. The film reaches its climax on a Sunday evening when, just as it is about to hatch thousands of young, a BBC crew discovers the monster high amongst the scaffolding inside Westminster Abbey. Quatermass manages to kill the organism by diverting London's power grid and electrocuting the monster. Lomax is relieved but worries about Quatermass's eagerness to explore space and his relentless search for knowledge.

"Well," he tells Quatermass, "this time you won. In my simple Bible way, I did a lot of praying. One world at a time is good enough for me." Having killed his former astronaut, Quatermass says nothing. As he walks away from Westminster Abbey, he pauses only to tell an assistant, "Start again." The film ends with the launch of a new rocket. Quatermass represents a human egotism run rampant that threatens the very existence of human civilization.

The postwar world of nuclear science and technology was often incomprehensible and certainly foreboding. In *Quatermass* Judith Caroon, seeing the rocket after its return, comments, "It's funny. It looks exactly the same. Yet, it's been, who knows how far. There isn't a word." Susan Sontag argues that the moral theme of 1950s science fiction films is the "the proper, or humane use of science versus the mad, obsessional use of science."[33] Both *The Quatermass Xperiment* and *Behemoth the Sea Monster* suggest the postwar British public's unease with nuclear weapons and with science generally. Both films also express this concern through Judeo-Christian concepts of human egotism and sin. "Stories of man-made catastrophes," writes one scholar of science fiction, "continue the ancient tradition of prophetic warning, by which sinful man is reminded of his disobedience and the wrath to come that his wrongdoing has earned." An Armageddon created by scientists rather than by God is no less the "consequence of our Original Sin."[34] Such concerns about the consequences and meaning of scientific inquiry can be traced back to the first development in nuclear science, the discovery of radioactivity in 1895. In his novel *Tono-Bungay* (1908), H. G. Wells worries about the combination of human ambition and nuclear science. The quantum leap in human power gained through nuclear weapons provided a tremendous potential for disaster that fueled "technological fantasies" and "fed the new apocalyptic imagination" that appeared in Aldous Huxley's *Ape and Essence* (1949). In Huxley's post-nuclear holocaust novel, the Arch-Vicar ridicules the scientists and technocrats. These "wretched slaves of wheels and ledgers," he says, "began to congratulate themselves on being the Conquerors of Nature. Conquerors of

---

33. Susan Sontag, "The Imagination of Disaster," *Against Interpretation and Other Essays* (New York: Farrar, Straus & Giroux, 1966), 216.

34. W. Warren Wagar, "The Rebellion of Nature," *The End of the World*, ed. Eric Rabkin, Martin H. Greenberg, and Joseph G. Olander (Carbondale: Southern Illinois University Press, 1983), 170; and Rabkin, Greenberg, and Olander, *The End*, viii.

Nature, indeed! In actual fact, of course, they had merely upset the equilibrium of Nature and were about to suffer the consequences."[35] Mid-twentieth-century writers and filmmakers increasingly saw scientists as "Epimetheus, unwisely accepting 'gifts' from the gods so that his curiosity may release a plague of troubles upon mankind."[36]

Concern only increased after the U. S. government acknowledged in 1953 that the superpowers possessed sufficient atomic firepower to annihilate the human species. In 1954 the United States provided film footage of the "Operation Ivy" hydrogen bomb test. Immediately there was a flood of articles, novels, and films about nuclear weapons. Grappling with the nuclear threat, many ordinary people sought time-worn explanations for the dangers they faced. What was most worrying was the tremendous power that rested in the hands of scientists and political leaders. For many, even natural occurrences no longer seemed natural: they were human in origin. In the wake of nuclear-test scares, it was reported that inhabitants of Seattle believed that the tiny pits they were finding in their windshields were caused by fallout from nuclear tests. In fact, the pits were the result of normal wear and damage caused by dirt.[37]

Science fiction films brought to the fore the tensions of the 1950s when the public was, as it were, torn between "unremitting banality and inconceivable terror." By the end of the 1950s, a sharper and more cynical mood was common in British films.[38] At the decade's conclusion Peter Sellers appeared in *The Mouse That Roared* (1959), which lampoons many of the hypocrisies and absurdities of the early Cold War period. The film features the multiple roles of Peter Sellers, who is a grand duchess, prime minister, and leader of the armed forces. To save its export trade in wine, the tiny principality of Grand Fenwick, founded in the fifteenth century by an English knight, declares war against the United States and plays the Cold War powers against one another. This film appeared in a Britain that had three years earlier suffered a humiliating defeat in the Suez Crisis and watched the young John Osborne's

---

35. Brian Stableford, "Man-Made Catastrophes," *The End*, 107; and Aldous Huxley, *Ape and Essence* (London: Chatto & Windus, 1967), 93.

36. Stableford, "Man-Made," 116.

37. Weart, *Nuclear Fear*, 187. Wagar estimates that among the 250 literary doomsdays published since 1914, the ratio of human to natural disasters is 2:1. He argues that this ratio marked an exact reversal of the earlier pattern (Wagar, "Rebellion," 141).

38. Sontag, "Imagination," 225. In part the greater cynicism reflected the easing of censorship rules. See James Robertson, *The Hidden Camera: British Film Censorship in Action, 1913–1972* (London: Routledge, 1989).

attacks on tired old Britain in *Look Back in Anger* (1956). *Behemoth the Sea Monster* shows the triumph of Anglo-American collaboration and science, yet suggests uncertainties that increasingly plagued British culture. *Behemoth the Sea Monster* and *The Quatermass Xperiment* express ambivalence toward science and technology, both of which are linked to present-day America. Concerns about science, particularly nuclear weapons, were often expressed by means of traditional Judeo-Christian concepts of human nature and sin. The nuclear monster films indicated the level of unease with atomic weapons and more pervasive worries about science and modernity. As one historian notes about *Seven Days to Noon*, "The film does not identify the Russians as the enemy; the enemy is modern life itself."

4. ALIENATION, SEX, AND AN UNSATISFACTORY ENDING
Themes and Features of Stories Old and New

Ralph J Brabban

Certain characteristics of storytelling are virtually universal throughout the record of telling stories. Among those characteristics are themes or features such as alienation, sex, and unsatisfactory endings. Whether in the recounting of ancient folk traditions or in the presentations of stories in new media, these themes and features play themselves out in many and varied ways.

Loneliness, or alienation and the search for belonging, has been one of those dominant themes in many ancient stories. It is also among the most common themes of the American imagination. From the classic story of the lonely Gilgamesh (one of the earliest extant narratives with a human hero) to the alienation and loneliness present in many of the works of countless modern authors (such as Hemingway and Faulkner), it is as if alienation and the search for repatriation are universal, but particularly central to the Western *mythos*. Many modern interpreters suggest that the common American ancestors came to this country as a response to their (often forced) alienation from their homelands; perhaps as a result, the ancient chord of a search for belonging is even more resonant to U.S. culture than to others. Regardless, alienation is and has been a common theme throughout history and is a common theme that strikes a chord in the American psyche.

Similarly, sex, sexuality, and the selling of sex are seemingly ubiquitous. Although sex is certainly not a new invention, contemporary American culture is saturated with sexuality and sexual images. The banality that sex sells is perhaps nowhere more obvious than in the marketing of our luxury and leisure items such as automobiles, fragrances, jewelry, or clothing. Modern media abound with examples. In this sense, the present is often seen as a continuation of the free-love era of the late 1960s. It is no coincidence that 1969 saw not only the modern seminal free-love event, Woodstock, but also saw the Academy Award's Best Picture presented to its first (and thus far only) X-rated film, *Midnight Cowboy*. But again, sex is nothing new. Modern promiscuity or the pre-occupation with sex has often been likened to the attitudes or decadence of ancient Rome, Greece, Babylon, or other previous civilizations. Stories of sexual adventures and intrigue abound even in such "staid" sources as the Hebrew Bible. The Book of Ruth is merely one example of a biblical book with a prominent sexual theme.

Additionally, a lack of closure or an ending that does not quite work or feels incomplete is a common feature throughout literature as well as in other contemporary media. Again, in the ancient story of Gilgamesh, the hero searches for immortality but finds it is not available to him as he wishes, but only posthumously via fame. So also, in the *Star Wars* saga George Lucas acknowledges that the final episodes—the ending of the story—will never be made. Science fiction fans will have to depend on themselves or others to make up what will undoubtedly be a multitude of endings. Lucas's story will never be told, at least as planned. It is with chagrin that the modern person realizes that "and they all lived happily ever after" is a fairy tale left behind in childhood, and not ever a reality for the present. As Augustine observed, "For these three do exist in the mind, and I do not see them anywhere else: the present time of things past is memory; the present time of things present is sight; the present of things future is expectation."[1] It is the human condition that the future will never become the present except as expectation or hope; the ending will always be incomplete.

With such themes or features as background, one might easily turn to compare any of a number of otherwise dissimilar works. This article will focus on a comparison of two works from different times and in different media: the biblical story of Ruth and the 1969 film *Midnight Cowboy*.

In this discussion there is no pretense that all aspects of the two works will or can be discussed. Only a limited number of meanings out of a much larger set can ever possibly be discovered. Nevertheless, this article will show that even such dissimilar works as these may have surprising connections.

---

1. Augustine, *The Confessions of St. Augustine*, trans. Rex Warner (New York: Penguin Putnam, 1963), 11.20.

MIDNIGHT COWBOY

When the American Film Institute announced its top one hundred American films of the twentieth century in 1998, one of the more surprising selections was number thirty-six, *Midnight Cowboy*. This film is the only one on the list that was originally rated "X" by the Motion Picture Association of America (MPAA), and it is the only film whose rating was later lowered (to an "R") without a single change in even one frame of the film.

Upon its release, *Midnight Cowboy* received rather mixed reviews, primarily due to its controversial content. One critic, for example, called it a "skillful, but ultimately pointless film exercise" and a "considerable step forward—or backward—into permissiveness."[2] It is perhaps significant that the film's competition in 1969 included *Easy Rider*, *The Wild Bunch*, *True Grit*, *Fellini Satyricon*, *The Prime of Miss Jean Brodie*, *Bob & Carol & Ted & Alice*, and *Z*. Sex, violence, and alienation seem to have been the dominant themes for the film industry that year.

Midnight Cowboy was based on James Leo Herlihy's 1965 novel of the same name. In many ways the film was true to the harsh mixture of loneliness and sex that Herlihy depicted, even though the plot was simplified by the deletion of a major plotline (including Tombaby Barefoot and Juanita). Such reductions are typical of modern film. As Browne notes, "'Popular cinema' is perhaps most clearly defined by the limited range of 'stories' it tells; the more 'simple' the story the more chance of successful theatrical release worldwide. Thus there is a 'folk tale' or even 'fairy tale' dimension to popular cinema. . . ."[3]

What is not simplified, however, is the feeling of loneliness the film captures from the book. This is nowhere more evident than when Joe Buck, the story's protagonist, is in Mr. O'Daniel's room expecting Mr. O'Daniel to be a procurer or manager for his sexual hustling, but instead finds he is a religious zealot who is as desperately lonely as Joe. O'Daniel yells, "They's no Beatitude for the Lonesome. The Book don't say they are blessed."[4] The lonesomeness of which O'Daniel speaks is the book's theme, and the film, like the novel, exudes an almost overwhelming feeling of sadness. Additionally, the film, like the novel, has only the thinnest hint of hope or completeness emerging at its conclusion.

---

2. Leslie Halliwell, *The Filmgoers Companion*, 6th ed. (New York: Hill & Wang, 1977), 486.
3. David Browne, "Film, Movies, Meanings," *Explorations in Theology and Film*, ed. Clive Marsh and Gaye Ortiz (Malden, Mass.: Blackwell, 1997), 16.
4. James Leo Herlihy, *Midnight Cowboy* (New York: Simon & Schuster, 1965), 137.

The film *Midnight Cowboy* is the story of a naïve Texan, Joe Buck (played by Jon Voight). The film begins with Joe preparing to quit his job at the local small-town diner where he is a dishwasher. He packs his bags, quits his job (without the fanfare for which he had hoped), and leaves to go to New York. There he anticipates that he will have great success as a male prostitute or hustler—a midnight cowboy.

When Joe reaches New York, he checks into a low- to moderate-rate hotel and begins to cruise the streets looking to pleasure women. Along the streets he is virtually ignored by everyone; he discovers that New York also has its down-and-out—alienated—populace. His only success is with Cass (Sylvia Miles), but even this success includes a reversal as Joe ends up paying her instead of getting paid by her.

After Joe leaves Cass, he goes to a bar where he meets the other main character of the film, Rico Rizzo (Dustin Hoffman), who is known as Ratzo. Ratzo, somewhat crippled but streetwise, chases off a transvestite who is hitting on Joe. Ratzo and Joe then strike up a conversation. Joe identifies himself as a hustler who needs a manager. Ratzo takes Joe to Mr. O'Daniel's hotel room (for a fee) on the pretense that O'Daniel (John McGiver) is such a manager. He is not. Joe, realizing he has been conned, flees, searching for Ratzo in order to strangle him.

As days pass, Joe continues to walk through the cinema district of New York; there he sees other men who are dressed as he. One is alone; another is surrounded by boys. With no income, Joe's funds soon run out; he is locked out of his hotel room and all his possessions are confiscated. Hungry and with no money, Joe goes back to the streets and allows a teenage boy to have oral sex with him in one of the movie theaters.

With nowhere to go, Joe wanders around and by chance sees Ratzo in a donut shop. Joe threatens Ratzo until he realizes that Ratzo is little better off than he is. Ratzo invites Joe to stay with him in a room in an abandoned, condemned tenement. The room has no electricity, but apparently does have water and gas. Joe and Ratzo develop a genuine friendship. They survive on the streets by Ratzo's wits: they steal food; Ratzo cooks. They also share their dreams: Joe still wants to be a hustler, apparently what he feels he is best at; Ratzo wants to go to Florida where his health will improve and he will become popular.

They determine that to accomplish their dreams Ratzo will help Joe; with the proceeds, they will go to Florida. Unfortunately, even clean clothes, polished boots, a steamed and blocked hat, and an address pickpocketed from a man leaving a gentleman's escort service do not give Joe the necessary decorum for his chosen profession. Their dreams go awry and their situation becomes worse. As winter comes and they have no heat, Ratzo gets sicker. Their tenement is destined to be demolished. So, to earn money, Joe returns to hustle in front of movie theaters and even to sell his blood to a blood bank.

While Joe and Ratzo spend an unusual moment in a restaurant, an eccentric couple (brother and sister) invites them to a party. Apparently, Joe's appearance was deemed abnormal enough to warrant an invitation to a psychedelic event. After they arrive, Ratzo determines that those present are "Wackos, they're all wacko,"[5] but he still eats all he can from the buffet, stuffs as much food as he can in his pockets, and generally steals whatever he can take. Meanwhile, Joe is introduced to marijuana, pills, alcohol, bizarre sexuality, and Shirley (Brenda Vaccaro). Shirley is what Joe has been looking for. She agrees to pay him $20 for his services, and they go back to her place. Afterwards, Shirley calls friends of hers and lines up future sexual encounters for Joe.

When Joe makes it back to the apartment, however, his hopes are crushed. Ratzo can no longer walk and doctors are out of the question. "Florida, just get me to Florida," he pleads. In desperate need of money, Joe goes back to the streets where he allows himself to be picked up by an out-of-town businessman, Towny (Bernard Hughes), only to beat the older man and rob him.

Joe and Ratzo get on the bus to go to Miami and anticipate the thirty-one hour trip. On the bus their roles shift; Joe begins to take care of the nearly helpless Ratzo. They agree that Ratzo should once again be called by his given name, Rico. Then, on the outskirts of Miami, Rico dies. Joe tells the driver, who pulls over and confirms Rico's death. "Is he kin to you?" the driver asks. Joe shakes his head, no. The bus continues into Miami, and Joe puts his arm around his deceased friend. The film ends as other passengers look back, then away, as they prepare to arrive at their destination.

One of the most obvious themes throughout the film is one of loneliness and a search for belonging. From the beginning, as Joe prepares to leave his small Texas town, it is evident that Joe has big dreams but no real sense of belonging. As the film progresses and the audience pieces together Joe's life from a series of flashbacks, it becomes even more obvious that much of the film centers on Joe's search for belonging. The flashbacks begin on Joe's bus trip to New York and extend throughout the film. Many are of his experiences with women that are not pleasant

---

5. Quotations from the film are my own transcription.

experiences; generally they exude a harsh feeling of sadness, failure, and abandonment. Joe was abandoned by his mother and raised by his grandmother, Sally Buck. Sally, however, is not much better at nurturing than was Joe's mother. Joe's memories show Sally repeatedly leaving him alone while she went out with one of her many male companions. The abandonment by Sally is complete when Joe returns after his stint in the army only to discover that Sally has died, no one has notified him, and he is left utterly alone.

Joe is also abandoned by his first love interest, Crazy Annie. Generally, Joe's memories of her are positive; Joe has a high opinion of his sexual prowess, and she is the one he remembers of his past sexual experiences. Still, his last memory of her is as she is being driven off in an ambulance to an asylum. Ultimately, Annie, too, abandons Joe.

New York is also a lonely place for Joe. There he walks the streets alone, on the one hand searching for female companions, but on the other hand, his day-after-day search seems aimless. There are women all around him in New York, but Joe cannot seem to find what he is looking for. When he is in his hotel room, Joe watches television, again alone. The programming he sees is telling. The programs are of lonely people. The film flashes back to Joe's childhood as his grandmother leaves him while he watches television. Back in New York Joe returns to watching a television program in which people dress up a dog in clothing in a way that seems cruel; Joe looks very sad. It is as if he identifies with being isolated and manipulated.

Joe's quest in New York is to find belonging. The means by which he plans to accomplish this is to use the only abilities he thinks he has—his sexual talents. "The only one thing I ever been good for's lovin'," Joe tells Ratzo. His sexual background, however, has not exactly been savory. His best memories are of his experiences with Crazy Annie. But even the best experiences are questionable. Annie tells him, "You're the only one, Joe," but the suggestions are that indeed, Joe is by no means the only one; other boys tell Joe, "Kissin' Crazy Annie, man, you better drink a whole damn drug store." Further, his memories of Sally hint at sexual abuse. In one flashback Joe massages his grandmother's neck. In another, Joe is in bed with Sally and one of her many male friends. In still another, Sally spanks him and prepares to give Joe an enema.

As a hustler, Joe is generally a failure. On the streets of New York, Joe tries to start conversations with women by using a very trite pickup line: he asks if they can direct him to the Statue of Liberty. After being turned down or ignored several times, Joe's only success is Cass. But even here the sex is rather unsavory and unfulfilling. Joe does not receive the status he had dreamed of. He follows her into her apartment with less status than her dog. He is virtually ignored while she first calls her husband (or boyfriend?). Joe and Cass's sex is mostly innuendo. In their rolling about the television remote is activated and the channels change. In one significant moment, the televangelist bishop asks, "Do you think God is dead?" Apparently for Joe, the answer is yes: God is dead and so are Joe's hopes. After Joe and Cass have sex and get dressed, Joe awkwardly asks Cass for money. Instead, she gets $20 from him for cab fare to her next appointment. Joe is apparently not a very good hustler.

It is only with Shirley that Joe's success approaches his dreams, but even in this instance Joe's temporary impotence leads to mild sado-masochistic behavior before his libido awakens. It is also sadly ironic that this success with Shirley leads to raising Joe's hopes as she arranges more encounters for Joe with her friends. Sadly, Joe's hopes are dashed by Ratzo's need to leave New York immediately.

This gritty side of sex even extends to somewhat overt homosexuality, a topic highly unusual for popular cinema, at least until this film. In two separate flashbacks of the same incident, Joe and Annie have sex in a parked car when they are interrupted by a gang of boys, who violently attack both of them. Annie tries to run away, but Joe is raped by the boys as he is held down on the hood of the car.

The episode with Mr. O'Daniel is filled with homosexual innuendoes. Speaking to Joe and wearing only a bathrobe, he says, "Why don't you and me get right down on our knees right now?" He then opens the bathroom door and instead of something pertaining to hustling, a gaudy, flashing shrine including a plastic Jesus appears along with a banner proclaiming "God Is Love." Only then does Joe realize that O'Daniel is not a pimp but a religious fanatic.

The interplay of language from sex to religion catches Joe and the audience off guard, but is a pattern for the film, as religion is often associated with disappointment, ambiguity, or the seedy side of life. Joe's flashbacks often confirm this. In this part of the film, after being duped, Joe remembers his baptism in a river as a child. Even as the event surrounds him, the implication is that the child is alone and unaffected. In an earlier scene, on Joe's trip to New York, Joe sees "Jesus Saves" on a barn roof and hears a faith healer (on his transistor radio) asking for money. Joe's religious ambiguity, alienation, and sexual drive are all intertwined throughout the film.

In another scene, this time in New York, when Joe is desperate for money, he goes to a theater and allows himself to be picked up by an adolescent boy. The boy promises Joe $25 to be allowed to have oral sex with him in the back of the theater. The film's director is not at all subtle at this point. Joe remembers Annie in an effort to gain sexual arousal, and the theater's science fiction feature shows the launching of a rocket into space as he climaxes. Later in the restroom, when Joe discovers that the boy does not have the money promised, Joe becomes even lonelier and more dejected.

The last homosexual episode involves Towny, a man in conflict with his homosexuality: "God, I loathe life. I loathe it." In Towny's hotel room, Joe beats up the older man in an unusual violent moment in the film. He steals the money he needs for the bus to Miami and shoves the phone in Towny's mouth, splattering some blood on his jacket.

There is little prurient or titillating about sex in *Midnight Cowboy*. It is harsh and unsatisfying in almost every portrayal in the film. Joe is obsessed with sex, but almost always frustrated by it.

Finally, the film ends without any satisfying resolution. On the bus to Miami, Rico, now completely immobile, experiences incontinence. Joe buys them both new clothes (including a shirt with floral palm tree patterns) at a rest stop and throws away the last of his cowboy clothes. Before getting back on the bus, a waitress asks Joe where he is from. He replies, "New York." The last vestiges of the midnight cowboy disappear when Joe tells Rico that he plans to get an outdoor job when they arrive at their destination. On the outskirts of Miami, Rico dies.

As with any other film, the audience does not necessarily have the right to (or even the desire for) the storybook ending that says "and they all lived happily ever after." Still, this film is ranked as one of the great American films, thirty-sixth on the AFI's all-time best film list. It is therefore necessarily part of the American *mythos*. Yet the audience is left wondering what the director (John Schlesinger) thinks is the American worldview. If this is a slice of life, then it is a very gritty slice that begins with loneliness and ends with loneliness. Hope is transient. Sex is a false means of finding fulfillment, and in it is no real hope or satisfaction. Religion permeates one's existence, but it tends to have more negative than positive implications for life. Also, life is episodic and always incomplete.

If this is a quest, the audience has been misdirected throughout the film. Joe's goals were subverted by Ratzo's dreams. The hopes of New York (broken hopes, nevertheless) have been given up for the uncertainty of Miami. Joe's dreams of sexual stardom are replaced by a hope for an outdoor job.

Further, with this ending Joe has no real repatriation. Indeed, his alienation could be further enhanced with this ending. After all, Joe's state has been returned to loneliness and alienation. He extinguishes his own dreams of sexual fame when he leaves Shirley. The only true friend he has found in his search for meaning has died. If Joe's status has changed from novice to caregiver, then, with Ratzo dead, for whom will he care? The story ends with a sense of uncertainty, with Joe, abandoning his own sexual ambitions, left with only someone else's hopes. The only one who may have gained repatriation is Ratzo, whose name reverts to Rico, but only as he nears death.

It looks like Halliwell was right after all. *Midnight Cowboy* is nothing more than a "skillful, but ultimately pointless film exercise."[6] But such a critique misses the harsh realism, honesty, and tragic form the film is attempting to capture. As critic DeWitt Bodeen notes,

> Although its details are sometimes sordid, *Midnight Cowboy*'s story is amusing, satiric, and often shocking, but in the end it is moving and poignantly tragic. It presents an honest portrait of some aspects of America, and in particular Manhattan. English director John Schlesinger's approach is far more accurate than an American director's might have been, in that he glosses over nothing, and thereby captures the essence of the country from Texas to New York to Florida.[7]

And, as Bodeen later observes, "Today [*Midnight Cowboy*'s] boldness, which once seemed vulgar and excessive to some, is scarcely offensive. Its ruthless realism is now appreciated, particularly because it helped establish a new trend."[8]

The American tragedy is that all too many people are lonely, searching for meaning and hope through sex, but are often unfulfilled. Perhaps such insights are not really new, though; perhaps *Midnight Cowboy* is picking up and extending much older trends. The film's (and the book's) Mr. O'Daniel finds no beatitude for the lonely, but one wonders if he could quote the Preacher, "All things are wearisome; more than one can express; the eye is not satisfied with seeing, nor the ear filled with hearing. What has been is what will be, and what has been done is what will be done; there is nothing new under the sun. Is there a thing of which it is said, 'See, this is new'? It has already been, in the ages before us" (Ecclesiastes 1:8–10).[9]

---

6. Halliwell, *The Filmgoers Companion*, 486.
7. DeWitt Bodeen, "Midnight Cowboy," *Magill's Survey of Cinema: English Language Films*, ed. Frank Magill, 1st series (Englewood Cliffs, N.J.: Salem, 1980), 3:1095.
8. Ibid., 1097.
9. All biblical quotations are from the New Revised Standard Version.

While *Midnight Cowboy*, in book and film, has numerous explicit references to the Bible, most of those references are to Jesus, his teachings
(as in the Beatitudes), to the organized church and its practitioners, or to
the cultural side of religion (television evangelists and slogans such as
"God Is Love" and "Jesus Saves"). A more subtle sharing of religious/
biblical themes, though, can be found (though almost undoubtedly
implicitly or covertly, at most) with the Hebrew Bible's story of Ruth.

RUTH

The biblical story of Ruth shares many of *Midnight Cowboy*'s dominant
themes. Both deal with abject loneliness—alienation and repatriation,
the search for belonging—and the acute and absolute sadness inherent
therein. Both deal with sex or sexuality in very open and (perhaps) unex-
pected ways. Both end in incomplete or unsatisfying ways. In both, these
three themes or features are inextricably entwined.

Ruth is very different from *Midnight Cowboy*. It is much more ancient,
it is from a significantly different culture than the America of the late
1960s, and it is a much briefer tale. Still, it deals with similar issues,
though, as would be expected, in different ways. The Book of Ruth is a
rather simple, charming tale, with definite folk qualities. It is a story with
a rather uncomplicated plot and a limited number of named characters.

Set in the time when judges ruled the land, the book tells the story of
a family that moves from their hometown, Bethlehem of Judah, to the
foreign country of Moab because of a famine. The family includes
Naomi, her husband Elimelech, and their two sons, Mahlon and
Chilion. In Moab the sons marry native women, Orpah and Ruth.
Within ten years the husband and two sons die. When Naomi hears that
the famine in Bethlehem has ended, she plans to return to her home.
The two daughters-in-law begin to go with her, but Naomi encourages
them to stay in Moab and to remarry. Ruth, however, would not do as
Naomi requested, but instead accompanies Naomi to Bethlehem.

Since it was time for the barley harvest, Ruth goes to glean in the
fields of Boaz, a relative of Elimelech. Boaz learns of Ruth's plight and
apparently out of compassion he encourages her to glean in his fields.
He tells his servants not to bother Ruth as she gleans, and at mealtime
he gives her a generous meal. Following this he instructs his servants to
drop additional grain for her to pick up. At the end of the day, when
Ruth returns to Naomi with a surprisingly large amount of grain, Naomi
encourages her daughter-in-law to continue gleaning throughout the
barley harvest as well as during the subsequent wheat harvest.

Naomi then encourages Ruth to dress up and secretively approach Boaz as he sleeps at his threshing floor. Ruth does as she was instructed. Boaz awakes, startled, and tells Ruth he will try to gain the right of redeemer (*go'el*) with her the next day, and encourages her to stay the night. Ruth leaves before dawn and returns to Naomi, but not before Boaz has given her more barley.

Boaz goes directly to the city gate; the next of kin passes by and Boaz convinces the man to sell him the rights and responsibilities that had been Elimelech's inheritance. With all this comes Ruth, and the responsibility to carry on Mahlon's name. Boaz marries Ruth. They conceive a son, Obed, who later became the grandfather of David.

In this story, as in *Midnight Cowboy*, also resides a theme of loneliness, alienation, and a concern for repatriation. Naomi and her family leave their home because of desperate conditions and live in an alien land, not members of the society there, but rather a family having the status of resident aliens. Tragically, the men die. Thereupon, Naomi hears that the famine has ended, and returns to her homeland. But even in coming back, Naomi does not find reintegration into society. Upon returning, "She said, . . . 'Call me no longer Naomi, call me Mara, for the Almighty has dealt bitterly with me. I went away full, but the LORD has brought me back empty; why call me Naomi when the LORD has dealt harshly with me, and the Almighty has brought calamity upon me?'" (Ruth 1:20–21) Her experiences while away have left Naomi bitter, unconnected.

What may not be apparent is that generally, Hebrew names have meanings, and that typically, in the Hebrew Bible, a person's name tells her/his essential character. Naomi means "pleasant," but she changes her name to Mara, "bitter." Because of her losses, her character changes and she become bitter. Unfortunately, the theme of alienation becomes fuzzy at this point, as the text continues to call her Naomi. It would be easier to follow the concerns of the theme of Naomi's alienation if one could determine at what point she regains her sense of belonging and subsequently changes her name back from Mara. But this does not occur; the interpretation is left open. One can only speculate if she regains her sense of belonging upon her return to her homeland or upon her family's redemption at the hands of Boaz. It seems more likely that something significant occurs at the end of the story, after Ruth and Boaz have a son, when the text says,

> Then the women said to Naomi, "Blessed be the LORD, who has not left you this day without next-of-kin; and may his name be

renowned in Israel! He shall be to you a restorer of life and a nour-
isher of your old age; for your daughter-in-law who loves you,
who is more to you than seven sons, has borne him." Then Naomi
took the child and laid him in her bosom, and became his nurse.
(Ruth 4:14–16)

Either Naomi gains some sense of return through becoming the nurse to
the child, or alternately, repatriation eludes Naomi throughout the story.

Indeed, Naomi's status and actions throughout the book are ambiguous, perhaps even suspicious. She encourages her daughter-in-law to
glean, whereby Ruth, not Naomi, becomes the household provider.
Naomi determines that Ruth has gleaned an extraordinary amount and
encourages Ruth to continue gleaning in Boaz's fields throughout that
harvest as well as the subsequent wheat harvest while the two women
continue to live together. During the harvest Naomi sends her daughter-
in-law effectively to seduce Boaz in order to gain security, ostensibly for
Ruth ("My daughter, I need to seek some security for you, so that it may
be well with you" [Ruth 3:1b]), but also for herself, as Boaz becomes
Naomi's redeemer as well as Ruth's.[10] And finally, when Ruth's child is
born, the women of the town say, "A son has been born to Naomi"
(4:17b). It appears that the surrogate grandmother has usurped the
child. This suspicious reading, questioning Naomi's motives, differs from
more traditional, devotional readings of the text.

Naomi is not the only character in the book who demonstrates the
theme of alienation. Much of the book implies Ruth's search for belonging. In Ruth's case, after her husband dies, she leaves her homeland out
of loyalty to her mother-in-law.

But Ruth said, "Do not press me to leave you or to turn back from
following you! Where you go, I will go; where you lodge, I will
lodge; your people shall be my people, and your God my God.
Where you die, I will die—there will I be buried. May the LORD do
thus and so to me, and more as well, if even death parts me from
you!" (Ruth 1:16–17)

From that point on, Ruth does as Naomi tells her. She supports her
mother-in-law with her work, she seduces and marries a provider, and

---

10. E.g., Ruth 4:5, 9.

she bears a requisite son. Yet throughout the story, the text is remarkably silent regarding her feelings, motives, or goals, though the reader might easily assume that Ruth is searching for meaning or belonging.

In fact, an intertextual reading suggests that Ruth can never find belonging in Israel. Deuteronomy 23:3 states, "No Ammonite or Moabite shall be admitted to the assembly of the LORD. Even to the tenth generation, none of their descendants shall be admitted to the assembly of the LORD." If one is to take the Deuteronomic code seriously, then, Ruth must live her life in Judah without any hope that she or her children (to ten generations!) could ever become a part of the society in which she has chosen to reside. It is quite inexplicable how the ending demonstrates that Ruth's great grandson is in fact David, the greatest king of Israel's history, the model of the messiah and messianic hope, and one who is particularly beloved by God. If the story of Ruth ends in hope, then it is only through discovering the rest of the story beyond the text that the reader can know of this hope. Instead, from the text alone, Ruth's status, like Naomi's, remains ambiguous. The tale itself shows loneliness or alienation of both major characters, but no explicit resolution to their situations.

Sex and sexual concerns also permeate the Book of Ruth. Most scholars agree that the concern for progeny through the process of levirate marriage, or at least something very similar to this process,[11] accounts for the marriage of Boaz to Ruth. Obviously, progeny demand sexual union.

A levirate marriage is the concern of two other biblical texts: the narrative in Genesis 38; and the law for such a marriage in Deuteronomy 25:5–10. Genesis 38 is the story of Tamar who marries Judah's son, Er. Er dies, and Judah's next son, Onan, is given to Tamar. The story continues: "Then Judah said to Onan, 'Go in to your brother's wife and perform the duty of a brother-in-law to her; raise up offspring for your brother.' But since Onan knew that the offspring would not be his, he spilled his semen on the ground whenever he went in to his brother's wife, so that he would not give offspring to his brother" (Genesis 38:8). Onan is put to death by God and Judah refuses to give his third son, Shelah, to Tamar out of fear for the life of his last son. The concern of how Er's lineage will be continued (the very reason for the existence of the levirate law) is satisfied when Tamar tricks Judah. She disguises herself as a prostitute and sleeps with the next closest male relative of Er (after Shelah)—Judah, her deceased husband's father. When Judah discovers that Tamar is

---

11. See, e.g., H. H. Rowley, "The Marriage of Ruth," *The Servant of the Lord and Other Essays on the Old Testament* (London: Lutterworth, 1952), 163.

pregnant, assuming she has committed what is deemed adultery, the truth is discovered, and Judah acknowledges "She is more in the right than I, since I did not give her to my son, Shelah" (38:26).

The second passage in the Bible, the law pertaining to the practice of levirate marriage, states:

> When brothers reside together, and one of them dies and has no son, the wife of the deceased shall not be married outside the family to a stranger. Her husband's brother shall go in to her, taking her in marriage, and performing the duty of a husband's brother to her, and the firstborn whom she bears shall succeed to the name of the deceased brother, so that his name may not be blotted out of Israel. But if the man has no desire to marry his brother's widow, then his brother's widow shall go up to the elders at the gate and say, "My husband's brother refuses to perpetuate his brother's name in Israel; he will not perform the duty of a husband's brother to me." Then the elders of his town shall summon him and speak to him. If he persists, saying, "I have no desire to marry her," then his brother's wife shall go up to him in the presence of the elders, pull his sandal off his foot, spit in his face, and declare, "This is what is done to the man who does not build up his brother's house." Throughout Israel his family shall be known as "the house of him whose sandal was pulled off." (Deuteronomy 25:5–10)

The concern for levirate marriage, then, is to perpetuate the lineage of one who has died without leaving behind a son. By combining the two passages mentioned, it is the responsibility of the next male kin to father a child with the widow. The child then becomes the heir of the deceased. Further, as Kalmin notes, "Through the levirate, society avoids a sociological misfit, the young childless widow. The levirate not only continues the line of the deceased, it reaffirms the young widow's place in the home of her husband's family."[12]

It is within the construction of the levirate marriage that the sexual union of Boaz and Ruth exists. But something has gone awry. Certainly, Boaz gains the legal right to be the *go'el*, or redeemer, from the actual next of kin (Ruth 4:7–12) in a ceremony not otherwise reproduced in the biblical text (but touching on the Genesis 38 passage, which also mentions the use of a sandal in the exchange of goods and rights). All

---

12. Richard Kalmin, "Levirate Law," *Anchor Bible Dictionary*, ed. David Noel Freedman, (New York: Doubleday, 1992), 4:296–97.

seems to follow what is prescribed and expected as Boaz states, "I have also acquired Ruth the Moabite, the wife of Mahlon, to be my wife, to maintain the dead man's name on his inheritance, in order that the name of the dead may not be cut off from his kindred and from the gate of his native place; today you are witnesses" (Ruth 4:10). However, in this passage, that Ruth is to be Boaz's wife subsequent to being Mahlon's wife suggests that Boaz has additional intentions beyond leaving behind an heir for Mahlon. Boaz intends to keep Ruth as his wife even after she bears a child.

Further, as noted from the passage in Ruth as well as the other biblical passages, the child should be recognized as the son of Mahlon (Ruth's deceased husband). Instead, the child's lineage is given in the text as the descendant of Tamar's son, Perez (from Genesis 38!) through Boaz (!), not Mahlon (Ruth 4:18–22). Boaz gets credit for the child. Further, nothing in the text even remotely suggests that the offspring should be traced to Elimelech. He had offspring, though they had died; he is not mentioned in the genealogy; and if Elimelech were to be the legal ancestor, the mother should be Naomi, not Ruth. Even the phrase "A son has been born to Naomi" (4:17b) is not usually interpreted as suggesting that Ruth is a surrogate child bearer for Naomi. Since Boaz is the father of Obed, one can only conclude that Boaz's sexual escapades with Ruth are not for any levirate purpose. It seems that Boaz's actions primarily ennoble his own sexual prowess, providing for his own progeny, and only secondarily bring security for Ruth and Naomi as they become part of his household.

The sex in Ruth is not just a genetic necessity or the means of sociological status for Ruth (and Naomi), however. Chapter 3 is charged with sexual language and innuendo. There, Naomi tells Ruth, "'Now wash and anoint yourself, and put on your best clothes and go down to the threshing floor; but do not make yourself known to the man until he has finished eating and drinking. When he lies down, observe the place where he lies; then, go and uncover his feet and lie down; and he will tell you what to do.' She said to her, 'All that you tell me I will do'" (Ruth 3:3–5).

Readers, then as now, cannot miss the sexual overtones of this passage. The overtones are enhanced by one's recognition that the Hebrew term for "feet" is occasionally used as "a euphemism for the pubic region."[13]

Ruth is instructed to wash, cover herself with oil, and put on specific clothing. Perhaps significantly, the order and terms are the same as in

---

13. Ludwig Köhler and Walter Baumgartner, *The Hebrew and Aramaic Lexicon of the Old Testament*, rev. Walter Baumgartner and Johann Jakob Stamm, trans. M. E. J. Richardson, 5 vols. (Leiden: Brill, 1994-2000), vol. 3, s.v. "*rgl*," 1185.

Ezekiel 16:8 and following, a passage in which a bride was given every luxury, but then went and "played a whore" (Ezekiel 16:15). Ruth is then told to uncover Boaz's feet (or genitals?). Then she is admonished to follow whatever instructions Boaz may give. And Ruth agrees to do all this.

As the story continues, Ruth "came stealthily and uncovered his feet, and lay down" (Ruth 3:7b). Boaz awakes at midnight; the text says he "was startled and turned over" (3:8). The roots for the Hebrew verbs are "to tremble"[14] and "to touch oneself."[15] The language is provocative. Certainly there is nothing graphic, but the innuendo is present.

Boaz then spreads his cloak to cover Ruth. "In Deut 23:1; 27:20; Ezek 16:8, the removal or the spreading of the 'skirt' of a man's robe over a woman is used as a euphemism for the consummation of marriage."[16] Again, exactly what is suggested is uncertain, but the sexual overtones are inherent in the language.

Ruth stays at Boaz's feet until before dawn at which time Boaz gives Ruth some more grain and sends her back to Naomi with the promise that he will attempt to gain the right of redeemer, or next of kin.

With a bit of study and upon a closer reading, this part of the story is startling. At the least, sexual innuendoes abound. At the most, there is seduction on the magnitude of an aggressive sexual professional.

At least one additional sexual reference emerges from the Book of Ruth in regard to taking a portion of the text out of its original context. The passage previously quoted, in which Ruth pledges her loyalty to Naomi, is often a part of contemporary wedding ceremonies: "Where you go, I will go; where you lodge, I will lodge; your people shall be my people, and your God my God" (Ruth 1:16b). While this is a beautifully poetic statement of fidelity, the modern person reads this text in a nuptial setting. Most modern weddings are not about platonic love; the fidelity promised by bride and groom includes fidelity, especially in sexual love. Yet the original setting was between Ruth and her mother-in-law in Ruth's search for belonging, with no sexual overtones.

It seems unlikely that most brides and grooms who use this text from Ruth would intentionally connect the relationship of Ruth and Naomi to the sexuality of the marriage setting. The result would be a homosexual (lesbian) relationship between Ruth and Naomi, which is clearly not what the text is about. Yet this is what is subversively suggested. Context is important.

---

14. Ibid., vol. 1, s.v. "*hrd*," 350.
15. Ibid., vol. 2, s.v. "*lpt*," 533.
16. Frederic Bush, *Ruth, Esther* (Dallas, Texas: Word Books, 1996), 164.

The final point of comparison between *Midnight Cowboy* and Ruth is Ruth's unsatisfactory ending. In addition to any uneasiness the reader may have in regard to the book's characters' lack of obvious repatriation, the levirate marriage that goes beyond the bounds of levirate responsibility, or the question of Obed's genealogy—which goes back to the wrong person—quite simply, the book does not end correctly. The biblical text gives a phrase that introduces an etymological etiology, but then does not follow through with a requisite name.

Etiologies are explanations regarding causes or origins. Of interest here are etymological etiologies, passages in which, generally, "proper nouns designating persons and places are given semantic interpretation based on phonic correspondences."[17] In an article in the *Journal of Biblical Literature*, Marks in his opening footnote lists six major sources, each of which purports to survey the numerous etymological etiologies of the narrative sections of the Hebrew Bible. Marks states that by conservative count, there are over eighty such etymologies (though no specific list is given). Indeed, the number limits the discussion only to explicit passages, usually with formulaic introductions, even though "the forms are often mixed or freely varied."[18] As Marks states:

> Typically the naming of a child will be recorded in the narrative past tense, "and she called his name Seth" (*sht*), followed by a subordinate clause which echoes some feature of the name, "for she said, 'God has appointed (*sht*) for me another child instead of Abel'" (Gen. 4:25). The naming of a place is more often preceded by an account of something that happened there, from which an inference is then drawn to its meaning: Lot pleaded with the angel to let him flee to yonder city, so "little" or "insignificant" (*mtsr*); "therefore the name of the city was called Zoar" (*tsr*) (Gen. 19:22).[19]

There are numerous such explicit passages. The number of etymological etiologies would balloon if more covert plays on names were included.

Etymological etiologies seem to be a subcategory of paronomasia or parasonancy, types of playful word associations that abound in the Hebrew Bible. Such wordplays are one of the most obvious and striking

---

17. Herbert Marks, "Biblical Naming and Poetic Etymology," *Journal of Biblical Literature* 114 (spring 1995): 21.
18. Ibid.
19. Ibid.

characteristics of classical Hebrew. It is almost as though the *joie de vivre* of the text is pointing out and playing on linguistic similarities. It is not difficult to find wordplays throughout the Hebrew Bible. Many are overt, with formulaic introductions, while others are subtler.

So, when a formulaic introduction is given, the reader's first tendency is to look for the wordplay. Indeed, if the wordplay does not ensue, there is a feeling of incompleteness and chagrin. One of the best examples of this incompleteness occurs at the end of the Book of Ruth: "Then Naomi took the child and laid him in her bosom, and became his nurse. The women of the neighborhood gave him a name, saying, 'A son has been born to Naomi.' They named him Obed" (Ruth 4:16–17a). The formula, here with the descriptive clause first, "A son has been born to Naomi," typically should lead to a wordplay with the name that follows. Unfortunately, it does not.

The problem is recognized in most commentaries, but generally, scholars throw up their hands with the problem and state that the text has somehow been reworked from its original context, whatever that might have been. It is generally recognized that by working backwards, the name should play off the Hebrew words "son" (*ben*) and the name "Naomi." From the formula, one might expect the son of Ruth to be named something like "Ben Naomi" or "Ben Naom" or even (by reversing the consonants of "Naomi") "Ben Yamin"—that is, Benjamin.

This last possibility leads to delightful speculation that the present story has been reworked from an original folk tale that supported primacy of the tribe of Benjamin through its national hero, Saul, but has been appropriated by a pro-Davidic faction for its own purposes. All this is speculation, however. The only thing certain from the story of Ruth as it now stands is that the ending does not work. "Obed" is the child's name, but is in no way related to the introductory formula. The Book of Ruth has a very unsatisfactory ending along with its themes of alienation and sex.

CONCLUSION

People in contemporary Western societies approach biblical texts by reading them through certain lenses. First (or early) readings are likely to be made with a certain amount of devotional or pietistic expectation. The texts are assumed to be "staid" and are read in that light. When one allows themes, features, or other characteristics of biblical texts to be compared with nonbiblical stories, however, new readings and new insights may appear. Such is the case with *Midnight Cowboy* and Ruth.

In both *Midnight Cowboy* and Ruth, the audience is left with alienated characters, uncomfortable sexuality (which borders on the explicit rather than just the implicit), and a feeling of incompleteness. Certainly, these characteristics play themselves out differently, as the cultures in which they originated are different. Still, after one watches *Midnight Cowboy* and then rereads the story of Ruth, the latter story becomes surprisingly similar to the former in the way it deals with alienation, sex, and incompleteness.

Ruth and Naomi are certainly alienated in the story, but nowhere in the text do they clearly regain meaning or belonging. Obed, the child that should be Mahlon's heir, does not clearly remain Mahlon's heir; he is absorbed into Boaz's family in the final genealogical listings: as a result, Elimelech's family ceases to exist. The reader is left with an over-all feeling of sadness that is more evident with each reading of the story. As much is left unstated in the text, the reader is also left with an uncomfortable feeling of ambiguity. As with *Midnight Cowboy*, none of the characters clearly gain what they seem to be searching for.

Additionally, as with *Midnight Cowboy*, the Book of Ruth has a significant sexual underpinning that is a part of the characters' searches for repatriation. Unfortunately, however, in both stories, although belonging is sought through sex, sex ultimately fails as a means by which this belonging can be found. With additional readings, the sexual content of Ruth becomes far more suggestive, and even homosexual themes are brought into the discussion. With these rereadings, the language of Ruth confirms definite sexual inferences that may not have been evident in the earlier readings. Ruth's nighttime encounter with Boaz becomes sexually provocative and seductive, and Naomi's motives appear highly suspicious, as if she were the manager that Joe Buck so desperately wanted.

Finally, rereadings of Ruth heighten the sense that the story is incomplete. "Obed" is the wrong name for the child; or perhaps he is the wrong child. The levirate marriage is not quite fulfilled. All is not right with this story. It is not just a pleasant devotional tale after all. It may have a far more significant function within the political and social structures of an ancient civilization.

As *Midnight Cowboy* tells of the seedy side of a particular part of American society in the late 1960s, Ruth may tell of emerging values of at least one part of a society as Judaism enters a predominantly Gentile world; alternately or even conjunctively, the story may tell of Davidic dynastic intrigue in late biblical Judaism. Ultimately, the parts that alienation, sexuality, and incompleteness play in the story of Ruth may demonstrate that this ancient culture is not as far removed from the contemporary reader as we might initially think.

5. COMING-OF-AGE IN *THE PRINCE OF EGYPT*

Jennifer Rohrer-Walsh

"But you know that we begin by telling children stories. These are, in general, fiction, though they contain some truth. And we tell children stories before we start them on physical training."

"That is so."

"That is what I meant by saying that we must start to educate the mind before training the body."

"You are right," he said.

"And the first step, as you know, is always what matters most, particularly when we are dealing with those who are young and tender. That is the time when they are easily moulded and when any impression we choose to make leaves a permanent mark."

"That is certainly true."

"Shall we therefore readily allow our children to listen to any stories made up by anyone, and to form opinions that are for the most part the opposite of those we think they should have when they grow up?"

"We certainly shall not."

"Then it seems that our first business is to supervise the production of stories, and choose only those we think suitable, and reject the rest."[1]

---

1. Plato, *Republic*, 2nd rev. ed., trans. Desmond Lee (London: Penguin, 1987), 2.377a–c.

INTRODUCTION

Plato's concern for selecting the appropriate literature for children can be extended to preadolescent reading as well. In particular, the coming-of-age story warrants careful selection because it is designed to mold and guide according to culturally acceptable standards. Charles Dickens affords the preadolescent Victorian reader a text that many would deem most appropriate. "Whether I shall turn out to be the hero of my own life, or whether that station will be held by anyone else, these pages must show. To begin my life with the beginning of my life . . ." introduces the most typical coming-of-age novel ever written.[2] Without question, *David Copperfield* exemplifies the characteristics of a classic coming-of-age novel as it traces David's childhood, adolescence, and adulthood. Despite this individual focus, Dickens also unleashes a social commentary of the Victorian Age. Although the reader follows the life of David Copperfield, it is always a life constrained by his British socioeconomic and cultural codes. This dual focus—on the individual and on his or her community—also appears in *The Prince of Egypt*, which traces Moses' life from his childhood river journey, through his adolescent sibling rivalry, to his adulthood leadership. As with *David Copperfield*, DreamWorks's individual focus is combined with a community focus: the saving of the Israelites.

A coming-of-age story never balances this dual focus: the individual focus dominates until the end. In *David Copperfield*, the reader's attention, sympathy, fear, disbelief, and hopes all hinge on David's personal successes and failures, not on how Victorian society influences him. In *The Prince of Egypt* the viewer's focus lies with Moses' coming of age, not on the Israelites' salvation.

Of course, the goal here is not to compare *The Prince of Egypt* to *David Copperfield* but rather to compare the children's movie to the Book of Exodus. In that comparison, the animated story weighs heavily on the individual side of the seesaw while the biblical story weighs heavily on the community side of the seesaw. This comparison does not imply that one position is right while the other is wrong. Even if there were an *Ur-David Copperfield* that wallowed in social satire, Dickens's individual-focus novel would not be wrong. It would simply stand as an alternate

---

2. Charles Dickens, *David Copperfield* (New York:. Collier, 1911), 1.

version—one that reveals much about Dickens, his society, and, most importantly, his coming-of-age character.

THE GENRE OF THE COMING-OF-AGE STORY

To come of age requires a delicate mixture of rebellion, assistance, discovery, and accommodation. On the one hand, adolescents must leave their nests, reject authority figures, break taboos, and fail. On the other hand, adolescents must acquire respect, accept their mentors, conform to norms, establish their new roles in a stable nest, and succeed. Arnold van Gennep describes the typical pattern of coming-of-age rituals: (1) separation; (2) transition; and (3) incorporation.[3]

Physical change and emotional turmoil trigger the separation stage that begins with the protagonist's journey. Leaving the nest guarantees the protagonist's isolation and freedom. No former restraints or restrainers control and confine the protagonist, who gleefully and swiftly ignores or violates the laws and codes. Yet the euphoric escapades and escapes from society's clutches are short-lived. As the former restraints dissolve, the former supports are also abandoned. Instability threatens adolescent glee.

Isolated from childhood home and community, the protagonist journeys to a new setting and must overcome obstacles with a mentor's assistance. This is not to say that the protagonist heeds the mentor's warnings and always follows the mentor's guidelines; but by the end of the coming-of-age story, the protagonist has at least begun to consider the mentor's advice for overcoming the obstacles. Typical obstacles revolve around a romance, athletic competition, ethical dilemmas, and personal tragedy. The audience witnesses the protagonist's tension, ambivalence, rebellion, alienation, and error. No type or degree of support guarantees success; deterrents abound.

This transitional stage features both support (mentor) and deterrents (obstacles) in order to encourage adolescent development. Mentor figures may appear to be antagonists at first but ultimately become the protagonists' best friends—at least during the transitional stage. Mentors promote growth by recalling past supports and memories, offering advice (often ambiguously), and foreshadowing outcomes. Mentors are not usually attractive characters and are frequently older, alienated

---

3. Arnold van Gennep, *The Rites of Passage* (Chicago: University of Chicago Press, 1960), 21.

members of society. Mentors are always wiser and more patient than protagonists. Once mentors promote the adolescents' growth, their purpose is served and they are dismissed from the plot. Even if the coming-of-age stories include them in the incorporation stage, this is only a gesture. They are not crucial past the transitional stage.

This transitional stage also features political, social, or religious hardships that impede, but do not prevent, adolescent development. Not everything in the adolescent's world changes, of course. For example, family members may still influence. However, changes, rather than constants, promote the protagonist's character reversal.

For instance, Hamlet, through five acts, transforms himself from Wittenberg scholar to divine scourge and avenger in order to commit regicide. *Hamlet* affords the perfect example of such an incremental and purposeful transformation, one that Stephen Greenblatt calls Renaissance "self-fashioning."[4] Hamlet must, through a series of Renaissance religious tests, convince himself that the ghost is a divine emissary and that Hamlet himself has been divinely chosen to kill King Claudius. This self-fashioning begins in Act I and continues for five acts, to the chagrin of T. S. Eliot, who finds Hamlet's indecision plodding.[5] Plodding it may be. But it is typical of the coming-of-age genre. This values shift defines the coming-of-age genre. Hardships offer the opportunities for this shift, and changes offer the opportunity to develop into adulthood. Without any hardships, a coming-of-age protagonist does not learn how to come of age independently—nor does the audience. Only through hardship, failure, and struggle can a protagonist recognize the decisions leading to adult development.

This is the typical mold of the coming-of-age genre; this mold relates to its pedagogical purpose. Although not explicitly stated in the story, the coming-of-age tale teaches the adolescent character, as well as the adolescent audience, to explore existential questions appropriately in order to develop a new value system acceptable for an adult community member. Ideally, every coming-of-age story affords a deeper self-knowledge in order to instruct the adolescent character, as well as the adolescent audience. Realistically, however, not all coming-of-age stories so instruct.

---

4. Stephen Greenblatt, *Renaissance Self-Fashioning* (Chicago: University of Chicago Press, 1980), 1.

5. T. S. Eliot, "Hamlet and His Problems," *The Sacred Wood: Essays on Poetry and Criticism* (London: Methuen, 1920), 101–102.

Should those non-pedagogical stories be excluded from the genre? Should *Heidi*, for example, be disqualified because Heidi learns positively nothing? After she is separated from her grandfather, she herself teaches several people life-altering lessons, but she herself learns nothing new. In fact, she is "the little child who shall lead them" (Isaiah 11:6).[6] Simba in *The Lion King* is a similar example. In that movie, Disney makes a spectacle of the land of *hakuna matata*—"no worries." The potential hero eats what he wants, plays constantly, follows no schedule, jokes with his pals, and rescues no one. Although he experiences no tests, he suddenly embraces the memory of his father, avenges his father's death, saves his homeland, and creates the next generation. As coming-of-age stories go, *Heidi* and *The Lion King* show their adolescents in fairly tension-free environments during the marginal stage. Perhaps they do not break the genre's mold, but they seriously reshape it.

This reshaping does not involve the ending, however, because all coming-of-age stories end with the adolescent's incorporation into the community. This reshaping involves only the degree to which the story tests the adolescent during the transitional stage. *Hamlet* and *The Catcher in the Rye* pose extremely high levels of tension throughout the transitional stage because of the many tests the protagonists must pass and the lack of support they receive. Those stories that test the least, like *Heidi* and *The Lion King*, offer little tension.

One can chart this tension along a wide spectrum. At the tensest end of the spectrum, the adolescent faces life-threatening tests and enjoys little support. At the middle of the spectrum, the adolescent faces manageable tests with the mentor's support. In the least tense end of the spectrum, the protagonist faces few tests and enjoys heavy support from the mentor.

A practical example may illustrate this spectrum. A mother receives a phone call from the police that her son has shoplifted a $10 item. She must decide the extent to which she will test or support her son. She may decide that there was no logical reason for the theft as his wallet held $75 that she had just given to him, so she will let him "rot" in jail overnight. Her son will experience a high level of tension and probably learn a hard lesson about accountability. Or she may suggest that her son call his uncle who will give him a good lecture, make him wait a few hours, and determine the

---

6. All biblical citations are from the New Revised Standard Version.

preconditions for posting bail. Her son will experience less tension and learn a mild lesson about gratitude and responsibility. Or she may race down to the jail, hug her son sympathetically, admonish him, and bail him out. Her son will experience little tension and learn dependence. The son's new knowledge depends on many factors, of course, but one factor is the amount of tension he experiences during this crisis. Tension is crucial for learning accountability. Many adolescent-development textbooks attest that after the age of three, only a significant emotional experience (like tension) has the power to change a person's values.

The degree of tension during the transitional stage should correspond to the coming-of-age story's purpose. If the purpose is to instruct the adolescent audience to combine wise advice with chutzpah, then the middle of the spectrum works. If the purpose is to instruct the audience to survive almost exclusively as individuals, then the tension should be the highest. If the purpose is to demonstrate dependence on a support system, then the tension should be the lowest. In this last case, when the adolescent leaves the nest, the wings are sturdy, the flight is programmed, and the destination is secured. Such is the case in *The Prince of Egypt*. There is little tension; therefore, the protagonist learns dependence more than accountability. This may not be typical of the genre; however, it is an acceptable adjustment. Like *Heidi*, *The Prince of Egypt* portrays "a little child shall lead them" protagonist, rather than an autonomous Esther in *The Bell Jar*.

Although the coming-of-age story's author may play drastically with the level of tension in the transitional stage, the author may not play with the result of the tension. The incorporation stage, as the name implies, finds the protagonist connected to a community. Success is guaranteed. If the level of tension has been high, this success may surprise the audience. It is no surprise, however, to the critic of a coming-of-age story. To all, critic and audience alike, incorporation comes as a relief. The first two stages of the coming-of-age story pit the adolescent against the world—nature, religion, school, and so forth—to test values and endurance, to reshape goals and beliefs, and to reposition the adolescent into society. Not until the end of this journey from adolescence to adulthood do individual needs balance with community needs. Not until the end of the journey does the audience learn how the individual succeeds in a particular society—both as an individual and as a society member. Unlike stories that emphasize the community's needs, such as myths, coming-of-age stories concentrate on the individual's personal growth.

THE PRINCE OF EGYPT AND EXODUS: SEPARATION STAGE

Adaptations are like gelatin creations. DreamWorks not only uses its own shape of mold (individual focus), but also substitutes and even adds new ingredients (content) to the Exodus story. DreamWorks's creation, once slid from the mold onto the plate, is still biblical gelatin—although it is a different flavor in a different shape. Who knows for sure if the content changes improve the original dessert or not? For that matter, who even notices all the changes? At the very least, every reader/viewer *experiences* the changes. For better or for worse, from beginning to end, the DreamWorks story differs dramatically from the original. DreamWorks remolds the shape from the community Exodus story into the individual *The Prince of Egypt* coming-of-age story.[7] DreamWorks also reworks the content by adding to and altering the plot as well as the characterization.

From the very beginning, *The Prince of Egypt* alters the biblical content of Exodus. For example, the movie makes no mention of the midwives who, having spared the Israelite males at birth, are blessed with children themselves. Further, it makes no mention of Pharaoh's rising fear about the multiplying Israelites. And it makes no mention of the daughter of Pharaoh hiding the son from the house of Levi for three months. Instead, DreamWorks casts the slavery of the Israelites against an animated background of looming clouds, creating a montage of Egyptian oppression coupled with the sound tract of "Deliver Us." The movie juxtaposes these lyrics with imposing Egyptian edifices. Nonetheless, both the biblical and animated versions begin with a focus on the community of the Israelites. The mold is the same although the ingredients differ.

As the basket with baby Moses floats away from his mother, the movie's story floats away from a community focus. DreamWorks elongates the Exodus narrative time that comprises two sentences (Exodus 2:3–4) to a three-minute scene that dramatizes every wave, every rocking, every near disaster of the basket's tumultuous journey on the Nile. Except for Miriam's prayer, "send a shepherd to shepherd us,"[8] the camera, the

---

7. For more information regarding the movie as a coming-of-age story, consult Bernard Brandon Scott, "Changing Genre and the Problem of Meaning: Moses and *The Prince of Egypt*" (paper presented at the annual meeting of the Society of Biblical Literature, Boston, Mass., 22 November 1999).

8. Quotations from the film, unless otherwise noted, are my own transcription.

music, and the narrative time focus on one character, Moses, not on the plight of the Israelites. Cinematically, DreamWorks sets the stage for its coming-of-age version of the Exodus story.

Those who know their Hebrew Bible will be most struck by the next scene, for it mixes a new ingredient into the recipe: sibling rivalry. Cecil B. DeMille's *The Ten Commandments* had already introduced this rivalry to the screen's audience. DreamWorks reintroduces the brotherly competition. For many fun-filled, rollicking minutes, the movie treats the audience to a wild chariot race with Moses and Rameses taunting each other and demolishing the hard work of the Israelite slaves. Notably, the viewer must recall that hard work; the director does not. If the first scene belabors the labors of the Israelites, the second scene highlights the high jinks of the boys. And boys, who will be boys, race their "cars" and boast of their speed. A few good-natured taunts are thrown in: "How would you like your face carved on the wall?" "Someday, yes." "How about now?" To most adults, Rameses and Moses act recklessly; to most children and teenagers, the pair play freely. The director creates and presents the race from the younger vantage point to portray the brothers' friendly competition. This is the nest Moses must leave in order to come of age.

The tree supporting this nest soon begins to shake. Pharaoh admonishes Rameses' recklessness: "I seek to build an empire [from] ancient traditions." "When I die, you will be the morning and the evening star." "One weak link can break the chain of a mighty dynasty." With his admonitions, Pharaoh returns to the original community focus: the Egyptian dynasty. Although Moses confesses and apologizes, Pharaoh dismisses him. Moses, after all, is not to be king, so he can afford to soothe Rameses: "You care too much." Rameses cannot afford such glibness. The plot has returned to a community focus; however, the community has changed from Israelite to Egyptian.

Exodus never considers Egyptian motives and fears. Never once does the Exodus story sympathize with the Egyptians, although often, especially in the first half of the movie, the DreamWorks version does. There is no need to puzzle over this variation. A community-focused story never changes sides: Exodus faithfully exalts the Israelites over the Egyptians. A coming-of-age story always changes sides: *The Prince of Egypt* begins with the stable Egyptian nest that Moses leaves in order to redefine himself in and by a new Israelite nest.

Enter woman. Male redefinitions often begin when a woman enters the picture. Pip in *Great Expectations*, for example, is never the same once

Estella comes on the scene. Jay Gatsby never recovers from his infatuation with Daisy. So too with Moses. Tzipporah, furious at being bound and dragged for public spectacle, first infuriates but soon captivates Moses. Tzipporah's entry, exit, and reunion are pivotal for a story with an individual focus. She will be Moses' wife. As wife, she will antagonize, console, question, inspire, and praise Moses. He will learn to redefine himself from a mischievous lad to a responsible husband through his relationship with her. In these respects, DreamWorks characterizes her as Moses' mentor. True, she is an unlikely mentor because she is not a social outcast, older, and unattractive. Perhaps God is a better candidate for the mentor role. With his burning bush, staff, edicts, and plagues, God directs Moses. However, this direction controls and guarantees Moses' success more than a mentor should. As mentor candidate, God stacks the deck rather than reviewing the rules or predicting the odds. Tzipporah remains a more typical mentor because she takes a more marginal role.

As a mentor, Tzipporah's first important task is to unwittingly lead Moses away from his Egyptian family. DeMille's *The Ten Commandments* dwells on their love affair. So too, the DreamWorks version capitalizes on their courtship. Already agitated by Tzipporah's arrival, as well as by his sister's announcement that he is an Israelite and her speculation that he may deliver her people, Moses is agitated enough to make inquiries. Once he learns the horror of the Israelite genocide and hears Pharaoh's explanation that "sometimes for the greater good sacrifices must be made," Moses interrogates his mother about his birth. When she confesses that he is adopted and attempts to comfort him by insisting that he has been sent by the gods, Moses has no rest. The Queen concludes, "When the gods send you a blessing, you don't ask why it was sent." She may not ask, but Moses does.

Insights from these three women, Tzipporah, Miriam, and the Queen, destroy Moses' pride that he is "a sovereign Prince of Egypt."[9] Further, they destroy his friendship with his brother. Finally, they destroy everything else secure about his place in the Egyptian community.[10]

In the Bible, Moses meets Zipporah (the movie's Tzipporah) in Midian, not in Egypt. The banquet scene, as well as the rest of the entire

---

9. Charles Solomon, *The Prince of Egypt: A Vision in Animation* (New York: Harry N. Abrams, 1998), 63.

10. For more information regarding the role of women in the movie, consult Alice Ogden Bellis, "Portrayal of Women in the Biblical Story of Moses and *The Prince of Egypt* (paper presented at the annual meeting of the Society of Biblical Literature, Boston, Mass., 22 November 1999).

courtship, does not exist in Exodus because it is absolutely irrelevant to the community focus of the biblical story. In Exodus the mentor is Jethro, who guides Moses toward a proper relationship with God and with the Israelites. Jethro values Moses not as an individual (son-in-law), but as a community's only hope.

Although there are many ingredient changes from Exodus to *The Prince of Egypt*, both versions have the same "final straw" that forces Moses to leave: Moses' murder of the Egyptian guard who is beating an Israelite slave. In the DreamWorks film, Moses accidentally and publicly murders. In Exodus, Moses deliberately and privately murders. It is only when he realizes that others know his secret that Moses flees.

THE PRINCE OF EGYPT AND EXODUS: TRANSITIONAL STAGE

As the saying goes, when one door shuts, another is opened. All three women have identified the door to Moses' Israelite heritage. With the murder, Moses opens it. At the end of the separation stage, Moses isolates himself from his childhood and adolescent supports to self-fashion into Israelite adulthood.

To repeat, coming-of-age stories *eventually* strive to balance the individual's self-fashioning with a new community role. To that end, Tzipporah in *The Prince of Egypt* links Moses to his Israelite lineage and to his place as savior of the race. Through their courtship, Moses learns to conduct himself, to dance and to dress, within his new community. The DreamWorks version remains focused on Moses, an individual who works in the Midian community seemingly oblivious of and unconcerned about the Israelite slaves, his people. Life is grand for him. Where are the worries prevalent in the transitional stage? Where are the tasks, trials, and tests? Once more, here is the land of *hakuna matata*. It is hard to find the obstacles in *The Prince of Egypt*, which is why there is little tension and, consequently, little instruction on how to come of age. Rather, Moses is like "the little child who shall lead them."

The burning-bush scene presents the only real tension in *The Prince of Egypt*. Charles Solomon explains:

> Moses' encounter with the Burning Bush is the spiritual turning point of the film. The interaction with God transforms Moses' understanding of himself and the world, and initiates the process of his full spiritual development. During his desert journey, he had completely abandoned his identity as an Egyptian prince.

Happily married to Tzipporah, he now lives contentedly as a shepherd among the Midianites, from whom he has learned a new system of values.[11]

The burning-bush scene destroys Moses' contentment. Hearing the voice of God, seeing the burning bush, and assimilating God's directives would unnerve anyone. Moses, as would anyone else, trembles. The DreamWorks animators deliberately tried to enhance the Exodus account of the burning bush with cinematic effects:

> The description of the Burning Bush in Exodus 3 is awe-inspiring and evocative, but the language does not provide concrete descriptions or well-defined images. The Hebrew Bible says simply that "the angel of the Lord appeared to him in flames of fire from within a bush" and that Moses "saw that though the bush was on fire it did not burn up" (Exodus 3:2, New International Version). The film-makers knew the encounter with God couldn't look like ordinary animated magic; clouds of sparkling dust wouldn't suffice for a divine miracle. . . .
>
> Effects artist Jamie Lloyd did extensive work on both the Burning Bush and the Angel of Death. He sought to unify the two effects visually, without making them identical. "In black-and-white, the Burning Bush looks very much like the Angel of Death. When we add color, it looks completely different. But the essence of the images is the same, so that each sequence refers to the other. This creates a constant design element whenever God is manifested."[12]

Clearly, DreamWorks intended to create a significant emotional experience with the animation of the burning bush. Moses is, of course, significantly moved:

> GOD: I shall teach you what to say.
> MOSES: You've chosen the wrong messenger.
> GOD: . . . Who made the deaf, the mute, the seeing, or the blind? Did not I? Now, go! Oh, Moses, I shall be with you—go to the King of Egypt.

---

11. Solomon, *The Prince of Egypt: A Vision in Animation*, 94.
12. Ibid.

With such assurance, it does not take long for Moses to fully recover. With little hesitation, with staff in hand, and with optimum courage, he departs from the burning bush, dances deliriously with his bride, shows off his magic staff, "saddles his horse," and rides with his wife to Egypt to do "the task that God has given [him]." Enduring only this one test, Moses experiences little tension. He learns little about accountability and much about dependence.

Once back in Egypt, Moses squares off with the priests in the "Playing with the Big Boys" scene:

> You're playing with the big boys now,
> Playing with the big boys now.
> Stop this foolish mission—
> Watch a true magician
> Give an exhibition how.
> Pick up your silly twig, boy,
> You're playing with the big boys now![13]

The song's playfulness undercuts any potential tension between Rameses, the reigning Pharaoh, and Moses, the up-and-coming savior.

Despite Rameses' pleas to rekindle their brotherhood and friendship and despite Rameses' pardon, Moses remains firm against Israelite slavery. Rameses' pleas do not test him; God guarantees his heroism. Throughout the plagues, Moses suffers the Israelites' wrath but remains firm. Their wrath is not a test for him; he never wavers. Moses confidently relies on his belief in the Israelite God and in his place as God's savior. The tension is at the lowest end of the spectrum. Stephen Schwartz, musical composer, speaks about Moses' faith:

> The other line that represents to me the essence of *The Prince of Egypt* is: "There can be miracles when you believe." Some believe that God makes miracles for us. Others believe we make our own miracles. In the end, miracles require an act of faith. Faith means that if we believe in and work hard toward our goals, not allowing ourselves to be discouraged or frightened, we can achieve things we never thought possible.[14]

---

13. Stephen Schwartz, *Through Heaven's Eyes: The Prince of Egypt in Story and Song* (New York: Penguin Putnam, 1998), n. p.
14. Ibid.

Faith, or some might say "dependence" on God, eases any coming-of-age tension for Moses. Schwartz's song "When You Believe" reflects his intention to privilege this dependence:

> There can be miracles
> When you believe—
> Though hope is frail,
> It's hard to kill.
> Who knows what miracles
> You can achieve
> When you believe
> Somehow you will—
> Now you will,
> You will when you believe.[15]

God is the key to Moses' success. God affords him confidence and guarantees his aggregation into the Israelite community

Only the burning-bush scene offers any test of Moses' confidence. Other than that, how Moses sustains his confidence and experiences a character reversal—from Egyptian prince regent to Israelite savior and Egyptian destroyer—is not pursued by DreamWorks, just as it is not an issue in *Heidi* and as it is flagrantly dismissed in *The Lion King*. Typically, a coming-of-age protagonist matures through the marginal stage due to confusion, sexual development, psychological growth, emotional turmoil, and values questioning. The adolescent character is torn between the lure of independence and the comfort of dependence. Afraid, the adolescent character self-fashions many inappropriate personas to mask this insecurity. Gradually, the loss of innocence is replaced with an appropriate, confident person's new value system and a new place in society. All these struggles during the typical marginal stage are purposeful and incremental.

Notably, *The Prince of Egypt* does not conform to this typical coming-of-age mold. Moses struggles little and is supported much, by God himself. Even the sibling rivalry that dominates the DreamWorks version does not unsettle him until God murders Rameses' son.

The remainder of the DreamWorks version follows this sibling rivalry. Moses and Rameses, once the best of friends, have become the

---

15. Ibid.

worst of enemies. They recall their boyhood antics. Of the two, though, only Rameses laments this change: "Why can't things be the way they were before?" Without remorse and with more than a modicum of malice, Moses fires back, "Rameses, your stubbornness is bringing this upon Egypt. Think of your son." Rameses threatens to finish his father's genocide program. Moses knows the threat signals the end of Egyptian domination and of their relationship. He arrogantly terminates the conversation: "Rameses, you bring this upon yourself."

Clearly, this is the protagonist's point of view with no attempt at sympathy for his rival. This entrenchment in the protagonist's perspective represents the genre. For a few examples, everything is seen, heard, and deeply felt through Jane Eyre, through Gene in *A Separate Peace*, and through Tom in *The Great Gatsby*. Coming-of-age writers employ the protagonist's perspective; thus, the narration could not be more personal. Even the violence is personalized as the night wind singles out one child after the next for murder. *The Prince of Egypt* personalizes the violence not as God's wrath against the Egyptians as much as Moses' wrath against Rameses.

To come of age, Moses must destroy their childhood relationship and triumph. Frequently, coming-of-age stories will alter the once-close friendship between the protagonist and the character who later becomes the antagonist. (Other antagonists are possible, of course: society, the protagonist's self, an adult authority figure, and so forth.) It makes perfect sense, within the guidelines of the genre, that Rameses should become the antagonist at the transitional stage. Onto Rameses, Moses unleashes all his complaints about the Egyptians' treatment of the Israelites. There is no mention of Moses' past misdemeanors, only of Moses' mischief switching the heads of statues. Egyptian Moses, after all, has changed to Israelite Moses. Now he views life completely through Israelite eyes, as Schwartz puts it in his song's title, "Through Heaven's Eyes":

> I have been asked what one lyric most expresses the essence of the film to me. I would say that there are two. The first is: "Look at your life through heaven's eyes." It is very easy in this world to judge ourselves by the standards of the society around us. . . . But just as Moses, who was as rich and powerful and privileged as could be, came to realize that these things meant nothing as long as he was being dishonest about who he was and as long as he was allowing others to be enslaved and denied their rights, we each

know somewhere inside us that our honesty about ourselves and our actions toward others are what truly count.[16]

Schwartz highlights the secular, personal ethic at stake. Moses' honesty to his heritage, coupled with Rameses' responsibility to his people, dissolves into a personal sibling rivalry during the transitional stage.

Exodus addresses none of this because the biblical story is not concerned with Moses' self-fashioning. Exodus values Moses only as God's choice. Everything that Moses does, avoids, speaks, and withholds has nothing to do with his own personal growth and has everything to do with God's purposes. Moses flees to Midian, defends the seven daughters of Jethro, is welcomed by their father who offers his daughter Zipporah in marriage, and produces a son, Gershom—all to guarantee his future place as God's chosen savior. "I have been an alien residing in a foreign land" (Exodus 2:22). But no more. Moses has found a new home and a new community.

Egypt loses its king and more heavily oppresses its slaves who cry to their God to recall "the covenant with Abraham, Isaac, and Jacob" (Exodus 2:24). This is the community focus of Exodus in which God repeatedly places Moses into a long and impressive lineage of Israelite predecessors:

> God said to Moses, "I AM WHO I AM." He said further . . . "Thus you shall say to the Israelites, 'The LORD, the God of your ancestors, the God of Abraham, the God of Isaac, and the God of Jacob, has sent me to you.': This is my name forever, and this my title for all generations. Go and assemble the elders of Israel, and say to them, "The LORD, the God of your ancestors, the God of Abraham, of Isaac, and of Jacob, has appeared to me, saying: I have given heed to you and to what has been done to you in Egypt. . . ." (Exodus 3:14–17)

Later, when Moses questions God, he hears a similar reminder of his place in the Israelite hierarchy: "I am the LORD. I appeared to Abraham, Isaac, and Jacob as God Almighty, but by my name 'The LORD' I did not make myself known to them" (Exodus 6:2–3). A litany of ancestral names bolsters Moses' confidence. God lists the heads of the ancestral

---

16. Ibid.

houses: the sons of Reuben, the firstborn of Israel and their families (Exodus 6:14). God follows with the families of Simeon, Levi, and so forth (Exodus 6:14–25). This litany is meant to socialize Moses—to show him that he is one among many. The litany is also meant to illustrate the daunting Israelite dynasty. Moses is one among a longstanding and far-spreading community of families. He is not an independent individual.

Although Exodus, like *The Prince of Egypt*, features dialogue between Moses and Pharaoh, the biblical version never introduces a theme of spoiled brotherhood. Pharaoh is not considered as an individual; he is simply an evil king of an unchosen community. In fact, he is never given a name. Exodus continues its concern for the Israelite community oppressed by the Egyptian community. Moses steadily defeats the Egyptians with one divine plague after another. Of course, more than the plagues contribute to Rameses' defeat; it is also his heart, hardened by God. Rameses never stands a chance. Both versions guarantee Moses' success from the beginning, proof that he is not being tested and that he is not learning heroic attributes, only dependence.

After the death of Pharaoh's son, the DreamWorks Moses attends to his personal feelings for his former brother/friend and juxtaposes them with his feelings for the Israelite community. DreamWorks visually intends this juxtaposition, as Charles Solomon notes:

> "When You Believe" is a complex sequence. Both the characters in the film and the audience watching it must shift among profound and often contradictory feelings. Moses has seen the man he loved as a brother holding the lifeless body of his son; he has also freed his people. The audience has experienced the destruction of Egypt, culminating in the Death of the Firstborn, and now must share the triumphant joy of the former slaves.[17]

"Let There Be Miracles" transitions from mourning to relief to joy. However, Exodus does not juxtapose the individual with the community focus. Exodus has no intention of valuing Rameses' grief or even Moses himself, beyond his communal role. Exodus simply and unabashedly celebrates God as Israelite savior.

---

17. Solomon, *The Prince of Egypt: A New Vision in Animation*, 126.

THE PRINCE OF EGYPT AND EXODUS: INCORPORATION STAGE

Exodus ends with God and his people, not with Moses and his people. Although Exodus considers privileging Moses' status, it rejects that idea. In Exodus 18, Jethro, Moses' father-in-law, cautions him against micromanaging:

> What you are doing is not good. You will surely wear yourself out, both you and these people with you. For the task is too heavy for you; you cannot do it alone. Now listen to me. I will give you counsel, and God be with you! You should represent the people before God, and you should bring their cases before God; teach them the statutes and instructions and make known to them the way they are to go and the things they are to do. You should also look for able men among all the people, men who fear God, are trustworthy, and hate dishonest gain; set such men over them as officers over thousands, hundreds, fifties, and tens. Let them sit as judges for the people at all times; let them bring every important case to you, but decide every minor case themselves. (Exodus 18:17–23)

Jethro and the text itself stress the need for a workable system, not for a charismatic leader. Therein lies the major difference between the two versions of the story, a difference uniquely suited to each version's purpose. In Exodus, Moses reports the instructions for Passover, the falling manna, the six days of bread gathering, the seventh day of solemn rest on the holy Sabbath, and the dietary laws. Exodus continues with the Israelites' prayer for water, Yahweh's direction to the water rock, the building of an altar, and the consecration of the firstborn. Then there is Yahweh's pillar of cloud by day and pillar of fire by night that separates the Israelites from the Egyptians. There is the parting of the Red Sea.

In Exodus 19, the Israelites enter the wilderness of Sinai and camp. Moses, beckoned by God, scales the mountain to hear the details of God's deal: "Now therefore, if you obey my voice and keep my covenant, you shall be my treasured possession out of all the peoples. Indeed, the whole earth is mine, but you shall be for me a priestly kingdom and a holy nation. These are the words that you shall speak to the Israelites" (Exodus 19:5–6). Thus, Moses journeys up and down the mountain, mediating between God and the people. So continues Moses, journeying back up the mountain, listening to the next set of God's edicts, journeying

down the mountain, informing the Israelites and improving their lives—
at least according to God's vision. These edicts involve prohibitions
(murder, idol worship, and adultery), ritual stipulations (rest on the
Sabbath), and ordinances (servitude of male slaves). For four chapters,
God informs Moses to inform his people of situation after situation to
be avoided or embraced. God is the spouse who instructs the other
spouse to call the doctor, the repairman, or the financial planner. During
the phone call, the caller must listen to constant instructions from the
spouse who, for whatever reason, could not make the phone call. God is
the non-calling spouse, with his prohibitions, stipulations, and ordinances to be passed on by the calling spouse. When the people act "perversely" (Exodus 32:7), Moses is sent to rescue them, Moses admonishes
them, Moses displays the new tablets, the people sin again, and God
sends a plague. During the last eight chapters of Exodus, the cult is
established and the connection with God is assured:

> Whenever the cloud was taken up from the tabernacle, the
> Israelites would set out on each stage of their journey; but if the
> cloud was not taken up, then they did not set out until the day that
> it was taken up. For the cloud of the Lord was on the tabernacle by
> day, and fire was in the cloud by night, before the eyes of all the
> house of Israel at each stage of their journey. (Exodus 40:36–38)

Exodus ends with the power and the protection of Yahweh, God of the
Israelites. Exodus ends with God's relationship with his chosen community.

Cecil B. DeMille's film *The Ten Commandments* nicely captures this
relationship, with its balance of power and protection. Although in
some scenes Moses looms large, he is always dwarfed by the booming
voice of Yahweh. Moses is significant only as Yahweh's emissary for the
Israelites in DeMille's production.

In sharp contrast, the DreamWorks film barely features the Ten
Commandments. Blink too long and the average viewer will not even
notice the tablets. In fact, the average viewer must already know that
what Moses is holding are the Ten Commandments. *The Prince of Egypt*,
instead, privileges Moses' triumph over Rameses in the parting of the
Red Sea. Solomon confirms this interpretation:

> "The Parting of the Red Sea" is the climax of *The Prince of Egypt*
> and the most taxing assignment the effects artists faced. "This film
> scared the heck out of me," Co-head of effects Don Paul admits. "I

couldn't visualize how on earth we'd do the Red Sea." The water had to move realistically and also be consistent with the look of the backgrounds, and the audience needed to be convinced that God was moving the sea in miraculous ways. The visuals would also have to compete with the famous scene in the Cecil B. De Mille *[The] Ten Commandments* and satisfy an audience used to viewing special effects in recent big-budget live-action films.[18]

Solomon includes at least seventy-eight storyboards and animated pictures of the parting of the Red Sea in *The Prince of Egypt: A New Vision in Animation*. In at least eighteen of those shots, Moses stands alone, either leading or triumphing. In only two pictures are Israelites present. This numerical analysis of the book's representation of DreamWorks's storyboards diminishes the importance of the Israelite community. In their explanation of the actual animated production, however, Solomon contradicts that assumption:

> During production, the filmmakers realized that they needed to do more than create dazzling spectacles for the parting of the Red Sea and the other big effects scenes. They needed to anchor the miraculous events in a human context, to give the audience a sense of what the Hebrews felt as they beheld those miracles. Director Steve Hickner explains: "We've tried to create a number of minor Hebrew characters, almost like bit players, whom the viewers will get to know through the story. The audience will recognize, say, an old woman who comforts a little girl. When the characters are finally free, the viewers will feel some attachment to the people and their ordeal. I don't think that's ever been done in an animated picture."[19]

In the drawing room, it was the intent to end the film with a dual focus on Moses and God's Israelites.

However, DreamWorks ends *The Prince of Egypt* focusing only on Moses. The once-Egyptian prince regent has become the new Israelite savior. At least on screen, it appears to be Moses, not the Yahweh of Exodus, who delivers. There is a brief shot of Rameses screaming

---

18. Ibid., 138.
19. Ibid.

"Moses! Moses!" and Moses sadly returning, "Good-bye, brother." To the bitter end, the sibling rivalry theme pervades. To the bitter end, *The Prince of Egypt* maintains its focus on the individual, on Moses against Rameses. True, Tzipporah remarks, "Look, look at your people, Moses. They are free." The shot spans out from a happy Moses to the saved Israelites, but only briefly. The film concludes with a long shot of Moses alone with his staff on the mountains, close to the heavens. With staff and tablets in hand, with his back to the audience, and with red gown waving in the breeze, Moses looks far, far down upon a blurred image (of the Israelites). He holds more than tablets and staff; he holds the claim of hero. The song "Deliver Us!" fades out. The song commands Moses, not God, to deliver. DreamWorks has prepared the audience for God's replacement. According to Bernard Brandon Scott, the movie does not feature God as a principal character; he is prominent in only three scenes: the burning bush, the night vapor, and the parting of the sea. In fact, continues Scott, God is less a character than a computer-generated graphic image.[20] Moses, not God, dominates the movie.

This Moses is the modern hero: personalized rather than homogenized. To view the DreamWorks film is to watch Moses leave the Egyptian nest and come of age in the Israelite nest, with few obstacles and much support. To view this film is to marvel at Moses, the charismatic hero. To view this film is to witness the historical release of the Israelites. But to view this film is not to learn *how* to come of age—unless personally selected by a divinity and guaranteed success lies within the viewer's future. It is, however, to learn what is valued: Moses' saving of the Israelites via his personal triumph over Rameses, his brother and former friend.

CONCLUSION

Is the change from the Exodus community perspective to a more, but not solely, DreamWorks individual perspective a sign of our times? Are there now more Lion Kings than Hamlets portrayed in narrative? Does society take little trouble to teach the ins and outs of growing from adolescence to adulthood? The temptation is to suppose that this tipping of the individual/community seesaw toward the individual is a cultural phenomenon. However, succumbing to that temptation would overlook the incredible

---

20. For more information regarding the liminal role of God in the movie, consult Bernard Brandon Scott, "Changing Genre and the Problem of Meaning."

success of the Harry Potter series, the popular response to the completion of the Star Wars trilogy, and the much-awaited cinematic arrival of Tolkien's *Lord of the Rings* series. These are all modern coming-of-age stories that teach the audience *how* to self-fashion and to become productive, respected, even heroic members of society. These well-received stories, unlike *The Prince of Egypt*, portray a high level of tension in the transitional stage and strike a balance between the importance of the individual and the importance of society in the incorporation stage.

Is there some logical explanation for the significant changes made by DreamWorks? Interestingly, Katzenberg notes his determination to respect the biblical text:

> From the outset, the filmmakers remained keenly aware of the responsibility they had accepted in bringing a Bible story to the screen. They understood that while they wanted the movie to be entertaining, they had to be respectful of the biblical source material and sensitive to the many millions of people of different religions for whom the story of Moses is a foundation of faith.[21]

Producer Penney Finkelman Cox attests that they "did extensive research, reading the commentaries, histories and philosophical texts that deal with Moses and the Exodus story."[22] In addition, "[T]he film-makers brought in two prominent biblical scholars to act as ongoing consultants. . . . In addition, they hired Tzivia Schwartz-Getzug, a civil rights attorney with a background in interfaith relations and religious studies, to serve as the liaison to the religious community . . ."[23]

Katzenberg confirms an incredible financial, time, and energy investment in order to understand Exodus:

> We asked religious leaders from every faith group, as well as theologians, scholars, archeologists and Egyptologists from around the world to come in, and invited their comments. I was concerned that trying to get a consensus from hundreds of people would constrain us, but actually, I am certain that our movie has been

---

21. In *"Prince of Egypt*: Production Notes," 25 [cited 25 September 2000], from http://moview.yahoo.com/shop?d=hv&id=1800019629&cfr=prod. This page is no longer available.
22. Finkelman Cox, in ibid., 25–26.
23. Ibid., 25.

qualitatively and quantitatively improved by the incredible diversity of opinion and observation we brought into the process.[24]

This investment would lead to speculation that the director was genuinely concerned about the Exodus version and sought to remain faithful to its mold and ingredients—its message and content. Clearly, DreamWorks strove to avoid offense to Jews, Egyptians, and so forth. In *The Prince of Egypt*, with attention drawn away from the communities' rivalry and drawn toward the brothers' rivalry, the chances for cultural offense are drastically minimized.[25]

Obviously, no such political correctness concerns Exodus. When any story devalues one community so completely, as does Exodus, in order to value another just as completely, it will give offense. The Exodus version would never avoid offense. This is a right-versus-wrong, us-versus-them story. Exodus exudes a community's pride and supports only one culture's codes.

In *The Prince of Egypt*, as in every successful coming-of-age story, what matters most is the adolescent. Every ideal adolescent audience member aligns with the adolescent protagonist who develops into adulthood. That adulthood will find the protagonist snugly fitting into a community. Schwartz notes this marriage of individual and communal focus:

> *The Prince of Egypt*, the story of Moses and the liberation of the Hebrew people from slavery, contains themes and ideas that are important to all people: the responsibility we each have to be true to ourselves, to treat others with respect and decency, and to do what we know is right—no matter how dangerous or difficult. To me this is the essence of morality. It became very important to me that the words to the songs of *The Prince of Egypt* express how I feel about these ideas.[26]

For Schwartz, Moses, the individual, is ultimately responsible to the Israelite community. A coming-of-age story will ultimately guarantee Schwartz his dual focus.

---

24. Katzenberg, in ibid., 25–26.
25. For more information regarding production research, see Everett Fox, "*The Prince of Egypt* from a Consultant's Point of View" (paper presented at the annual meeting of the Society of Biblical Literature, Boston, Mass., 22 November 1999).
26. Schwartz, *Through Heaven's Eyes*, n. p.

Although Moses is a hero in both versions, he is a different kind of hero in each. In Exodus, Moses resembles Aeneas in *The Aeneid*. Moses is driven from the onset to succeed, to lead, to save. In both stories, the individual counts for little. However, in *The Prince of Egypt*, the individual counts for everything. In *The Prince of Egypt*, Moses resembles Gilgamesh in *The Epic of Gilgamesh*. Moses must leave behind friendship and seek his fair amount of fame as a just leader. Arguably, Gilgamesh differs from Moses in that the Sumerian hero is tested and learns from his mistakes, while the movie hero automatically displays heroic qualities. However, *The Epic of Gilgamesh* and *The Prince of Egypt* are both similar coming-of-age stories because they focus on the protagonist's journey to redefine his role in a community. As typical coming-of-age stories, they privilege the individual over the community focus.

The DreamWorks version of the story of Moses fits one purpose while the Exodus version fits a different purpose. Neither purpose is particularly more appropriate. It is only the snugness of the fit that is appropriate. *The Prince of Egypt* snugly fits a coming-of-age story's individual focus with little tension during the transitional stage. The protagonist comes of age learning little about accountability but much about dependence (faith). Ultimately, the adolescent merges into society. Exodus fits for a community focus just as snugly. In it, Moses is first and foremost Yahweh's emissary to the Israelites.

To view, compile, and critique the changes is not to criticize, but only to appreciate them. If the purpose for telling the tale changes, so too must the mold and contents change. *The Prince of Egypt*, intending to depict the coming-of-age of Moses, most appropriately privileges the individual over the community. The DreamWorks version of the Exodus story marries purpose with form. An audience member could ask for no more. Plato himself could not insist on more.

6. SITCOM MYTHOLOGY

George Aichele

LEVELS OF REALITY

[T]he cinema is fascinated by itself as a lost object as much as it (and we) are fascinated by the real as a lost referent.[1]

Walter Benjamin describes the motion picture as a "mechanical reproduction" that deprives the representation of the authority or "aura" with which it was invested by the "work of art."[2] This aura derives from the unique existence of any original artwork, such as a painting, which gives authenticity to that work and binds it to a tradition. Although this aura functions in a primarily aesthetic manner in the modern world, it originates in the ritual importance of the work of art, and this ritual significance remains in some vestigial way associated with the work's aura.[3] In contrast, the mass-produced and mass-experienced, mechanically reproduced work of art replaces both the ritual and aesthetic functions with a

---

1. Jean Baudrillard, *Simulacra and Simulation*. trans. Sheila Faria Glaser (Ann Arbor: University of Michigan Press, 1994), 47.

2. Walter Benjamin, *Illuminations*, trans. Harry Zohn (New York: Schocken Books, 1968), 221. Benjamin regards all photographs as lacking in aura. Roland Barthes argues that some still photos do possess a kind of authenticity (he calls it the *punctum*), but he agrees that this is lost in the moving picture (*Camera Lucida*, trans. Richard Howard [New York: Hill & Wang, 1981], 3, 55, 78, 89).

3. *Illuminations*, 223–24.

political function, and "[w]hat is lost is the original, which only a history itself nostalgic and retrospective can reconstitute as 'authentic.'"[4]

The movie *Pleasantville* explores ideological aspects of the mechanically reproduced artwork that is the televised situation comedy, and it does so by means of the mechanically reproduced artwork that is the popular feature film. In other words, *Pleasantville* does not reproduce a work of art, but instead it simulates yet another reproduction, a televised situation comedy or sitcom. The doubling of media and of reproduction plays an important part in both the expression form and the expression content of this movie.[5] A fictional story depicts the relationship between fictional stories and reality. It makes explicit the duplicity involved in any narrative. Through this referential loop, the movie continually calls attention not only to the fictional status of the TV show, "Pleasantville," but to its own fictionality as well. It challenges not only the traditions and ideologies within which the early TV sitcoms functioned, but also those that inform any mechanically reproduced work of art, including itself.

Pleasantville is set in the late 1990s world of middle-class, suburban America. The movie's narrative world realistically mimics a contemporary suburban, middle-class neighborhood in the United States. Early in the movie, in a rapid sequence of brief scenes, high school teachers describe for their classes the grim state of affairs in the world at present and in the near future. These descriptions apply as well to the actual world, the primary world in which the film's audience lives. The movie's principal characters are also realistic ones, and they live in realistic situations. David and Jennifer Wagner are fraternal twins growing up in a broken home. David is a teenaged "nerd" who spends all of his spare time watching 1950s-era television shows on an "oldies" TV cable channel not unlike the real-life channel, Nickelodeon. Jennifer is a "valley girl," interested only in boys and fashions, and in each of those objects only as means to greater popularity with her clique of girlfriends. Both of them are ignored by their forty-something mother, who is desperately trying to regain her own lost youth and to deal with the fact that her life is not turning out at all the way that she had planned.

---

4. Baudrillard, *Simulacra*, 99, discussing Benjamin.
5. This distinction derives from Hjelmslev. See Seymour Chatman, *Story and Discourse: Narrative Structure in Fiction and Film* (Ithaca, N.Y.: Cornell University Press, 1978), 22–24, for a summary of Hjelmslev's views.

The extraordinary exception to this realism occurs when both David and Jennifer are miraculously transported into the narrative world of a fictitious television series from 1958. This TV series is also titled "Pleasantville," and it is also set in middle-class suburban America, in a town also called Pleasantville. The use of the same name for the movie, the TV show, and the town highlights the importance of the various "levels of reality"[6] in this story. To reduce confusion, I refer to the movie as *Pleasantville* (in italics), to the television show as "Pleasantville" (in quotes), and to the town as Pleasantville.

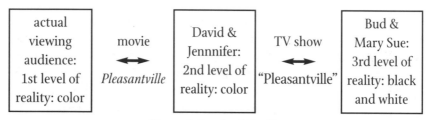

Figure 1. Levels of Reality

Pleasantville exists within the actual, primary world of the movie's audience. I call this the first level of reality. *Pleasantville* is one movie among numerous others in our world. This movie depicts a second level of reality, the fictional but realistic secondary world inhabited by David and Jennifer. "Pleasantville" exists within this secondary world as one TV series among many others. Other TV shows, actual series from the 1950s, are mentioned by name in the movie, although they are not shown on the screen. Finally, Pleasantville exists within a third level of reality, the fantasy world represented in "Pleasantville."[7] However, Pleasantville is not merely one town among others; it is unique, initially at least, because there are no other communities in the world of "Pleasantville." The expansion of this world to include other communities is one of the changes that occurs as the story of *Pleasantville* unfolds.

---

6. Italo Calvino, *The Uses of Literature*, trans. Patrick Creagh (New York: Harcourt Brace Jovanovich, 1986), 101–21.

7. See J. R. R. Tolkien, "On Fairy Stories," *The Tolkien Reader* (New York: Ballantine, 1966), for further discussion of both "primary world" and "secondary world." See also Benjamin, *Illuminations*, 217–51. One could call a third level world such as that of Pleasantville a "tertiary world," but its ontological status remains that of a secondary world. Realism is not reality, nor is fantasy non-reality: "there is no antipathy between realism and myth. It is well known how often our 'realistic' literature is mythical (if only as a crude myth of realism) and how our 'literature of the unreal' has at least the merit of being only slightly so. The wise thing would of course be to define the writer's realism as an essentially ideological problem" (Roland Barthes, *Mythologies*, trans. Annette Lavers [New York: Hill & Wang, 1972], 136–37).

What is reproduced in this movie is itself a fictional reproduction, and this has important consequences for both its form and its content. It is important that these levels of reality be kept distinct, even when they spill out into one another. The distinction between "Pleasantville" and Pleasantville is crucial to the distinction between expression form and expression content at work in *Pleasantville*. The fictional reality represented in the TV show is at two removes from the primary world of the movie's viewers. Pleasantville is a town in a fantastical secondary world ("Pleasantville") that in turn appears within a realistic secondary world (*Pleasantville*); in this sense, it is the least "real" of all the levels. However, although Pleasantville is the least realistic of the three reality levels, it is the most important one in the overall story of *Pleasantville*. All the important events in the movie take place in the fantastical town of Pleasantville. In the third-level reality of Pleasantville, David and Jennifer come of age and come to terms with their *Pleasantville* lives, because it is there that mythologically significant transformations and transgressions occur.

It is common in fantastical narratives for a magical gate or passage-way to connect the realistic world to the fantasy one. In this way, the two worlds are connected but also kept distinct. Familiar examples of this sort of fantasy structure include *Alice in Wonderland*, *Peter Pan*, and *The Wizard of Oz*. The story of *Pleasantville* also begins in this way. The Wagners' television set and the TV show appearing on it function as a gateway between the world of the movie and the world of "Pleasantville." Nevertheless, in this case the boundary between reality and fantasy is eventually inverted and blurred, and finally it collapses altogether. Following David and Jennifer's transfer into the TV show, the realistic world begins to appear in the world of Pleasantville, much to the discomfort of the town's inhabitants. Thus this story is not merely about multiple levels of reality, but also about the possibly of interference and exchange between the various levels.[8] The transfer of the characters David and Jennifer from the second level of reality to the third level initiates this exchange, but its ramifications extend far beyond them.

The difference between these levels of reality is signified graphically in the movie's discourse by the contrast between the fully colored world of *Pleasantville* and the black-and-white world of "Pleasantville." The invasion of realism is represented in the discourse of the movie through

---

8. For additional examples see George Aichele, "Two Forms of Meta-Fantasy," *Journal for the Fantastic in the Arts* 1, no. 3 (1988): 55–67.

the gradual penetration of color images into the black-and-white TV-show world. In this respect, *Pleasantville* may be compared to the movie version of *The Wizard of Oz*. In that movie, color represented the fabulous, magical realm of Oz, and the dull everyday realities of Kansas appeared in black and white. The shift back and forth between monochrome and color was quite abrupt and startling, as was the shift between the worlds of Kansas and Oz. Only Dorothy (and the viewer) was aware of this media shift at the beginning and end of the movie, so it served both as an index of a shift in reality and connoted that the dream fantasy of Oz was preferable to the waking reality of Kansas.[9]

In *Pleasantville*, the effect is quite different. The initial shift from the second-level reality to the third level one is abrupt, but from then on, as realism gradually invades Pleasantville, patches of color increasingly spread into the monochromic screen images. The inhabitants of Pleasantville are aware of this increase in the colorfulness of their world, and they react to it in various ways. Unlike *The Wizard of Oz*, the use of both color and monochromic images is not only essential to the discourse of *Pleasantville*, but it plays an important part in the story as well. Expression form itself becomes expression content, and transformations of content change the form. Eventually, Pleasantville is entirely colored, so that when David returns to his home at the movie's end, the reality shift involves no media shift at all. The fantasy world has become a real one.

LIMITS OF THE PLEASANT

[T]he whole visible world is perhaps nothing more than the rationalization of a man who wants to find peace for a moment. An attempt to falsify the actuality of knowledge, to regard knowledge as a goal still to be reached.[10]

In contrast to the realism of *Pleasantville*, "Pleasantville" does not accurately represent the primary world of America in the 1950s. Indeed, the

---

9. Even earlier, DeMille used "two-tone" color in the scene of Jesus' resurrection in *The King of Kings*. Several other movies have combined color and black and white, in various ways. The British "counterculture" movie *If…* did so simply because the producers ran out of money about halfway through the filming and had to finish the movie using black-and-white film. Because scenes were filmed out of narrative sequence, the finished movie switches back and forth fairly often. Even so, the media shifts in *If…* are curiously suggestive.

10. Franz Kafka, *Parables and Paradoxes*, trans. by Willa and Edwin Muir et al. (New York: Schocken Books, 1958), 33.

world of this television show is quite unrealistic. In addition, there is no pretense in *Pleasantville* of a return to the 1950s, and the simulation of an old sitcom provides a perspective on the present-day world, not that of the past. Although "Pleasantville" realistically imitates a 1950s sitcom, the movie audience (at the time of its release in 1998) and the movie's characters, David and Jennifer, react to both the TV show and the town depicted in it in terms of values and beliefs of people living in the 1990s, that is, with irony and amusement. However, what the 1990s audience finds funny is not necessarily what the 1950s audience found funny. Characters and situations seem unrealistic to present-day viewers in ways that they did not to the original viewers of the actual shows in the 1950s. Certain behaviors and ways of speaking seem old-fashioned. Clothing and hairstyles from the 1950s tend to appear strange or ugly now, while the automobiles and popular music have acquired respectability and "classic" status.

Nevertheless, it is precisely in its unrealistic qualities that "Pleasantville" most realistically imitates the world of TV sitcoms. The TV show within the movie is strongly reminiscent of black-and-white TV favorites from the Eisenhower era, such as *Father Knows Best, Leave It to Beaver,* or *Ozzie and Harriet.* Several of these actual TV series are mentioned by name in the first few minutes of the movie, and reruns of them can still be seen on cable networks such as Nickelodeon. These actual sitcoms present a highly distorted version of reality, quite like that of "Pleasantville." Thus, although the fantasy world of "Pleasantville" appears in the midst of the realistic world of *Pleasantville,* that happens simply because it is a television show and, in reality, TV shows are often unrealistic.

The actual 1950s TV series, such as the ones mentioned above, represent not the way the primary world actually was, but rather the world as white middle-class Americans wanted it to be. These shows typically feature a white, middle-class, nuclear family living in a homogeneous suburban neighborhood. The father and mother both live in a happy, peaceful, and monogamous relationship. All members of the family depict conventional gender and generational roles. These shows reflect a white, patriarchal, Protestant, middle-class myth of America, and in that sense they serve as ideological mirrors of desire. The sitcoms are not realistic depictions of actual life, but rather utopian dreams of what that life should be. In other words, these shows represent a fantastical secondary world, a narrative assembled from bits and pieces of the actual, primary world but rearranged according to the desires of the viewing audience, or at least according to the TV producers' understanding of those desires.[11]

The ideology reflected in these shows was not merely a dream, but it was also a stimulus to action and a goal to be actively sought. Many real-life people (including my own parents) moved to the burgeoning American suburbs in the 1940s and 1950s with the dream of living in a Pleasantville of their own, a place in which the unpleasantness of racial or economic exploitation could be kept always out of sight from the very ones who profit most from that exploitation. Pleasantville represents exactly the sort of town that these people wanted to live in: a place where drug abuse, broken families, homosexuality, class or race conflict, and crime are unknown, and where docile teenaged children always respect and obey their parents. Pleasantville is the place where there is no unpleasantness at all.

"Pleasantville" represents a stable and homogeneous utopia. This little world truly is a pleasant one in many ways. The weather is always sunny and calm, catastrophes never occur, and the sole function of the fire department is to rescue the occasional stranded cat. There is neither poverty nor unemployment—marginalized people apparently do not exist—and every family has its own clean and spacious house and yard. As David notes, "nobody's homeless in Pleasantville."[12] Harmony reigns in "Pleasantville," perhaps because there is no evidence of political, religious, lifestyle, racial, or cultural differences. The mayor holds impromptu court in the barbershop or the bowling alley, but these irregular meetings are innocuous because there are never any serious matters to discuss. Everyone in Pleasantville knows and likes everyone else, and each weekly episode of the show ends happily. "Pleasantville" is suitable for the whole family to watch, and it represents wholesome, middle-class American "family values."

However, pleasantness has its price, and it is a high one. Pleasantville exists in a world of its own. It is indeed a paradise, surrounded not by physical walls (Genesis 2:8; 3:23–24) but by narrative limits: an Eden

---

11. Interesting exceptions to this tendency include *I Love Lucy*, in which the Cuban musician, Desi Arnaz, played Lucille Ball's husband, and *The Honeymooners*, in which the marital relationship was stormy and the characters belonged to the working class. In *My Three Sons*, there was no female mother figure. Both *I Love Lucy* and *The Honeymooners* also had urban, apartment settings, unlike the suburban, single-family houses that were common in 1950s sitcoms. However, these sitcoms also reinforced bourgeois values. More recent sitcoms no longer follow such simplistic patterns, but they remain highly utopian and unrealistic, for the most part.

12. Quotations from the film are my own transcription.

from which humanity was never exiled, a kind of reverse ghetto. The inhabitants are trapped in mythic reiterability.[13] Pleasantville is truly utopia (Greek *ouk topos*, "nowhere"), because its inhabitants are only dimly aware of a world beyond the town's outskirts. Indeed, whether a larger world exists at all in "Pleasantville" is uncertain. The streets do not connect to other streets, towns, or cities. The inhabitants have heard of the Mississippi River, but because the roads loop back on themselves, they have no way to go to see it. Likewise, the people all know what color is, and the words for different colors, even though they have never seen any colored thing. When color starts to appear in their monochrome world, they call it "real" color.

The world of Pleasantville is limited in other ways as well. Adult women do not work outside their homes, unlike their husbands. Instead they stay at home and fix meals. The women play bridge, and the men bowl. The occasional unattached adult (such as the soda-shop owner, Mr. Johnson) is charmingly eccentric, and never a threat or challenge to the marital norm. Younger women become cheerleaders and bake cookies for their boyfriends, who play basketball and never miss a shot. The high school team always wins, although where the other teams come from is not clear. Despite (or perhaps because of) the apparent universality of heterosexuality, the word, "sex," and any sexual activity beyond the occasional kiss on the cheek are unknown. Married couples sleep in separate beds. The teenagers go to Lovers' Lane, but only to hold hands and talk. In the soda shop or their cars, they listen to the bland music of Perry Como and Johnny Mathis.

In *Pleasantville*, David and Jennifer Wagner are forcibly transported from the realistic social chaos of the late 1990s into the tidy utopian world of Pleasantville. This transgression of the limits of reality is effected by a marvelous TV remote controller, which is supplied to them by a mysterious TV repairman who admires David's knowledge of the TV series. When David and Jennifer are translated from their full-color world into the monochromatic "Pleasantville" reality, they become native "Pleasantville" characters, Bud and Mary Sue, the adolescent children of mild-mannered civic leader George Parker and his wife Betty. No one notices the changed appearance of Bud or Mary Sue—unlike more recent sitcoms, where cast changes are often written into the script in

---

13. See Umberto Eco, *The Role of the Reader* (Bloomington: Indiana University Press, 1979), 112–22.

various ways, in 1950s sitcoms, changes in the cast frequently went unnoted in the show. However, the clash of cultures that results when David and Jennifer's realistically depicted 1990s ideas, attitudes, and actions inevitably collide with the insipid world of 1950s sitcoms leads to disruptions of the TV show's scripted order.

David is a big fan of "Pleasantville," and initially he wants to stick closely to the scripts, which he already knows by heart. In his world, "Pleasantville" is forty years old, and long since in syndicated reruns. Nevertheless, precisely because David knows in advance how each episode will turn out, his behavior as the "Pleasantville" character, Bud Parker, is changed. The Pleasantville natives, like most fictional characters, are unaware of the script that controls their lives and presumably think they act out of free will. In contrast, David's knowledge of the script allows him to deviate from it, but this difference affects the story in ways that he cannot predict. Despite his love of "Pleasantville," David's knowledge as an expert viewer of the series causes him to react to situations in ways different than any native "Pleasantville" character would.

In spite of himself, David brings changes into the world of "Pleasantville." Early in the story, he must decide whether or not to encourage Jennifer (as Mary Sue Parker) to go out with Skip, the handsome high school basketball hero, as the script requires, although David knows that Jennifer will probably not merely hold hands with Skip, contrary to the script. Since Skip is a native of the "Pleasantville" world, he is completely ignorant of sexual matters, and he is not at all ready for a sexually active woman such as Jennifer. Unlike David, Jennifer is not a "Pleasantville" fan, and she hates her imprisonment in the "pasty" 1950s TV world. She will do almost anything to get out of it and back to the colorful 1990s, including seducing Skip.

> JENNIFER: We don't belong here.
> DAVID: If we don't play along we can alter their whole existence.
> JENNIFER: Maybe it needs to be messed with.

Jennifer wants to return to the second-level reality of *Pleasantville*, and she does not mind rearranging the "Pleasantville" world if that will result in her return. Sex is introduced, first among the teenagers on Lovers' Lane and then in the bedrooms of the adults, as married couples begin to buy double beds (which never appeared in 1950s sitcoms). Nevertheless, "it's not just the sex," as David says. His own relationship (as Bud) with Mr. Johnson, in whose soda shop he works, inexorably draws David in directions that the native Bud would never have gone. Both David's and Jennifer's affection for Betty Parker, their "Pleasantville" mother, also have this result; their relationships to Betty simultaneously press both of them to further violations of the "Pleasantville" scripts. Thanks to transgressions such as these, the teenagers of the town discover rock 'n roll and jazz music, as well as the novels of Mark Twain, D. H. Lawrence, and J. D. Salinger, among others. Many of the town's inhabitants are eager to learn about a world where the roads do not simply loop back on themselves but "just keep on going." An escalating sequence of narrative imbalances ripples out through the peaceful town of Pleasantville, and a wide range of repressed desires are unleashed as the lives of the Pleasantville inhabitants deviate further and further from the "Pleasantville" scripts.

These script deviations are accompanied by the appearance of color in the monochrome world of "Pleasantville." In other words, the narrative alterations introduced by David and Jennifer are accompanied by the appearance of the realism of *Pleasantville* in the midst of the fantasy that is Pleasantville. With each new deviation, the amount of color on the movie screen grows, and although the hue and placement of the emergent color—a deep red rose blossom, a lime green automobile—may seem arbitrary, it is hardly random. The play in this movie between color and monochrome film media is not just a clever techno-trick, nor is it only a metaphor. The film's use of both color and monochromic images highlights the cinematic medium itself in a way that is essential to the story. It is both symbolic and iconic, to use the terminology of C. S. Peirce. An image of the world in color is inherently more realistic than the same image in black and white, and the vivid colors that gradually spill out onto the movie screen and especially onto the characters' skins increase the actual realism of the image on the screen. The colors also symbolize deep changes in the characters. They are associated with stronger emotions and commitments, and richer perceptions. As David says, "they just . . . see something inside themselves."

Some of the townspeople eagerly embrace the new world of color and deviation from the script. They also discover that they are deeply unhappy in their bland, monochrome lives. Thanks to Jennifer's instructions, Betty discovers the pleasures of her own body and becomes "colored," in a remarkable negative transfiguration. She also uncovers her own deep dislike for her underprivileged status as a woman and housewife in Pleasantville. With David's help, Mr. Johnson discovers that he doesn't have to do everything in the soda shop always in the same tightly scripted order, and he realizes that he really wants to be a painter. Both Betty Parker and Mr. Johnson discover within themselves desires that their lives should somehow be other than they currently are. In both cases, these desires take them beyond the safe world of 1950s middle-class American conventions into dangerous places and alternative lifestyles.

Other inhabitants of the town respond to the disruptions in the script and especially to the appearance of color in their world with fear and anger. Like George Parker, Betty's husband, these townspeople are comfortable with their tightly scripted reality and are deeply resistant to the escalating sequence of changes. As a result, the changes have an acutely divisive effect on the Pleasantville community.

> GEORGE PARKER: "It'll go away" (referring to his wife's newly colored skin).
> BETTY PARKER: "I don't want it to go away."

However, Betty is fearful of appearing with her colorful skin in public, and David comes to the rescue by applying monochrome "makeup" to her face. Betty's decision to "pass" as "white" is understandable. Some of those who remain "white" violently attack the newly "colored" people and anything associated with them. Eventually the "white" people hold a town meeting (to which only "true citizens" of Pleasantville are welcome) in which the mood is initially ugly, but where the people eventually decide (in liberal, middle-class fashion) that violent action will not solve the problem.

Like many white middle-class Americans of the 1950s and 1960s, the Pleasantville inhabitants are uncomfortable with the changes in their world, but many of them are equally dismayed by the violence that arises in reaction to these changes. By this point in the movie, the realism that has emerged in Pleasantville has replaced a great deal of the non-realism that was typical of 1950s TV sitcoms. Those sitcoms never seriously addressed issues such as racial, sexual, or lifestyle difference, even though by the late 1950s Americans were increasingly aware of these and related matters. By 1958, nuclear weapons were being actively and frequently tested by both sides of the Cold War, and many Americans were digging bomb shelters in their basements. Sputnik had orbited the Earth, and the United States was losing the "space race." Fidel Castro and his followers were about to make big changes in Cuba. More to the point, the Civil Rights movement was well underway, and the United States was beginning to get involved in the very controversial war in Vietnam. Rock 'n roll, with its roots deep in the music of black Americans but sometimes performed and always eagerly purchased by a whole generation of suburban white teenagers, was coming into its own as a cultural force. It was also during the late 1950s that color television sets and programs became widely available.[14]

A FLAW IN EDEN

[C]oloring the world is always a means of denying it (and perhaps one should at this point begin an inquiry into the use of color in the cinema). . . .
[C]olor is an artifice, a cosmetic (like the kind used to paint corpses).[15]

Pleasantville repeatedly establishes parallels between the town library, Lover's Lane, and the soda shop, with its innovative music. As sites of adolescent social encounter and sexual experimentation, Lovers' Lane and the soda shop clearly belong together; it is also not surprising that Lovers' Lane and the soda shop serve as major beachheads of the color invasion. It is less obvious why the local library should also be so marked, but the townspeople rightly perceive both the soda shop and the library to be dangerous sites of novelty and rebellion. Both of them become popular gathering spots for the newly colored people, and both of them are eventually destroyed by enraged mobs of "white" people.

In a crucial episode, David takes Margaret Henderson, another native "Pleasantville" character, out to Lovers' Lane. Both Margaret and David are still in black and white. Margaret has already deviated from the TV script on her own, because she is supposed to be the girlfriend of another character, who is appropriately named Whitey. Because of David's unscripted heroic actions (teaching the firemen how to fight an equally unscripted fire), Margaret is attracted to him instead of to Whitey. After

---

14. The videotape for *Pleasantville* begins with a series of still images and instructions to adjust the "color level" of the television set. In the mid-1950s, my father worked on the patent rights for some of the new color TV technology. As a result, we had a color TV in our house long before most other people in our Pleasantville-like community. Color programming was rare in those days, and we often invited neighbors or friends over to watch the amazing new phenomenon with us (not unlike gatherings of people to listen to radio programs a generation earlier). The technology was still undependable, and this invariably resulted in agonizing moments when we struggled to adjust the color level of the TV set, often without success.

15. Barthes, *Mythologies*, 94; *Camera*, 81.

they arrive at Lovers' Lane, David and Margaret sit by the lake with several other young couples who are reading books and talking quietly together. Impulsively, Margaret runs to pick a bright red apple from a tree in the park, which she offers to David with a smile, saying, "Go ahead, try it."

Prior to this point, the movie's plot has been generally simple and linear, but now the montage cuts rapidly back and forth between this episode and several others, which are presumably occurring simultaneously. These concurrent episodes are as follows:

1. Jennifer sits alone in her room, reading a book. Skip appears outside her window and asks her to join him for another sexual rendezvous. She declines, saying that she'd rather study.
2. George Parker comes home from work to find his house dark, his wife missing, and no dinner on the table. George runs to the bowling alley, where he encounters the mayor and other male friends, who are righteously aghast at his story.
3. Betty Parker visits Mr. Johnson at the soda shop. He ends up painting her portrait, and eventually (on the soda shop window) her nude, fully colored body reclining on the bar of the soda fountain.

In each of these interwoven scenes, a significant alteration in the order of things has occurred. The valley girl becomes the serious student. The husband finds his home abandoned and in disarray. The housewife and the soda jerk become bohemians.

This juxtaposition suggests that these three scenes belong together with the Edenic encounter of David and Margaret, and furthermore, that the cinematic allusion to the story of Adam and Eve is by no means incidental. Each of the four scenes indicates major changes in the lives of characters arising from the intrusion of David and Jennifer into the "Pleasantville" world and the consequent color revolution. Immediately after this complex of scenes begins, the uniformly pleasant weather ceases and it starts to rain in Pleasantville. This storm further ties all four of the interrelated scenes together. George gets soaked as he runs to the bowling alley. In their respective locations, Jennifer, Betty, and Mr. Johnson all look out of windows and notice with pleasure the change in the weather. In contrast, David calms the fears of the teenagers caught out in the storm at Lovers' Lane. It has never "really" rained before in paradise, and the native inhabitants look upon this new phenomenon with ignorance.

The rain is the product of a mild thunderstorm, and no Noachian flood results. This storm is no punishment for sin. David and Margaret have merely been kissing, in contrast to the torrid lovemaking between Skip and Jennifer earlier in the story, and the apple that David takes from Margaret is just an apple. In contrast to the biblical Eden story, the eating of this fruit is a *good* thing, and it is the woman, not the man, who is transformed when she offers it to him, because Margaret soon becomes "colored." Both Jennifer and Mr. Johnson also become "colored" during the storm. David's own color transformation must wait until he defends his "colored" mother from a gang of thugs led by Whitey. David remains a "white" man, but his desire for Margaret has finally overcome his desire to follow the "Pleasantville" script.

The scene between David and Margaret at Lovers' Lane is not the first time that the biblical story of Eden is referenced in *Pleasantville*. When David brings an art book from the library to the soda shop to encourage Mr. Johnson's desire to paint, the book falls open to a colorful painting of Adam and Eve, hands covering their nakedness, fleeing in shame and misery. After the rain, numerous references point to the Eden and Flood stories. Most obviously, the comically wrathful TV repairman tells David that his acceptance of the apple from Margaret has decisively changed everything. Referring to "the deluge" and "bolts of lightning," the repairman shows David (and the movie's viewer) a replay of Margaret offering him the apple.

> REPAIRMAN: "You don't deserve to live in this paradise. . . . I'm going to put this place back the way it was, and we're going to make everybody happy again."
> DAVID: "I can't let you do that."

David and the repairman both admire "Pleasantville," but they want quite different things for the people there. David defies the power of the repairman and eventually defeats him.

Pleasantville presents a story of encounter with forbidden knowledge—that is, knowledge that opens the eyes[16] (Genesis 3:7) and from which there is no turning back. Like the repairman, David and Jennifer are supernatural beings in relation to the world of Pleasantville. Unlike him, they are actively present in that world, not merely watching it from outside.

---

16. "Evidently a different nature opens itself to the camera than opens to the naked eye—if only because an unconsciously penetrated space is substituted for a space consciously explored by man" (Benjamin, *Illuminations*, 236–37).

The roles of David and Jennifer in the transformation of Pleasantville are similar to that of the hero of Gnostic redeemer myths, and a dualistic metaphysics is implied by the movie's multiple levels of reality. The twin redeemers descend from second-level *Pleasantville* to enlighten the ignorant people of third-level "Pleasantville" and deliver them from their enchantment by oppressive powers.[17] However, the knowledge that David and Jennifer bring to the people of Pleasantville is not offered either as temptation or as revelation. At no point do David or Jennifer inform the "Pleasantville" natives that they (the natives) are merely fictional characters, or that they (David and Jennifer) know how the "Pleasantville" scripts run. Nevertheless, Jennifer and David's knowledge redeems the inhabitants of Pleasantville, and it is the truth, although the saving knowledge that these redeemers bring does not provide escape from an evil or fallen world. There can be no (fantastic) escape from this world because it is already utopia, the place to which one escapes. Instead, the entire world is transformed from within. The fantasy world of Pleasantville is "redeemed" as it becomes more realistic.

After the storm, a brilliantly colored rainbow arches over the black-and-white town and suggests a promise of good things to come. However, despite the movie's explicit (albeit amusing) depiction of divine wrath, and in contrast to the biblical text (Genesis 9:12–15), in *Pleasantville*, the rainbow after the storm signifies a broken covenant, a departure from paradise. The people of Pleasantville have broken their implicit covenant with the TV repair deity—that is, they have strayed far from the script—and they choose in favor of the new ways and the more colorful world introduced by David and Jennifer. Furthermore, unlike the usual reading of the biblical story of Eden, it is good that they do so. The changes that Jennifer and David bring, directly through their own actions and indirectly through their effects on others, are all presented by the movie as good things. These effects include individual freedom and spontaneity, diversity, creativity, and hedonism. They may be summarized as willingness to deviate from the script.

The successful color revolution in Pleasantville does not result in shame and misery, but rather in a world noticeably closer in its complexity and diversity to the everyday, primary world in which we actually live—a world that for all its faults is far more desirable than the monochrome and monotone world of "Pleasantville." Paradise is the place where one

---

17. Compare John 1:1–14, and Gospel of Thomas ("the twin") 28, 50, 61, 77.

must follow the script without deviation, and it is eventually replaced in this movie by a messier but more human (and humane) world where "nothing is supposed to be." Even the transgressions of Betty and Mr. Johnson, quite outrageous in terms of 1950s middle-class morality, are vindicated in the movie's conclusion. Nevertheless, although the happy ending of the movie justifies the broken covenant, it is not an unambiguous vindication. The pleasant illusion of freedom has been replaced by harsher circumstances. From now on, the people of Pleasantville must write their own scripts and suffer the fear and uncertainty that accompany such responsibility.

David and Jennifer have also been changed by Pleasantville. Here lies the greatest contrast to the redeemer myth. The redeemers have themselves been redeemed. Although she initially despised the world of Pleasantville, Jennifer decides to remain in the third-level reality, where the roads now connect to other communities and other possibilities, and where she will have to face the same challenges and obligations that a young woman would have to face in the second-level world of *Pleasantville*, or in our world. Jennifer's decision to stay in Pleasantville requires that she abandon her former valley-girl lifestyle. Conversely, David leaves his "Pleasantville" mother, Betty, and his Pleasantville girl-friend, Margaret, to help his *Pleasantville* mother through her midlife crisis. David's departure from his beloved world of "Pleasantville" and return to the grimmer world of *Pleasantville* also suggest a deep change in him. He no longer wants to flee from reality, and now he is eager to attempt the sort of changes in the "real" world that he has made in the fantastic one. David's and Jennifer's choices are presented as the considered decisions of adults who, because of their experiences in Pleasantville, have come a long way from their initial, narcissistic adolescence.

THE LOST REFERENT

What is life, after all, but a caravan of lifelike forgeries?[18]

Roland Barthes says of the still photograph, "The choice is mine: to subject its spectacle to the civilized code of perfect illusions, or to confront in it the wakening of intractable reality."[19] A similar choice is presented

---

18. Robert Coover, *Pricksongs and Descants* (New York: Penguin, 1969), 111.
19. *Camera*, 119.

by this moving picture. Like the TV shows that it mocks, *Pleasantville* reinforces elements of middle-class ideology: individual freedom, optimism in the face of an uncertain future, and traditional humanistic values, such as tolerance, compassion, and fair play. In addition, despite the movie's technical play with the cinematic medium and its postmodern play with levels of reality, its treatment of the Eden story is hardly novel. The position of the Eden story at the beginning of the biblical canon connotes that without the transgression that it narrates, the rest of the biblical story would be unnecessary. The eating of forbidden fruit sets the stage for greater events to come.

Such would be the "civilized" reading of this movie. However, as Barthes says, another reading is possible. The reference to the Eden story in the movie is closely tied to the collapse of levels of narrative reality into one another: the fantastic becomes real, color invades the black-and-white world, and expression form becomes expression content. The cinematic rewriting of the biblical stories of Eden and the Flood in *Pleasantville* not only juxtaposes them, but it also recycles them in a way that challenges the Christian reading of those stories.

Christian theologians describe the eating of forbidden fruit by Adam and Eve as the original sin. This sin condemns humanity (the descendents of Adam and Eve) to an inherited condition of universal unworthiness, from which only the undeserved sacrifice of Christ can deliver them. The theologians ignore the possibility, suggested in the biblical text itself, that the primal fault appears much earlier in the Eden story. God puts two supernatural trees in the garden, and these trees separate knowledge from life (Genesis 2:8–9). As a result, the garden is divided at its center and cannot be single: the garden itself is diabolic. The potential for disharmony in (and liberation from) paradise appears in this duality, which, once begun, continues to spread. The eating of forbidden fruit only occurs after humanity itself has been divided, also by God (Genesis 2:21–22). In other words, God creates the situation in which the humans will be tempted and must then be driven from the garden. God is as responsible for the humans' transgression as is the serpent, and arguably even more so.

Furthermore, the duality is not merely in the garden, but in God himself. God and the serpent are not enemies, but allies. The serpent is one half of a fundamental split within God, corresponding to the divided trees.[20]

---

20. See John Dominic Crossan, "Felix Culpa and Foenix Culprit," *Semeia* 18 (1980): 109; and George Aichele, *The Limits of Story* (Chico, Calif.: Scholars, 1985), chap. 2. See also Gospel of Thomas 23, 61, 72. Some scholars suggest that in an earlier form of the Eden-myth, Adam and

According to Umberto Eco, this fault also appears in the language of Eden—that is, God's perfect language.[21] God's authoritative and creative Word brings with it its own inevitable misunderstanding and transgression. It makes lies and fictions possible. This language is inherently ambiguous and fictional, and it encourages an uncontrolled play of metaphors that undermines the binary oppositions that are crucial to the significance of any message. The original sin is linguistic. In their own emerging ability to play with language, Adam and Eve become like God (Genesis 3:22).

Like Adam, David in "Pleasantville" is an ordinary human being, and like the serpent (Genesis 3:4–6), David in *Pleasantville* brings forbidden knowledge—supernatural knowledge—to Pleasantville. Margaret as Eve tempts David as Adam, but only after (and because) David as the serpent has already tempted her. Insofar as David is the one to whom Margaret offers the apple, he is placed in a peculiar position. He is simultaneously the supernatural tempter and the human being. David here corresponds to Tzvetan Todorov's understanding of the fantastic as narrative undecidability between the marvelous and the uncanny.[22] This accounts for the encounter between David and the TV repairman described above, in which David refuses to allow the restoration of paradise. God splits in two and this tears Eden apart, but it also opens a space for a nonutopian, uncertain, human world. The old sitcoms go their way, and a new, more colorful day arrives. By the movie's end, a sadder-but-wiser deity drives off in his repair van.

Pleasantville interprets the biblical story of Eden as a contest between finite, thoroughly human gods. The supernatural TV repairman defends the ideological status quo of the sitcom and insists that the script must be obeyed at all costs. The sitcom script is the inflexible law, the divine will. The repairman wishes to keep the people of Pleasantville in a state of pleasant ignorance, the oppressive ignorance that makes paradise possible. His will is thwarted by David and Jennifer, who are

---

Eve were gods, and so were the trees (Ludwig Köhler, *Old Testament Theology*, trans. A. S. Todd. [Philadelphia: Westminster, 1957]; and Gerhard von Rad, *Genesis*, trans. John H. Marks [Philadelphia: Westminster, 1961]). Many variants on the Eden story in recent popular literature rewrite the respective roles of man and woman, or of humans and God. For some recent examples, see John Crowley, "The Nightingale Sings at Night," *Novelty, Four Stories* (New York: Doubleday, 1989), 1–34; and Neil Gaiman and Terry Pratchett, *Good Omens* (New York: Ace Books, 1990), vii–ix. See also Kafka, *Parables*, 29–33.

21. *Role*, 90–104.

22. Tzvetan Todorov, *The Fantastic*, trans. Richard Howard (Cleveland: Case Western Reserve University Press, 1973), 41–57.

able to defy him successfully and to transform the fantastic "Pleasantville" world, to make it more realistic, because they are incarnate in that world and he is not. Although the repairman possesses the marvelous power to transfer David and Jennifer from *Pleasantville* to "Pleasantville" and back again, once he gives that power to them, he cannot stop them from making fundamental, irreversible changes in Pleasantville.

Eco claims that the Edenic language is dominated by the "poetic function,"[23] and therefore its messages are "aesthetic" and self-referential. Much as in Eco's account of Adam and Eve, *Pleasantville* also plays with "language"—that is, with the cinematic medium itself. The characters in *Pleasantville* apparently watch many of the same TV shows that we do, although there are some differences, such as "Pleasantville" itself. The residents of Pleasantville also own TV sets; perhaps they also watch situation comedies on them. Such shows would entail another (fourth) level of reality, although David uses TV sets to communicate from the third-level reality of Pleasantville to the TV repairman, who remains within the second-level world of the movie. However, the poetic function is most apparent in the movie's many frames in which colored and monochromic images appear side by side on the screen, including the temptation scene between Margaret and David. Each of these complex images makes the audience aware that we are watching a movie, a simulation.

The explicit interplay between various levels of reality in this movie generates a paradox. The confusion of names and the manipulation of the medium create a referential feedback loop through which the movie interrogates its own reality and therefore also the reality inhabited by its viewers. David and Jennifer change the world of Pleasantville, but they are also changed by it. If such exchanges can occur between the second and third levels of reality, can they not also occur between other levels, including our own? These exchanges between levels suggest that even the world inhabited by the movie's audience may not be the very first level. Could it be that we and everything in our world are also merely simulacra and mechanically reproduced illusions, shadows on the cave wall of yet another level of reality, observed by yet other beings in some medium that we cannot imagine, because we *are* it? Might the so-called "primary world" of everyday life as we know it be itself just another "level of reality," another fictional, ideological construct?[24] Or is our

---

23. See Roman Jakobson, *Language and Literature*, ed. Krystyna Pomorska and Stephen Rudy (Cambridge, Mass.: Belknap Press of Harvard University, 1987), 69–70.

24. See Baudrillard, *Simulacra*. This possibly infinite regress appears even more explicitly in other recent movies, such as *The Matrix*, *The 13th Floor*, and *eXistenZ*.

supposedly non-fictional world impermeable to fictional beings? The gnosis offered by David and Jennifer to the Pleasantville inhabitants is also offered to the film's audience—and the simulation and fictionality that are inherent in any story, and that are raised to a higher degree by the mechanically reproduced electronic media of film and television, are likewise imputed to the audience's primary world. "The process will . . . put . . . models of simulation in place and . . . give them the feeling of the real, of the banal, of lived experience, to reinvent the real as fiction, precisely because it has disappeared from our life."[25]

Pleasantville radically secularizes the biblical Eden story, even as it critiques the sitcom mythology. Although a paradise, Pleasantville was never especially innocent. Instead, it was bland and pasty. What it needed was to become more colorful, in other words, more realistic. The use of color both symbolizes and iconically enacts the intrusion of realism into a nonrealistic world, and the alignment of color with realism also connotes the goodness and desirability of the changes that occur.

In addition, and unlike other interpretations of the Eden story, in this movie redemption is not a one-way gift. Instead, it is an exchange. The redemptive exchange takes place not only between Margaret and David, but also between levels of reality. For both David and Jennifer, the fantasy world transforms the realistic world, and vice versa. Underneath the allure of the fantastic lies a desire for reality, and it is only by passing through fantasy that they encounter reality—different realities, as it happens. The ideological relation between the realistic and the fantastic is exposed and inverted, and the fantastic becomes real. The moment in the movie where that inversion is most apparent, where it appears in the discourse of the movie itself, is the moment when monochrome Margaret gives monochrome David a bright red apple.

25. Baudrillard, *Simulacra*, 124.

7. NON-SENSE
Total Recall, Paul, and the Possibility of Psychosis

Roland Boer

What might be the relationship between the film *Total Recall*, based on a story by Philip K. Dick, and the New Testament, especially the figure of Paul as narrative and epistolary figure? My argument is that the deeper structure of both the film and the New Testament texts is that of psychosis, but that the connection between them is necessarily mediated through the wider work of Philip K. Dick and the analysis of psychosis in both Freud and Lacan. That is to say, the connections between *Total Recall* and the New Testament, between Arnold Schwarzenegger and St. Paul, only become clear in the light of psychoanalysis itself. I base this discussion on the Lacanian point that it is precisely through anachronistic juxtaposition—in this case of *Total Recall* and the New Testament texts of Paul—that the "truth" of both emerges.

In short, my argument is that the classic patterns of psychosis appear in *Total Recall*, which is to be expected since it is drawn from a text by Philip K. Dick, whose work as a whole, especially in the concerns over memory, history, the subject, and religion, is distinctly psychotic. But the decisive moment is his own "revelation" that saw a shift in his last three novels—*VALIS*, *The Divine Invasion*, and *The Transmigration of Timothy Archer*—to explicitly religious matters as he tried to make sense of a major spiritual experience. However, the treatments of psychosis that inform my analysis are those of Freud and Lacan, along with the critiques by Macalpine and Hunter, and Walker. All these discussions deal with a central text in psychoanalysis: Daniel Paul Schreber's *Memoirs of My Nervous Illness*, whose psychosis is remarkably similar both to that of

Dick himself and to that of St. Paul. But there is a final twist in all of this: it is not so much that Paul's texts exhibit all the signs of psychosis, which they do, but that the very possibility of psychosis and its key terms (see below) are provided by Paul's religious terminology in the first place. And so my argument comes full circle, arguing that the expression of psychosis in *Total Recall* is based, in a mediated fashion, on the New Testament itself. A particular characteristic of my discussion is that, like some key ideas of psychoanalysis, the analysis is based in written texts, whether those of Dick, Schreber, or those concerning Paul, both narratives about him in the Book of Acts and epistles reputedly by him. In other words, I take the "lives" reconstructed from the texts as other texts in their turn, which then number among the texts I am studying.

My argument moves through five stages with psychosis as the unifying theme. I begin with the film *Total Recall*, identifying the major features of the film that suggest psychosis. From there I locate the film as one outcome of the science fiction work of Philip K. Dick, widely regarded as a key figure in the genre itself. Dick's own theoretical reflections on his work provide the lead into the theories of Freud and Lacan on psychosis, both of whom were fascinated by the memoirs of Schreber. The next part of the paper compares the psychotic texts of three nuts—Dick, Schreber, and St. Paul—before moving to a Lacanian reading of the film and of Paul. I close by drawing *Total Recall* and Paul into each other. Throughout I have attempted to follow the model of Freud himself in his "Psychoanalytic Notes on an Autobiographical Account of a Case of Paranoia (Dementia Paranoides) (Schreber)," in which he describes the crucial symptoms themselves before proceeding to an analysis. Of course, my description inevitably sets up the possibility of the analysis, but the symptoms themselves are sufficiently central to make the procedure workable.

THE FILM

The film is based on Philip Dick's short story "We Can Remember it for You Wholesale," a story of memory implants, erasure, and undercover spy activity focused on Mars. But my interest is, to begin with, the film itself. In characteristic Dick-like twists, it opens up a whole series of questions about memory and the subject, for its story is that of lowly quarry worker Doug Quade, played by Arnold Schwarzenegger, who, as an escape from his life on a grim and dismal Earth, seeks a cheap and trouble-free holiday at "Recall," where a series of drugs provide a memory of the trip of one's choice. For Quade, however, the process itself partially breaks open a repressed or erased memory of another existence in which he was a key political operator on Mars, wanted by both the ruler of Mars, Cohaagen, and the rebels, led by Kuato. From then on Quade must avoid elimination by everyone around him, from his "wife" to his construction coworkers. Having made his "real" way to Mars, he becomes involved in the fight for a "free"—liberal and capitalist—Mars, represented materially in the fight over breathable air.

So much for the basic plot, but I want to focus on a number of features that problematize what appears to be a straightforward science-fiction story. The film begins with a sequence on Mars in which Quade and an as-yet-unidentified female walk together on the surface of the planet, only to fall down a cliff and die from asphyxiation when their helmets break open. It turns out to be a "dream," but it will be echoed at the close of the film in a very different setting. The preliminary function of the dream in psychosis is a crucial feature to which I will return.

Further, what Quade thought was a quiet life as a lowly quarry worker turns out to be an elaborate setup by forces that wish to keep him quiet. His memory has been erased (although repression is the better term here, for it continually shows itself in dreams and in the selection of the "holiday" itself), and all of those around him, including his wife and coworkers, turn out to be part of the conspiracy. In other words, Quade becomes the center of a conspiracy as large as the solar system itself. When it seems he is becoming aware of the situation, everyone whom he trusted attempts to eliminate him. This is of course a classic persecution complex that is invariably narcissistic—everything happens with the subject at its center.

The film, as one would expect from anything based on Philip Dick, makes the whole situation much more complex—it is never quite clear what constitutes reality, which memory is valid, what belongs to the realm of dreams, and which of Quade's identities might be the true one. The first sequence of the film, Quade's dream, later turns out to have an element of "reality" about it, and the narrative continually questions whether Quade's former quiet life is not in fact "real" and whether his secret-agent persona is not a dream, a paranoid fantasy of grandeur. But this is also a characteristic element, because paranoia builds in defense mechanisms for precisely such questions: the subject perpetually deals with the objection that he or she is experiencing paranoia and constructs protective mechanisms, perfectly logical within the system itself, for dealing with such objections. Thus, in a sequence on Mars, a psychologist appears at his hotel-room door, telling him that he is experiencing a schizoid embolism, a paranoia that has gone into freefall based on the holiday drugs of the Recall agency. In order to prove his point—that the psychologist has been built into the holiday memory for precisely such an occurrence—he produces Quade's wife (Sharon Stone), who urges him to forget the dream and come home. Quade almost succumbs until he sees a drop of sweat on the psychologist's cheek: this apparently verifies the "reality' of the current situation, without questioning why a drop of sweat could not be part of a paranoid system. In other words, the paranoid has a whole series of "reality" checks that work only for him or her.

Another point in the film that is important for my analysis is the moment when Quade removes the tracking device from his sinuses, following instructions, narrated by himself, that he has left for himself on a portable computer should just such a situation arise. But this other is not Quade but "Hauser," the key political operator on Mars. Hauser appears to Quade as if in a mirror, the computer screen itself, and the scene functions as an extraordinary moment when the mirror image talks back to the subject. There are two elements of this sequence in the film that interest me: the removal of the oversize tracking device in a birth-like sequence by means of forceps through his left nostril, and the doubling effect of the Schwarzenegger character. It appears as if this character helps himself to escape from his persecutors, who follow his movements via the tracking device, yet it later turns out that Hauser has doubled the conspiracy, working not for the Martian rebels under Kuato, but for the monopolistic ruler of Mars, Cohaagen. What we have here is a troubled doubling that can be described as the mirror-stage— the computer screen is the mirror of another Quade. Yet, the mirror-stage not only sets up recognition of the subject—who becomes a subject by the removal of the large ball from his sinuses—but also of opposition to himself. This scene is central for my reading of the film as psychosis, because the move from the mirror-stage (in Lacan, "the Imaginary") to the realm of symbolic meaning is blocked in psychosis.

The Quade character also functions in the standard redeemer format. But the redeemer is never straightforward. In classic eschatological logic, he threatens to destroy the world at the same time he raises the possibility of saving it. Quade's acts almost bring to ruin the plans of the rebels on Mars, bringing about the death of Kuato, but in the end he "saves" Mars from the dominion of the totalitarian Cohaagen, providing the free air, i.e., life, that everyone deserves. In psychosis a person experiences both the fear that he has done something that will destroy the world and the perception that he is crucial to its salvation.

The final point I want to highlight in the film is the frenetic repetition of male birthing sequences. With the women in the film denied any maternal function—they are coded as conventionally masculine, athletic, and violent—the males provide the sources of birth. Thus, in the scene to which I have already referred—the removal of the oversize tracking device from Quade's sinuses—the grimace of pain replicates that of a birth sequence, even to the point that what Quade removes from his nose (itself a transference from the lower region to the upper region of the body) constitutes his own subjectivity. I will return to this scene, but there is also the major birth scene in which the rebel leader, Kuato, emerges from the waist of his lieutenant, covered with the fluids of birth and taking over the body and consciousness of his lieutenant who, after the birth pangs, closes his eyes in exhaustion. Kuato, clairvoyant that he is, then proceeds to bring to birth Quade's own memories of his former life—except that the whole function of memory has now been thoroughly problematized. When danger threatens, Kuato returns to the womb, ready for his next rebirth.

The whole of the film's closure is engulfed with male birth; immediately following Kuato's invocation of Quade's memory, the camera moves into a cave-like area that the viewer can read as Quade's own mind/womb.[1] Only when the shot pans out and the voices and bodies of Cohaagen and his goons appear do we realize that we are in the remembered cavern of an alien-built reactor under a pyramid mountain. Not only does much of the final sequence take place in the various tunnels and passages of underground Mars, the reactor itself hovers over a vast glacier that awaits its own meltdown in order to release the much-desired oxygen to the planet. The film's closure may be read in two ways: after the struggle to activate the reactor, Quade and the woman—Melina, who appeared in the opening dream—are thrust out onto the planet's surface through a red tube. As they begin to asphyxiate, the reactor does its job, melting the glacier and ejaculating clouds of steam into the atmosphere, crowned by the huge spurt out of the pyramid mountain itself. Our first option is to read this as a birth sequence out of the reactor cave—womb—and into the harsh environment of the planet; not only is such a birth enabled by the ejaculation sequence, the

---

1. As with much of this paper, this observation comes from discussion with Julie Kelso.

planet itself becomes livable through the ejaculation to end all ejaculations. Mars becomes engulfed in sperm. Alternatively, Quade and Melina are sucked back into the womb—the surface of Mars—whose hostility is neutralized through the massive injection of sperm. Only then does the Edenic sequence become possible, because the film closes with Quade and Melina looking out from a rise over a paradisiacal valley, the first couple in a new world who have already begun the process of repopulating it. In this reading, the desire for a return to paradise becomes a desire for the return to the womb. The final scene of course echoes the opening "dream," because Quade and Melina walked on Mars's surface in the first dream, although in pressure suits. Now they walk freely. The film possesses an unavoidable mythological dimension, especially its closing sequence, particularly in the way a *deus ex machina*—the alien-built reactor—enables closure.

I have of course deliberately selected certain items from the film that will enable my subsequent analysis to move forward, but it also seems to me that they constitute the major elements of the film. That it should be read as an example of the particular form of psychosis known as paranoia (the other type is schizophrenia) will become clearer as I proceed. First, I want to make the connections to the work of Philip Dick, who is still known for the ideas around which his stories were built, no matter how rough or stimulant-induced they might be.

PHILIP K. DICK

One of the more regular descriptors of Dick's work has been that of paranoia. The self-description as schizophrenic or schizoid-effective[2] is perhaps more facetious than anything else, but Dick's own heavy drug use (up to one thousand Methadrine tablets per week in 1971[3]) exacerbated any genetic predisposition to psychosis, especially paranoia. My move to biography should not be taken in the sense of an older biographical criticism, in which the author's life and situation provided the interpretive key to the text; nor should it be understood on the model of an earlier psychoanalytic criticism that sought to analyze authors based on their texts. Rather, as I have indicated above, the biographies themselves form one more text for discussion.

---

2. Philip K. Dick, *The Man in the High Castle* (Harmondsworth, England: Penguin, 1965).
3. Lawrence Sutin, *Divine Invasions: A Life of Philip K. Dick* (New York: Harmony, 1989), 176.

However, before I make the biographical move explicit, let me connect the short story on which *Total Recall* was based to Dick's work more generally. Sprinkled throughout this work are the themes that eventually appear full-blown in the final three theological novels.[4] Much of his earlier and later work abounds with conspiracies and plots, perhaps the most sustained being *A Scanner Darkly*. Written after he had moved beyond drugs, it traces the way Bob Arctor, a drug agent, finally spins out of control on the drugs he is supposed to track down. But it is the dialogues between Arctor and his roommates, Jerry Fabin and Rick, that follow the patterns of meaningless psychotic dialogue to which I will return in my discussion of Lacan and Freud below.

Another example of the explicit concern with paranoia comes in *Clans of the Alphane Moon*, in which psychiatric patients have been sent to one of the moons in the Alphane system and manage to form a society based on a clinical psychiatric division of labor. While the main plot concerns the interactions between the Terran CIA and the Alphanes, there is the appearance of the telepathic Ganymedean slime mold, Lord Running Clam, and the arrival of the "Normals" at the end to set things right. But it is the clans themselves that are more intriguing: Pares, paranoids who are the official leaders and live in Adolfville; Manses, manics who are the inventors and fighters and live in DaVinci Heights; Skitzes, the schizophrenics who are visionary mystics living in Gandhitown; Heebs, the hebephrenics who function as manual laborers and ascetic mystics and also live in Gandhitown; Polys, polymorphic schizophrenics whose fluctuations provide them a modicum of happiness; Ob Coms, the obsessive compulsives who carry out useful tasks; and the Deps, depressives who live in the Cotton Mather Estates and seem to have no role, being avoided by everyone.

Apart from the schizophrenic theme of *The Martian Time Slip*, focused on the small-time repairman Jack Bohlen, a one-time schizophrenic who still lives with the effects of schizophrenia, my other major example of the pre-religious Dick novels is *Eye in the Sky*. Here, after an explosion at the Belmont Bevatron, eight people fall through the Proton Beam Deflector to the floor, the effect of which is to allow one after the other to construct worlds of their own making, worlds based on religious fanaticism, psychotic paranoia, sexless prudishness, and the

---

4. See also Patricia S. Warrick, *Mind in Motion: The Fiction of Philip K. Dick* (Carbondale, Ill.: Southern Illinois University Press, 1987), 168–69.

Communist party line. As each person comes to consciousness from the floor, his or her own world takes over until the "real" world returns.

Dick's work is also concerned with related phenomena, such as nature and the construction of reality, memory, and the human subject—the latter mostly through cyborgs and androids. Indeed, science fiction provides a lumber-room of possibilities for approaching such subjects, although Dick's genius was in constructing distinctive narratives with their own peculiar twists. As far as the content is concerned, these texts deal explicitly with paranoia and schizophrenia, the two psychoses, but what interests me most about Dick is the wholesale shift to religious questions in his last works, although these are by no means absent in his earlier writings.

But let me move to the religious works via another question that will turn out to be crucial for the psychosis itself. My initial step here is to make a critical move from Dick's own work, namely, the "crack in space" or reality, after the novel by the same name. In a whole range of texts he works away at the question of what "reality" might be, returning time and again to the potential that what appears to be "real" is in fact a construct that will eventually show its flaws. A breakthrough occurs in which another "reality" appears, although it is not clear that the new reality is any more real than the one that has just broken down. The question is central to *Eye in the Sky*, as it is to the follow-up to *The Man in the High Castle*,[5] in which a fiercely guarded porthole in time provides access to the Nazi past. In *The Crack in Space* itself, a potential solution to chronic overpopulation and unemployment—where citizens, especially blacks, are frozen and live in suspended animation—appears with a rent in space that seems to open out to another world suitable for human conditions but without people. The crack becomes a focus of political intrigue and multinational competition, but whether it is hostile or not remains an open question, although the black presidential candidate, Jim Briskin, stakes his political career on the possibility of a solution.

Precisely this "crack in reality" also characterizes the film *Total Recall*, because Quade's "real" world breaks down through a drug-induced slippage that sees his constructed world collapse and the other one emerge. The reason for picking up the question of the "crack in reality" is that, apart from the links with Lacan, it takes a distinctly religious

---

5. See Lawrence Sutin, ed., *The Shifting Realities of Philip K. Dick* (New York: Vintage, 1995), 175–82.

turn at certain points, especially in Dick's later work. In *The Cosmic Puppets*, the reality of the small town of Millgate in Virginia where the main character, Ted Barton, grew up, has been radically altered, so that he can scarcely recognize it any longer. However, the new reality maintains its hold with difficulty, the ghosts of those living in the older reality perpetually appearing and items that have disappeared may be recovered, if only for a short time. In this case, the new real is built upon the old, former objects transformed into very different items. But these two realities are part of a cosmic struggle between the forces of good and evil, named after the Zoroastrian gods Ormuzd and Ahriman (names that recur in his later *Exegesis* and in Schreber as well[6]). This divine construction and adaptation of reality also emerges in "The Adjustment Team," where a somewhat weary God is engaged in subtle shifts in the nature of earthly reality in order to bring human beings to cooperation rather than conflict. Sections at a time undergo such changes, except that the hero in this case wanders in upon one of God's "adjustment teams" as they go about a sectoral change, witnessing precisely such a "crack in reality." In *A Maze of Death*, Dick seeks to produce a rational explanation for religious phenomena, where the various characters who are placed on a planet, Delmak-O, together find that it is an experiment in a "reality" that keeps shifting about. The characters die one after the other as they try to use each other's perceptions to make sense of what is happening. It turns out they are the crew of a damaged rocket ship, dreaming one in a series of polyencephalic dreams to try to stay sane as they float through space. Dick provides an elaborate religious schema in which Gnosticism, neo-Platonism, and Christianity come together: the Metufacturer is the creator (God), the Intercessor the one who lifts the curse of creation through sacrifice (Christ), the Walker on earth who gives assistance (Holy Spirit), and the Form Destroyer, the one that generates entropy (Satan, Demiurge, and so forth).

The most extensive text is of course *VALIS*, in which Dick himself, as Horselover (literal translation of the Greek *philippos*) Fat (translation of the German *Dick*), appears as the subject of a revelation, a direct communication by a laser-like beam of pink light from a divine being. The "crack in space" has become a source of religious vision and, most

---

6. See Daniel Paul Schreber, *Memoirs of My Nervous Illness*, trans. Ida Macalpine and Richard Hunter (Cambridge, Mass.: Harvard University Press, 1988), 19. References to Schreber's text follow the standard practice of referring to the page numbers of the original German text preserved in the margins of the English translation.

importantly, the communication of divine knowledge of the real, as Dick puts it himself. The text is replete with a Christlike child, a subsequent incarnation, and excerpts from the text of Dick's extensive *Exegesis*, which sought to produce a religious mythology of the universe and human existence that he believed was communicated to him by God. This chronically difficult text becomes an autobiographical moment in Dick's corpus, because it is his first effort to deal with his own religious visions of 1974. But let me stay with the novel itself, as well as the two related novels, *The Divine Invasion* and *The Transmigration of Timothy Archer*.

Although given to visions earlier in life, such as the hostile metallic face that filled the sky in 1963 that became the source of *The Three Stigmata of Palmer Eldritch*,[7] and although he was interested in Gnostic thought at around the same time, *VALIS* is the first full-blown work in which Dick's visions found fictional form. The length of time it took to write (five years) was a significant change from his frenetic production of earlier years, but his energy had gone into the *Exegesis* itself. I will focus on particular dimensions of the novel, since both its content and the "experience" with which it seeks to deal are distinctly psychotic. There are, to begin with, the rays of pink light from the artificial intelligence (AI) that provide information to Horselover Fat. The heliotropic dimension is crucial here, although it appears in muted form. Further, the split between two characters that seem to be the same person—Horselover Fat and Phil Dick—has already appeared in my discussion of *Total Recall*. Horselover is crazy, but he is the one who writes the "Exegesis" in the novel, the content of which is none other than selections from the revelations Dick himself felt he had experienced. The "Phil" of the novel scoffs and criticizes Horselover's visions and his "Exegesis," but in the end is unable to convince him. By the end of the novel, Horselover and "Phil" coalesce into one person at the hands of the Christ-child (who subsequently dies), only to split at the end as Horselover continues seeking signs of the messiah. Again, the basic psychoanalytic category of the mirror-stage appears at this point, which is in the realm of the Imaginary. However, the replication of the mirror-stage is a symptom of psychosis itself, because the subject tries to pass into the Symbolic stage (the realm of signifiers, language, and law) by other means.

In fact, the sheer length of *VALIS*, in comparison to Dick's other novels, the long stretches in which theological ideas appear, and the selection

---

7. See also Sutin, *Divine Invasions*, 127–28.

from Dick's own *Exegesis* as an appendix—entitled "Tractate: Cryptica Scriptura"—is central to this effort to pass into the Symbolic. Also of note is the language used by the "God" AI to impart knowledge to Horselover Fat: it is Koine Greek, which Horselover himself has never learned but now understands. This relates directly to the "basic language" in which Schreber heard God speaking to him (see below).

Other characteristic features include the importance of dreams for *VALIS*: Horselover Fat obtains most of his information from nightly dreams, the content of which he records in his "Exegesis." The double pattern of global destruction and salvation appears: in order to save the world from destruction, the three characters, Horselover, Kevin (searching for truth), and David (the conservative Christian), go to see Eric and Linda Lampton, rock stars living in Sonoma. Kevin and David, particularly as their names form part of the initials for Philip K. Dick himself, may also be read as a further splitting of the main character, as "hypostatized qualities . . . of the Father, Dick the novelist."[8] As the self-styled "Rhipidon Society"—the "Fish Society" (*rhipidos* means "fan" and signifies fish who have fan-like fins)—they visit the Lamptons only to find that Valis is a device that fires information from the Ablemuth star system. More significantly, Valis and Linda Lampton have produced a baby daughter, Sophia, who is the fifth savior and the first in female form. While Sophia enables "Phil" to shed the Horselover persona, she later dies from a laser beam that attempts to gain information from her head. I have spent a moment with this plot section not only to show the destruction-redemption pattern, but also to indicate the kind of associations and plot loops that take place. There is an internal logic, but the reader must agree to enter it.

Here again, in the story of Sophia, the birthing sequence appears. Although Linda is a bearer of the baby—the Christian associations cannot be avoided here—the source is of course the AI godlike VALIS itself, identified in Dick's "exegesis" as Jesus Christ. Once again, a male birth fantasy appears in a psychotic text, but it is in *The Divine Invasion*, which Kim Stanley Robinson suggests may be read as the novel written by Horselover Fat,[9] that a full-blown savior story appears. Here, in a story in

---

8. Robert Galbraith, "Salvation-Knowledge: Ironic Gnosticism in *Valis* and *The Flight to Lucifer*," *Science Fiction Dialogues*, ed. Gary Wolfe (Chicago: Academy Chicago, 1982), 119; see also Warrick, *Mind in Motion*, 171.

9. Kim Stanley Robinson, *The Novels of Philip K. Dick*, Studies in Speculative Science Fiction 9 (Ann Arbor, Mich.: UMI Research Press, 1984), 117.

which layers of reality peel off, particularly through the various narrative shifts surrounding Herb Asher, and then play against each other, the messiah—Emmanuel—is to be born of Rybys Romney, having been impregnated by Yah. Herb Asher (*Ehyeh asher ehyeh*) accompanies Rybys to an Earth dominated by Belial. But Rybys dies, Herb is placed in cryonic suspension due to his injuries, and Emmanuel is born prematurely through a synthowomb, brain-damaged, forgetting that he is God until his female half, Zina Pallas, restores his memory and they heal the cosmos together. Symptomatic here is the removal of the mother and the replacement of her womb by a prosthesis, which allows a fully male birth, as well as the androgynous godhead—Emmanuel and Zina—in which the maternal body is drawn up into the divine figure and is thereby able to save the world.[10] In *The Transmigration of Timothy Archer* such an appropriation operates in a different but more complete fashion, for here the soul of the dead Timothy Archer—a bishop with less-than-orthodox ideas who dies in the Judean desert searching for *anokhi* ("I") in the form of a magic mushroom—comes to inhabit the schizophrenic Bill Lundborg. Angel Archer, the daughter of Timothy, narrates the story. Not only do we have a female God-figure, but in the process of making her narrator, woman is removed from the process of birth itself—males merely need to transmigrate.

Finally, in *VALIS*, Dick attempts to deal with perceived objections to the psychosis through the separation of Horselover and "Phil," because the latter offers objections to Horselover, who must continue to assert the validity of what he has seen. The overt consciousness that it is in fact psychosis and the effort to deal with that knowledge in the form of meeting objections is characteristic of psychosis itself. In the end, however, it is the search for what is "real" that characterizes both the novel and Dick's *Exegesis*. I will move on to Lacan's notion of the Real in a moment, where it will shift ground somewhat, but the importance for Dick is the way the Real emerges from the crack in reality as a religious psychosis.

So far I have sought to trace the key elements of both *Total Recall* and then the wider work of Philip Dick, since the film itself is based on one of his short stories. The crucial link, it seems to me, is religion, particularly in the later work of Dick, because the patterns of psychosis in this work carry through those of his earlier works and through the film itself. Whereas until now I have been concerned with a film and written fiction,

---

10. See further Warrick, *Mind in Motion*, 182–83.

from here I move into theory before passing into the biographical texts of Dick, Schreber, and Paul.

FREUD AND LACAN

It is time to bring in the theoretical material of Freud and Lacan in a more consistent manner. By now it should be obvious that in their writings psychosis relies heavily on Christianity, especially the content of the New Testament. Horselover Fat hears God speak in Koine; the redeemer figure is inevitably modeled on Christ, as is the God of psychosis, with its own mutations. In fact, in both Freud's and Lacan's analysis, the question of God looms large.

In what follows I provide a summary of a much more detailed argument over psychosis in psychoanalytic literature, restricting myself to Freud and Lacan. The key elements of psychosis that Freud finds in the *Memoirs* of Schreber include delusions of persecution, especially the "soul-murder" at the hands of his analyst Flechsig and then the attacks of God, erotomania, jealousy, megalomania, the eschatological dimension of a fear and hope of the end of the world, hypochondria, the connection between God as father and the sun, God as both beneficent and malevolent, the construction of an alternative or substitute reality, but above all the belief by the psychotic subject that he is in some way a redeemer figure and undergoing a process of emasculation in order to become God's female partner.[11]

Rather than focus on the usual motif of the redeemer figure, Freud stresses Schreber's desire to be God's female counterpart, finding that both elements "are linked in his assumption of a feminine attitude towards God."[12] On this basis, Freud develops at length the argument that psychosis involves a repression of homosexual desires that returns with renewed force in another form, at the point of fixation—a moment when an instinct falls outside the normal path of development and remains behind in a more infantile stage—which is the precursor to repression

---

11. Sigmund Freud, "Psychoanalytic Notes on an Autobiographical Account of a Case of Paranoia (Dementia Paranoides) (Schreber)," *Case Histories II*, The Pelican Freud Library, 9:131–223, ed. Angela Richards, trans. James Strachey (Harmondsworth, England: Penguin, 1979 [1911]), 148–49, 171–74, 189–91, 193, 200–203, 207–208, 211–14, 220; "Neurosis and Psychosis," *On Psychopathology*, The Pelican Freud Library, 10:209–18, ed. Angela Richards, trans. James Strachey (Harmondsworth, England: Penguin, 1979 [1924]); and "The Loss of Reality in Neurosis and Psychosis," *On Psychopathology*, 10:219–26.
12. Freud, "Psychoanalytic Notes," 167.

proper. However, by not allowing these wishes to emerge into conscious-ness, the subject uses various defenses in order to make the wishes appear otherwise. For Schreber, the fixation that precedes the repression is on his father and elder brother, subsequently transferred to his analyst Flechsig, and then to God. However, the defense against the recognition of this latent homosexuality takes the form of the fantasies of being persecuted by these figures and then of being transformed into a woman.

The central item here, which is where Lacan picks up his develop-ment of Freud, is the Oedipus complex, although in a negative register. In response to Oedipal conflict, specifically the danger of castration at the hands of the father, the (male) child identifies with his mother and takes on her role through the very process of abandoning the mother as an object of love. There is a failure to move from the stage of autoeroti-cism or narcissism, in which the subject's own body is the love object, to "object-love," the focus on another person of the other sex as the object of love.[13] This alternative path leads to the choice of a sexual partner with the same genitals. In other words, in refusing the central feature of the Oedipal conflict, sufferers of psychosis fail to become part of the whole drama. This is where the contradiction of psychosis manifests itself, because the castration anxiety remains paramount. Whereas the child wishes to identify with the mother, that is, to be transformed into a woman, which requires castration, the threat of castration is rejected by homosexuality. Yet, homosexuality itself, in the process of rejection, recognizes and perpetually repeats the desire for castration. For Freud this is none other than *Verleugnung*, or disavowal, the result of the endeavor by psychotics "to protect themselves against any such sexual-ization of their social instinctual cathexes."[14] The illness is then the result of the disavowal of what Freud calls latent homosexuality, which then explains the desire to become a woman and a redeemer figure.

Lacan[15] offers the most extended analysis of psychosis, covering the whole of his third seminar in 1955–1956, and this work provides the

---

13. Ibid., 197–98.

14. Ibid., 200.

15. Readings of Lacan are notoriously difficult, especially if we seek to focus on the content. Thus interpreters will either apologize for the inevitable distortions, citing Lacan's fragmen-tary and elliptical style (Samuel Weber, "Introduction," *Memoirs*, xlv), or move quickly to cite other interpreters of Lacan (Michelle Boulous Walker, *Philosophy and the Maternal Body*, 53). An alternative reading that begins with the form of Lacan's text is not possible here, but see Fredric Jameson, "Imaginary and Symbolic in Lacan: Marxism, Psychoanalytic Criticism and the Problem of the Subject," *The Ideologies of Theory* (Minneapolis: University of Minnesota Press, 1988), 1:75–115.

most detailed way in which the film, Dick's writing and biography, Schreber, and Paul all relate as instances of psychotic discourse. Lacan is of course committed to explicating the logic of Freud's own work, so he must take the Oedipal complex—what Lacan terms Freud's "quilting point," the sewing-in of signifier and signified to create meaning[16]—as a central feature. However, for Lacan the dialectical categories of Imaginary, Symbolic, and Real must also be central to any analysis, so he comes to the following conclusion. Since the psychotic refuses to enter or "forecloses" the Oedipus complex, he is unable to move by the usual means into the Symbolic, the realm of signification and therefore of language and the law. The subject does not experience the quilting point of the Oedipus conflict, so signifier and signified do not connect, do not provide the link so that meaning and thereby language might operate. Instead, signifiers relate directly to other signifiers and not to signifieds. In order to deal with and find another path into the Symbolic, the subject generates an alternative language, the "non-sense" of psychotic speech and writing. In doing so, the subject senses that the Real—that which is inaccessible yet constitutes the very ground of the subject's existence—has crashed in, quite specifically in the figure of God as Other. But this Real becomes a substitute, that which takes the place of the Real.

What then of castration and latent homosexuality? For Lacan, the fear of castration becomes the phallic signifier, which in the Imaginary produces identity and draws everything into it. However, in the inseparable realm of the Symbolic, the phallus is simultaneously that which signifies lack, that item that is extraneous to the system yet provides the core of its viability. But in psychosis the phallic signifier does not come into play: since the subject is unable to enter the Symbolic by the usual means of the Oedipus complex, the signifier of lack cannot produce the absent register by which language operates. Therefore, the psychotic seeks to compensate by the incessant production of an alternative linguistic structure. With the quilting point of the Oedipus complex gone, the signifiers run amok.[17]

Finally, Lacan transposes Freud's analysis of latent homosexuality into what he calls, following Freud, not "repression" (*Verdrängung*) or "disavowal" (*Verleugnung*), but the "foreclosure" (*Verwerfung*) of the

---

16. Lacan, *The Psychoses*, 268.
17. Lacan also begins to argue in the third seminar of 1955–56 that the production of language more generally operates in this fashion, that the constitutive lack of language itself is the Oedipus Complex.

Name-of-the Father. Castration and the Name-of-the-Father are of course closely connected in psychoanalysis, but Lacan's move was to make such a connection symbolic. In particular, the Name-of-the-Father is the dead father, the one the son kills in order to take his place in the Oedipus complex. For only a dead father, one who has subsequently become "God," can become a symbol. Freud elaborated on this point in both *Totem and Taboo* and *Moses and Monotheism*, but Lacan emphasizes that it is not so much primal history but a myth of symbolic necessity. With the father dead, the Name-of-the-Father can be distinguished from the father and thus be that which constitutes the Symbolic itself. Again, we find the same logic as that of the phallus: it is precisely what is absent, empty, that ensures the coherence of the Symbolic system, whether it be law or language. In other words, when the Name-of-the-Father disappears, the threat of castration that pushes the subject into the Symbolic has also evaporated. In place of castration, all that remains is a hole or tear in the Symbolic: symbolization has no basis. In psychosis, therefore, the signifier signifies nothing: the signifier is constituted by a hole, by lack.[18]

The connection with Philip Dick's notion of the "crack in space" or in reality draws curiously near to Lacan's formulation, because in Dick's work the constantly shifting "reality," the layers that continually peel off, may be read as nothing other than the Real in psychotic texts, especially since it functions as a substitute for the Real of usual symbolization. But Lacan's analysis is by far the most detailed of all the texts, although the key features remain the absence of the usual procedure through the Oedipus drama, the phallic signifier, and the foreclosure of the "Name-of-the Father." Given that these are crucial features of the production of psychotic language and writing, I will invoke them at particular moments in my discussion below. Let me close by drawing attention to the presence of God in the literature on psychosis. Freud emphasizes the theological nature of Schreber's text[19] and for Lacan God is a crucial feature in the text, as any reading will soon indicate.[20] In other words, the

---

18. It is from here that the Real makes its presence felt: rather than being the absent cause of the Symbolic, the Real merges into the Imaginary without the dialectical mediation or structuring function of the Symbolic. In both the essay in *Écrits* (179–225) and seminar on *The Psychoses*, Lacan stresses the importance of the relation between the Imaginary, Symbolic and the Real. Here may be found his most detailed statement on the dialectical relation between them; see especially the diagrams and discussion (*Écrits*, 195–97, 211–14). A fuller discussion of these diagrams is another task.

19. Freud, "Psychoanalytic Notes," 152–62.

20. See especially Lacan, *The Psychoses*, 59–72, 258–70.

language of psychosis is unavoidably theological (as is the analysis of Lacan, although that is a topic for another essay), a feature that surprisingly receives less-than-adequate attention.

In my reading of Schreber, Dick, and Paul that follows, with a final loop back to the film, I will draw on particular features of the psychoanalytic discussion of psychosis, particularly the symptoms (dreams, hypochondria, the role of the sun, megalomania, paranoia, the distortion of reality, and conspiracy theories), but especially the key features of male birthing, the redeemer figure, the production of language itself, especially in written form, and the explicit theological nature of the psychotic's language and writing.

INTERTEXTUAL CORRESPONDENCE

Let me see if I can set up sufficient correspondence between the texts of Schreber, Dick, and Paul, as well as that of the film, to show that they are indeed psychotic, although the surprise is how close they in fact are. It is as if Paul in particular becomes part of a psychotic brotherhood, a coterie of crazy religious types who all believed that God had spoken to them and therefore they were, of course, the most important individuals in human history. My interest is in the textual nature of this material, because in each case we have a written text for analysis—the *Exegesis* of Philip Dick, the *Memoirs* of Daniel Paul Schreber, and the New Testament texts of Paul. The only variation is the film, and the medium itself generates different possibilities for reading.

The initiatory moment of the dream or vision begins the process. Not only in the film does the Edenic dream of Quade and the (at that stage) unknown woman set up the film itself, but in Schreber, the first sign of the second and more intense bout of psychosis appears in a dream, halfway between waking and sleeping: "it really must be rather pleasant to be a woman succumbing to intercourse."[21] In Dick and Paul, the narrative is slightly different. Both "experience" a blinding vision in which VALIS/Jesus Christ/God (Dick) or Jesus Christ/God (Paul) makes his first contact. For Dick this was initially a vast hallucination over February and March 1974 that subsequently took the form of blinding pink beams, rays, and phosphene graphics that communicated with him,[22]

---

21. Schreber, *Memoirs*, 36.
22. Sutin, *Divine Invasions*, 214, 218.

whereas for Paul it was "a light from heaven" that flashed around him (Acts 9:3; see Acts 22:6 and 26:13). Subsequently he hears Jesus for the first time, "Saul, Saul, why do you persecute me?" (Acts 9:4; 22:7; 26:14 with a variation) and engages in discussion with him: "'Who are you, Lord?' he asked. 'I am Jesus, whom you persecute,' the voice said. 'But get up and go into the city, where you will be told what you must do'" (Acts 9:5–6; see the variations in 22:8, 10; 26:15–16).[23]

Already in the visions of Dick and Paul the heliotropism characteristic of psychosis appears. Freud reads this as a replacement for the father/God. For Dick, the blinding pink light beamed from VALIS (the Vast Active Living Intelligence System) becomes a constitutive feature of the divine communications, for a time at least. Later the information comes to him in dream content. Schreber's *Memoirs* repeatedly make use of the sun motif; he identifies God with the sun, stares at it for long periods of time, and communicates/talks with this sun/God. The film also has some key heliotropic moments, especially when Quade and Melina spurt out of/are sucked back into the surface of Mars. In the harsh glare of the Martian surface, they face death by asphyxiation and loss of atmospheric pressure until the clouds of steam bursting from the mountain provide them and everyone else with much-desired breathable air. And then there is the penultimate scene of the ejaculatory pillar of steam or smoke from the mountain that evokes its double, the pillar of fire.

A further symptom is the persecution complex, closely tied in with conspiracy theories. I have already noted this in the film, but it is a comprehensive feature of Schreber's text with the "hastily constructed men," those around him whom he believed did not exist except for his own immediate perusal, the belief that Flechsig was out to kill him or that the nurse that bathed him wished to drown him, and finally that God desired his death. In Dick, the "raid" on his house put him in constant fear of a whole range of people, including the FBI, the KGB, and himself, but he also believed that he had been programmed to die,[24] that he was under constant suspicion for his novels (both the anticapitalism of *Ubik* and the anti-Communism of *Flow My Tears, the Policeman Said*). In Paul's case, the persecution is double-edged, for not only does he suffer at the hands of those who numbered him with them in their persecution

23. Biblical quotations are from the Revised Standard Version unless otherwise noted.
24. See Philip K. Dick, "Selection from *Exegesis* (c. 1975–80)," *Philip K. Dick: Contemporary Critical Interpretations*, ed. Samuel J. Umland (Westport, Conn.: Greenwood, 1995), 328, 322.

of the fledgling Christians (Acts 9:23–25 and repeatedly thereafter), but in his epistles it is precisely his sufferings at the hands of others that become the hallmark of Christian authenticity, a cause for boasting (2 Corinthians 6:4–10; 11:23–29). Here the first hint of a significant inversion in my analysis begins to appear, for in valorizing suffering and persecution, Paul provides an insight into the structure of persecution in psychosis itself.

Persecution overlaps considerably with hypochondria: Dick's constant fear that he was under investigation and the subject of plots by Nazis and Communists, his agoraphobia, provide the context for his concerns about his own mental and physical health, manifested most typically in the self-diagnosis of ailments and of their treatment by various concoctions of drugs and vitamins, as well as by the belief that he was programmed to die through Christ's interference with his genetic coding.[25] Schreber's hypochondria is legendary. His first illness was diagnosed as hypochondria, whereas in his second illness his constant focus on his body rendered not only a process of emasculation but also a long list of ways God attacked his body. These include the removal of beard and moustache, change in body stature, replacement of his heart, attacks of his lungs, compression of chest, removal of stomach, the tearing and removal of gullet and intestines, putrefaction of the abdomen, the immobilization of the muscles, attacks on his eyes and skeleton, until his is a martyrdom that can only be compared with the crucifixion of Jesus Christ.[26] But what of Paul? He is in good company, for the mention of "thorn" in his flesh (2 Corinthians 12:7), something that he felt troubled and hindered his work, becomes again a mark of God's blessing, the validation of all that he writes. In the film, the virtual impossibility of a hypochondriacal Arnold Schwarzenegger generates a significant shift: the various ailments and weakness that Dick, Schreber, and Paul see in their own bodies spread out onto the bodies of others, especially the rebels. In the shady nightclub on the edge of the colony, replete with bad air that causes the deformities in the first place, the rebels manifest in their bodies—claw-like arms, triple breasts, deformed heads that generate psychic powers, stunted growth, and ultimately the male birth of Kuato himself—all the signs of psychotic hypochondria.

I have already mentioned the inherent megalomania of psychosis—an overwhelmingly male condition—in which the central character is

---

25. Ibid., 322.
26. See Schreber, *Memoirs*, 148–61, 293.

the crux on which salvation and knowledge turns, sometimes superior to God,[27] leading us into the redeemer figure. And in each case there is a bifurcation of redeemer figures: on the one hand, the redeemer is external to the psychotic, inevitably and explicitly Jesus Christ. Thus Schreber is concerned about a redeemer who will, not unexpectedly, save the world, although in Schreber's case he himself will give birth to this figure. For Dick the major redemptive figure of his *Exegesis* is Jesus Christ, although, along with a host of others, such as Zoroaster, Mani, Buddha, and Elijah, he is more of a superior redeemer, VALIS itself—"Christ seems to have been an actual terminal of this computer-like entity."[28] Both his *Exegesis* and the final three novels turn endlessly around this question. Not unexpectedly, Jesus is the central figure of Paul's theological reflections, *ad nauseam*: the resurrected Jesus is the only valid position for the church, he has divine status as part of God, and Paul is his chosen instrument. In *Total Recall*, however, there is no explicit Jesus Christ, although Kuato, perpetually reborn in childlike form, does fill the role. But the film indicates the other side of the bifurcated redeemer figure. Quade himself saves Mars, claiming a more Adamic than christological identity. So also with the rest of this psychotic bunch, for Schreber in the end sees himself as the redeemer, as the one who will save the world by giving birth, believing the "continuation of all creation on our earth rests entirely on the very special relations into which God has entered with me."[29] In a similar fashion Dick takes on more and more of the role of the redeemer in his own person, for this supernatural entity loans Dick a part of his spirit. Alternatively, Dick sees himself as merged into the mystical Corpus Christi[30] because he has been granted the special gnosis, the knowledge that will lead others to salvation. Immortal, he becomes the "champion of all human spirits in thrall."[31] And so it is with Paul: studiously avoiding any reference to the life of Christ that appears in the Gospels, particularly the parables and teaching of Jesus, Paul assumes this role for himself. This self-proclaimed apostle-come-lately (1 Corinthians 15:8–9) is the one who provides the convoluted teaching in place of Jesus, with whom he claims a special relationship, and it is this knowledge that provides the true path to salvation.

---

27. See ibid., 188.
28. Dick, "Selection from *Exegesis*," 327.
29. Schreber, *Memoirs*, 215.
30. Dick, "Selection from *Exegesis*," 323.
31. *Exegesis*, quoted in Sutin, *Divine Invasions*, 215.

If the redeemer figures in our psychotic texts resemble each other, then a similar coherence appears with the desire for male birthing. Paul himself, the one who suggests that "men" may marry if they cannot control their passions, argues that the ideal state for "men" is above such male-female sex (1 Corinthians 7:1–7). Instead, he preserves for himself the role of giving birth to a comprehensive doctrine and to the church. Christians of course are those who are "born of the spirit," "sons of God" (see below), a creative process that bypasses the womb; but it is the church as the female partner or bride of Christ that makes explicit the wish for a female identity. I have already spoken of the overrun of birthing sequences in *Total Recall* above, specifically the removal of the tracking device from Quade's sinuses and the multiplication of wombs, seminal ejaculations, and new birth with which the film closes. In these cases it is Quade himself who gives birth, who triggers the escape from or return to the womb noted above. And then there is Kuato, the rebel leader, who emerges from the side of his male lieutenant who undergoes birth pangs in order to bring Kuato forth. A central feature of Schreber's text is his process of "unmanning," the bodily transformation into a woman that enables him to become God's female partner, comparable to the Virgin Mary, and with whom he will give birth to a new race of human beings. But Schreber also asserts that spontaneous generation or parentless generation happens frequently at the hands of God.[32] Dick's own delusion has him take on the persona of a woman, embodied in the figure of Angel Archer in *The Transmigration of Timothy Archer*, who narrates the story of the transmigration of Timothy Archer's soul to Bill Lundgren. The AI he hears is female, whether Artemis/Diana, Aphrodite, Athena/Minerva, St. Sophia, or his dead sister Jane.[33] In the end, Dick is fascinated by the process of spiritual and bodily rebirth, *ex nihilo*, that he himself experiences: "'Thomas' was not born in my brain but born in my body, e.g. my hands and tongue."[34]

Yet I want to stress that although the discussion of psychosis has focused on these various symptoms, especially the redeemer figure and male birthing, Lacan's own analysis moves in another direction, namely the production of language itself. As I indicated earlier, for Lacan the psychotic does not pass through the crucial phase of the Oedipus complex that provides the connection between signifier and signified and

---

32. Schreber, *Memoirs*, 4 n. 1; 241–42, 251–55, 278–83, 288.
33. Sutin, *Divine Invasions*, 214.
34. Dick, "Selection from *Exegesis*," 340.

thereby the production of meaning required for language, the realm of the Symbolic. The psychotic thus produces what appears to be "nonsense" in an effort to overcome this foreclosure. My own point is that the language inevitably becomes theological, of a somewhat heterodox but internally consistent Christian form. For Schreber the key lies in nerves and in the posterior and anterior realms of God;[35] for Dick in Gnosticism[36] and in the explanations characteristic of science fiction (DNA coils, Artificial Intelligence, and so on); and for Paul it is, of course, Christology, heterodox from a Jewish perspective.[37] This production of language takes on two forms: the language in which God speaks to the person in question, and the texts themselves. As for God, it seems that he chooses to speak in a special language, which in Schreber's text is the "basic language" in which sentences remain unfinished, a high German loaded with euphemisms, often abusive.[38] For Philip Dick this becomes Koine Greek, a knowledge of which was enabled by the divine artificial intelligence that beamed him information, but which also mouthed obscenities to him over the radio and presented him with printouts, books, pages, and galley proofs in his dreams.[39] Did Paul also hear Christ speak in peculiar language? At least he speaks of "things that are not to be told, that no mortal is permitted to repeat" in his heavenly holiday (2 Corinthians 12:4), if not of the very private language of glossolalia.

The production of written texts, emphasized by Lacan as well as by Walker and Weber, is the other dimension of the denied path to the Symbolic. Psychotics do not always produce written texts, although there is a logic that indicates they should do so, especially if the process has its own internal coherence. Thus Schreber speaks not only of a book or notes written down for him by creatures given human shape,[40] but he also writes his memoirs that then become the foundation text for understanding psychosis, replete with a curious and shifting style, critical analysis, and a theological system. Philip Dick moves from his "prolific" writing of science fiction to writing his *Exegesis*, a handwritten text that

---

35. See especially Schreber, *Memoirs*, 6–32.

36. See Dick, "Selection from *Exegesis*," 331–33; Warrick, *Mind in Motion*, 179–81.

37. "The paranoiac is the most rigorous of metaphysicians. The typical paranoid outlook is thoroughgoing, internally logical, never trivializing, and capable of explaining the multitude of observed phenomena as aspects of a symmetrical and observed totality" (Carl Freedman, "Towards a Theory of Paranoia: The Science Fiction of Philip K. Dick," *Philip K. Dick: Contemporary Critical Interpretations*, ed. Samuel J. Umland (Westport, Conn.: Greenwood, 1995), 8.

38. Schreber, *Memoirs*, 13, 216–18.

39. Sutin, *Divine Invasions*, 218, 219.

40. Schreber, *Memoirs*, 126–27.

seeks to record the revelations he felt he had experienced, their meaning, and the possibility of a logically consistent theological system. In Dick's case, this writing ran to eight thousand pages of handwritten text, produced between his first episode in 1974 until his death in 1982 (see the samples at the end of *VALIS* and *Exegesis*). It will then come as no surprise that Paul's own lengthy letters to the various churches fall into the same category, especially since they also are an effort to make sense of his own "communication" with God. Once again we find an effort to produce a coherent system, and in terms of the form of Paul's writing there is nothing to distinguish it from the writing of Dick or Schreber. The psychotic logic of such writing carries through into the "Pauline" letters, because the process finds closure difficult if not impossible. Paul, it seems, is in good company; his own writing may be understood as an effort to overcome the inability to move into the Symbolic by the usual means of the Oedipus complex: the result is the production of nonsense.

This production of nonsense may then be understood, as I have suggested above, as the breaking in of an alternative Real. Normally the absent cause that keeps the symbolic structure intact, that which constitutes the system by its very exclusion, the Real in the case of psychosis cannot constitute the Symbolic because the psychotic does not access the Symbolic in the usual fashion. Thus the Imaginary and the Real collapse into one another: God, normally out of the picture and yet constitutive of it, suddenly appears as the Other. Given that psychotics do not lose their ability to think critically, reflections on the Real become intense. Schreber feels that the divine rays have destroyed the whole world around him and that he is the only one left as his old reality crumbles. Those who do appear become "fleeting-improvised-men,"[41] placed there for his convenience only to disappear when they are no longer needed. Paul also finds that his old reality has gone, that what is real to him is the realm of Christ and God, that this world itself will soon pass away for the greater reality of the return of Christ and the eschaton. And from his earliest writing Dick obsessed about the question of reality. By the time of the "Exegesis," he felt he had finally found the Real:

> Year after year, book after book & story, I shed illusion after illusion: self, time, space, causality, world & finally sought in (1970) to know what was real. Four years later, at my darkest moment of dread & trembling, my ego crumbling away, I was granted dibba

---

41. Ibid., 127, 255–56.

cakkhu [enlightenment]—& although I didn't realize it at the time, I became a Buddha. ("The Buddha is in the park") [AI voice message]. AI illusion dissolved away like a soap bubble & I saw reality at last—&, in the 4½ years since, have at last comprehended it intellectually—i.e. what I saw & knew & experienced (my exegesis)."[42]

TOTAL RECALL AND PAUL

It is through the Real that we return to *Total Recall*, because the real life of Quade is always open to question. Is he really Hauser, the double agent working for Cohaagen? Or is Quade himself real, denying what looks like his earlier identity? Or does Quade assert himself against the Real that shows up in his double? This is a consistent feature of Dick's writing from its earliest moments, giving it its own spin. What I will do in this final section is offer a strictly Lacanian reading of the film that indicates its continuity with Paul, Schreber, and Dick himself.

The two categories of specific language production and the possibility of writing do not appear in the film. However, without reiterating the various symptoms that I have already covered, let me begin with the Oedipus complex, the crucial quilting point of the Symbolic.

Although there is no explicit moment that may be identified as Oedipal, the film is saturated with the problem. To begin with, the only significant female figures are far from maternal: Quade's wife is one of the conspirators assigned to watch him and kill him if necessary, and Melina is both a sex worker and rebel militant. The only hint of female maternal function is the momentary glimpse of the three-breasted mutant woman that Quade meets in the rebels' nightclub while he is searching for Melina. The women, then, have had the maternal systematically removed from their representation. Further, there is, as in Schreber's text, a replication of father figures. Cohaagen, the exploitative and tyrannical leader of Mars, is the most obvious father figure, especially when he is later seen with the arm of Hauser—Quade's double— around his shoulders. Hauser, then, represents what a successful passing through the Oedipus drama will effect: an identification with and usurpation of the father in response to the threat of castration represented by the mother. Not so for Quade, who refuses to identify with Hauser and thereby takes Cohaagen as his father figure. But there are other father

---

42. *Exegesis* entry September 1978, quoted in Sutin, *Divine Invasions*, 234.

figures, including the "real" husband of Quade's wife. He works for Cohaagen and is engaged in the immediate surveillance of Quade, moving to kill him when Quade threatens to break out of his constructed life. And then there are the aliens, the unknown and absent figures who have built the reactor that will enable the melting of the vast glaciers under Mars's surface and create a breathable atmosphere. The alien often replaces God in science fiction, particularly when appearing not in person but in the form of superior technological relics that humans must in some way activate to survive.

Quade, then, shows all the signs of not having passed through the Oedipal drama. The clearest sign of this lies in the replication of mirrors—the mirror-stage that is central to the Imaginary. For Lacan, the mirror-stage provides the first moment of identification for the subject—when the subject recognizes the image as his or her own, the moment of the first constitution of the subject. Lacan consistently identifies the Imaginary as something that humans share with animals: his examples of the mirror-stage draw upon various patterns of animal behavior. The recognition by an animal of another of its own species triggers both sex and conflict, depending upon whether the other is of the same sex (male) or of the other sex (female). But the mirror-stage also raises the first question about identity that opens up the possibility of the Symbolic, because what the subject sees in the mirror also appears to hide something crucial; the subject suspects that something is hidden. Thus animals and young children will peer behind the mirror to locate that something. This is a feature of the Symbolic, in which the excluded item, that which does not compute in the system, is precisely the thing that keeps the system together. For Lacan this absent cause is variously the phallus (for signification and language), the Real, or the lack.

In *Total Recall* the mirror-stage sequence takes place when Quade opens the computer screen to see himself. Except that the mirror talks back to him as Hauser, his double that claims to be the "real" him. The computer/mirror proceeds to give him instructions about how to survive and get to Mars to carry out his assigned role. The very fact that the mirror talks back provides the promise of the Symbolic, because the something that is felt to be missing in the mirror now makes its presence felt. However, there are two problems. First, the mirror that talks back indicates a short circuit in the system—the Real cannot break through in this fashion in the context of the Symbolic. It must remain hidden, out of sight, below the horizon, for only then can it provide the coherence of the system, whether of language, law, or whatever. This is the first major signal of psychosis in the film, because in psychosis the Real breaks in, unmediated by the Symbolic, and speaks, often in the form of God. The second problem is that Hauser instructs Quade on how to remove the tracking device from his sinuses. Apart from the birthing analogy, and even apart from the feminization of Quade with the carefully arranged towel on his head, Quade must remove that which keeps his current "reality" in place. The tracking device allows his watchers to follow his every move, especially when he is trying to escape; it is the hidden item that enables Quade's world to make some sense. The removal of the device by means of forceps and agony may be understood as the removal of what Lacan calls *objet petit a*, that item that cannot be included within the system that at the same ensures its coherence. *Objet petit a* functions, then, in the same way as the Real, as the lack or phallus. By removing it, Quade blocks any possibility of moving into the Symbolic. This means of course that the "Real" that speaks to him in the mirror is a substitute Real, constructed in place of the Real now gone.

From this point on, Quade remains stuck in the Imaginary, as it were, and it is here that Lacan locates the defense against the homosexual tendency, narcissism, and megalomania: "the ego's enlargement to the dimensions of the world is a fact of libidinal economy which is apparently located entirely on the imaginary level."[43] The replication of the mirror-stage is part of the lock in the Imaginary, because Hauser returns to speak with Quade on a screen in Cohaagen's office on Mars. Having unwittingly enabled the security forces to access the rebels and kill Kuato, Quade and Melina are brought before Cohaagen only to have Hauser appear on screen and congratulate Quade on carrying out the double agent's mission. Yet Quade refuses the identity, becoming instead the means of achieving the rebel's desire—free air for everyone. But this alternative identity can only be an effort at compensating for the impossibility of the Symbolic.

The final element of the incomplete Oedipal process appears with the various birthing scenes, all of which feature Quade himself. From the removal of the tracking device, through the rebel leader Kuato, whose role Quade himself takes over, to the double womb of the alien reactor and Mars itself, Quade gives birth. By placing his hand in the reactor trigger, he and Melina burst forth from the womb to be born again on a renewed Mars; but then they are also sucked back into the womb that becomes a new Eden, a paradise that is nothing other than a return to the womb. In

---

43. Lacan, *The Psychoses*, 312.

other words, Quade has taken on the maternal function by not having passed through the Oedipal complex. Having refused the possibility of castration and thereby having failed to identify with the father, the only figure remaining with whom he can identify with is the mother. In the film the birthing sequences are the clearest instance of such a process.

But what of the phallus, since for Lacan its role is central to both the Imaginary and the Symbolic? In the Imaginary, the phallus provides the point of coherent identity for the subject, the object into which all may be drawn, whereas in the Symbolic it becomes the signifier of lack, the absent item that produces signification, that is, language. In other words, in the Symbolic, the fear of castration (which emerges first in the Imaginary) becomes the reality of castration, because the phallus no longer appears. Again, the link between these two inseparable functions of the phallus is the Oedipal drama. It is not coincidental that Schwarzenegger plays the role of Quade—his phallic status is one of the most overplayed dimensions of his "acting." This "condom with muscles" perpetually reiterates his phallic status: Melina grabs his crotch in the first moments of their meeting; he destroys the drilling machine that threatens to kill Melina and himself by means of a huge phallic drill; and the film closes with massive seminal ejaculations of life-giving steam from the melting glacier until it is all drawn together in the huge ejaculation from the mountain under which the reactor is housed. Yet, I want to focus on an earlier scene in which Quade's gun is the quintessential phallic object. When he first begins to realize that all is not as it seems—after his unsuccessful drug-induced holiday and after the effort to shoot him in his apartment—Quade runs, without purpose, through a security screen. We have already seen such a screen earlier, in which all that remains opaque are the subject's bones; now, Quade's gun, tucked into his pants, flashes red on the screen and alarms sound. Here we have the phallus highlighted for us on the screen. Quade emerges with gun in hand and, inevitably, shoots his way out of trouble. But what interests me about this scene is that the screen functions as another marker of the mirror-stage, except that now it sees more than is within him. And in the mirror-stage, the realm of the Imaginary, the phallus is that which provides the overwhelming coherence of identity and draws everything into it. For Quade, the phallus is not the phallic signifier, that absence upon which signification is based. He remains locked out of the Symbolic.

Finally there is the foreclosure of the Name-of-the-Father, the failed identification with and effort to replace the father that is the result of the Oedipus complex. Such a foreclosure leaves a hole or tear in the Symbolic—

there is nothing left that can structure the process of symbolization. It is not so much a case of producing a symbolic replacement of the dead father that can then enable symbolization, but the very absence of the Name-of-the-Father itself. The result of this in Schreber is a perpetual shifting in an effort to overcome such a foreclosure, moving from his own father to his elder brother to Flechsig and then to God. In *Total Recall* there is a similar shuffle by a bewildered Quade: at first Hauser seems to provide a way forward, then Kuato, then Cohaagen, and finally the aliens. But in each case Quade does not find the Name-of-the-Father; each one proves to be an unstable basis upon which to begin to construct a process of symbolization, and the effort to overcome the foreclosure of the Name-of-the-Father fails. The result is the psychosis of the film itself.

There is one final move to make in such a psychoanalytic reading, but in doing so I move outside the film itself to Schwarzenegger. Is it not possible that the effort to overcome the inability to move into the Symbolic manifests itself in the "actor" Arnold Schwarzenegger? In other words, the success of the film—as psychotic—relies precisely on Schwarzenegger's inability to act: his lack of ability, his woodenness, the dreadful delivery of lines, the comical effort to express emotion, makes him peculiarly appropriate for such a film. In a dialectical inversion, Schwarzenegger becomes the absent cause of the film's psychotic narrative, the ultimate failed effort at symbolization.

But how does all this connect with the psychotic narrative and texts of Paul in the New Testament? *Total Recall*, as I have argued, is one element in the much wider production of the work of Philip Dick, whose writing and personal life provide a classic case of psychosis. In order to make this point I also brought in the *Memoirs* of Schreber and the theoretical analyses of Freud and Lacan, which in their turn enabled a reading of the film as psychosis. But it is Dick himself that provides the immediate link, for in his psychosis he believed he was taken back into the world of first-century Judea, the time of Paul and the early church as well as of the Gnostics he loved. Often he saw this first-century world and the time in which he lived as simultaneous realities. At times he felt he was Simon Magus in the Book of Acts, or Thomas, or that Thomas was in him,[44] the character of the Gospels who doubts Jesus' resurrection appearances (more psychotic narratives?). If this was his mortal side, then as "Firebright" he was immortal.[45] And the Artificial Intelligence, the female

---

44. Dick, "Selection from *Exegesis*," 340.
45. See Sutin, *Divine Invasions*, 211.

mechanical voice of VALIS, Christ himself, spoke to him in Koine Greek. Indeed, Dick felt that he had lived or did live in the time of the Book of Acts, in which Paul is the central character. Paul's letters profoundly influenced Dick's reflections, as did the Gospel of John.[46] And one of the works he planned to write was the "Acts of Paul."[47] He hints that in some way he himself wrote the Books of Acts, giving birth to this text as God:

> Put a third way, suppose a normal person wishes to know what is in the Book of Acts. He must locate a copy and read it. But this meta-mind simply knows the contents of the Book of Acts (if he is to know it at all). How does he know it? Because he found that he had written it, and thus read it. Then he checked with a copy of the Book of Acts to corroborate that it is indeed the Book of Acts. But when and where and how did it originally enter his mind? There is no answer to that: it is *ex nihilo*: without cause.[48]

Apart from the particular symptoms of psychosis that I identified earlier in Paul's texts, is there also a deeper logic of psychosis here as well? Again, with Paul there is no clear narrative of the Oedipus complex, although the traces of its failed completion are everywhere to be found. Let me begin again with the mirror-stage: in Paul, as in *Total Recall*, it appears in the replication of two Pauls—although in Acts, one is Saul, the other Paul. Saul is the one who breathes "threats and murder against the disciples of the Lord" (Acts 9:1), who goes to Damascus to bind and bring back to Jerusalem any who belong to "the Way" (Acts 9:2). After his initial psychotic vision, the Christians who encounter him are incredulous, but accept him as one of their own. Saul then disappears from the narrative at Acts 9:30, only to reappear momentarily at Acts 11:25, 12:25, and 13:2. By Acts 13:9 the inversion takes place: "But Saul, who is also called Paul. . . ." For the remainder of Acts he is Paul, but the mirror switch happens precisely before he utters his first words in Acts 13:10–11, a curse of blindness on Elymas the magician that is immediately enacted. We might read the Saul/Paul opposition as the split Jewish/Christian Paul of the epistles, for at times he plays up his own Jewishness only to undermine it (see Galatians 1:13–24). Another way of putting it is that these two narratives from Acts and Galatians—

---

46. Dick, "Selection from *Exegesis*," 331, 336.
47. Sutin, *Divine Invasions*, 206.
48. Dick, "Selection from *Exegesis*," 347.

who is to say which is fiction?—play upon each other. For a Lacanian reading, this is none other than the mirror-stage, the constitutive feature of the Imaginary. Does Paul then pass into the Symbolic? Does what was present in the mirror cease to provide a unitary identification for the subject to become instead the absent cause of the Symbolic, the realm of language and the law? Given the renaming from Saul to Paul immediately before his first words are uttered, the initial impression is that the Symbolic does indeed play a role and that the split subject of the Symbolic order, the one whose subjectivity is determined by a constitutive lack, has appeared.

Other indications suggest that this is not the case. The narrative of Paul's first encounter with Jesus Christ, with its bright light and divine voice, is the most obvious. Here we have the substitute Real appearing; the Real that provides the basis of the Symbolic through its absence disappears altogether and the subject attempts to identify another Real as a compensation. But we do not need to resort to Acts alone for such a divine encounter: in the counter-text of 2 Corinthians 12:1–4 Paul speaks of being "caught up to the third heaven—whether in the body or out of the body I do not know, God knows" (2 Corinthians 12:2). From there he was brought up into paradise (12:3) and "heard things that cannot be told, which man may not utter" (2 Corinthians 12:4).

But there is another signal in the text of Paul's letters where he deliberates over the relationship between the Law and grace. In Romans 2:12–3:31 Paul undertakes a complex maneuver to show how the Law is both annulled and taken up to a higher level in the new doctrine of justification by faith through grace. In the end he seeks to show how justification by faith, or grace, absorbs the Law into itself: "Do we then overthrow the law by faith? By no means! On the contrary, we uphold the law" (Romans 3:31). Yet at the same time Paul uses a number of arguments to show how the Law is inadequate: knowledge of the Law makes one so much more culpable and responsible (2:12); the Law brings the wrath of God (4:15); the only road to justification through the Law is by doing it, but this is impossible (3:20); thus the only function of the Law is to provide a knowledge of sin (3:20; 7:7) or an incentive for sin (7:8–12); all those who rely on the works of the Law live under the curse of the Law (Galatians 3:10, 13). In the end, he argues that Christ allows one to bypass the Law, that Christians are "not under law but under grace" (Romans 6:14; see 3:21). Further, since justification and righteousness cannot come through the works of the Law, the only solution is to find an alternative source: "For we hold that a man is justified

by faith apart from works of the law" (3:28). The final move is to argue
that this is not such a new thing—Abraham too was justified by faith, a
faith he had before he was circumcised. Abraham's righteousness was
then not a result of the Law but of faith, because his justification took
place before the mark of the Law, circumcision, appeared on his penis
(4:1–15). Paul has systematically undermined the Law, outflanking it in
both time and salvific promise.

I have explored this issue at some length because for Lacan the law is
one element of the Symbolic, that which is structured by a crucial lack,
namely, the transgression itself. But what Paul manages to do in this section of Romans is replace the Law entirely with the notion of justification
by faith in Jesus Christ: "For Christ is the end (*telos*) of the law, that every
one who has faith may be justified" (Romans 10:4). It seems to me that
Paul is not so much providing an argument for the existence of the Law
itself in Lacanian terms as trying to produce an alternative to it. In other
words, his argument in Romans is an effort at another language, another
road of access to the Symbolic, and in doing so he must negate the
Symbolic itself. That it is in the end also nonsense has not always been
said of Paul: rather, his astute theological mind is able to come up with
logical non sequiturs, such as: justification by faith in Jesus Christ provides righteousness apart from the Law, but this means that the Law is
upheld. In this respect there is no qualitative difference from the theological nonsense of Schreber or Philip Dick.

Yet I do not need to restrict myself to the rational Paul to find the
attempt to provide a signifying system as a compensation for the
Symbolic. Not only does he hear "things that cannot be told, which man
may not utter" (2 Corinthians 12:4), but the divine language of the early
Christians, the language of the Holy Spirit, is none other than glossolalia:
"For one who speaks in a tongue speaks not to men but to God; for no
one understands him, but he utters mysteries in the Spirit" (1
Corinthians 14:2). Except that he seeks to curb such excesses, preferring
the gift of prophesying, or at least that the gift of interpreting the nonsense of glossolalia may also be sought (1 Corinthians 14:13). Paul is
overly conscious of the nonsense of glossolalia. Although he speaks in
tongues more than all of them (1 Corinthians 14:18), he prefers that
words of the mind, not of the spirit, be used (1 Corinthians 14:19). As I
indicated earlier, this divine language is of the same type as the "basic
language" of Schreber and Dick's revelations in Koine Greek.

Perhaps the strongest mark of a failed Oedipal drama, but also of the
foreclosure of the Name-of-the-Father, is the prevalence of birthing

images, most of them focused on Jesus Christ. One of the leitmotifs of Paul's letters is that Christians become "sons of God" (*huioi theou*; Romans 8:14) or "children of God" (*tekna theou*; Romans 8:16), through the spirit of God or through Jesus. Indeed, the "spirit of sonship" (*pneuma huiothesias*; 8:15) enables the believer to cry "Abba! Father!" (*Abba ho pater*; Romans 8:15). They become one with Jesus as fellow heirs of God (Romans 8:17). So what we end up with is that Jesus or the Spirit gives birth to the Christians, who then become siblings of Jesus as sons of God: Jesus is both their father and their brother. This is nothing other than the foreclosure of the maternal body characteristic of psychosis and the attempted replacement with a male birthing process, alternatively described as creation: "if anyone is in Christ, he is a new creation (*ktisis*)" (2 Corinthians 5:17). This then opens up the possibility of being resurrected, raised from the dead, being reborn in heaven (1 Corinthians 15:12–28): Jesus then enables a double birth, one the process of becoming a Christian and the other the birth into heaven. Just when it seems that the gender of the first Christians has been clarified—as sons of God—Paul shows some ambivalence. He speaks of the Corinthians or the whole Corinthian church (the text itself is ambivalent at this point) as the bride, or virgin, of Christ: "I feel a divine jealousy for you, for I betrothed you to Christ to present you as a pure bride (*parthenon hagnen*) to her one husband" (2 Corinthians 11:2). The sexual tone is somewhat effaced by this translation, for it may also be read as "chaste virgin" or "unmarried girl." So Paul becomes a marriage broker and the gender identity of the Christians ambiguous: are they "sons" of God or "virgins" of Christ? Is Paul then among their number as a believer? Perhaps, but the process of "emasculation" and re-forming as a woman is something that comes through strongly in Schreber's psychosis and formed one of the reasons for Freud's assessment of latent homosexuality. For Lacan such material indicates the failed Oedipal drama and the subsequent identification with the mother since the father ceases to be a point of identification—Lacan's foreclosed Name-of-the-Father.

So far, however, the identification with the mother, or appropriation of maternal functions, has been reserved for Jesus Christ rather than for Paul himself. Yet, what happens throughout both the narrative of Acts and the epistles is an identification with Christ, a merging of their identities that sees Paul as the divine figure. Thus, in Acts Paul curses a man to blindness (13:10–12); heals the sick, even by pieces of cloth brought away from his body (19:11–12); is recognized along with Christ by the demons (19:15); raises the dead (20:7–12); rides a boat through a storm

(Acts 27); and is impervious to the poison of vipers (28:1–6). In this last piece of extraordinary prowess, the result of Paul's nonchalant flick of the snake into the fire is that the Maltese locals "said he was a God (*theon*)" (28:6). The internal logic of this appears also in Paul's letters, where his rampant christocentric focus gradually merges his own being with Christ's: "I have been crucified with Christ; it is no longer I who live, but Christ who lives in me: and the life I now live in the flesh I live by faith in the Son of God, who loved me and gave himself for me" (Galatians 2:20). He begins to bear on his body "the stigmata of Jesus (*ta stigmata tou Iēsou*)" (Galatians 6:17). And so, as Christ, he can exhort the Thessalonians to "become imitators of us and the Lord" (1 Thessalonians 1:6).

In the end it is Paul who is the redeemer, the one who dispenses salvation, gives birth to the new Christians, and enables their rebirth in paradise, where he, incidentally, has already been. But is this really fair to Paul? It seems to me that the infamous passage about marriage and the "temptation to immorality" for which marriage is a safety rail puts Paul squarely in with the male mothers. Here he writes: "It is well for a man not to touch a woman" (1 Corinthians 7:1), but due to *porneia*, prostitution, immorality, and so on, he condescends that men and women should marry in order to avoid such a dreadful state. In a moment of profound pastoral understanding, he says: "I wish that all were as I myself am. But each has his own special gift from God, one of one kind and one of another" (1 Corinthians 7:7). Traditionally read either in eschatological terms or as a justification for a celibate clergy, the "gift" (*charisma*) also removes Paul from male-female relations. Given my earlier point about his appropriation of Christ's maternal appropriation, his argument becomes another part of the failed Oedipal complex in which the troubled identification with the maternal body is the outcome.

For Lacan, the function of the phallus, or more specifically castration anxiety, is part of the Oedipus complex and thereby part of the interaction between Imaginary and Symbolic. In Paul, the phallus itself, or rather castration anxiety, emerges as the incessant repetition of the question of circumcision and Paul's concern with his own penis. With a rare succinctness, Romans 2:25–29 outlines his point, linking it closely with the Law. He begins, characteristically, with the loaded statement that circumcision is fine if you obey the Law, but since he has already indicated that this is not possible, we can anticipate what is to come: breaking the Law (the default position) becomes uncircumcision (Romans 2:25). He has already shuffled away from physical circumcision to its apparent symbolic status. From there he suggests that an uncircumcised man who keeps the Law will therefore be regarded as circumcised. Again, the possibility is foreclosed by his earlier argument about the Law, but it carries his current point forward another step, which is to suggest that circumcision is not something outward or external (*en toi phaneroi*) nor in the flesh (*en sarki*) (Romans 2:28). Circumcision is then "of heart in spirit" (*peritomê kardias en pneumati*) (Romans 2:29; see Galatians 5:2–12; 6:11–16)—all very well in the move to subsume Judaism, but what this argument shows is a comprehensive effort to cope without the Symbolic phallus. For Lacan the fear of castration (and Freud drew his initial discussion of castration anxiety from circumcision in the Hebrew Bible) appears first in the Imaginary when the male subject first recognizes that his mother is castrated. At this point the phallus functions as a unifying field, drawing everything into itself. However, with the Symbolic the fear of castration is nothing other than the awareness that one is already castrated. That is to say, the Symbolic can only operate in the absence of the phallus, the empty signifier or signifier of lack. Yet in this text Paul has systematically avoided the Symbolic because circumcision is that already effected castration. By shifting to a circumcision of the heart, Paul is seeking to construct an alternative Symbolic field and signifying system to the one that has been closed to him. It is not for nothing that his discussion of circumcision is closely tied up with the Law; his treatment of the Law, as I argued above, is an effort to bypass the Law, a feature of the Symbolic, by grace. Circumcision of the heart follows the same logic.

Finally, there is the foreclosure of the Name-of-the-Father. First appearances suggest that Christ fills this role for Paul, especially in his effort to usurp Christ's role: this would indicate the son's identification and supersession of the dead father. Yet, is it not the obsession with Christ that marks the foreclosure of the Name-of-the-Father? The very fixation on a divine figure as a replacement for the father figure is one of the key marks of psychosis. For Paul, Christ is both the figure of intense erotic fixation as well as the one who gives birth and allows Paul to do so. In fact, Paul shuffles his father figures much like Schreber: at times it is Adam, at others Abraham, and then, most commonly, Christ.

So it seems that the figure of Paul that emerges from Acts and the letters is one of a psychotic nut: he travels from church to church, blathers nonsense (glossolalia), bears a circumcised heart, performs miracles, hears Christ in a bright light and speaks with him, travels to paradise, sees Christ as giving birth to Christians (which he himself would like to do), all the while constructing a theological system that will form the basis of the church, to which he gives birth.

In all of this there is a final dialectical twist that Paul himself provides. I hinted at it a little earlier in my discussion of hypochondria and persecution complexes, but it is not so much that we may read the narrative of Paul's life—however fictional the Book of Acts or his letters may be—as psychotic after the work of Freud and Lacan on psychosis. We can and must do this, but the possibility of psychosis—its experience in all its many features, the content of those experiences, and the texts that were generated from them, as well as the possibility of locating a deeper psychoanalytic theory for psychosis—comes from the New Testament itself, and especially from Paul. In other words, the narrative and texts of Paul provide the enabling moment of psychosis as a specifically Western and Christian psychological pathology. Without Paul, psychosis would not exist—at least not in the form and content in which we now understand it. Thus, it is ultimately Paul, mediated through Schreber, the analyses of Freud and Lacan and others, and the writings of Philip Dick, who provides the very possibility of a psychotic film like *Total Recall*.

Yet, this leaves Paul somewhat high and dry, a psychotic before his time, who himself enables psychosis. But what, dare I ask, of the literary and cultural context from which these texts arise? Here I pick up Frederic Jameson's point that texts function as responses to determinate social situations and contradictions, yet they may also be said to create such situations in the first place insofar as they articulate a situation and become an exemplary reaction to it. "From this point of view, the response may be said to structure and bring to being for the first time an objective situation lived in a confused and less awakened fashion by their contemporaries."[49] Context then becomes what is generated by the text in question at the same time as it begins to work on it and to alter it. The figure of "Paul," generated by the texts in question, functions in such a capacity. Not only does he think and operate like any other person in the ancient world—they were all psychotic in this sense, expressing everything in religious terms—but he also responds to the situation with such clarity that he brings forth the "psychotic" core of religion, which was, after all, Christianity.

---

49. Jameson, "Imaginary and Symbolic in Lacan," 78.

8. GAZING AT IMPOTENCE IN HENRY KING'S *DAVID AND BATHSHEBA*

Julie Kelso

But the LORD said to Samuel, "Do not look on his appearance or on the height of his stature, because I have rejected him; for the LORD sees not as man sees; man looks on the outward appearance, but the LORD looks on the heart." (1 Samuel 16:7)[1]

I was thinking that in the Bible, for example, there must be passages in which the eye confers the *baraka* or blessing. There are a few small places where I hesitated—but no. The eye may be prophylactic, but it cannot be beneficent—it is maleficent. In the Bible and even in the New Testament, there is no good eye, but there are evil eyes all over the place.[2]

INTRODUCTION

David and Bathsheba is Henry King's "somewhat unclassically classic 1950s epic."[3] Recently biblical scholars David Gunn and Cheryl Exum have given it critical attention. Despite the fact that both Gunn and Exum foreground the figure of Bathsheba in their examinations of

---

1. All biblical quotations are from the Revised Standard Version.
2. Lacan, *The Four Fundamental Concepts of Psychoanalysis*, ed. Jacques-Alain Miller, trans. Alan Sheridan (London: Vintage, 1998), 118–19.
3. Bruce Babbington and Peter William Evans, *Biblical Epics: Sacred Narrative in Hollywood Cinema* (Manchester and New York: Manchester University Press, 1993), 70.

painterly and filmic texts, their interpretations of King's film are remarkably different. For Gunn, *David and Bathsheba* is a film that can be situated within the classical cinematic genre of the woman's film.[4] But he also points out, "something is happening in this movie that is exploiting the fundamental ambiguities of the social and ideological forces that created the genre in the first place." Gunn observes that *David and Bathsheba*, as a woman's film, encodes "the tension between the emerging desire of women as subjects . . . and the latent anxiety of men as subjects over the impending collapse of their privileged status."[5] And yet, the film extends beyond the boundaries of the woman's film. The typical woman's film enforces the renunciation of desire by the female lead, or she may be subject to filmic sanctions such as separation from her lover or death.[6] However, in this film, Bathsheba's desire is satiated, and the ending is happy.

Cheryl Exum, on the other hand, is concerned to show how *David and Bathsheba*, as an example of the classical cinema and its inherent phallocentrism, produces an objectification of the female body (Bathsheba's) for the viewing pleasure of the spectator. The film rearticulates in visual form the relationship between the male gaze and power present in 2 Samuel 11, a relationship that for Exum exonerates the narrator/spectator from any guilt associated with the explicit voyeurism at work in both. Exum resists what she believes the phallocentric structures of the film ask of the male and female spectators. That is, to assume the male position constructed by the filmic text as "ideal" and to contemplate, without guilt, the eroticized object of the female body.

In dealing with biblical texts represented in paintings and films, visual or scopic relations must be broached. Exum and Gunn both raise questions as to the status of some "gaze" in looking at these visual renderings throughout history, be it David's, Bathsheba's, and/or the spectators (including themselves). To do so they engage to a certain extent

---

4. *David and Bathsheba* contains many of the dominant themes and motifs of the woman's film, such as sexuality, family, marriage, the desiring woman, the woman in love, the "waiting" woman, and the male protagonist as artist (David Gunn, "Bathsheba Goes Bathing in Hollywood: Words, Images, and Social Locations," *Semeia* 74 (1996): 93–95). For a more general discussion on the themes of the woman's film, see Mary Ann Doane, *The Desire to Desire: The Woman's Film of the 1940s* (Bloomington: Indiana University Press, 1987), 96–122; and Jackie Byars, "Feminism, Psychoanalysis, and Female-Oriented Melodramas of the 1950s." *Multiple Voices in Feminist Film Criticism*, ed. D. Carson, L. Dittmar, and J. R. Welsch (Minneapolis: University of Minnesota Press, 1994), 93–108.

5. Gunn, "Bathsheba Goes Bathing," 96.

6. Ibid., 95.

with film theory. Since a number of biblical scholars are turning to Hollywood, redefining the boundaries of biblical studies in the process, certain problems concerning theory have inevitably arisen as a result.[7] Since my own essay is in some sense a response to Exum's analysis of *David and Bathsheba*, particularly her appropriation of Mulvey, the first issue I will address in this essay is Mulvey's argument and an outline of the major criticisms directed against her thesis since the essay was first published in 1975. Furthermore, with this essay I want to focus exclusively on the film, touching upon the biblical text only tangentially, rather than taking a comparative approach that brings the ancient verbal and modern filmic narratives together. A consideration of filmic narrative as a distinct narrative form necessarily entails a detailed consideration of theories concerning cinematic specificity.

The more recent challenges to the apparatus theories of the 1960s and 1970s, coming from critics who are best described as "Lacanian," interest me here. With the help of Joan Copjec and Slavoj Žižek, I want to examine the film according to Lacan's elaboration of the relationship between the subject and representation, or the subject of the scopic realm. In the first section of this essay I give an overview of Lacan's theory of the gaze, along with a summary of Copjec's critique of the "gaze" as it appears in classical film theory. She argues that classical film theorists, while claiming to be dependent on Lacan in their theorization of the relationship between the apparatus, the spectator, and the gaze, are rather quite dramatically at odds with Lacan. Classical film theory has argued that the spectator identifies first with the gaze of the camera and then with the gazes of the characters. As such, the spectator comes to be sutured into the world of the film as its "subject," with meaning arising at this very juncture. For Lacan, the gaze is not simply "the look." Nor is the gaze situated within the image as the mirrored reflection of the spectating subject. Instead, the gaze is situated beyond representation, rendering the subject of vision an *object* within the scopic realm. In identifying with the gaze, the subject is situated within the scopic realm as external to itself and at odds with its environment. The effect of the gaze is traumatic, not reassuring, as film theory would have it—it is that

---

7. A number of the contributors to the recent *Semeia* volume, *Biblical Glamour and Hollywood Glitz* (Alice Bach, ed., *Semeia* 74 [Atlanta: Scholars, 1996]) dealing with gender codes in Hollywood films, either mention Laura Mulvey's Lacan-inspired essay "Visual Pleasure and Narrative Cinema" or analyze the films with Mulvey's thesis as the unacknowledged basis of their critique.

"lost object" (*objet petit a*) that ensures the subject never encounters the "real" of its being. And yet, it is this very lack that constitutes the subject of language, the subject able to apprehend its world, to make meaning of it. Furthermore, the spectating subject is *always* guilty. In the scopic realm, the subject is always culpable, guilty of the same deception with which it faults its representations.

This discussion allows me to bring Lacan "into the picture." I argue that this Lacanian gaze can account for a gaze that is notably absent in Gunn and Exum's readings of the film. This is the gaze of that unseen and unseeable biblical character known by various names (one of which cannot be spoken): God. The film presents David's impotent attempts to avoid paying the debt that must be paid to the God who has seen him, chosen him, and anointed him "king of Israel." David must be king—it is his destiny as the anointed one. However, the entire film presents David's futile attempts to get an answer as to why he was chosen. While he never explicitly asks the question, "Why am I what you say that I am?" or "What is it about me that made you choose me in the first place?" his disillusionment with kingship and his feelings of inadequacy express this question toward an unseeable God who will always refuse to answer because there is no answer. Here, the work of Slavoj Žižek becomes crucial. For Žižek, this hysterical question is the only possible answer to a more traumatic question in the Jewish religion: "What does God want from me?" The ending of *David and Bathsheba*, which sees David paying his debt and sacrificing his "life," is in fact the assertion of the Christian answer to the Jewish dilemma of the enigma of God's desire, best summed up by Lacan's "*Che vuoi?*" "What does the Other want from me?"

Bathsheba plays a crucial role in all of this. Again drawing from Žižek, this time from his elaboration of the relationship between imaginary and symbolic identification, I will show that Bathsheba is positioned as a subject of the gaze and that her positioning allows David to identify with that very gaze to enjoy his own hysterical impotence. This is itself an impotent attempt by David to delay the debt that will have to be paid to his terrifying God. In both the bathing scene and the "crisis" scene (the scene where David remembers the death of Jonathan), Bathsheba is pushed into this position almost to block out the unbearable trauma that is the effect of the gaze of God: the "death" of the subject's "being." And so, unlike Exum who wants to insist that it is the image of Bathsheba's body that is the problematic feature of the film, I will argue that, ironically, it is Bathsheba's *gaze* that is troublesome from a feminist perspective. I say ironically, because in classical film theory (as for both Gunn and Exum), it is the holder of the gaze who is also the holder of power.

Finally, in all of this, David takes on the guilt that is rightly but impossibly God's. Focusing again on the "crisis" scene, but this time in relation to the penultimate scene where David remembers through a "dream" the moment of his anointing (having been struck unconscious by placing his hands on the ark of the covenant), I argue that these are fantasmatic attempts to avoid the real source of his trauma: God himself. The death of Jonathan stands in for the source of David's guilt. But this itself merely sidesteps the real guilt that floods the film: David will give up his desire and fully take on his mandate as king of Israel.

I

Explicit in Exum's analysis is a reliance upon film theorist Laura Mulvey's analysis that the classical cinema functions smoothly through its construction of a stable, heterosexual male viewing position as the "ideal" position from which to view the film. For Mulvey, one important aspect or quality of this cinema, in terms of its success, was its skilled and satisfying manipulation of visual pleasure. Said to be an elaboration of Lacan's theory of the gaze, derived from his work on the mirror-stage, Mulvey argues that film narrative functions according to the direct relation between power and looking:

> Unchallenged, mainstream film coded the erotic into the language of the dominant patriarchal order. In the highly developed Hollywood cinema it was only through these codes that the alienated subject, torn in his imaginary memory by a sense of loss, by the terror of potential lack in fantasy, came near to finding a glimpse of satisfaction: through its formal beauty and its play on his own formative obsessions.[8]

Mulvey's thesis is largely a response to the theorization of the cinema as "apparatus," coming out of British and French film theory of the 1960s and 1970s. Perhaps the most influential of these theorists was Jean-Louis Baudry. In his essay "Ideological Effects of the Basic Cinematographic

---

8. Laura Mulvey, "Visual Pleasure and Narrative Cinema," *Narrative, Apparatus, Ideology: A Film Theory Reader*, ed. Philip Rosen (New York: Columbia University Press, 1986), 200.

Apparatus," Baudry argues that it is through the cinema's basic mechanics of representation and their arrangement (projector, screen, camera movements, editing, and the immobile spectator) that an ideological position is produced. The position is that of the transcendental subject, whereby the spectating subject perceives itself to be centered as the basic source of meaning in the visual field. He insists that the cinematic apparatus is the direct descendant of the perspectival model developed in the Renaissance. Renaissance painting constructed a centered space, with the center of this space coinciding with the eye. This monocular-centric construct is repeated in the cinema through the "eye" of the camera. It is monocular vision that is said to map the space of an ideal vision. In other words, the spectator is situated at that geometrical point within the image as the subject of the image. The cinema is therefore situated as the culmination of a particular Western ideological project. The subject constructed by the cinema is seen by Baudry to be the transcendental subject of Western philosophical idealism.

Furthermore, at the cinema, the transcendent subject, who can view the homogeneity of "all Being" from afar, is a disembodied subject, tied to the wandering eye of the camera. Rather than setting up a multiplicity of viewing positions for the subject, the camera produces a singular subject effect. One of the techniques for producing this seemingly coherent subject position in relation to the filmic representation is the shot-reverse-shot alternation. The effect of such a technique is what is known as the "suture" or "sewing" of the viewing subject into the film's enunciation. This process of "sewing-in" serves, by necessity, to fill in the gap left by the text, as the source of cinematic enunciation is absent from, or invisible in, the text. In place of the absence in the text, the subject is produced by means of such a mechanism of optical point of view.[9] This process of subject positioning is said to "sew-up" the conflicting subjectivities of the actual viewer into an imaginary harmonious whole by allowing identification with the gazes of the characters in the film.

Baudry further explored this fundamental process of identification using certain ideas of Jacques Lacan, in particular, his work concerning the "mirror-stage."[10] According to Lacan, two orders or registers exist out of which the ego of the infant is formed. The Imaginary order comprises an axis of identification for the subject. Here the ego emerges through identification with the specular image of another. This identification

---

9. Annette Kuhn, *Women's Pictures: Feminism and Cinema* (London: Verso, 1993), 53.
10. Jacques Lacan, *Écrits: A Selection*, trans. Alan Sheridan (New York: Norton, 1977), 1–7.

with the image of another reassures the subject, falsely, that it is a stable and unified subject. Disruption of the reassuring aspects of the Imaginary[11] occurs through the subject's entry into the second order—the Symbolic. The child enters the order of pre-established structures of language and social laws over which it has no control. The axis of the Symbolic is one of desire or lack as the child becomes separated from its first love-object/mother to hold a distinct position in the wider network of established symbolic and social structures. Whereas Imaginary relations are dualistic (the subject and the (m)other), the Symbolic functions according to three fields of exchange—the subject, the other, and the Other. This "Other" is made up of the systems of signification and social inscription. For entry into the Symbolic, there is an inevitable price to be paid. No longer can the subject be defined solely by the reflection of some other. Instead, its definition is reliant upon the substitutive and displacing logic of signifying systems. So according to Lacan, it is a lack that constitutes the desire or being of the subject.

For Baudry, as with much of the French and British film theorists of the 1960s and 1970s, the medium of film best fulfills the ego's illusory quest for an image of itself as a stable and unitary subject. It does so, according to Baudry, because of its ability to reconstitute the misrecognitions of specular identity that emerge at the "mirror-stage" of subject formation. The cinema, with its arrangement of projector, darkened hall, and screen, successfully reconstructs the situation necessary for the "mirror-stage" to be released (again):

> This psychological phase, which occurs between six and eighteen months of age, generates via the mirror image of a unified body the constitution of at least the first sketches of the "I" as an imaginary function. . . . But for this imaginary constitution of the self to be possible, there must be—Lacan strongly emphasizes this point—two complementary conditions: immature powers of mobility and a precocious maturation of visual organization (apparent in the first few days of life). If one considers that these two conditions are repeated during cinematographic projection—suspension of mobility and predominance of the visual function—perhaps one could suppose that this is more than a simple analogy. And possibly this very point explains the "impression of

---

11. The splitting of the subject is said to have both reassuring and alienating effects, the latter because the ideal image is only achievable through some other person and place than its own.

reality" so often invoked in connection with the cinema. . . . In
order for this impression to be produced, it would be necessary
that the conditions of a formative scene be reproduced. This
scene would be repeated and reenacted in such a manner that the
imaginary order (activated by a specularization which takes
place, everything considered, in reality) fulfils its particular function of occultation or of filling the gap, the split, of the subject on
the order of the signifier.[12]

So, because the subject misrecognizes itself within the idealizing config-
uration of the image, the spectator imagines itself as this unified subject.

For Mulvey, however, this transcendental subject is always, in the cinema, a male subject. Because under patriarchal order the processes of
psychosexuality and identity construction are imbalanced across the
sexes, pleasure in looking is split between active/male and passive/
female. The male is the active bearer-of-the-look, while the female is the
object of the look, to the point that the image of woman is said to connote
"to-be-looked-at-ness."[13] However, because both voyeuristic scopophilia
and narcissistic scopophilia are said to be defense mechanisms against the
male subject's recognition of his own inadequacies, the image of a "castrated other"—both for the male character "in" the film and the male
who is viewing the film—will always evoke the anxiety it originally signified: castration anxiety. So, according to Mulvey, the pleasure associated with male looking can also contain a threatening component. And in
patriarchal culture, it is the image of "woman" that crystallizes the paradox: "the look, pleasurable in form, can be threatening in content."[14]

Because the formal preoccupations of the classical narrative cinema are
said to "reflect" the psychical obsessions of the society that produced it, the
possibility of the subjecthood of "woman" within the advanced representation system of the cinema (so dependent on the mobilization of the look,
both within the diegesis of the film, and that of its spectators) is nil.

[W]oman's desire is subjected to her image as bearer of the bleeding
wound, she can exist only in relation to castration and cannot tran-
scend it. . . . Woman then stands in patriarchal culture as signifier

12. Jean-Louis Baudry, "Ideological Effects of the Basic Cinematographic Apparatus,"
Narrative, Apparatus, Ideology: A Film Theory Reader, ed. Philip Rosen (New York: Columbia
University Press, 1986), 294.
13. Mulvey, "Visual Pleasure," 203.
14. Ibid., 202.

for the male other, bound by a symbolic order in which man can live out his fantasies and obsessions through linguistic command by imposing them on the silent image of woman still tied to her place as bearer of meaning, not maker of meaning.[15]

Furthermore, this structuring of the look and looking, in narrative cinema, is said to contain a contradiction in its own premise. While the male characters of the classical narrative cinema act to push the narratives forward, to maintain the flow of the narrative (taking the *male* spectators along with them), the image of "woman" constantly threatens the unity of the diegesis "and bursts through the world of illusion as an intrusive, static, one-dimensional fetish."[16] So while the spectator becomes caught up in film narrative through voyeuristic/narcissistic identification (the relation of looking and identification), the image of "woman" operates on the side of spectacle, and as such threatens the flow of the narrative by temporarily bringing it to a halt so that the image may be contemplated erotically. As object of the look, "woman" thereby not only evokes the pleasurable aspects of looking, but also the dangerous, with narrative constantly working to eradicate the threatening aspects of looking through its restoration of what can be considered the "conservative" status quo. The main assumption here is that the classical cinema is directed to a male spectator, or that the cinematic text constructs the male viewing position as the ideal vantage point from which to view the film.

Relying upon Mulvey's thesis in her own essay leads Exum to argue that the body of this filmic Bathsheba is seen through and controlled by the male gaze. In controlling representation, men produce images for the pleasure of other men. Thus, the discourse of the cinema is a phallocentric discourse, in which man is the bearer of the look and woman is the object of the look, with the very image of "woman" connoting "to-be-looked-at-ness."

While both David and Bathsheba are said to be guilty (the former, of voyeuristic desire, and the latter, exhibitionism), the viewer (male or female) is free to gaze upon the body of Bathsheba without guilt. Because the spectator is given the specific privilege, in relation to looking during Bathsheba's bathing scene, of seeing more than David can see, the spectator is not identified exactly with David and therefore escapes wearing the guilt which is his and Bathsheba's.

---

15. Ibid., 199.
16. Ibid., 209.

Furthermore, while Exum argues that a male spectator is constituted by the cinematic address, she also speculates upon the question of how a female spectator responds to such a situation (whereby the filmic text makes no space for the female point of view). For Exum it is a matter of resistance. In this particular instance, "the narrative strategy of allowing us to look guiltlessly and, if we wish, to blame the woman at the same time is the premise behind the story's representation in painting and film."[17] What is needed, according to Exum, is attention to the gendered nature of both representation and interpretation, thereby allowing for the possibility, particularly for the "female" spectator, of resisting "the phallocentric premises of the text and its visual representations."[18]

But what does Exum mean by "phallocentric premises of the text"? Like Mulvey, for Exum the cinematic gaze is said to be phallic in that it situates an ideal, masculine viewing position, with woman as the object of that gaze.

> The male viewer of the paintings and the films, like the male reader of the biblical story, is invited to take David's symbolic position as the focalizer of the gaze: he can look through David's eyes; he can fantasize himself in David's place. . . . The male spectator is invited to identify with the male protagonist and to desire the female image. The female spectator is also invited to look at the female image with the *phallic power of the gaze*, yet we are identified with that image.[19]

The film functions through its construction of stability and coherence with respect to its designation of male as "bearer-of-the-look" and female as "object-of-the-look." In the end, Susan Hayward's Bathsheba is the passive object of an all powerful, controlling male gaze, largely due to Exum's acceptance of Mulvey's assertion that the classical cinema works according to an assumed male viewer, or at least constructs such an ideal viewing position that *thoroughly* sutures the spectating subject as the subject of the film. The gaze here is that point of spectatorial identification, the point where the subject of representation comes into being, the point from which the film makes sense. For Exum, following

---

17. J. Cheryl Exum, *Plotted, Shot and Painted: Cultural Representations of Biblical Women* (Sheffield: Sheffield Academic Press, 1996), 53.

18. Ibid., 52.

19. Ibid.; emphasis added.

Mulvey, this point is "phallic" because it is a position constructed as masculine. And it is against this constructed subject position, she argues, that we must resist.

Apart from the feminist criticism directed at Mulvey's failure to account for the female spectator[20] and her subsequent postulation of the transvestitism of female spectatorship—where the female spectator identifies with the male hero,[21] feminist film theorists have mainly challenged the monolithic account of classical Hollywood film. Janet Walker argues that this monolithic view fails "to account for the spaces of female resistance that give rise, for example, to classical film texts that depart in places from the model, to radically other sorts of pleasurable filmic representations, and even to critical writing such as Mulvey's own."[22] However, the most convincing critique of not only Mulvey's theoretical position but also of the supposedly psychoanalytically informed apparatus film theories in general, before and after Mulvey, comes from Joan Copjec.

In "The Orthopsychic Subject: Film Theory and the Reception of Lacan," Copjec argues that film theories of the apparatus draw from only certain aspects of Lacan's theories concerning representation and the subject based on a metaphoric of the "mirror-stage," where the screen is equivalent to the mirror in that the images presented on the screen are accepted by the viewing subject as its own. As Copjec points out, film theory ignores Lacan's more radical insight whereby the mirror is conceived as screen, repressing other elements from his work that would problematize what she believes is an unacceptable definition of narcissism that is attributable neither to Freud nor to Lacan. She convincingly argues that "apparatus" film theory relies more on Foucault's

---

20. See Teresa De Lauretis, *Alice Doesn't: Feminism, Semiotics, Cinema* (Bloomington: Indiana University Press, 1984).

21. Laura Mulvey, "Afterthoughts on 'Visual Pleasure and Narrative Cinema' inspired by *Duel in the Sun,*" *Feminism and Film Theory*, ed. Constance Penley (New York: Routledge, 1988), 69–79.

22. Janet Walker, "Psychoanalysis and Feminist Film Theory: The Problem of Sexual Difference and Identity," *Multiple Voices in Feminist Film Criticism*, 84. See also Byars, "Feminism, Psychoanalysis," 97; Mary Ann Doane, *Femmes Fatales: Feminism, Film Theory, Psychoanalysis* (New York: Routledge, 1991), 42–43; Judith Mayne, "Feminist Film Theory and Criticism," *Multiple Voices in Feminist Film Criticism*, ed. D. Carson, L. Dittmar, and J. R. Welsch (Minneapolis: University of Minnesota Press, 1994), 54–57; Diane Waldman, "Film Theory and the Gendered Spectator: The Female or the Feminist Reader," *Camera Obscura* 18 (1988): 80; and especially Tania Modleski, *The Women Who Knew Too Much: Hitchcock and Feminist Theory* (New York: Methuen, 1988). Modleski argues that certain Hitchcock films present a highly unstable masculine viewing position, along with multiple positions of viewer/character identifications that cross gender boundaries. Exum is certainly aware of these discussions.

elaboration of the panoptic gaze than on Lacan, despite its fascination with Lacan's mirror-stage.

As outlined earlier, theorists who conceive of the cinematic apparatus as a mirror do so following Lacan's work on imaginary relations from his earlier essay, "The Mirror Stage as Formative of the Function of the I." However, the later Lacan of *The Four Fundamental Concepts of Psychoanalysis* reconceives the relationship between the subject of vision and its surrounding environment, including representations, through the metaphor of the *stain*. To reconceive this relationship, Lacan develops Roger Callois' thesis on mimicry. Callois was unconvinced by the usual argument that animals and insects adapt to their environment for self-preservation, largely due to the observation that the stomachs of predatory birds were found to contain as many insects said to be protected by mimicry as those not.[23] Rather than a manifestation of intentional will, mimicry is found to be an uncontrollable merging with the surrounding environment, a radical loss of its own being. For Lacan, this best explains the relationship between the modern subject of vision and both its own representations and its surrounding social and cultural environment. The perceiving subject is split between its own being and the mask it presents to the world for the purpose of being seen within that very world. The subject is both seer and, using Lacan's term, a "picture."[24] So the subject of the visible realm for Lacan is split between both active and passive, seer and that which is seen.

For film theorists, the model that best explains the scopic realm, and in particular the relationship between the seeing subject and its representations, has been that of geometric perspective, developed during the Renaissance (see above). However, in *Four Fundamental Concepts*, Lacan explicitly refuses to accept that geometric perspective alone explains how a subject comes to make meaning out of its visual world: "I am not simply that punctiform being located at the geometrical point from which the perspective is grasped. No doubt, in the depths of my eye, the picture is painted. The picture, certainly, is in my eye. But I am not in the picture."[25] The geometric laws of the propagation of light map space only, not vision. Lacan refers to Diderot's *Lettre sur les aveugles à l'usage de ceux qui voient* (Letter on the Blind for the Use of Those Who See), which shows that the geometrical space of vision is reconstructable

---

23. Lacan, *Four Fundamental Concepts*, 73.
24. Ibid., 106.
25. Ibid., 96.

and imaginable by a blind man.[26] So, the single triangle drawn by geo-metrical perspective (see Figure 1; this is the triangle with "The subject of representation" at its apex) cannot explain that which it claims, that is, how the subject understands, makes meaning of, what it sees. For Lacan, another triangle that intersects the first structure of the scopic field is required (Figure 1). This diagram brings the field of the signifier into play.

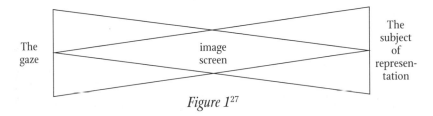

Figure 1[27]

Language and sign systems account for making meaning in the scopic realm, not optics (light):

> I must, to begin with, insist on the following: in the scopic field, the gaze is outside, I am looked at, that is to say, I am a picture. This is the function that is found at the heart of the institution of the subject in the visible. What determines me, at the most pro-found level, in the visible, is the gaze that is outside. It is through the gaze that I enter light and it is from the gaze that I receive its effects. Hence it comes about that the gaze is the instrument through which light is embodied and through which . . . *I am photo-graphed.*[28]

This may sound remarkably similar to the film theoretical (and Foucauldian) notion of the subject as the fully constructed realization of some external, organizing structure. But Copjec astutely points out that a reading of Lacan that sees in this statement a confirmation of the Foucauldian position that the gaze determines the absolute visibility of the subject within the perceptual grid fails to account for the hyphen that splits the term photo-graphed into photo (light) and graph, which she says is, among other things, a fragmentary form of the Lacanian "graph of desire." Through hyphenation, Lacan is describing the subject

---

26. Ibid., 86.
27. Ibid., 106.
28. Ibid.

of the scopic realm as a split subject.[29] What this second triangle accounts for is the interference of the signifier within the optical figuration of the emission of light. Copjec states that for Lacan, it is semiotics, not optics, that accounts for the structure of the visible domain and the positioning of the subject in relation to it.[30]

Because signifiers are material, referring to each other rather than to some preexisting signified, the subject's encounter with representation is fraught with problems. The visible field is not clear or translucent, but ambiguously and disturbingly opaque. Something is not visible.[31] It is this sense of something concealed, of a deception at work, that situates the subject of vision as a desiring subject, the subject whose desire is projected towards its representations to ask, as Copjec puts it, "what is being concealed from me? What in this graphic space does not show, does not stop *not* writing itself?"[32] For Lacan, representation (be it a painting, a film, and so forth) is then a "trap for the gaze."

The distinction between the gaze of film theory and the Lacanian gaze needs to be made. Film theory has suggested that the spectating subject, convinced of the adequacy of filmic representation as its own image (the spectator as "master" of the image), thereby thoroughly identifies first with the "gaze" of the camera (the monocularcentric vision that positions it at the geometric perspectival point), then with the image. As Copjec puts it, because the subject is convinced that it has been adequately reflected on the screen, "[t]he 'reality effect' and the 'subject effect' both name the same constructed impression: that the image makes the subject fully visible to itself."[33] This subject, who sees itself in its entirety, with nothing hidden, is of course the subject of the panoptic apparatus. In film theory, as in Foucault, the gaze is that point from which the subject is made completely visible to itself and to others through the structures of the apparatus. Although film theory states that this is a *misrecognition* by the spectating subject (as is specular identification according to Lacan), it is still a process that is said to operate without failure.

---

29. Joan Copjec, "The Orthopsychic Subject: Film Theory and the Reception of Lacan," *October* 49 (1989): 67–70.

30. Ibid., 68.

31. Lacan refers many times to Merleau-Ponty's attempt to rethink vision in terms of what remains hidden in *The Visible and the Invisible* to develop his thesis of the subject trapped within a visible field in which it can only see from one point, never able to see itself from the point from which it is seen.

32. Copjec, "The Orthopsychic Subject," 69.

33. Ibid., 59.

This is far from the Lacanian relationship between subject and representation as he later theorized it in *The Four Fundamental Concepts of Psychoanalysis*. The relationship between the "I" and the "gaze" is far more complex than the relationship posited by theorists who maintain the mirror-like relationship between the subject and representation. First, the preexistence of the gaze accounts for the fact that "I see only from one point, but in my existence I am looked at from all sides."[34] In other words, the gaze is prior to the subject, mapping the subject within the world as both that which sees and that which is seen. The subject has no control over this gaze, but is instead situated as one of its objects, one of "the seen." Furthermore, this subject within the visible cannot occupy that position from which it is seen. The gaze in Lacan is, therefore, not simply equivalent to the vision of the subject. The gaze also marks that *impossible* point from which I see myself seeing. The Lacanian gaze marks the very impossibility of the subject *ever* seeing itself entirely. Remember that in mimicry, the subject is split between its being and its external mask, the very process of which reveals the passive, objective status of the subject within the visible, an object *seen*. The subject suspects with almost paranoid suspicion that there is a difference between its "real" internal self and its external representation. So too, the effect of representation is a subject convinced it is being deceived, that beyond the material surface of representation is some thing-in-itself. That which appears to be invisible, left out of, or concealed by the field of representation is the *Lacanian* gaze, "the *absence* of a signified; it is an *unoccupiable* point, the point at which the subject disappears."[35] The effect of signification upon Lacan's modern subject (be they filmic representations, or the sociocultural environment itself) is traumatic, not reassuring, because signification, seeming to hide something, convinces the subject that it is always cut off from the "real" of its being (known in Lacan as the barred subject). The subject is situated within the scopic realm as external to itself. The gaze, then, is something that is both a part of the subject (as subject, able to see and make meaning) and something removed from the subject (the subject unable to see itself entirely). This is why Lacan refers to the gaze as *objet petit a*, the object that, because it is forever lost, prevents the subject from ever encountering itself as "real." Thus the subject of representation is an alienated subject, cut off from itself by the external and a priori status of the gaze:

---

34. Lacan, *Four Fundamental Concepts*, 72.
35. Copjec, "The Orthopsychic Subject," 69.

> [T]he interest the subject takes in his own split is bound up with that which determines it—namely, a privileged object, which has emerged from some primal separation, from some self-mutilation induced by the very approach of the real, whose name, in our algebra, is the *objet a*. In the scopic relation, the object on which depends the phantasy from which the subject is suspended in an essential vacillation is the gaze.[36]

While Lacan insists that beneath the material veil of signifiers there is nothing at all, this does not mean that the subject can easily dismiss this through some conscious awareness of the illusory nature of representation. This very opacity of signifiers *founds* the subject. For Lacan, the subject is constituted by lack, by the very impossibility of ever encountering itself as "real." The opacity of signifiers, the very failure of language to "reveal all," is the *cause* of the subject's being, its desire. According to Copjec's reading of Lacan, "[t]he subject is the effect of the impossibility of seeing what is lacking in the representation, what the subject, therefore, wants to see. Desire, in other words, the desire of representation, institutes the subject in the visible field."[37] And as Lacan himself puts it, "if I am anything in the picture, it is always in the form of the screen, which I earlier called the stain, the spot."[38]

One of the main agendas in Copjec's essay is to show exactly how different are film theory's and Lacan's conceptions of the gaze. The subject of representation, as film theory would have it, identifies with the gaze and finds itself positioned as the very source of meaning. The subject is satisfied that it has seen itself as the idealized, fully stable subject, master of all it sees. Representational systems, like all sociocultural systems, thereby construct the subject fully and adequately. The subject is thus the realization of language, of the law. For Lacan, however, the gaze marks the very failure of language to ensure the meeting of reality and representation. As such, representation appears to conceal the real, and it is through identifying with the gaze, with the absence of meaning within the field of signification, that the subject comes about. The subject is thus the effect of the law and not its realization.

This then leads Copjec to point out the difference between the Lacanian notion of narcissism and that of film theory. Film theory

---

36. Lacan, *Four Fundamental Concepts*, 83.
37. Copjec, "The Orthopsychic Subject," 70.
38. Lacan, *Four Fundamental Concepts*, 97.

argues that the harmonious integration of the spectating subject through successful processes of identification is narcissistic. The subject perceives itself within signifying systems to be fully and adequately represented, and is *satisfied*. This account relies upon a definition of narcissism that sees the subject fall in love with the image before it as its ideal image. The relationship between the subject and the social is therefore harmonious in this account. Yet, in psychoanalysis, narcissism has an *unbinding* effect. The narcissistic relation between subject and self is *disruptive* of other social relations. This is a long way from the subject in complete harmony with social representations, as film theory has long maintained.

According to Lacan it is not that the image before the subject satisfies its need for an ideal image of itself. In fact, the image fails, *necessarily*, to convince the subject that it is that unified, specular totality. Rather, narcissism is the belief that one's being, which representation fails to register, must be more than the image presented. What is loved in the self image is that which exceeds the image. This means that the subject is far from harmonizing with its environment, far from seeing itself *fully* within the idealizing configurations of representation. Instead, as both the subject and object of seeing, a subject split between its being and its external mask, the subject is inscribed within all representational forms as a stain, as the failure of signification.

And so for Copjec, the more radical insight from Lacan (whereby the mirror is a screen) offers a more comprehensive theorization of the subject of vision and as such should be taken up by film theorists. It is the

> suspicion of deception that must necessarily be raised if we are to understand the cinematic apparatus as a *signifying* apparatus, which places the subject in an external relationship to itself. Once the permanent possibility of deception is admitted (rather than disregarded, as it is by the theory of the panoptic apparatus), the concept of the gaze undergoes a radical change. For, where in the panoptic apparatus the gaze marks the subject's *visibility*, in Lacan's theory it marks the subject's *culpability*. The gaze stands watch over the *inculpation*—the faulting and splitting—of the subject by the apparatus.[39]

While for Exum it is only Bathsheba who is both image and bearer of the look, if we begin to examine the film with the Lacanian split subject

---

39. Copjec, "The Orthopsychic Subject," 65.

in mind, the complexities of David's subjectivity begin to surface. David is split between his symbolic mandate as king and what he believes to be the "real" David, David the man. David is both the subject who sees, a subject of language who reflects upon his own inner being, and a subject seen and judged. The all-controlling gaze is in this film—as in the biblical texts—the gaze of a God who sees beyond the signifying surface into the heart and mind. More than once in his seminars on the gaze, Lacan turns to discuss the God of the Hebrew Bible, a God who makes humans in his own image yet refuses images of himself to be made. The biblical texts are seen to manifest the fundamentally alienating effects of a gaze beyond signification, a gaze that is at the same time the very cause of the symbolic status of the people.

II

David and Bathsheba shows repeated concern for the discomfort and self-doubt felt by David towards his role as king of Israel. The film presents a male protagonist who is disillusioned not only with kingship but also with his own ability to fulfill such a role. The familiarity of his royal surrounding is lost, and the male subject is in crisis. This crisis is elaborated as that discrepancy between David the "man" and David the "king."

Throughout the film, much narrative space is given to the expression of doubt, by David and other characters, concerning David's kingship. In the first scene of the film, we hear how David has gone along with Uriah into battle. This is a transgressive act by David, prompting Joab to state, with exacerbation, "King, king of all Israel out there in the darkness exposing himself to the enemy. Crawling on his belly like a common soldier."[40] David is not acting like a king should. On his return from the battle, in a tent on the outskirts of the city of Rabbah, David remarks that the days of his warriorhood are over, ending when he became king. In these first two scenes kingship is clearly, in David's eyes, a far less heroic station than that of warrior. Mockery of kingship is the focus of the following scene. In his throne room, King David receives a visitor from Egypt who brings greetings from the Pharaoh. David delivers his sarcastic reply in a manner that manifests his boredom and disillusionment with the role of king, saying (quickly and mechanistically), "The king of Israel warms himself in the sun of the Pharaoh's regard."

---

40. All quotations from the film are the author's own transcription.

Having been given the gift of a jeweled knife, David whispers to his loyal attendant Abashai, "My cousin (the Pharaoh) probably hopes that I will cut my throat with this." David not only mocks his own role as king, he alludes to the fraudulent nature of the role of autocrat in general.

Having dealt with these public matters and left his throne, David is confronted by his two sons, Amnon and Absalom, who are quarrelling over the ownership rights of a vineyard. David, having promised all of the vineyards of a particular region to Amnon, has given the largest of these to Absalom. Both demand justice. Here the roles of father and king have come into conflict. As a father, David has favored Absalom, but as a king, he must ensure that the vineyard goes to the heir to the throne— Amnon. With both children demanding justice, David realizes, "[N]o matter how I decide, I am unjust." He must, however give the vineyard to Amnon, because, as he tells Absalom, "had it become known that I had favored you, it would weaken him (Amnon) in the eyes of the people. . . . With our people the law is everything." These two archetypes of male law (king and father), rather than sitting comfortably in the figure of one man, are the source of discord. Because "the law is everything," and hierarchically the king is the ultimate guarantee of law—in some sense above the father—David reluctantly follows the rules that make and keep him king.

The fraudulent nature of kingship that this narrative seeks to express is brought to a head in the following scene between David and his wife, Michal. When Michal sarcastically remarks, "How graciously you give your royal approval," David responds, "Your sarcasm is wasted. We both know that royalty is a fraud." After Michal suggests that it was no fraud when her father was king, David agrees with her by saying that Saul was "every inch a king." In response to Michal's quick reply—"And his successor every inch a fraud"—David can only agree with her. So while David alludes to the masquerade of symbolic status, he does suggest that there are some who genuinely fit the role. David's problem is that he fails to see himself in such a way.

All of this occurs before David's sighting of Bathsheba. After David has sent for her, the two are dining together in his room. Having realized their desire for each other is mutual, David tells her: "I am only a man, Bathsheba. I need someone to understand that." Believing that her expectations would be high, considering that he is the king, David warns Bathsheba of his weakness—he is *only* a man. In the following scene, the lovers are relaxing in an idyllic pastoral setting. In a conversation with the old shepherd, it is revealed that the old man, who is maimed, fought a battle for the king. When David inquires if it was for David that he fought, the shepherd sharply replies, "Not him! The king, King Saul." Furthermore, when David queries the shepherd over his remorse that with both Saul and Jonathan dead there was no one fit to take the place of the king, telling the shepherd that Israel put David on the throne, the shepherd loses his temper saying, "Saul was king and Jonathan should be king today."

On the enunciative level, much is made of David's lack of success, indeed authenticity, as king. While other characters (Michal, Joab, Nathan, the old shepherd, Absalom) also question David's ability to be king, David himself no longer believes in his capability. Indeed, this 1950s Hollywood fascination with the "man" David, that is, the man "inside" the king (or as Slavoj Žižek puts it, the "positive person of the Master"), reveals the gap between the actual person who is king and the place of power he occupies. As Žižek points out, the visibility of this gap is possible only because of what Claude Lefort has called the "democratic invention."[41] The traditional master's authority is granted according to some transcendent reason (the king, for instance, being the anointed of God), and as such, all those who occupy the position are entitled to do so because of some divine decree. With the "democratic invention," the locus of power is now an empty place. The person who occupies the place of power within a democracy does so because "the people" as such say that it is so. As Žižek states, "what then becomes visible with 'democratic invention' is the gap that separates the positive person of the Master from the place he occupies in the symbolic network—with 'democratic invention,' the place of Power is posited as originally *empty*, occupied only temporarily and in a contingent way by different subjects."[42]

It is possible, then, to see the inherent tensions in *David and Bathsheba* as deriving from the forced encounter of an ancient narrative that contains an understanding of leadership as "God-given" and a modern, democratic understanding of leadership as "people-given." In other words, David has to justify his mandate in terms *beyond* God. And yet, as a filmic version of a text that is deemed fundamental to the American notion of the sacred, the integrity of the biblical text must be maintained. David must be "the anointed of God" *and* he who is

---

41. Slavoj Žižek, *The Ticklish Subject: The Absent Centre of Political Ontology* (London: Verso, 1999), 192.
42. Ibid.

deemed worthy according to public opinion. According to Lefort, where under a traditional, pre-democratic mode of leadership there is no gap between the man and the symbolic position he inhabits (there is something *in* the king that specifically makes him ruler; a divine addition to the man that makes him more than a man and therefore not a man at all), under democracy there can and must be cause to doubt. The leader is a human being subject to the scrutiny of others.

So in the film we are presented with a King David who is caught in the process of both self-surveillance and the surveillance of others. In both cases there is the suspicion that there is something exceeding "the king," something not fully represented by the mandate. Here, of course, it is the suspicion that this excessive feature, not contained within symbolic representation, is an inadequacy or lack. David must come to realize, however, that he is given the symbolic mandate through the anointing, the transference of some divine "thing." Throughout most of the film he struggles against the burden of the mandate. This struggle can be read as more than just David's loss of the merciful and kind God of his youth, as the film with all its Christian overtones wants to stress. David is questioning the reason for his mandate, searching for answers beyond the mandate, asking if there is something essential to David that can account for God's choice. The question that perfectly describes David's problem is: "Why am I what I am?" The conclusion of *David and Bathsheba* sees David return to the original moment of his anointing through a dream/memory sequence. In the end, David must confront the cause of his symbolic designation to find that that excessive feature is in fact a divine addition that has nothing to do with the "real" David whatsoever: he is the anointed of God, destined to be king. As such, he owes a debt to God. David must surrender his "being," surrender any pretense to the "essence" of David, to be fully interpellated as "king."

Žižek points out this "question to the Other," from the subject who does not know why he or she is situated in this specific symbolic position, is the question of the hysteric.[43] But this question to the Other is itself the hysterical answer (the only answer) to a prior question: "*Che vuoi?*" "What does the Other want from me?" The subject is given a place within the intersubjective network of symbolic relations precisely by being tied to a signifier (the Lacanian definition of the signifier being what "represents the subject for another signifier"). But because this

---

43. Slavoj Žižek, *The Sublime Object of Ideology* (London: Verso, 1989), 113.

mandate is always arbitrary, having nothing to do with the "real" qualities of the subject, the subject can never know why he or she inhabits
that place. This second question to the Other is the articulation of a
failed interpellation, a failure of the subject to assume the symbolic
mandate without questioning the reason why he or she is there. Lacan
puts the failure this way: "Why am I what you're telling me that I am?—
that is, which is that surplus-object in me that caused the Other to inter-
pellate me, to 'hail' me as . . . (king, master, wife . . .)?"[44]

For Žižek, this terrifying, unknowable desire of the Other is exemplified by the Jewish God, the God who forbids any image of himself that
would allow the Israelites to construct a fantasy that would "fill out" the
empty void. He states:

> [B]efore the pact with God they were a people like any other, no
> more and no less corrupted, living their ordinary life—when sud-
> denly like a traumatic flash, they came to know (through Moses . . .)
> that the Other had chosen them. The choice was thus not at the
> beginning, it did not determine the "original character" of the
> Jews. . . . Why were they chosen, why did they suddenly find them-
> selves occupying the position of a debtor towards God? What
> does God really want from them? The answer is—to repeat the
> paradoxical formula of the prohibition against incest—impossi-
> ble and prohibited at the same time.[45]

Returning to the gaze, the Israelites come to be "God's chosen" only
because of the a priori gaze of a God who sees all. From then on, they are
faced with the traumatic understanding that God sees them and chooses
them (and as such carves out a place for them in the symbolic), but
refuses to give them an answer as to why he chose them. The Law then
functions as an attempt to know the impossible, to know what the Other
wants from them. In the film, David states: "With our people the Law is
everything. It is in their bones." This "thing" that is "in the subject more
than the subject" is only installed as an effect of the event. In other
words, while the reason for the original call of God is unknowable, the
Law is an attempt to fill in the gap, to account for the Israelites as "God's
chosen," and to alleviate the alienating effects of a God that refuses to

---

44. In ibid.
45. Ibid.

answer. This is precisely how the filmic drama is resolved. In the same way that the Law is "in the bones" of the Israelites, David must come to realize that God will never give him an answer as to why he is king, because there is no answer other than that this frustrating Other has chosen him. To alleviate the unbearable nature of this faceless God, David returns to the moment of his anointing, the moment that David can rationalize God's irrational choice with a fantasy of divine addition to his person. It is this and this alone that makes everyone call him "king." Before God's call and God's gaze upon his heart, there can be no articulation of a feature of David that accounts for God's choice. Like the Law, the anointing is an effect of the call. Interestingly it is Bathsheba who tells David that his "life is marked out on a certain course. Even [he] cannot change it. It is God's design." David can only submit to a destiny over which he has no control.

For most of the film, though, David is stuck on this question, "What is it that makes me that which You say that I am, king of Israel?" In seeking to answer the question, David can only see his own pathetic failure. Indeed, his impotence. Cheryl Exum argues that David (and therefore the spectator who identifies with this male gaze) is that stable and unified subject able to master all that he sees, including Bathsheba. I now want to look at the scopic relations in *David and Bathsheba* in light of the film's narrative attempts to alleviate the alienating effects of the Israelites' relationship with their God. In other words, to understand the logic of looking in this film, the analysis must address the impossible gaze of God. In doing so, it becomes clear that Bathsheba is more than an object for the male gaze. Her own gaze comes to function in the service of the male subject split by this "evil eye" of God, as a means for David to avoid the debt that must be paid. The most stunning staging of this split subject occurs in what I will call from now on the "crisis" scene. This is the scene on Mount Gilboa where David remembers the death of Jonathan.

III

Following the scene where David and Bathsheba are relaxing in the pastoral area surrounding Mount Gilboa is a lengthy scene that has David facing the ghosts of his past. In this scene, David is traumatized by the memory of the death of Jonathan. Having left Bathsheba to sleep (although the spectator is aware that she is awake and has risen to follow him), David ventures out into the evening and sees Mount Gilboa in the near distance. The camera follows David as he ascends to the top of the mountain, to the site of the bloody battle where Jonathan was killed. Accompanied by a rather foreboding musical score, David comes across some of the remnants of that war—first, an old ruin of what was once a chariot; second, a dagger with its blade broken in half.

At the top of the mountain, the camera at first holds David in a medium close-up. The camera zooms in as David bends down to pick up the dagger, tilts down to focus on the dagger in David's hand and then up to David's face, in close-up, as he looks down upon it. David raises first his eyes, then his head, to look off to the right of the camera. The screen darkens so no light appears on David's face. As this occurs, the sounds of battle begin with a trumpet fanfare, horses, and the screams of men. The scene is set for David's remembering to take place.

David's face is in extreme close-up and it fills the screen in darkness, with a bright light appearing in his right eye resembling the projector's light in a cinema. This same eye, however, also takes on the qualities of the cinematic screen as the lights begin to flicker, suggesting the movement of the figures of war whose screams are heard. This shot lasts for forty-four seconds, the longest still shot in the film, and ends, following a scream on the soundtrack, with David's own passionate crying out, "Jonathan!" A quick zoom out to a medium close-up shot precedes David's second cry of "Jonathan!" at which time he raises the broken dagger in his hand above his head as if he himself were taking part in a battle at that time. But he is not. His traumatic remembering becomes "real" enough to convince him that he is participating in the battle and that he can intervene to prevent the death of Jonathan.

With a sharp ending of the battle soundtrack, David is brought back to "reality." He lowers the dagger and looks suddenly off to his left, his attention caught by a bright light that has appeared. As he sits down, the camera again zooms in to his face. It then cuts to Bathsheba standing nearby. David, however, is unaware of her presence and unaware of her gaze. While the camera is on Bathsheba, David (out of frame) can be heard saying, "How are the mighty fallen, in the midst of the battle." The camera then cuts back to David in medium close-up with Bathsheba in the background; she is looking at David as he studies the broken dagger. David begins to speak. As he does so, he moves off to the right of the screen space, saying, "Oh Jonathan, thou wast slain in thine high places." David has moved out of frame, leaving only Bathsheba in the background, reminding the viewer of the importance of her witness to this scene. The next shot is again of David as he continues to speak—"I am distressed for thee my brother, Jonathan. Very pleasant has thou been unto me. Thy love to me was wonderful, passing the love of women." He then looks down to the dagger, saying, "How are the mighty fallen, and the weapons of war perished." He throws down the dagger and the scene ends.

The first feature of this scene that interests me is the rendering of David's memory in a way that recalls the cinematic machinery. The trauma of war, experienced through David's remembering, is registered through the visual representation of David as the site of the conflation of the cinematic machinery with the spectator himself. The light that shines from his right eye bears a remarkable resemblance to the projector's light at the rear of a cinematic theatre. This same eye, however, takes on the qualities of the cinematic screen, with the flickering movements of the light suggesting the movement of figures on a screen. The use of such allusions to the cinematic apparatus imply a visual rendering of memory, and this conflation ensures that David, as a spectator of his own memory, is seeing and experiencing what his camera/eye allows him to see and experience. The mechanisms of the cinematic apparatus are depicted as having collapsed onto the form of David, the effect of which is the inclusion of David into the world of his memory (just as in classical film theory, where the cinematic spectator is said to enter the world of the film as its subject). David's remembering becomes so "real" that he is caught up in the illusion of that reality. The memory/image of the war (which only he can see) convinces David, both psychologically and physically, that he is a participant in that very "reality."

In this scene of the staging of memory, David is effectively depicted as the spectator of cinema as theorized by classical film theory. What he sees is a war, with the death of Jonathan unfolding before his (and only his) very eye. As such, he represents the "ideal" spectator of the type of film we, the spectators of *David and Bathsheba*, are ourselves watching. Except in this film-within-a-film, like Bathsheba we are unable to see what David sees.

On the other hand, despite the depiction of David as the "successful" spectator, within the narrative structure of the film itself this same male subject is marked by his failure to identify with his symbolic position of power. In this scene, the obvious symbol of failure is the broken dagger that David clutches as his vivid recollection takes place. The meaning of the broken dagger and its relationship to symbolic impotence becomes clearer when contrasted with the use of a dagger and spear as signifiers of male adequacy earlier in the film.

A dagger was given to David by the Pharaoh of Egypt. David discards it, seeing it as a potential threat to his life. He gives it to Absalom, who carries it in every scene in which he appears for the rest of the film. It is Absalom who believes that he should be the next king, as do the people of Israel. The dagger (in its complete, "uncastrated" form) is aligned with the character "the people" believe is an adequate king. Likewise, the spear of Saul (the only king the old shepherd would acknowledge), hanging on David's wall, serves the same purpose. Michal even taunts David with it, saying, "Do you think that hanging his spear on your wall will make you royal?" David, however, can only be associated with the incomplete, "castrated" weapon. He refuses these prosthetic artifices, symbols of complete symbolic identity and power. His impotence is dramatized in the "crisis" scene when he raises the useless weapon as if in battle. On the one hand, David is "master" of all he (and he alone) sees. He misrecognizes himself in the fantasy/memory scene before him as a subject participating within the unfolding drama. He is that transcendental subject, he who sees and understands all, he who is the very source of meaning within his visual field. But he actually (in diegetic time and space) is in no danger. Nor can he have any effect. The power of his gaze here is no power at all. The spectators and Bathsheba witness this impotence of his gaze.

Why does this imaginary identification with his own fantasy/memory text rendered in scopic terms, where David can situate himself at that point of coherence and see himself as "warrior," take place and then fail to sustain itself? And what is the function of this light toward which David turns and then ignores? To answer these questions I first need to broach the relation between imaginary and symbolic identification.

According to Žižek, imaginary identification is identification with that image in which we appear likeable to ourselves, the image representing "what we would like to be." The feature with which we identify does not have to be a positive or powerful feature. It can be identification with weakness or failure. Symbolic identification is identification with the place from which we are observed. It is that point *"from where* we look at ourselves so that we appear to ourselves likeable, worthy of love."* In the former, the subject, as subject of the look, confronts the image, while in the latter, the subject places itself within the visual realm as an image looked at. The two are not, however, mutually exclusive, because "imaginary identification is always identification *on behalf of a certain gaze.*" The question that needs to be asked of the subject playing a role is, *"for whom* is the subject enacting this role"?[46]

---

46. Ibid., 105–6.

If in this scene David can stage an imaginary relationship of coherence with his image and then fail, it is necessary to ask, "for whom is David staging this?" Or, in Žižek's terms, in returning to this traumatic moment, in repeating the encounter with what is deemed an unpresentable (not visualized for the spectator) horror, for what gaze does he humiliate himself, does he reveal his impotence? Who is it that appears in that position from which David can enjoy himself in the very process of impotence? The answer, of course, is Bathsheba. David insists on calling Bathsheba "Beloved," the meaning of the Hebrew word/name for David. Michal charges David with self-love when she says "David, meaning beloved. David the beloved of David." Bathsheba is then David, the beloved of David. But to get to this positioning of Bathsheba in the place David identifies to sustain his enjoyment, I need to look at how the narrative and specular constructions work to bring it about.

It is necessary to remember that when David is dining with Bathsheba a few scenes earlier, we are told that Bathsheba knew that David would see her bathing. She says to him, "Before you went away, I used to watch you every evening as you walked on your terrace. Always at the same hour, always alone. Today I heard you had returned." Immediately David realizes that *he* has been seen. The very act of seeing Bathsheba as she bathes is preempted and made possible only by a gaze outside of himself. Remember that for Lacan, this a priori gaze that institutes the subject within the visible, that founds the subject, is also that which marks the failure of a subject's representations, its mask for the world, to be united with the "real" of its being, forever and necessarily lost. The gaze institutes the "death" of the subject's "being" or, using Lacan's phrase, the "original murder of the thing."[47] Indeed, this is David's problem. Unsatisfied with David the king, suspecting there is more to him than meets the eye (with all of this registering as inadequacy), David cannot assume his symbolic position. The disconcerting and alienating effect of the a priori gaze, an unoccupiable position (that position of the terrifying God who sees all), is sought to be mollified by positing an actual, visible subject—Bathsheba. Bathsheba tells David: "The man I watched from my window was not the king, but a man whose heart is well worth the sharing." Bathsheba becomes, then, that subjective position from which David can masochistically enjoy[48] his

47. Jacques Lacan, *The Seminar of Jacques Lacan: Book I: Freud's Papers on Technique*, ed. Jacques-Alain Miller, trans. John Forrester (Cambridge: Cambridge University Press, 1988), 174.

48. For Lacan (ibid., 172–74) the masochistic outcome is located at the juncture between the Imaginary and the Symbolic. Thanks to Scott Stephens for directing my attention to this.

own failure through blotting out, or rather delaying, the alienating "gaze" of a God who demands his debt be paid. Even toward the end of the film, when David hesitatingly moves to arm himself with Saul's spear to protect Bathsheba from the hordes who want her dead, Bathsheba cries "No, David!" and hands him the harp instead.

It is no surprise then that Bathsheba should make her appearance in the crisis scene at precisely the moment that David can no longer sustain his imaginary image of himself as virile warrior, about to step in to save Jonathan. Bathsheba watches as David clutches the dagger in the aftermath of a hysterical, impotent outburst. This lack, that Bathsheba is prepared to valorize or see as a positive feature of David's identity beyond that of the king, serves a rather obvious agenda. Bathsheba verifies for David that he is *not* only a man, but that he *is* a man, with all his failings and for her/him that is more than enough. Rather than reading Bathsheba's scopic control as a progressive or perhaps proto-feminist feature of the film, it can be seen that "woman" is actually asked to step in to give coherence to the broken male by ameliorating the alienating effects of the unseen gaze, by allowing him instead to enjoy his failure rather than to assume fully the mandate at the cost of his "being." Curiously, however, what Bathsheba is witnessing is the inevitable "death" to come.

Given that *David and Bathsheba* was made six years after World War II, when America was still in a stage of recovery, it is possible to read this appropriation of a female gaze for the benefits of male subjectivity as an attempt to deal with a traumatic feature—beyond the horrors of the recent war itself—that postwar American masculinity had to deal with: the mobilization of a female workforce.[49] David Gunn makes this point in his analysis of the film. However, he prefers to see in the ambiguities of the film, particularly in Bathsheba's bathing scene, signs of the tensions arising out of the emergence of the female subject and the anxiety of men on the brink of the collapse of their subjective status.[50] Bathsheba's cheeky looks toward the camera/viewer are read as possible signs of an emergence of woman as desiring subject. However, with Lacan's theory of the relationship between the subject of vision and representation, it becomes apparent that in the bathing scene, like in the "crisis" scene, Bathsheba serves to abate the alienating effects of the gaze on the male subject. In the end, Bathsheba's crime, her adulterous desire

---

49. Kaja Silverman, *Male Subjectivity at the Margins* (New York: Routledge, 1992), 64.
50. Gunn, "Bathsheba Goes Bathing," 96–97.

for David, means little next to her willingness to believe in David the man with all his shortcomings, beyond his symbolic measure, and give positive form to that symbolic position of scopic enjoyment that David needs to sustain his *impotence* in the face of the debt to be paid. The question now to be asked is: Why is David guilt-ridden?

The "crisis" scene and the penultimate scene that has David rendered unconscious by touching the ark of the covenant and then "dreaming" of his youth need to be read together to answer this question. First, both depict David's memory in scopic terms. The former has David "see" his memory in cinematic form, while the latter is "dreamed"—this time it is visualized for the spectator. Given the scopic coherence of these two memory scenes, what purpose do they serve within the larger narrative framework? On the surface, the two scenes seem to contradict each another. In narrative terms, the "crisis" scene demonstrates the guilt felt by David because of Jonathan's death, a memory that suggests the cause of David's psychological dilemma. The dream sequence, on the other hand, brings the film to its conclusion by pushing "loss of faith" as the cause. David need only re-find his faith in the gentle and merciful God of his youth to quiet the deity's anger (a contradiction in itself). In such a reading, the "crisis" scene becomes superfluous to the narrative, a mark of narrative excess or indulgent editing on the part of the director, given the repeated references throughout the film to the loss of faith in the God of David's youth. Returning to Lacanian theory, however, it can be seen that on the contrary, the two scenes are crucially related.

The dream has David see himself as the young shepherd boy anointed by Samuel and then as the fearless boy who defeats Goliath. David is the young warrior, not yet king, but already God's chosen. Jonathan appears in the dream as his friend, prepared to give his own life to save David's. This small feature connects with the "crisis" scene, but the connection is still weak. Furthermore, the dream itself appears somewhat extraneous. By approaching the ark and thereby entertaining the possibility of death, the same fate of the ark bearer much earlier in the film, David seems to convince God that he is willing to trust him entirely on the matter, that his faith has returned. Why then the need for the dream sequence? Surely, after David's long, passionate prayer to God immediately before his potentially suicidal act, the survival of David could easily be granted without the dream sequence. God has simply believed through the prayer itself that David's faith has been restored.

David must face in the dream that original moment, that primary traumatic encounter with the God who has seen into his heart and has called him. To delve into the biblical text briefly, while in 1 Samuel 16:12, immediately prior to the anointing, it is stated that David "was ruddy, and had beautiful eyes, and was handsome," it is the narrator's gaze, not God's, that is present here. In his essay "David is a Thing," a reading of the David narratives that introduces Žižek's argument that "The King is a Thing," Roland Boer seems to confuse the two gazes.[51] While he acknowledges that it is the narrator who is drooling, the immediate anointing that follows is read as Yahweh's identification with this mortal gaze. This contradicts the earlier assertion that God looks on the heart. But could it not be that Yahweh is anointing because it is he who can see *beyond* this appearance, beyond the gaze of man, which cannot go beneath the surface, the difference between the gaze of man and the gaze of God already stated in 1 Samuel 16:7? Given the attempts in the filmic presentation to avoid the gaze of God, it is now possible to read this narrational comment as an attempt to sidestep the gaze of God, knowable only through its traumatic effects, and to pathetically (hysterically?) assert the only signifiable gaze—the gaze of man. Returning to the film, what is "discovered" there in his dream is the apparent source of his guilt. In being the anointed of God, David is responsible for the symbolic death of Jonathan, who can now never take up his position as king of Israel.

Earlier the old shepherd tells David that "Saul was king and Jonathan should be king today." If David were to assume his symbolic mandate, without questioning what it is about his character that made God choose him, then God becomes responsible for the displacement of Jonathan within the Symbolic. It is a petulant God indeed who chooses based on a gaze he is unwilling to show, ensuring "his people" are forever anxious about their status. By asking the question, David bears the burden of the guilt that is impossibly God's. The "crisis" scene quite logically follows. David repeats the traumatic encounter by re-narrativizing it in a way that avoids the fundamental trauma itself. Instead of facing the terrifying call of this God, David convinces himself that he is responsible for Jonathan's actual death—that it is the cause of his guilt. David wants to believe that war, not God, is the source of his trauma. Again, in doing so David removes the guilt from God.

---

51. Roland Boer, "David is a Thing," *The Labour of Reading: Desire, Alienation, and Biblical Interpretation*, ed. Fiona C. Black, Roland Boer, and Erin Runions (Atlanta, Ga.: Society of Biblical Literature, 1999), 172. See Slavoj Žižek, *For They Know Not What They Do: Enjoyment as a Political Factor* (London: Verso, 1991).

However, a feature of the "crisis" scene resists interpretation. What can be made of the light that appears just as David's (cinematic) memory ceases and his impotence is enacted? This is the light that appears suddenly and towards which David turns. He looks at it quizzically and sits down. Bathsheba then makes her appearance in the background, followed by David's monologue of shame: "Oh Jonathan, thou wast slain in thine high places. I am distressed for thee my brother, Jonathan. Very pleasant hast thou been unto me. Thy love to me was wonderful, passing the love of women. How are the mighty fallen, and the weapons of war perished." Following his failed attempt at intervention into the scene of Jonathan's death, David expresses his sense of personal guilt at being unable to thwart the death of the one who loved him. This light appears without narrative function except to signify, like the abrupt explosion of Jonathan's name from David's mouth, the failure of signification (the cinematic image with only David as a spectator) to fully integrate its spectator into its world through imaginary identification.

Returning to Lacan, the light may be read as the mark of the gaze within the scopic field, a gaze that renders the subject gazing as also a subject gazed upon, itself a picture to be looked at. If we read this scene as a self-reflexive comment upon the relationship between the spectator, the apparatus, and the gaze, then we can make sense of the guilt that is David's (and analogously our own as spectators). Believing that there is more to "David" than his symbolic mandate can offer (that representation necessarily fails because it cannot include the "being" of the subject), constantly questioning the Other as to why he is king, he is caught in the scopic field as an object looked at or, as Lacan would have it, a picture. As such, like representation, there is something concealed by his externality; there is a deception at work. Lacan states explicitly, in a discussion of Sartre's voyeur who feels himself "caught in the act" simply by hearing the sound of rustling leaves behind him, that we do not apprehend the gaze originally in the relation of subject to subject. It is not a seen gaze (the sighting of someone watching) but a gaze imagined by the subject in the field of the Other. "Is it not clear," he states, "that the gaze intervenes here only in as much as it is not the annihilating subject, correlative of the world of objectivity, who feels himself surprised, but the subject sustaining himself in the function of desire?"[52] The subject searches representation for its mysterious "truth," believing itself to

---

52. Lacan, *Four Fundamental Concepts*, 85.

be deceived by representation, all the while being something that represents for all others, something deceiving. And according to the biblical logic of this film and of the Hebrew Bible, the name of this gaze that splits the subject, that renders it both a subject and an object (in the case of both the individual and the nation), is God. But it is the final scene that provides the key to David's guilt.

When the boy David fights Goliath, he is struck in the side by a spear. After he has finally hit Goliath in the forehead with a rock from his sling, David puts his fingers in his side only to find blood. Of course, the Christlike reference here cannot be avoided (although here on the right side, not the left). Nathan has told David that it is "through faith alone" that David can appease God. So David approaches the ark, sitting before it in prayer. In this prayer David procures the gaze of God, saying: "Look not on the sinner who comes before thee, but on the boy that was, who loved thee and who would have died for thee. Make my heart as his. Let the boy live again in his innocence. Grant him thy mercy and *take this David's life*." He offers his "life," instead taking on the innocence of the boy who questioned nothing of God, the innocent subject successfully interpellated. But this is not the *heroic* sacrifice that the film wants to suggest. This Christian "sacrifice" is here, as Žižek puts it,[53] an attempt to "gentrify" the enigma of the Other's desire (the "what does God want from me?"). The reference to love in the final prayer is important. Again, following Žižek on Lacan, "love" and "sacrifice" are attempts to fill in the gap in the Other, in the desire of the Other, by offering ourselves to the Other as the object of its desire. In this sense, the sacrificing subject fills in the gap, alleviating the traumatic enigma, the empty space that is the desire of God. For Lacan, love is an interpretation of the desire of the Other and a fundamental deception. Žižek states:

> [T]he answer of love is "I am what is lacking in you; with my devotion to you, with my sacrifice for you, I will fill you out, I will complete you." The operation of love is therefore double: the subject fills in his own lack by offering himself to the other as the object filling out the lack in the Other—love's deception is that this overlapping of two lacks annuls lack as such in mutual completion.[54]

---

53. Žižek, *The Sublime Object*, 116.
54. Ibid.

So what appears to be a contradictory conclusion (David happily takes his place as king—despite the constant struggle with that very position throughout the film—and he gets to keep Bathsheba) is actually the Christian answer to the Jewish anxiety around the traumatic effects of their unknowable God. The final sentence, uttered by Nathan, is a testimony to this: "No man can ever hope to know the real nature of God. But he has given us a glimpse of his face." Again, the reference to the face of God cannot conceal that it is this aspect of God—he who sees us but refuses to show his face and chooses us but refuses to say why—that is traumatic and that needs to be alleviated. The Christian answer is love and sacrifice. So ultimately, David's sacrifice is nothing more than the debt that must be paid. David, in submitting to his destiny, gives up on his desire. Incidentally, this "giving ground to one's desire" is the only guilt acknowledged by Lacan, the only thing for which one can be guilty.[55]

In the film God is both that which determines the subject through the call and through the gaze and that which terrifies the subject. Only for most of the film, David refuses to give up on his desire, insisting on asking the question of the hysteric, "Why am I what you say that I am?" and in the process taking on the guilt that is God's: the symbolic death of Jonathan. Bathsheba is situated to alleviate the traumatic gaze of God, delaying as such the payment of the debt. She is not strictly analogous to the gaze (rendered by the light in the "crisis" scene), but takes on its primary feature: she renders David an object within the visible field. She does not, however, fault David as does God. She is at the position from which David can sustain himself as a subject of desire, a subject asking questions of his symbolic mandate. Finally, David pays the debt that all along he (and Bathsheba) knows must be paid. Before this he has staged the masochistic enjoyment, through identifying with the gaze of Bathsheba, of his impotent attempts to avoid the inevitable payment demanded by the terrifying Other. He is simply and mind-shatteringly God's chosen; there is nothing he can do about it. This is why in the end Bathsheba may live—she no longer provides David with any enjoyment whatsoever. Lost forever, he is now with God. A more Christian ending to this Jewish dilemma could not have been written. Except, of course, by "Jesus" himself.

---

55. Jacques Lacan, *The Ethics of Psychoanalysis*, ed. Jacques-Alain Miller, trans. Dennis Porter (London: Routledge, 1992), 319.

9. WHY GIRLS CRY
Gender Melancholia and Sexual Violence
In Ezekiel 16 and *Boys Don't Cry*[1]

Erin Runions

I start with an inkling that perhaps Ezekiel 16 and Kimberley Pierce's 1999 film *Boys Don't Cry* have something to say to each other. Certainly they are both texts about repeated, excessive, and fatal sexual violence; beyond that, it might be said they really have nothing to do with each other. Nonetheless, the task that I have set for myself, here and elsewhere, is to consider how like scenes in Bible and film can be read together productively. To my mind, the framing, focus, and staging of each can illumine what might otherwise go unnoticed in the other. Such a comparative endeavor may seem an impossible leap over millennia and cultures, destined to miss its mark and fall into an abyss of wild analogies and generalities. However, I have higher hopes for this kind of reading, largely because the Bible is still read as a definitive text, and so the world it projects becomes part of culture and may be influential on the same level as film. While it is not my intent to set out the points of convergence and divergence in the way that religious and filmic texts operate within culture, I start out on the premise that both contribute to, reinforce, and occasionally challenge norms in contemporary constructions of gender. As a feminist critic concerned with working against

---

1. My choice of theory and the kinds of arguments made are indebted to the readings and discussions that were part of the seminar "Psychoanalysis and Ethics" at Columbia University (spring 2001), cotaught by Ann Pellegrini and David Eng, which they graciously allowed me to audit. My focus on melancholia and trauma and my attempt to link them is the immediate result of the attention directed toward these themes in the seminar. Pellegrini's comments about the film in more informal conversations have also been helpful in my thinking through the issues.

the harmful effects of binary gender norms, I find it pertinent not only to examine the internal gender dynamics of culturally potent texts, but also to look at the ways they are read and identified with, as well as how they might be read and identified with differently.

Along these lines, reading together the unlikely candidates of Ezekiel 16 and *Boys Don't Cry* leads me to draw connections between sexual violence, gender melancholia, and trauma. More precisely, I would like to show that the sexual violence in both film and text is the acute and traumatic outworking of what Judith Butler has called the gender melancholia at work in heterosexual identity. Put another way, these texts, when read together, show the traumatic nature of heterosexual identification, enacted through the matrix of social relations. I am less interested in the psychic make up of the characters in these texts than what the details of these two culturally influential texts might reveal about the social construction of gender. The proposition of heterosexual identification as a kind of socially enacted traumatic neurosis—to put it a little too bluntly—is one that can only be tentatively sketched out within the limited space allotted here, and will require more detailed attention later. Moreover, due to constraints of form, I cannot engage the extensive range of psychoanalytic and critical theory that exists on these questions. Rather, I simply work through a few theoretical links and connections that I have noticed in a limited number of texts, specifically as I see them relating to the question of gender melancholia and its impact on social relations.

As indicated, *Boys Don't Cry* and Ezekiel 16 are remarkably similar in portraying graphic and traumatic sexual violence against women: stripping, beating, murder. However, the significant differences between the two are what lead me to consider gender melancholia in relation to sexual violence and trauma. The film—with its central transgendered tragic hero—highlights questions of gender (is this really about violence against a woman?), while the text—with its male competition played out in violence against the female beloved (is this really about Yahweh's love for Jerusalem?)—brings the question of motivation for sexually violent rage to the fore. These differences can be put to work, somewhat paradoxically, as a kind of mutually heuristic binding agent, bringing the two texts together in an exploration of the formation of heterosexual gender identity and its relationship to violence. Bearing both the similarities and differences in mind, I proceed first by offering a negative assessment of each text, which I then soften in a negotiation with each through an exposition of gender melancholia, my application of it to the texts, and consideration of what these texts might say about gender melancholia and trauma. Finally I look briefly at the way readers have identified with these texts in order to think about how reading this way might urge readers to interrogate the kinds of identifications and fore-closures that form their own positions within gender.

TRAUMATIC TEXTS?

Ezekiel 16 is one of the most disturbing texts of the Hebrew Bible for those concerned about violence against women. Many feminist biblical critics have worked to expose the depths and implications of the misogyny and violence in Ezekiel 16.[2] In brief (because others have done the work of detailed exposition), Yahweh chastises Jerusalem for idolatry, which is repetitively figured in terms of a woman's sexual appetite for her neighbors, the nations—she is accused not only of "whoring" but *worse* of giving gifts to her lovers, of pursuing them (16:23–44). She is com-pared with her mother, an unnamed Hittite, and her erring sisters, Sodom and Samaria, and found to be infinitely more wanton (16:44–52). As if it were not enough that Jerusalem's cultic practices are construed, condemned, and shamed as too-free feminine sexuality, criminalizing women's sexuality in the place of idolatry, the text takes it that extra mile and *punishes* her sexually too: Yahweh strips her and fur-ther incites her lovers and her enemies against her, gathering them to stone and cut her to bits (16:35–42). Somehow she lives on through all of this and is told repetitively to bear her shame, and never to open her mouth again (16:63).

---

2. Katheryn Pfisterer Darr, "Ezekiel," *The Women's Bible Commentary: Expanded Edition*, ed. Carol A. Newsom and Sharon H. Ringe (Louisville, Ky.: Westminster/John Knox, 1998); J. Cheryl Exum, *Plotted, Shot and Painted: Cultural Representations of Biblical Women*, (Sheffield: Sheffield Academic Press, 1996); Julie Galambush, *Jerusalem in the Book of Ezekiel, the City as Yahweh's Wife* (Atlanta: Scholars, 1992); Peggy L. Day, "The Bitch Had it Coming to Her: Rhetoric and Interpretation in Ezekiel 16," *Biblical Interpretation* 8 (2000): 231–55; Linda Day, "Rhetoric and Domestic Violence in Ezekiel 16," *Biblical Interpretation* 8 (2000): 205–30; Johanna Stiebert, "Shame and Prophecy: Approaches Past and Present," *Biblical Interpretation* 8 (2000): 255–75; Mary E. Shields, "Multiple Exposures: Body Rhetoric and Gender Characterization in Ezekiel 16," *Journal of Feminist Studies in Religion* 14 (1998): 5–18; Carol J. Dempsey, "The 'Whore' of Ezekiel 16: The Impact and Ramifications of Gender-Specific Metaphors in Light of Biblical Law and Divine Judgment," *Gender and Law in the Hebrew Bible and the Ancient Near East*, ed. Victor H. Matthews, Bernard M. Levinson, and Tikva Frymer-Kensky (Sheffield: Sheffield Academic Press, 1998); Renita J. Weems, *Battered Love: Marriage, Sex and Violence in the Hebrew Prophets* (Minneapolis: Fortress, 1995).

How to deal with such violence and misogyny in a purportedly sacred text?[3] Some feminist critics, without trying to redeem the passage, have made a call to read this text differently, so as not to justify contemporary violence against women or other groups or to highlight and work against contemporary problems of conjugal violence.[4] To my mind this kind of rereading is the only option for dealing with the text, since it is still firmly fixed within the biblical canon, and since that canon still operates as authoritative in many communities. The challenge is to create a tradition of reading the text differently so that it becomes another kind of cultural influence. What then if this text were to be read, as the film seems to be, as a text with something interesting to say about the construction of gender identity?

There are in fact more similarities between *Boys Don't Cry* and Ezekiel 16 than one might imagine. Like the biblical text, the film portrays a woman (Teena Brandon), though living as a man (Brandon Teena), who pursues lovers throughout small town Nebraska, giving them gifts and pleasure. Brandon returns to his pleasures time and time again, almost reveling in the variously motivated chases this provokes from angry men. After hooking up with new friends in one of these pursuits, he ends up in Falls City, in love with the local Lana Tisdel, and buddies with his killers-to-be, John Lotter and Tom Nissen. As in the biblical text, her/his sexual behavior—which plays out in flirtations of all kinds and then in passionate lovemaking to Lana—is rewarded with excessive sexual violence by John and Tom, after she is identified as Teena Brandon by the police. They strip her, beat her, rape her, and kill her. So, like the biblical text, the film depicts the shaming of a woman, here double shame because it exposes a female to male transgenderist as a woman, "the pussy" he tries so hard not to be.

Though *Boys Don't Cry* is ostensibly a film about a transgendered man, at the end of the day it hits home as a film of violence against a *woman* who defies heterosexual norms of gender. The film starts out with Brandon as a young man confidently wooing women, but by the end of the film we are in no doubt that Brandon Teena is in fact a woman; the film goes out of its way to show it. In an extended scene, Brandon is stripped, her womanhood revealed in a long zoom-in on her

---

3. Shields notes that this is "the only text banned from use in the synagogue (*Meg.* 4:10; *b. Hag.* 131)" ("Multiple Exposures," 5–6); so also Steibert, "Shame and Prophecy," 268.
4. Shields, "Multiple Exposures," 18; Dempsey, "The 'Whore' of Ezekiel 16," 76 n. 28.

vagina (unusual in film in any case, and unusually long here). In an even more protracted scene, she is beaten and raped twice (by John followed by Tom), forcing us to witness her penetrability. Following the rape, the film continues to expose her as a woman, revealing her unbound breasts as she speaks to the nurse who examines her, and showing her curves in the shower (this in a mainstream, soap-commercial type pose—shot from behind and headless, with a focus on thighs and hips, off balance, on one leg). Then, before Brandon can possibly have time to recover, Lana is engaging her sexually as a woman. "You're so pretty," Lana initiates, to which Brandon replies in high femme fashion, "You're only saying that 'cause you like me."[5] Not long after this moment of first-time lesbian romance, we see Brandon's head blown off in the film's traumatic climax, as John "takes care of a coupla' dykes." Thus the film forces Brandon to admit what he does not believe is true, fulfilling the wish of his frustrated cousin, "You are not a boy! . . . You are not a boy! . . . Why don't you just admit that you are a dyke?!" Though Brandon replies, "Because I'm not a dyke," the film apparently thinks it knows better.[6]

However similar the film might be to the biblical text, it has not been subjected to feminist critique in the same way. Whereas feminist biblical critics have argued that enough is enough with Ezekiel 16, that it is profoundly unhelpful as a religious metaphor let alone as a culturally influential text, the acclaim for the film has been almost entirely positive. The reasons for the film's amnesty from feminist critique, as far as I can see, are threefold. First, the main subject of the film is the tragic end to a conflicted transgendered life, which makes it both unusual and iconic for people who are interested in questions of gender identity,[7] thus giving the film a place in the world of alternative film. Second, the film depicts a true story, which makes it seem like an honest specimen of truth telling, rather than a fictional figment of misogynist imagination. And

---

5. Quotations from the film are my own transcription.

6. It seems from an interview in *Gay and Lesbian Review Worldwide* that perhaps Kimberly Pierce viewed Brandon primarily as a woman crossing gender lines (rather than primarily as a man with the wrong genitals). She says—and it is interesting to notice the use of pronouns and the order she chooses to use for name and surname here—"I really fell in love with this kid Teena Brandon, who one day put a sock in her pants and a cowboy hat on her head and reinvented herself into her fantasy of a boy and then went out and passed . . . and then after it all came crashing down, and Brandon found a deeper truer self" ("Putting Teena Brandon's Story on Film: An Interview by Francesca Miller" [fall 2000], 40). This deeper truer self that Pierce sees in Brandon, it would appear from the film, is a female, lesbian self.

7. See Vernon A. Rosario, "Transgenderism Comes of Age," *Gay and Lesbian Review Worldwide* (Fall 2000): 31–33.

finally, the film's director, Kimberly Pierce, identifies as queer, as does its feminist producer, Christine Vachon;[8] there may be some tacit understanding that queer feminists would not produce something damaging to women, or that they might stand outside the patriarchal loop.

But to my mind, "truth telling" (which somewhat ironically is how the Bible has traditionally been read) and "authorship" are not enough to grant the film absolution from feminist critique: I see no inherent radical political program in watching in detail—as entertainment—the violence that *really happened* to a wo/man. Nor do I think that an author's self-stated identity guarantees an alternative message. The question for me—as with my question of the biblical text—is whether this film has something interesting to say about gender identity and the violence that surrounds gender transgressions. At one level it seems that it does not, because it frames the story in a very traditional way (apart from the twist of gender and the inclusion of lesbianism at the end): two boys battle it out over a girl, one boy wins, the other boy loses and is punished (but here—grafting in another very traditional story—punished for sexual "misdemeanor" in the same fashion as are many women). But perhaps there is more complexity than first meets the eye, and this I would like to explore with the help of Butler and Ezekiel 16.

Indeed, the plot of the biblical text is slightly more elaborate than that of the film and may provide a way into thinking about the dynamics in the film. In Ezekiel 16, the two competitors (Yahweh and the nations) attack the object of their desire (Jerusalem), rather than each other (whereas in the film the contested object of desire, Lana, is one of the few who remains both alive and unincarcerated). Elsewhere, I have argued using the theory of René Girard on mimetic desire and violence that this complexity in the biblical text suggests that perhaps Jerusalem is violently barred from her desire for the nations because it mimics, and so competes with, Yahweh's (possibly homosexual) desire for the nations.[9] Over the years since the time of writing that essay, I have come to see that one of the problematic implications of the argument is that it might be read as predicating violence against a woman upon homoerotic desire, instead of upon misogyny and heterosexual misconduct.

---

8. Pierce, "Putting Teena Brandon's Story on Film," 39; Erika Muhammad, "Independent Means," *Ms. Magazine* (February/March 2000): 76–77.

9. Erin Runions, "Violence and the Economy of Desire in Ezekiel 16.1–45," *Prophets and Daniel: A Feminist Companion to the Bible*, ed. Athalya Brenner (Sheffield: Sheffield Academic Press, 2001).

Further, my argument there depended upon the idea that Yahweh's love for Jerusalem was not sexual, but parental (or both). Though I do not think this latter implausible, it may also be useful to think through the more traditional and predominantly accepted understanding of Yahweh's love for Jerusalem as (hetero)sexual.

However, I still believe the basic instinct of that essay—to relate the strange working of the plot to questions of sexual and gender identity— to be on track; but I now find it more important to take into consideration the unconscious working of heterosexual gender identifications as they relate to violence, and it is here that Butler is informative. I worry that the argument I make here runs the same risk of being read as blaming violence on homoerotic desire—given that Butler predicates heterosexual identification on disavowed homosexual attachment—and that I argue that heterosexuality, thus formed, gets lived out violently. However, I want to be clear that it is not the actual same-sex attachment that I am accusing here, but rather the socially formulated prohibition against homosexuality that comes before and causes the loss, for which the heterosexual world need take responsibility.

GENDER MELANCHOLIA

Judith Butler's writing on gender melancholia—to give a brief and simplified summary here of the basic lines of the theory with which many feminist and cultural critics are by now familiar—is an attempt to engage and move beyond structuralist and psychoanalytic accounts that separate biological sex from gender. In contrast to these accounts, whereby patriarchal law is understood to impose itself on essential raw nature, sex, to produce gender, Butler wants to see sexed bodies as equally discursively constructed. In other words, she sees "sex" constructed in the same operation in which gender and sexual orientation are also constructed. This proposition moves away from the reliance of feminism on essentializing (Western) conceptions of sex and gender, particularly femininity. Instead, patriarchal law is conceived of as a kind of culturally bound set of psychic processes serving to establish norms and prohibitions that inaugurate and regulate the means by which people come to identify and live out their gender and sexuality. In interrogating structuralist (Lévi-Straussian) and psychoanalytic (Freudian, Lacanian) notions of the incest taboo as a founding moment for heterosexual assignments of sex and gender, Butler asks whether there might be another taboo operating in the construction of sex and gender, an even more primary taboo, against homosexual attachments.[10]

Working through Freud's influential works, "Mourning and Melancholia" and *The Ego and the Id*, Butler aligns the incest taboo with mourning, and the homosexuality taboo with melancholia. For Butler following Freud, mourning represents a gradual and healthful letting go of a lost love object, a loss that is acknowledged. Melancholia, on the other hand, represents the inhibition of grief, a disavowal of loss, and an internalization of the lost loved object in a way that continues to haunt the bereaved. In other words, in melancholia the lost loved object is "set up inside the ego," or *incorporated* into the ego.[11] Such an internalization, Freud tells us, manifests itself as an identification with the lost loved object. This unavowed loss and subsequent identification is made manifest through melancholic self-reproach and depression. Self-reproach, which to Freud seems exaggerated and out of proportion in melancholic subjects, is a result of the ambivalence that the patient feels toward the lost loved one (love *and* anger), and represents the rage that should properly be directed toward the lost loved one, but is instead internalized.

In *The Ego and the Id*, Freud takes the mechanism of melancholic loss further to think of the inward-turned loss as actually forming parts of the ego. The ambivalence toward the lost object is understood to be configured

---

10. Judith Butler is at pains to point out that homosexual attachment is not something that comes "before" cultural constructions of sex and gender; it is a possibility opened up *within* culture, but on the margins and powerfully foreclosed from dominant culture (see *Gender Trouble: Feminism and the Subversion of Identity* [London & New York: Routledge, 1990], 77–78).

11. Freud uses the word "introjection," but later theorists, including Butler, have called this "incorporation," following the distinction elaborated by Nicolas Abraham and Maria Torok between introjection and incorporation. Introjection, Abraham and Torok suggest, is the process within mourning in which the object is known to be lost, and can thus be spoken of and represented. Incorporation, on the other hand, is the establishment of the lost object in such a way that it cannot be acknowledged, and cannot be represented; it is "anti-metaphorical" (Nicolas Abraham and Maria Torok, "Introjection—Incorporation: Mourning *or* Melancholia," *Psychoanalysis in France*, ed. Serge Lebovici and Daniel Widlöcher [New York: International Universities Press, 1980 (1972)], 9–10). Abraham and Torok call this a kind of encryption: "grief that cannot be expressed builds a secret vault [crypt] within the subject" (ibid., 8; see also Abraham and Torok, "A Poetics of Pyschoanalysis: 'The Lost Object—Me,'" trans. Nicholas Rand, *SubStance* 43 [1984 (1978)]: 4–5, 10–13). This crypt, Abraham suggests, can house either the subject's own secret, or a disavowed secret inherited from others (Abraham, "Notes on the Phantom: A Complement to Freud's Metapsychology," trans. Nicholas Rand, *The Trial(s) of Psychoanalysis*, ed. Françoise Meltzer [Chicago: University of Chicago Press, 1988 (1978)], 75–80).

both as *identification* (ego-ideal) and as *critical agency* (super-ego).[12] As Butler puts it, the ambivalence is "set up as internal parts of the ego, the sadistic part [the super-ego] takes aim at the part that identifies [with the lost object], and the psychically violent drama of the super-ego proceeds."[13] The super-ego, or critical agency, acts tyrannically against the object set up inside the ego (the ego-ideal).[14] In fact, as Butler points out—and this will be important to my own eventual argument—in melancholia the super-ego becomes the agent of the death drive, "a kind of gathering-place for the death instincts."[15] The super-ego, Freud tells us, also "has the task of repressing the Oedipus Complex," that is, of forbidding incest.[16]

Following this trajectory, Butler suggests that the heterosexual incest taboo represents forbidden objects of desire which, because they are known, are grievable and therefore within the realm of mourning. On the other hand, the strong cultural prohibition on homosexual desire, she argues, produces melancholia by creating disavowed same-sex attachments, and therefore ungrievable, lost loved objects ("I never loved, therefore I never lost").[17]

In elaborating the relationship of the lost loved object to the formation of the super-ego—a relationship that both film and biblical text also articulate—Butler shows that Freud comes to understand melancholia as constitutive for the ego and the super-ego. Melancholia, therefore, is the condition of possibility for mourning. Thus, for Butler, gender melancholia can be read as the condition of possibility for heterosexual norms: the melancholic, disavowed loss created by the taboo on homosexual attachments prepares the way for the incest taboo that governs heterosexual gender. Put another way, in order for the grievable incest taboo (in Freudian terms, the Oedipus complex) to operate, the child has first to identify with the same-sex parent, so as to compete for the opposite-sex parent. According to the logic of the system then, this

---

12. Though Freud does not delineate the different functions of the super-ego in *The Ego and the Id* where the notion first appears, in later writings he distinguishes the various roles of the super-ego, in which the ego-ideal operates as the ideal standard by which the critical agency judges the ego; see J. Laplanche, J.-B. Pontalis, *The Language of Psycho-analysis*, trans. Donald Nicholson-Smith (New York and London: Norton, 1973 [1967]), 144–45.

13. Butler, *The Psychic Life of Power*, 189.

14. Sigmund Freud, *The Ego and the Id*, vol. 19, *The Standard Edition of the Complete Psychological Works of Sigmund Freud*, trans. James Strachey (London: Hogarth, 1961 [1923]), 51.

15. Ibid., 54; cited in Judith Butler, *The Psychic Life of Power*, 188.

16. *The Ego and the Id*, 34.

17. *The Psychic Life of Power*, 138–40, 147.

initial identification is accomplished through a loss, that is, the ungrievable loss caused by strong cultural prohibitions against sexual attachments to the same-sex parent (homosexual taboo), which also at the same time *sets up* the prohibition against incest.

Moreover, for Butler this operation not only forms gender identifications, but also constructs *sex* at the same time. The lost object, as it is incorporated into the ego, she suggests—building on Freud's statement that the ego is "first and foremost a bodily ego"[18]—"literalizes the loss *on* or *in* the body" *as a sexed body*, as "the facticity of the body, the means by which the body comes to bear 'sex' as its literal truth."[19] In other words, one of the ways in which the loss comes to haunt the bereaved is as "sex." In this way Butler is able to move away from an understanding of sex as the a priori to gender; for her, sex and gender are part of one and the same melancholic operation.

VIOLENCE AND GENDER MELANCHOLIA

Both *Boys Don't Cry* and Ezekiel 16 might be said to portray the kind of identification with the lost object that is operative in gender melancholia. The gender identifications made in film and text can be read as the incorporations of lost loved parental objects. If Brandon is understood as identifying as a heterosexual man, and Jerusalem as a heterosexual woman, then following the theory that I have laid out, it is not surprising to find that these sex/gender identifications can be correlated to the loss of same-sex attachments. In each case we find parental loss: Jerusalem's mother abandons her in the field and Brandon's father, it is revealed at the end of the film, is lost to him before he is born. Not only is Jerusalem's mother—the unnamed Hittite—lost, but any remaining

---

18. *The Ego and the Id*, 26.
19. Judith Butler, *Gender Trouble*, 68. For an interrogation of Butler on this point, see Jay Prosser, *Second Skins: The Body Narratives of Transsexuality* (New York: Columbia University Press, 1998), 27–44. Prosser takes issue with what he sees as Butler's "displacement of sex from material interiority into fantasized surface" (ibid., 44). As I read it, his concern is with establishing the reasons why material sex might need to be changed in order to match up with what Freud calls the bodily ego (what Prosser calls interior perceptions of sex); Butler's emphasis on discursivity seems, to Prosser, to render sex abstract and imaginary, and therefore easily accommodated in whatever body one finds oneself. Though I do not read Butler (or Freud on the bodily ego) in quite the same way, Prosser's insistence on the need for transsexuals to change the materiality of their bodies is part of an important critique of what he calls queer theory's appropriation of transsexuality (ibid., 31)—the use of transsexualism as a deliteralized metaphor for "the essential inessentiality" (ibid., 14). Such an appropriation refuses transsexuals' need to literally change their bodies.

attachment to her, or grief over her loss, is foreclosed by the open deri-
sion of Hittite identity and the prohibition against Israel mixing with
other nations.[20] In this sense, the loss is the double loss of which Butler
speaks: a loss that cannot be avowed or grieved. In Brandon's case,
though, the death of his father before his birth makes the loss a literal
never, never (never loved, never lost), therefore also ungrievable in a way.

These losses seem to precipitate gendered identification. Certainly
the biblical text makes much of Jerusalem's identification with her
mother (in spite of not knowing her). As an insult, Jerusalem is told how
alike she is to her mother: "all who recite proverbs against you will recite
one saying, 'Like a mother her daughter. The daughter of your mother,
you are one who loathes her husband and her children'" (Ezekiel
16:44–45).[21] Likewise, Brandon, born—as he tells Lana—a "girl-girl,"
takes on the identity of a man, arguably an identification with his lost
father. The filmic depiction of identification formed with the lost object is
both less and more obvious than in the biblical text. On one hand, the film
does not make much of this identification. There are hints, though, that it
may be operative: in one of the film's more nuanced details, Brandon
reveals an internalized identification with his father by offering—in a
quiet moment, without his usual bravado—to sing Lana to sleep with a
song that his (never known, never loved, never lost) father taught him.
On the other hand, it might be said that Brandon has quite obviously
incorporated the lost father into/as a heterosexual male identity.
Indeed, he might be seen as an example *par excellence* of the literalizing
effect of the lost same-sex attachment on and in his body, as "sex." Of
interest here though is that Brandon, born a biological girl, has later
taken on heterosexual male identity, so the primary loss of a "same-sex"
attachment is in some sense retroactive. This of course bears out the
notion that "primary" loss is not original or foundational as much as
negotiated within and through culture.

Arguably, then, both film and text demonstrate the working of gendered and sexed identifications as structured through a disavowed loss.
But, following from this, it is interesting that neither Brandon nor
Jerusalem seems to engage in much self-reproach, signifying anger at the
incorporated lost object, as one might expect of melancholic dispositions

---

20. For comment on the conflation of racism and misogyny here, see Dempsey, "The
'Whore' of Ezekiel 16," 62–63, 77.

21. Translations of biblical texts are my own.

(in fact, we do not get any of Jerusalem's internal dialogue at all). Indeed, for the most part, Jerusalem and Brandon appear well-nigh "shameless" in their (hetero)sexual pursuits: the biblical text goes on at length about Jerusalem's willingness to make herself available to her lovers (Ezekiel 16:23–34), and Brandon seems always to be on the make, unabashedly using the women who fall for him for food, shelter, and money. There are a few brief moments in the film, however, that let slip at least a little hostile judgment upon the internalized heterosexual male object with self-deprecating comments. During the ritual of dressing—binding his breasts, inserting his penis, slicking his hair—Brandon looks in the mirror and (approvingly) tells himself, "I'm an asshole." Later he responds to Lana's question, "What were you like, before all this, were you like me, a girl-girl?" with "Ya, like a long time ago, and then I guess I was just like a boy-girl, *then I was just a jerk*. . . . It's weird, finally everything felt right."

But as Freud points out, there is a kind of ambivalence in melancholia whereby the melancholic subject is both reproach-filled and unabashed about it. In this fashion, Brandon's professions, though reproachful, are accompanied by a distinct lack of regret—and one gets the feeling that Jerusalem would have no regrets either, if she could speak. But this too fits with Freud's description of the melancholic, who, he says, exhibits a remarkable lack of shame. As he states it, "feelings of shame in front of other people . . . are lacking in the melancholic. . . . One might emphasize the presence in him of an almost opposite trait of insistent communicativeness which finds satisfaction in self-exposure."[22] So perhaps this shameless but at points derogatory self-display that Brandon and Jerusalem exhibit might be enough to make the case for the operation of gender melancholia in these texts.

Both texts also depict another kind of brutal reproach that culminates in self-abasement. This reproach comes from the outside but finally extorts self-reproach. In the film, John and Tom first shame Brandon by stripping him and exposing his "true sex," then reproach him verbally, "you know you brought this upon yourself,"[23] and finally

---

22. Sigmund Freud, "Mourning and Melancholia," *The Standard Edition of the Complete Psychological Works of Sigmund Freud*, vol. 14, trans. James Strachey (London: Hogarth, 1957 [1917]), 247.

23. As an interesting counterpoint to my argument here, I might note that in the film, we witness Brandon—in response to this shaming revelation of his "lack" of manhood—step out of his body and look on, as the man he knows himself to be. This could be read as an instance of the by now rather banal psychoanalytic "truth" that the phallus stands in for lack. Or, alternatively,

degrade him further through rape and beating. Their threat to kill him if he reports the rape seems finally to wrest the sarcastic but self-reproachful response from Brandon: "Of course, I mean, this is all my fault, I know." The same pattern of verbal and physical shaming followed by self-reproach also occurs in the biblical text. Before Yahweh gathers the nations against Jerusalem to strip and batter her, he verbally reproaches her, calling her "whore," "weak of spirit," "adulterous," "worse than other whores," and all other manner of insult.[24] In response to her abuse by Yahweh via the nations, Jerusalem is said to acknowledge her wrongdoing (self-reproachfully), to accept Yahweh's covenant, and to remain silent (although as Shields points out, we never actually hear her giving voice to her penitence[25]).

I would suggest that these scenes are in some way reminiscent of the violent drama of the super-ego. Indeed, John, Tom, Yahweh, and the nations might be seen as standing in for the super-ego, performing the function of the tyrannical critical agency through physical shamings and verbal abuses that ultimately lead Brandon and Jerusalem to some form of self-reproach. Not only is condemnation threefold (physical shaming, verbal reproach, and self-reproach), in both cases death is the final reproach (though somehow Jerusalem lives on after being cut to bits).[26] Thus the tyrannical male figures in these stories can be read as powerfully critical agencies that enforce self-reproach on the part of the melancholic heterosexual figures. And like the super-ego, they seem also to represent a gathering place for the death instincts, driving their reproaches unto death. It appears then that gender melancholia manifests itself in these texts through reproachful super-egos, as expected, but in a slightly altered, externalized form. This externalization of painful processes within the ego, I will argue presently, is similar to what happens

---

it could be read as Eve Kosofsky Sedgwick might read it, as a queer and liberating response of identity formation in response to shame ("Queer Performativity: Henry James's *The Art of the Novel*," *GLQ: A Journal of Lesbian and Gay Studies* 1 (1993): 12–15). This might point to the role that shame plays in enforcing the loss of same-sex attachments, and therefore in shaping subsequent identifications.

24. Linda Day points out that this kind of language is typical of batterers who use insults like "'dirty slut,' 'whore,' 'bitch,' 'stupid,' 'cunt,' 'slave,' 'dummy' . . . with great frequency" ("Rhetoric and Domestic Violence," 220).

25. Shields, "Multiple Exposures," 7.

26. Shields argues that a similar thing occurs in Ezekiel 23, where Oholah and Oholibah live on in spite of being killed because they are necessary "as warnings (*object* lessons) to other women . . . [and] as testaments to YHWH's power and identity" ("Identity and Power/Gender and Violence in Ezekiel 23," *Postmodern Interpretations: A Reader*, ed. A. K. M. Adam [St. Louis, Mo.: Chalice, 2001], 149).

in traumatic neurosis; but first I would like to consider other ways in which Brandon and Jerusalem might also represent externalized interior processes within the melancholic formations of heterosexual identity.

To this point, I have tried to show how these texts can be said to depict heterosexual identifications under attack by other, external, tyrannical figures. But significantly, these aggressors, as also heterosexual, must likewise operate within the matrix of gender melancholia. Their identities too would be constructed through loss, identification, and judging critical agency. It might make sense, then, to see how their cruel actions work out their own gender melancholia. I would submit that as much as Yahweh, the nations, John, and Tom can be read as inhabiting the role of super-ego, so also can Brandon and Jerusalem be read as standing in for the lost loved objects of their tormentors (particularly John and Yahweh, on whom the texts focus). In other words, Brandon— as the ideal handsome, kind, and daring man—and Jerusalem—as the ideal nation—might be said to be incarnations of John's and Yahweh's own disavowed same-sex attachments, turned into ideal points of identi- fication. In fact, these disavowed attachments might be unacknowledged bonds between John and Tom, or between Yahweh and the nations. Certainly some critics have hinted that the relationship between Tom and John betrays some kind of repressed love relationship;[27] and I have already floated the possibility that Yahweh desires the nations. If these loves are disavowed and so lost, they might also be set up, here externally, as points of heterosexual identifications that can then be both loved and berated. The sticking point here is that rather than being male points of identification, as one would expect, Brandon and Jerusalem are destroyed as women, the "worst kind" of women at that (whores and dykes).

REPUDIATING FEMININITY

Perhaps this can be seen as a moment within the formation of hetero- sexual male identification that Butler calls the repudiation of femininity. On the way to establishing heterosexual desire through identification with the same-sex lost object, the melancholic heterosexual male must prove that he is not a woman. Butler describes it thus:

---

27. Donald Moss and Lynne Zeavin, "Film Review Essay: The Real Thing? Some Thoughts on *Boys Don't Cry*," *International Journal of Psychoanalysis* 81 (2000): 1228. John Gregroy Dunne's story in *The New Yorker* also hints at this ("A Report at Large: The Humboldt Murders" [13 January 1997]: 44–52).

> Becoming a "man" within this logic requires repudiating femi-
> ninity as a precondition for the heterosexualization of sexual
> desire and its fundamental ambivalence. . . . Indeed the desire for
> the feminine is marked by that repudiation: he wants the woman
> he would never be. *He wouldn't be caught dead being her*: therefore
> he wants her. . . . One of the most anxious aims of his desire will
> be to elaborate the difference between him and her, and *he will*
> *seek to discover and install proof of that difference.*[28]

Both film and text, it seems to me, show male figures performing exactly
this kind of work; in repressing their own same-sex attachments, and
establishing identifications with them as masculine ideals, they must
first thoroughly abjure their femininity.

At the very least, reading along these lines makes some sense of several
peculiarities in the biblical text: that is, the strange working of the plot
whereby Jerusalem's competing lovers gang up on her rather than on
each other; the fact that Jerusalem lives on, even after being cut to bits;
and finally, an odd spelling that occurs throughout the chapter. As mentioned earlier, one of the points where film and text do not match up is
in the treatment of the "the object of desire." Where in the film, Lana—
the contested object of desire—remains unharmed, in the biblical text
Jerusalem is destroyed. But if the primary object of desire in the biblical
text is actually not Jerusalem, but the male nations—for instance the
sons of Egypt, whose "largeness of flesh" seems to be of some interest to
Yahweh (v. 26)—then Jerusalem's role can be understood differently. If
this same-sex attachment to the male nations is disavowed, which clearly
it is, and so lost, it makes sense (within the logic of gender melancholia
at least) that a replacement nation is set up as a point of identification.

Though the figure of a beloved nation (Jerusalem, and also Samaria
and Sodom in Ezekiel 16:46–52) may be the perfect stand-in object for
the lost love, the question remains as to how to make sense of her femininity.[29] That Yahweh identifies himself with the nation of Israel, and in
particular with the city of Jerusalem, is so much received theological

---

28. Judith Butler, *The Psychic Life of Power*, 137, emphasis added.

29. Freud writes: "The analysis of melancholia now shows that the ego can kill itself only,
if, owing to the return of the object-cathexis, it can treat itself as an object" ("Mourning and
Melancholia," 252). Figuring the nation as woman-as-sexual-object may be a convenient and
culturally accepted way of doing this. For elaboration on the point of objectification of the
women in Ezekiel 16 and 23, see Shields ("Multiple Exposures," 13; "Identity and
Power/Gender," 146–49).

wisdom. But as Shields points out in a discussion of the sister passage to this one, Ezekiel 23, Yahweh's identity as a powerful deity is dependent on Jerusalem as a political entity; he is nothing without her. There is therefore a strange conflation that occurs between the abuser/abused, subject/object, masculine/feminine.[30] This is one of the reasons, Shields argues, that Jerusalem lives on although she has been killed; she is an essential part of Yahweh's identity. In a sense, he cannot be "caught dead" being her. Yet as Shields notes, Jerusalem's continued life also poses a continual threat to Yahweh's power. This threat, I would suggest, resides at least partially in her feminine identification, that thing that Yahweh must repudiate (within himself) in order to disavow his love for the nations and to complete the accompanying masculine identification.[31]

Of particular interest with respect to the overlap in identity between Yahweh and Israel is a strange linguistic quirk, which produces an ambiguity between first-person verb forms (describing Yahweh) and second-person feminine verb forms (describing Jerusalem). Eight times in the chapter, the written consonants (Ketib) spell the first-person singular suffix form ("I, Yahweh"), but are vocalized as the second-person feminine singular suffix form,[32] and corrected in the margins (Qere) to the second-person feminine consonantal form ("you, Jerusalem") (vv. 13, 18, 22, 31a, 31b, 43a, 43b, 51).[33] While this orthographical oddity may simply be, as scholars maintain, an archaic second-person form,[34] it is curious that it occurs with such frequency in the chapter. The high concentration of the ambiguous form in this particular chapter is at the very least suggestive of an uncertain identification between Yahweh and Jerusalem. In the most notable of these occurrences, an ambiguity appears between Ketib and Qere as to whether you (Jerusalem) or I (Yahweh) put "my incense" before the images of lovers (v. 18), whether you or I build your

---

30. "Identity and Power/Gender," 151.

31. For a different kind of psychoanalytic reading, in which this rage is read as Ezekiel's rage against his own mother expressed in the metaphor of Yahweh's rage against Israel, see David J. Halperin, *Seeking Ezekiel: Text and Psychology* (University Park: Pennsylvania State University Press, 1993), 160–67.

32. This form does not occur again in Ezekiel, though a related form occurs in Ezekiel 36:13 in which the second-person feminine singular pronoun (*'t*) is spelled with a yod at the end (*'ty*), but is vocalized as usual. However, this spelling of the second-person feminine suffix form does occur elsewhere in the MT, particularly in Jeremiah (e.g., Jeremiah 2:33; 3:4, 5; 4:19; 31:21; 46:11).

33. The reverse occurs in v. 59, with the feminine form corrected to the first-person form.

34. Walther Zimmerli, *A Commentary on the Book of the Prophet Ezekiel*, vol. 1, trans. Ronald E. Clements, Hermeneia (Philadelphia: Fortress, 1979 [1969]), 325 n. 13; John W. Wevers, *Ezekiel*, The Century Bible (London: Thomas Nelson, 1969), 122 n. 13; Wilhelm Gesenius, *Gesenius Hebrew Grammar*, ed. E. Kautzsch (Oxford: Clarendon, 1910), §44.

high places (v. 31a), whether you or I go beyond the call of duty for a regular prostitute (v. 31b), and whether you or I have a hand in devising your abominations (vv. 43b, 51). With this ambiguity in place, the speech of Yahweh sounds very much like that of the self-deriding melancholic, accusing himself of wrongdoing while at the same time accusing the lost loved object.

The film has fewer ambiguities overall. However, one aspect that stands out as somewhat difficult to decipher is the relationship between John and Brandon. Clearly Brandon is both in awe and jealous of John. But John, as opposed to what one might anticipate in response to a newcomer in a small town, is immediately friendly and warm with Brandon (Tom is much more the bully we might expect). He fights Brandon's first fight with him; he jokingly shows him how to throw a punch; he tells him of his love for Lana; he sets him up to (dis)prove his manliness in bumper skiing; and he directs him in a car chase, leaning over his shoulder and telling him how and where to drive. Indeed, there are moments, in long, close-up camera shots of John's face, when it seems that John looks at Brandon with genuine love and tenderness. This kind of attitude is not reflected at all in his relationship with Tom, although the film hints that they do have some kind of a special bond ("I'm the only one who can control that fucker," says Tom). But if Brandon, as a point of masculine identification, can be seen as holding the place of John's (incorporated) lost love for Tom or other men, John's mentorship of Brandon might begin to make some sense.

Although on the surface the film mobilizes John's anger at Brandon as jealousy over Lana, perhaps John's tendency to push Brandon into danger is telling both as a kind of identification and as judgment upon that identification. In setting Brandon up to bumper ski, he tells him that he "can do it . . . don't let 'em scare you," and then (judgingly) that he "can do better than that," not satisfied. Strangely, as he introduces Brandon into the game, he pulls off his own shirt as if he were introducing himself: "this here's a mean prize fighter up from Lincoln . . . very tough" (this comes as a voice-over while John leads Brandon toward the truck; it is not clear who actually says it, or if it is just in John's head). After Brandon's failed attempts to stay upright aboard the hurling truck, John commends him with what could also be read as an ominous, foreshadowing threat, "you're one crazy little fucker, whadd're we gonna do with you?" Later, he urges Brandon on in a reckless car chase, head close, voice low, again somewhat beratingly ("c'mon ya' pussy, go faster,

y'cocksucker . . . don't stop, don't stop, go faster, go faster"). At one point
he mysteriously leans over (in response to Brandon's "I can't see") and
looks as if he will fix something (but what?), or perhaps as if to touch
Brandon between the legs (though we can't see that either), before he leans
back in orgasmic bliss. Yet once they have been stopped by the police, John
lashes out at Brandon, "don't you never pull that shit again . . . you got me
stopped by the fuckin' cops." It is as if Brandon lives out John's fantasies
for him, but also takes the heat for them (fantasies that include making
love to Lana, although this without John *literally* in the background).
Little wonder, then, with this kind of male identification being established, that when John finds out that Brandon is actually a woman, he goes
ballistic,[35] frenziedly seeking to establish proof of the difference between
himself and Brandon (the "pussy"), with whom he has identified.[36]

THE TRAUMA OF GENDER MELANCHOLIA

These texts might be seen as aptly depicting the workings of gender
melancholia. But beyond reading film and text simply as parables of
individual psychic processes, I think that it may be possible and even
helpful to consider these texts as cultural renditions of the psychic workings of the social order. I would tentatively suggest, therefore, that these
texts reveal sexual violence as the *social outworking* of gender melancholia. More specifically, they seem to depict the violent drama of the super-
ego, acting as the gathering place for death instincts, externalized and
enacted by others also affected by gender melancholia. This kind of
reading picks up on the notion, advanced by Butler at the end of *The
Psychic Life of Power*,[37] that the social metaphors in Freud's writing make
way for a consideration of the relation of the psychic to the social (Butler
notes that Freud uses language of institution and polity to describe the
psyche[38]). Butler seems to see this relation along the lines of ideological

---

35. Several reviewers open up the question of masculine identity and violence without pro-
viding answers as to what within heterosexual masculine identification gives rise to such rage
(Moss and Zeavin, "The Real Thing?"; Melissa Anderson, "The Brandon Teena Story and *Boys
Don't Cry*," *Cineaste* 25, no. 2 (2000): 54–56; Stuart Klawans, "Rough and Tumble: *Fight Club,
Boys Don't Cry, The City*," *The Nation*, 8 November 1999, 32–36).

36. Perhaps then, Pierce's decision to play up Brandon's femininity and lesbian sexuality at
the end of the film counters this violent repudiation of femininity.

37. *The Psychic Life of Power*, 178–98.

38. Ibid., 178.

interpellation, that is, the means by which (ideological) social prohibition becomes an effaced imprint on the psyche.[39] But another possible way to look at it might be to consider how these kinds of interior psychic relations come to be externalized and lived out on the level of the social.[40]

To this end, I have found it productive to think about the film and the biblical text alongside the muted connection that appears between melancholia and traumatic neurosis when *Beyond the Pleasure Principle* and *The Ego and the Id* are read together. I have already outlined the connection, drawn out by Butler, that Freud makes in *The Ego and the Id* between melancholia and the death drive, whereby for the melancholic the super-ego acts as a gathering place for the death instincts. Given that Freud develops the idea of death drive out of his consideration of trauma and loss in *Beyond the Pleasure Principle*, it seems natural to speculate on the relationship between trauma and melancholia, then specifically on gender melancholia.

In trying to understand why the ego will withstand unpleasure in spite of the pleasure principle (by which instincts continuously seek satisfaction), Freud begins *Beyond the Pleasure Principle* with a discussion of the compulsion to repeat. He notices—in the famous example of his grandson's game of *fort-da*[41]—that children, in their play, will repeat unpleasurable experiences as a way of renouncing instinctual satisfaction, but also as a way of mastering certain unpleasant experiences. What I would like to notice here is that the unpleasant experience of reality that the child deals with in this game—reality that gets in the way of instinctual satisfaction—is the unpleasant experience of loss, both of the child's mother (leaving the room) and of the child's father (at the front).

This discussion of unpleasant but productive repetition then leads Freud into a discussion of trauma and traumatic repetition compulsion, whereby a person who has been traumatized engages in a similar process of uncannily repeating the traumatic experience in order to master it. Freud speaks of trauma particularly in terms of fright as a forceful stimulus for which the external protective system of the ego is unprepared. The

---

39. Ibid., 190–98.
40. Judith Butler makes a related but differently focused argument in *Excitable Speech: A Politics of the Performative* (New York & London: Routledge, 1997), where she looks at how both social and psychic prohibitions on homosexuality are at once internalized and externalized (119–26).
41. Sigmund Freud, *Beyond the Pleasure Principle: The Standard Edition with a Biographical Introduction by Peter Gay*, trans. James Strachey (New York: Norton, 1989 [1920]), 12–17.

ego then works to shore up the breach in the ego's protective shield by repeating the unpleasurable experience in order to master it.[42] The actual experience of trauma is so sudden and so violent that it is repressed; therefore, it returns in alternate forms (dreams, etc.). As Cathy Caruth puts it, since trauma cannot be known, traumatic repetition is always the attempt to reclaim a "missed experience."[43] As an aside here, this already makes a rather obvious connection to melancholia, which is often precipitated by a loss for which an individual is unprepared, and in which the loss is unknown or repressed.[44]

Moving on from the discussion of trauma in *Beyond the Pleasure Principle*, reflecting more generally on why it is that individuals are driven to repetition, particularly of past unpleasurable experiences, Freud concludes that human organisms are essentially conservative, seeking a return to the past. Thus Freud rounds out his discussion of unpleasurable repetition by proposing the notion of death drive, that urge in the ego to return to "an earlier state of things,"[45] which is ultimately death. In a sense, in the death drive the ego works to restore what has been lost to it in the passing of time.

Building from Freud's discussions of repetition of unpleasurable experience (culminating in the development of the notion of death drive), I would suggest—and perhaps this is an obvious point, but I think it still bears mention—that they are all based in some sense on the idea of mastering loss.[46] The melancholic's tendency to berate herself can be seen as one means of trying to master this loss, just as the traumatized individual constantly reencounters the trauma as a way of trying to master the "lost" encounter.[47] My point, lest it remain obscure, is that

---

42. Ibid., 26–39.

43. Cathy Caruth, ed., *Trauma: Explorations in Memory* (Baltimore: Johns Hopkins University Press, 1995), 60–63.

44. Freud, "Mourning and Melancholia," 245.

45. *Beyond the Pleasure Principle*, 45.

46. This same muted connection between the death drive, trauma, and incommensurable loss (melancholia) appears in Caruth's work. At one point she calls the death drive "the traumatic 'awakening' to life. Life itself, Freud says, is an awakening out of a 'death' *for which there is no preparation*" (Cathy Caruth, *Unclaimed Experience: Trauma, Narrative, and History* [Baltimore: Johns Hopkins University Press, 1996], 65, emphasis added). Likewise her discussion of trauma as awakening is developed out of Freud's famous story of the grieving father who dreams of his dead (lost) son calling to him, "Father, father don't you see I'm burning" (*Unclaimed Experience*, 8–9).

47. Freud's description of melancholics' enjoyment of their suffering ("Mourning and Melancholia," 251) is remarkably like his description of the child's enjoyment of the game of loss and recovery.

melancholia, traumatic neurosis, and the death drive are all similar in their repetitive attempts to deal with loss, and that the kind of loss that provokes melancholia can therefore be said to be in some way traumatic. Thus, Freud's appellation of the super-ego as a gathering place for the death drive goes beyond just describing its destructive impulse. It might be said that in the unpleasurable experience of the super-ego's judgment upon the lost object, the ego in some senses puts itself in the position where it must, once again but in a different form, try to master the unpleasurable experience of loss.

Following from this connection between melancholia and trauma, I would make the parallel link between trauma and the loss of same-sex attachments that gives rise to gender melancholia. That is, part of the reason that the loss of the same-sex love is disavowed—as with a loss that brings on melancholia rather than mourning—is the ego's (culturally enforced) unpreparedness for this loss, and unwillingness to accept it. Further, if, as Butler argues, this loss is constitutive for heterosexual iden-tification, then perhaps the loss of same-sex attachments can be seen as a constitutive trauma, which the ego, via the super-ego, seeks to master.

I belabor this point because to my mind it establishes the ground-work for thinking about how gender melancholia might operate on a social level. What is interesting in Freud's discussion of trauma, and—as I think these texts show—is applicable to gender melancholia, is the fact that while at times the ego relives the trauma actively, through dreams, at other times these repetitions occur as if by chance, as if by some external demonic force that causes the ego to constantly confront the same traumatic experience.[48] This, he hints, but does not develop as fully as one might like, is because when internal unpleasures become too great "there is a tendency to treat them as though they were acting, not from the inside, but from the outside, so that it may be possible to bring the shield against stimuli into operation as a means of defence [*sic*] against them."[49] Given my discussion of the film and text, I would sug-gest that when the super-ego's threats become too great, then perhaps they are externalized and acted out on the level of the social. Indeed, Freud writes in *Inhibitions, Symptoms and Anxiety* that the "loss of an

---

48. *Beyond the Pleasure Principle*, 22–25, 43.
49. Ibid., 33.

object . . . and the threat of castration are just as much dangers coming from outside as, let us say, a ferocious animal would be."[50]

This kind of social outworking of psychic processes may be possible because of the liminality of the ego. As others have pointed out,[51] in *The Ego and the Id*, Freud also describes the ego, particularly the system perception-consciousness within the ego, as a (bodily) surface that forms a borderline between internal and external perceptions and processes.[52] He writes, "A person's own body and above all its surface, is a place from which both external and internal perceptions may spring."[53] Moreover, the ego mediates between internal and external "excitations" and processes. It would seem that at points, external excitations can be rolled into the ego's work, and perhaps stand in for unpleasurable internal excitations. As part of the ego (the borderline between the external and internal worlds), the super-ego's judgment can possibly seem to occur from the outside.

The way that gender melancholia seems to function socially, in the two texts I have discussed here at least, suggests that the primary loss of same-sex attachments can operate in the same way as Freud describes traumatic events; that is, giving rise to uncanny, repetitive, seemingly demonic encounters with destructive forces. Here the self-reproach to which the melancholic is inclined seems to come from without, as life-destroying danger. These might be thought of as repetitive encounters (repetition compulsion) with the externalized super-ego, also called the death drive, as a result of the traumatic event of the loss of the loved object. Perhaps this makes sense of why, in the film, Brandon repeatedly seeks out and revels in unpleasurable chase scenes,[54] and in the text, Jerusalem is said to repeatedly take pleasure in the very thing that angers Yahweh most. The larger implication here is that this reading points to the rather unfortunate conclusion that if

---

50. *Inhibitions, Symptoms and Anxiety: The Standard Edition with a Biographical Introduction by Peter Gay*, trans. James Strachey (New York: Norton, 1989 [1926]), 77.

51. E.g., Prosser, *Second Skins*, 40–41; Judith Butler, *Bodies That Matter: On the Discursive Limits of "Sex"* (London & New York: Routledge, 1993), 58–59.

52. *The Ego and the Id*, 24–27.

53. Ibid., 25.

54. Interestingly—in thinking about the connection between dreamwork and trauma—the film begins with what Pierce calls a "dream sequence" (Danny Leigh, "Boy Wonder," *Sight and Sound* 10 [March 2000]: 20), which includes moments from the car-chase scene.

gender melancholia produces the norm (heterosexuality), as Butler suggests it does, then the norm inherently lends itself to violence, and traumatic violence at that.

READERLY IDENTIFICATIONS

In summary, I have tried to show that both Ezekiel 16 and *Boys Don't Cry* do indeed have something interesting to say about the construction of gender. I have tried to indicate how both texts demonstrate Butler's conception of gender melancholia lived out on the level of the social, as the traumatic reenactment of the primary loss of homosexual attachments. More specifically, I have tried to show how these texts lay out the ways in which the construction of heterosexual identifications and identities, predicated as they are on a traumatic loss, lend themselves to violent externalizations of melancholia.

There is an added layer of complexity in all of this, however, when readerly identification is taken into account. Earlier I mentioned that, identifying as a woman, I initially experienced *Boys Don't Cry* as a text of terror, even traumatic,[55] and to this I would most certainly add Ezekiel 16. But as commentary shows, other readers have engaged with these texts differently, more positively. A number of feminist biblical critics have shown how male scholars writing about Ezekiel 16 identify with Yahweh and see Ezekiel 16 as fundamentally about Yahweh's goodness and Israel's depravity.[56] Likewise those writing about the film have shown how many viewers, both straight and transgendered, have identified with Brandon as a male hero, charmer, and especially, daring self-inventor.[57]

Yet, if these texts can be said to mirror each other in some way—and I hope I have shown that they do—then read together they might provide an eye-opening reflection of readers' favored points of identification. For instance, if those readers who identify themselves with Yahweh can see

---

55. The film magazine *Premiere* ranks *Boys Don't Cry* among one of the twenty-five most dangerous films ever made (Glen Kenny, "Extreme Cinema: The 25 Most Dangerous Movies Ever Made," *Premiere* 14 [February 2001]: 92–97).

56. L. Day, "Rhetoric and Domestic Violence," 224–27; P. Day, "The Bitch Had it Coming to Her"; Runions, "Violence and the Economy of Desire."

57. Rosario, "Transgenderism," 31; Michael Giltz, "Hilary's Journey," *The Advocate* [cited 28 March 2000]; available from http://www.advocate.com/html/ stories/808/808_cvr_hilary.asp; Kimberly Pierce, "Brandon Goes to Hollywood," *The Advocate* [cited 28 March 2000]; available from http://www.advocate.com/html/stories/808/808_cvr_peirce.asp; also Anderson, "The Brandon Teena Story," 54; Moss and Zeavin, "The Real Thing?" 1227; Xan Brooks, "Boys Don't Cry," *Sight and Sound* 10 (April 2000): 44.

that Yahweh is much like John and Tom (all of whom may be much like readers' own super-egos), then perhaps they might find this reflection disconcerting enough to consider loosening their identification with Yahweh. Likewise, those (especially straight) film viewers who identify with Brandon (as a straight man) might see that he is not that different from Jerusalem, and that both are figures of repudiated femininity and disavowed loved objects. Perhaps this might further interrogate opinions about the revered American ideal of self-invented heroes, and shed light on the violence and exclusions that support the "extolled virtue . . . [of] the 'self-made man.'"[58]

Moreover, both texts are structured in such a way that they invite divided identifications. As Shields points out, readers, as addressees of the biblical text, are invited to identify with whores, but (especially if readers are male), there is "pressure . . . to identify with YHWH" and therefore to identify as both women (whores) and men (Yahweh).[59] Likewise, Linda Day suggests that perhaps in refusing to acknowledge Yahweh's behavior as problematic, commentators, although taking the part of Yahweh, are in a sense identifying with abused *women* before they decide to leave their partners.[60] I would also add that the reversibility of the pronouns *I* and *you* in Ezekiel 16, not to mention the ambiguity between the first- and second- person forms discussed above, also lend themselves to this kind of transgendered cross-identification.[61]

A similar kind of thing might be said to occur in the film as well. In an interview, film director Pierce states that she deliberately tried not to demonize Tom and John, but to characterize them so that the audience could identify with them as well as with Brandon.[62] In this way, viewers are given a wide range of identifications: cruel straight men, ideal straight man, and abused woman (or in psychoanalytic terms: critical agency, ideal identification, and repudiated feminine). Readers are also invited to consider and perhaps to identify with a wide range of sexual preferences: as men liking women, as women liking women, as men liking men.

---

58. Anderson, "The Brandon Teena Story," 54.

59. "Multiple Exposures," 150.

60. "Rhetoric and Domestic Violence," 227.

61. For a more in-depth look at what role forms of address might play in forming readerly identification, see Erin Runions, "Called to Do Justice? A Bhabhian Reading of Micah 5 and 6:1–8," *Postmodern Interpretations: A Reader*, ed. A. K. M. Adam (St Louis, Mo.: Chalice, 2001), 158–61; and Erin Runions, *Changing Subjects: Gender, Nation and Future in Micah* (Sheffield: Sheffield Academic Press, 2002).

62. "Putting Teena Brandon's Story on Film," 40.

By way of parting reflection, I might say that by opening up these various kinds of identifications for readers, these texts might possibly also begin to unearth the disavowed primary attachments underlying readers' gender identifications. In other words, these texts might provide a way of "tracing the ways in which identification is implicated in what it excludes."[63] Going one step further, I would ask whether these varied openings for readerly identification in both film and text mean that the experience of engaging with these texts can mirror the melancholic structure of their characterizations. If so, it would seem that read together, Ezekiel 16 and *Boys Don't Cry* remind readers that every heterosexual identification—in the words of Brandon Teena—is a gender identity crisis.[64]

---

63. Judith Butler, *Bodies That Matter*, 119.

64. The film picks up and makes several uses of this phrase with which Brandon explained himself to the Falls City sheriff after his rape. This horrifying interrogation, in which the sheriff harasses and accuses Brandon, is aired in the documentary *The Brandon Teena Story*, directed by Susan Muska and Greta Olafsdottir.

10. MEETING PATCH AGAIN FOR THE FIRST TIME
Purity and Compassion in Marcus Borg, the Gospel of Mark, and *Patch Adams*

Jeffrey L. Staley

In December 1998 Universal Pictures released the Tom Shadyac-directed film *Patch Adams*, a screenplay written by Steve Oedekerk and based on the life story of Hunter Adams (played by Robin Williams), a medical doctor and founder of the alternative healthcare facility, *The Gesundheit Institute*.[1]

Although the movie did fairly well at the box office, garnering the top position in gross receipts in its first two weeks and staying in the top ten for a month and a half, reviews of the film were mixed. Some found the plot overly pedantic and the tone of film syrupy sweet. James Berardinelli's review is typical of the critical reviews during its first few weeks out: "Failed efforts [at melodrama] like *Patch Adams* spend too much time trying to reduce the audience to tears through a series of cheap, transparent ploys. . . . *Patch Adams* is the kind of film that will work for an audience that's just interested in having an emotional experience (with a happy ending) without caring how obviously or clumsily they are manipulated."[2] Other reviewers, however, were kinder. For example, Steven Scheer wrote: "Indeed, all those reviews of the movie that pan Patch on the grounds that they want serious doctors rather

---

1. A description can be found at *The Gesundheit Institute* [cited 20 May 2001]; available from http://patchadams.org/.
2. James Berardinelli, "*Patch Adams*: A Film Review," 1998 [cited 20 May 2001]; available from http://movie-reviews.colossus.net/movies/p/patch.

than clowns, overlook not only the whole point of the movie, but also the fact that Patch is not simply a clown but a serious and highly competent doctor-to-be. . . ."[3]

Despite the mixed reviews, I have used the film in undergraduate New Testament classes numerous times over the past few years. In this setting, I have discovered that a more thoughtful and complex reading of the film is produced when it is viewed in the intertextual framework of Marcus Borg's *Meeting Jesus Again for the First Time* and the Gospel of Mark. As I shall show below, all three of these texts deal in significant ways with the "politics of purity and compassion."[4] Both *Patch Adams* and the Gospel of Mark also explicitly address the dangers involved with crossing purity boundaries in the name of compassion. And finally, these two narratives—one ancient, and one modern—offer an implicit critique of Borg's compassionate Jesus, who apparently can "challenge" and "attack" a purity system without endangering his own life or the lives of his followers.[5]

Like the Gospel of Mark, *Patch Adams* opens by evoking the metaphor of life as a journey. We see Hunter Adams on a bleak, midwinter bus ride and hear his musing voice-over: "All of life is a coming home . . . all the restless hearts of the world, trying to find a way home"[6] (cf. Mark 1:2–3; 6:8; 10:32, 52; 11:8; 12:14). Then Hunter, still musing, quotes a dictionary definition of home. Home is both "a place of origin, and a goal; a destination," he says (cf. Mark 10:28–30).

Borg rightly argues that the journey motif is central to both Judaism and Christianity,[7] and as Steven Scheer reminds us in his review of *Patch Adams*, the film's opening "recalls the *Odyssey*, the ultimate or archetypal coming home story in classical literature."[8] But Hunter Adams's

---

3. Steven C. Scheer, "Patch Adams" [cited 20 May 2001]; available from http://stevenc-scheer.com/patchadams.

4. Marcus Borg, *Meeting Jesus Again for the First Time: The Historical Jesus and the Heart of Contemporary Faith* (New York: HarperSanFrancisco, 1994), 53, 58.

5. Ibid., 53–58. I have written elsewhere of Borg's nonthreatening Jesus. See my *Reading with a Passion: Rhetoric, Autobiography, and the American West in the Gospel of John* (New York: Continuum, 1995), 122–27. It is quite remarkable how carefully Borg skirts the historical and political issues related to Jesus' death. The only explicit references to his crucifixion are found in footnotes (cf. Borg, *Meeting Jesus Again*, 31; 89 n. 3; 140 nn. 24, 25).

6. Quotations from the movie are my own transcription.

7. *Meeting Jesus Again*, 133–36.

8. Scheer, "Patch Adams."

words clearly express something more than a literal return home. They also reflect the idea of searching and finding one's true place in the world, because a few sentences later Hunter invokes the opening words of Dante's *Inferno*: "In the middle of the journey of my life I had lost the right path"—a path which he was to find eventually "in the most unlikely place."[9]

Like the Gospel of Mark, which tells us virtually nothing about the early life of Jesus and opens with an adult Jesus being baptized by John, the film *Patch Adams* introduces us to an adult Hunter Adams who tells us little about his life before his "call." In Hunter's own words, "My father died when I was nine. He was in the army. He wasn't home much . . . I moved seven times in the last year. I've had several jobs. Nothing seemed to fit. I don't seem to fit." But through a series of humorous circumstances "in a most unlikely place" (the psychiatric ward of Fairfax Hospital), Hunter Adams finds he is able to help patients on the road to wholeness. His epiphany—or "baptism," if you will (cf. Mark 1:9–11)—comes through the insight of a wild-eyed genius and philanthropist, Arthur Mendelson, who, like Hunter, is a self-committed psychiatric patient. Arthur encourages Hunter to look beyond the ordinary and "see what no one else sees. See what everyone else chooses not to see. See the whole world anew, each day" (cf. Mark 8:22–25; 10:46–52). And when Hunter puts a sticker over a hole in Arthur's leaky paper cup,[10] Arthur gives him a new name: "You fixed my cup. I'll see you around . . . Patch" (cf. Mark 2:21).[11] "Patch" leaves with Arthur Mendelson's words echoing in his ears: "I fancy you are well on your way."

---

9. Adams's given name, "Hunter," is certainly no less fortuitous than "Patch," the nickname Arthur Mendelson later gives him (cf. Mark 2:21), because Hunter is on a personal quest to find his life calling (cf. Mark 1:17).

10. Scheer notes "It is also interesting . . . that Patch gets his new name when he repairs a leaking paper cup with a piece of self-adhesive strip that was originally meant for another purpose" ("Patch Adams").

11. As in Mark 9:41; 10:38–39; and 14:23, 36, cups play a metaphorical role in *Patch Adams*. For example, during Hunter's initial interview in the mental hospital, Dr. Prack's preoccupation with stirring his coffee makes Hunter conscious of the fact that the doctor is not listening to Hunter's explanation of his failure to "fit in." Not coincidentally, it is when Hunter fixes Arthur Mendelson's leaky cup that he catches a vision of the way the world could be and learns that "not fitting in" could also be viewed as a gift: a gift of seeing "what no one else sees." Later on, while drinking a cup of coffee with Truman Schiff in the University Diner, Patch has his vision of a "free hospital," and echoes Arthur Mendelson's words to "look beyond the objects . . ."

*(The real) Hunter "Patch" Adams with Kosovo refugee
camp children, Macedonia, 1999*

The rest of Hunter "Patch" Adams's life will be spent literally patching up broken people—making them well—for he soon checks out of the mental hospital and enrolls in Virginia Medical University. The remainder of the film deals with Patch's years of schooling, his purity system-shattering pranks that challenge those authority figures whose goal is to "train the humanity out" of first-year students, his romance with fellow medical student Carin Fisher, his dreams of starting an alternative hospital, and his eventual graduation.

In the process of tracing Patch Adams's journey toward "home" and wholeness, the film focuses on the rigorous "purity codes" (as Marcus Borg would call them) of four American institutions. These are the mental institution, the university, the food industry (meatpacking), and the hospital. Curiously—and most helpfully for its use with undergraduate students—religious purity codes only rarely intrude in the film's story line.[12] Finally, toward the end of the film a fifth "institution" makes its appearance—the counter-cultural, alternative, "anti-institution" of Patch Adams's Gesundheit Institute—a healing community without boundaries, rules, or apparent purity codes. Ironically, it is precisely because of the institute's lack of boundaries that Carin, Patch's soul mate and lover, is brutally murdered.

The term "purity code" was not invented by Marcus Borg, although he uses the term in a helpful way to describe how Jesus fits into—or more accurately does not fit into—the sociopolitical world of Second Temple Judaism. Quoting Jerome Neyrey,[13] who in turn summarizes the work of Mary Douglas,[14] Borg argues:

> [A] purity system "is a cultural map which indicates 'a place for everything and everything in its place.'" Things that are okay in one place are impure or dirty in another, where they are out of place. Slightly more narrowly, and put very simply, a purity system is a social system organized around the contrasts or polarities

---

12. Toward the end of the film when Patch is contemplating suicide after Carin's death, he speaks accusingly to God (Patch's address is always to "you"—he never uses the word "God") and evokes the Sabbath command. "You rested on the seventh day," Patch complains, "Maybe you should have spent that day on compassion."

13. Jerome H. Neyrey, "The Symbolic Universe of Luke-Acts: They Turn the World Upside Down," *The Social World of Luke-Acts: Models for Interpretation*, ed. Jerome H. Neyrey (Peabody, Mass.: Hendrickson, 1991), 275.

14. Cf. Mary Douglas, "Deciphering a Meal," *Implicit Meanings: Essays in Anthropology*, ed. Mary Douglas (London: Routledge & Kegan Paul, 1975), 249–75.

of pure and impure, clean and unclean. The polarities of pure and impure establish a spectrum or "purity map" ranging from pure on the one end through varying degrees of purity to impure (or "off the purity map") at the other. These polarities apply to persons, places, things, times, and social groups.[15]

In Borg's analysis, Jesus practiced a "politics of compassion" rather than a "politics of purity," and thus he consciously and consistently challenged the boundaries of the Jewish map of purity. For Borg, Jesus' actions "shatter[ed] the purity boundaries of his social world."[16] While Borg's cultural depiction may appear oversimplified to a serious anthropologist, his borrowing of Mary Douglas's purity polarities is useful in that it provides Bible readers and interpreters of ancient cultural artifacts a framework for quickly classifying biblical behavior and social phenomena.

For example, Borg writes: "Purity was political because it structured society into a purity system."[17] And later on, "Purity systems are found in many cultures."[18] Both of these statements can be easily misconstrued if the reader were to surmise from them that purity is not necessarily political today, and that there are cultures lacking purity systems. However, both of these latter construals would be wrong. Thus, in reworking Borg's book for my undergraduate students, I tell them to write in their copies of *Meeting Jesus Again*: "Purity is *always* political because it structures societies into purity systems," and "Purity systems are found in *all* cultures."

One can only begin to appreciate Mark's dangerous story of Jesus in all its richness when one becomes conscious of the purity codes in one's own culture and the political ramifications of challenging their pervasive power. And by reading the Gospel of Mark intertextually, against the background of Marcus Borg's work and *Patch Adams*, a number of significant purity-code connections begin to appear. First, it becomes readily apparent that the four central institutions of American purity

---

15. *Meeting Jesus Again*, 50.
16. Ibid., 55, 56, 60.
17. Ibid., 50.
18. Ibid. As Borg is quick to note, he is heavily dependent upon Jerome Neyrey's essay, "The Symbolic Universe of Luke-Acts." However, Neyrey writes much more inclusively than does Borg, saying, "*All* people have a sense of what is 'pure' and what is 'polluted,' although just what constitutes 'purity' and 'pollution' changes from culture to culture" ("The Symbolic Universe of Luke-Acts," 274, emphasis added).

and conventional wisdom[19] that Patch challenges (the mental hospital, the university, the meatpackers' convention, and the medical hospital) also appear at the beginning of Mark's gospel—albeit in different form. These purity codes are evident in the challenges to authority raised by Jesus' exorcisms (3:20–30), his teaching (1:21–22, 27; cf. 11:27–33), his eating with "sinners" (2:15–17; cf. 7:1–14), and his healing the sick (1:40–45; 2:1–12). Secondly, both *Patch Adams* and Mark's gospel closely link masculinity and racial/ethnic identity with purity and hierarchical power. In Mark, the male scribes, priests, Pharisees, and Jesus' twelve disciples are part of the traditional locus of Jewish power and conventional wisdom. They are the ones who most often challenge Jesus' claim to authority (cf. 1:42; 2:6, 16; 3:6, 13-19; cf. 10:35–40). So also in the film, each of the four authoritative institutions puts males in positions of power, speaking in the language of conventional wisdom.

In the film, the code of purity, with its attendant authoritative wisdom figures, is symbolized by white men wearing white jackets (cf. Mark 9:3; 16:5). Dr. Prack, the psychiatrist in the mental hospital, Deans Walcott and Anderson—both in the classroom and in the hospital—and the meatpackers, all wear white coats. The only other people to wear white are the multiracial/multiethnic staff at the Fairfax Hospital psychiatric ward and the multiethnic/multiracial nurses in the teaching hospital, who are all clearly on a lower level than the doctors. However, Patch and Carin also wear white T-shirts on significant occasions. Patch wears white on the day he decides to leave the mental institution to pursue a career in medicine, and Carin wears white the day she risks her life for Patch's vision of compassionate healing. Furthermore, Patch and his first disciple, Truman Schiff, are only able to transgress the boundary of the hospital's purity codes by donning meatpackers' white smocks and covering the meatpacker insignias or "patches" with their hands. Finally, Carin confesses her desire for the conventional code of purity and wisdom when she says to Patch, "I want the white coat. I want for people to call me doctor more than anything." Patch reiterates this perspective

---

19. Borg describes "conventional wisdom" as "the dominant consciousness of any culture" that "provides guidance about how to live"; is "intrinsically based upon the dynamic of rewards and punishments"; and "creates a world of hierarchies and boundaries" (*Meeting Jesus Again*, 75–76; see also 69-70, 75–77). There is an obvious connection between a culture's "conventional wisdom" and its "purity codes." For example, Borg discusses social hierarchies and boundaries under the subheadings of both "purity system" and "conventional wisdom" (ibid., 51–52, 75–76).

when he defends himself before the state medical board: "You can keep me from getting the title and the white coat," he proclaims, "but you can't control my spirit."

But like Jesus and the women of Mark's gospel, Patch's new community—his "free hospital"—challenges the hierarchical social constructions and the conventional wisdom symbolized by the white coats. Patch shares his vision with Carin halfway through the film. There will be ". . . no titles, no bosses; people will come from all over the world . . . [it will be] a community where joy is a way of life; where love is the ultimate good" (cf. Mark 9:33–37; 10:17–22, 31, 35–45). Significantly, Carin's response is more relevant to Mark than to Borg's *Meeting Jesus Again*: "I'm scared to death," she whispers prophetically. "Breaking the rules, people get hurt" (cf. Mark 8:31–36).

It is not surprising to find trust concerns closely related to the attacks on hierarchical (male) power in both Mark and *Patch Adams*. The word "trust" or "faith" (*pistis/pisteuein*) is richly evocative from the very beginning of Mark's gospel (cf. 1:15; 2:5; 4:40; 5:34, 36; 9:23–24, 42; 10:52; 11:22–24, 31; 13:21; 15:32), and in *Patch Adams* the theme is the focus of Dean Walcott's inaugural lecture to Patch Adams's entering class of medical students. Here issues of authority, trust, and children are clustered together in much the same way as they are in Mark's gospel.

> "First, do no harm," intones Dean Walcott, quoting the Hippocratic Oath.
> But "What is implicit in this simple precept?" he asks.
> "An awesome power. The power to do harm.
> "Who gives you this power?
> "The patient. A patient will come to you at his moment of greatest dread and will say, 'Cut me open.'
> "Why? Because he trusts you. He trusts you the way a child trusts. He trusts you to do no harm. The sad fact is, human beings are not worthy of trust. . . . No rational patient would put his trust in a human being."

Dean Walcott's words will prove to be prophetically true later when Carin finally puts her whole trust in Patch's ideals and goes off into the night to answer Larry Silvers's cry for help. Tragically, Carin is murdered by the one she goes to help. As a result of her risk-taking trust, she becomes the film's paradigm of fear, anxiety, and costly faith—sort of a composite of all the unnamed women of Mark's gospel (5:25–35; 7:24–30; 12:41–44; 14:3–9; 15:40–41, 47; 16:1–8). The night before Carin dies, she confides in Patch the reason why she finds it so difficult to trust any man—even Patch, the film's Christ figure. It is due to her lifelong sexual abuse at the hands of men. Ironically, the only explicit quotation of Scripture occurs the morning after Carin has been murdered, when Patch recites "O, ye of little faith" to Truman (Matthew 8:26; cf. Mark 4:40).[20]

Images of spiritual rebirth abound in the film the evening before Carin is murdered, when she is finally able to put her faith wholly in Patch. With Van Morrison's song "Into the Mystic" playing in the background[21] and torches burning in the night breeze, Carin reveals her tortured past to Patch with a story of how she would "look out [her] bedroom window at the caterpillars" when she was a little girl, envying them. Because "no matter what they were before, no matter what happened to them, they could just hide away and turn into these beautiful creatures that could fly away completely untouched." The camera then fades out with Patch and Carin embracing. When it refocuses it is morning, and we are looking at Carin from Patch's perspective as he watches her sleeping, wrapped in white sheets. A stained-glass butterfly hangs by a thread in the window above Carin's bed as sunlight washes the room.[22]

The butterfly, of course, is a well-known symbol of hope and new life; in the Christian tradition, it represents the resurrection. So the symbolism is not to be missed when, a few days after Carin's murder, Patch himself faces his ultimate test on a mountaintop (Mark 9:1–13). As he contemplates suicide,[23] a butterfly suddenly lands on his leather doctor's satchel, his heart, and his finger. Symbolically Patch's passion, his hands, and his vocation are renewed by this divine visitation.

All three texts under consideration—the Gospel of Mark, Borg's *Meeting Jesus Again for the First Time*, and *Patch Adams*—focus on purity

---

20. The only other explicit allusions to the Bible are when Patch says to the hospital nurses, "Hi! I'm John the Baptist. Any calls?" (cf. Mark 6:25–28); and when Patch tells Dean Walcott that the only rule that applies to him is the "Golden Rule" (cf. Mark 12:33).

21. The first line of the song goes: "We were born before the wind . . . "

22. The first time Carin appears in the film she is wearing a butterfly brooch on her jacket collar. On her second appearance she wears butterfuly earrings.

23. The film opens with Patch committing himself to a mental institution because of his suicidal tendencies.

codes and on the alternative politics of compassion. But the film and the Gospel of Mark reflect a more realistic picture of the dangers involved when crossing purity boundaries in the name of compassion. Patch makes this perfectly clear as he mourns Carin's death with the words, "I taught her the medicine that killed her." Of course, Mark's Jesus is pursued and eventually crucified in part because of his challenges to the core symbols of Jewish purity (Mark 3:6; 11:15–19; 13:1–3; 14:58).

Although Patch himself does not physically die because of his compassionate boundary-busting behavior, it is obvious that Carin's death figuratively represents his own. This is seen most clearly when he contemplates suicide after her murder and in his recitation of Pablo Neruda's "Sonnet 17"[24]—a recitation that brackets Carin's death. Patch begins the poem at a surprise birthday party he throws for her, then continues the poem the morning of the day she is murdered, as she lies in bed with the stained-glass butterfly hanging above her. Patch finally finishes the poem a few days later, after Carin's funeral, reading the closing lines over her coffin.

Thus, Patch, whose life is totally bound up with Carin's life, "dies" when she dies,[25] and is "resurrected" when the butterfly (her spirit? a holy spirit?) lands on his doctor's satchel. The theological significance of Patch's passion narrative—his "death and resurrection"—is also emphasized by a sudden appearance of God language in the film. For sandwiched between Patch's final fragmentary recitations of Neruda's sonnet are four apparently insignificant but crucial divine interjections:

1. The night before Carin dies she says, "God, Patch, it's amazing just what you've done with this place . . . "
2. The next morning Truman exclaims exasperatingly to Patch, "We don't even have any gauze, for God's sake."
3. Then, the following morning when Dean Anderson is forced to tell Patch of Carin's murder, he says, "Christ, Patch, I'm sorry."
4. The fourth use of God language comes just when Patch has decided to abandon his free hospital. Truman vehemently reacts to Patch's leaving with, "God, you're so self-indulgent!"

---

24. See Pablo Neruda, *100 Love Sonnets*, trans. Stephen Tapscott (Austin: University of Texas Press, 1986), 39.

25. Patch is shown sleeping on a porch swing the morning after Carin has been murdered, thus reflecting the closing lines of Neruda's poem: "so close that your eyes close as I fall asleep."

These four "kuriosities," as I call them,[26] define Patch as a Jesus-like savior figure in much the same way that Mark's characters use the word *kurie* (cf. 7:28; 10:51; 11:3; 12:9) to overdetermine the reader's association of the word *kurios* with Jesus.[27] The Markan reader is never quite sure if the word *kurie* means "sir," "master," or "Lord"—or all three, when Jesus is the addressee. But regardless of how the word should be understood, it is still closely connected to Jesus. So also with the cinematic kuriosities ringing in the viewers' ears: they should not go unnoticed, because Patch later speaks in phrases reminiscent of Jesus in Mark 10:43–45. During his final defense speech before the state medical board, Patch concludes by saying, "I want to become a doctor so I can serve others. And because of that I've lost everything. But I have also gained everything." Patch's "death" and "resurrection," like that of Jesus in Mark's gospel, is thus mysteriously redemptive. It will also prove to be renewing and empowering for the host of people who pack the balconies at the state medical board proceedings and who will follow in his wake (cf. Mark 13:9–13; 16:7).

In Borg's terms, Patch, like Jesus, practices a politics of compassion that is nurtured by an alternative wisdom tradition. The difference, of course, is that the primary source and mode of Patch's alternative wisdom and compassion is his own wacky sense of humor, whereas Jesus' alternative wisdom and compassion seems to be nurtured by the ancient Hebrew prophets and his own profound sense of God's presence.[28] Usually Patch claims no special authority for his actions, but at times he can argue that the AMA lends supports to his outrageous behavior.[29] Likewise, Mark's Jesus occasionally claims that Scripture supports his boundary-breaking activity and his challenging metaphors (2:25–28; 10:2–9; 12:18–27, 35–37). However, most often the authority of Mark's

---

26. By my careful reckoning there are only three other passing references to God in the film. The first is a divine interjection made by Patch close to the beginning of the film, and the final two occur in Patch's defense speech before the state medical board. The only reference to Christ in the film occurs when Dean Anderson tells Patch of Carin's murder. And the only time Patch is called "son" is during his "trial" before the state medical board (cf. Mark 14:61–62).

27. This rhetorical device, which I have termed a "kuriosity," is most evident in the film *The Matrix*, where all the divine interjections of the film are directed at "Neo," who turns out to be "the One" who saves humanity. The same phenomenon occurs in other recent Hollywood films as well.

28. Borg, *Meeting Jesus Again*, 31–36, 47–49.

29. For the most part, *Patch Adams* and the Gospel of Mark share a common distrust of doctors (Mark 2:17; 5:26).

Jesus is simply rooted in his own voice and deeds (2:10, 28; 7:14–15; 10:10–12, 23–27).

Unlike the Gospel of Mark, not all the purity codes that Patch flaunts are transgressions in the name of compassion. *Patch Adams* is a comedy; and some of Patch's words and deeds are intended simply to elicit belly laughs from the audience. For example, Adams spends most of a psychiatric ward "sharing time" making crude jokes about the possible meanings of the catatonic patient "Beanie's" upraised arm. Patch mocks the eating rituals of the meatpackers' convention with outrageous jokes and a ridiculous speech. And the giant papier-mâché spread legs that he builds for the "medical seminar/retreat for the Fellowship of the American College of Gynecologists" is little more than a sophomoric prank. Like a lot of humor, this physical joke challenges cultural purity codes, but offers no serious critique of the medical profession.

Some of the more obvious places where Patch challenges cultural purity codes are at the points of status transformation—those rituals related to entering and exiting the four institutions represented in the film.[30] For example, Patch transgresses the status transformation rituals of entering and exiting the psychiatric ward by committing *himself* to psychiatric care and then simply leaving when he deems he is "cured." He desacralizes the holy moment of the initiatory psychiatric interview with his rude sexual jokes that Dr. Prack totally misses. Dr. Prack, the "ritual elder" ostensibly in charge of Hunter Adams's status transformation, thus will have no control over the change that occurs in Patch's life while he is on the psychiatric ward. Furthermore, one of the symbolic objects of Patch's ritual separation—a simple, metal-frame bed—is misused as a bunker to protect him and his roommate Rudy from an attack of invisible squirrels. Through this unsanctioned "therapy" session, Rudy is strangely "cured"; and so is Patch, who discovers from this experience the healing power that comes from helping others. Patch's lack of respect for transformation rituals runs through to the conclusion of the film when, during the graduation ceremony of his medical school, he moons the dean and the crowd.

---

30. Mark McVann, following Victor Turner, defines "the elements of a status transformation ritual" as involving "(a) the initiands, who undergo the change of role and status, (b) the ritual elders, who preside over the ritual, and (c) the symbols (or *sacra*) of the world which the initiands learn during the ritual" ("Rituals of Status Transformation in Luke-Acts: The Case of Jesus the Prophet," *The Social World of Luke-Acts: Models for Interpretation*, 336).

The Gospel of Mark does not flaunt status transformation rituals the way that *Patch Adams* does. Instead, Mark simply omits from his narrative the normal Jewish transformation rituals and their attendant symbols of purity. For example, in contrast to the Gospel of Luke, Mark does not list Jesus' genealogy, mention his circumcision, or name his father. In contrast to the Gospel of Matthew, there is no naming ceremony for Jesus. And in contrast to the Gospel of John, at the end of Jesus' life no one properly prepares Jesus' body for burial.

Patch's blatant disregard for transformation rituals and their underlying purity codes has no direct parallel in the Gospel of Mark. However, his crazy antics in the hospital's oncology ward do raise issues of critique and compassion that are closely allied with Mark.[31] While there are virtually no dangers associated with Patch's crossing of boundaries in the meatpackers' convention or in the psychiatric ward, Patch's boundary-busting compassion in the teaching hospital constantly gets him into serious trouble with the "authorities" (Dean Anderson and Dean Walcott). For example, he crosses the purity boundaries of time and place by being in the wrong place (the hospital) at the wrong time (before his third year of medical school). Patch does the wrong things (he talks to patients about everyday concerns and pretends to be a clown) and misuses "sacred" things (he uses enema bulbs for noses, bed pans for shoes and hats, and hospital beds as bucking broncos). All this in the name of compassionate healing.[32] Similarly, Jesus, in the Gospel of Mark, crosses the purity boundaries of time and place (Sabbath, 2:23–3:6; temple, 11:15–17), things and actions (7:1–23), and persons and groups (1:40–44; 2:15–17; 5:21–43). All in the name of divine compassion.

The special edition videocassette of *Patch Adams* includes a twelve-minute postscript entitled *The Medicinal Value of Laughter*, which introduces the viewer to the real Hunter Adams, Tom Shadyac (the film's director),

---

31. After he has been caught one last time trespassing in the children's oncology ward, Patch lectures Dean Walcott on the medicinal importance of humor. And when Patch is called into the dean's office the next day, Walcott accuses of him of thinking "the rules [don't] apply to you." Patch replies, "Not all the rules, sir. But the Golden Rule—I think that applies to everyone—don't you?" Tellingly, all the hospital children shown in the film were actual "Make-a-Wish Foundation" children suffering from various types of cancer.

32. Patch argues before the state medical board, "If we're going to fight a disease, let's fight one of the most terrible diseases of all—indifference. . . . You treat a disease, you win, you lose. You treat a person, I guarantee you, you always win, no matter what the outcome. . . . The professors you respect, the ones who aren't dead from the heart up, share their compassion. Let that be contagious."

and Mike Farrell (the film's primary producer). In the threefold reading framework that I have proposed above, the short documentary becomes an important addition to the intertextual weave of Borg's book and the Gospel of Mark. As with Borg's reconstruction of the "pre-Easter Jesus"[33] the viewer discovers that there are significant differences between the film version of *Patch Adams* and Hunter Adams's actual life story. For example, Robin Williams's Patch Adams character is much older when he enters medical school than the real Hunter Adams was. But Mike Farrell argues, "[T]he film is based on a true story. The facts as they are laid out in the story—most of them are based in Patch's reality. Some of them are extrapolations, some happened at different times; some of them happened with different people; some of the people are compilations . . . " And Tom Shadyac adds, "The movie is really an 'inspired by' story. It's not *exactly* Patch's life, but just about everything that happens in the movie happened to Patch—just over a longer period of time . . ." Using Shadyac's phrase, Borg would probably argue that the Gospel of Mark—and all the gospels—are "inspired by" stories that condense, exaggerate, and build composite characters and scenes, all in the name of the spirit of its central character, Jesus. And just as Marcus Borg struggles to separate out the "pre-Easter Jesus" from the "post-Easter Jesus" and tries to balance the requisite truth claims of the historian and the theologian, the producer, the director, and the "pre-Easter" Patch Adams wrestle with the truth claims of their narrative reconstruction. *The Medicinal Value of Laughter*, directed by J. M. Kenny, functions as a delightful and helpful intertextual aid for engaging readers of Mark and Marcus Borg in questions of the relationship between "historical" truth and narrative truth.

In conclusion, viewing *Patch Adams* intertextually with *Meeting Jesus Again for the First Time* can help people see the pervasive and persuasive powers of purity codes in contemporary American culture. Viewing *Patch Adams* intertextually with *Meeting Jesus Again for the First Time* and the Gospel of Mark also helps people move beyond surface-level critiques of the film that merely focus on its storytelling devices and its emotional tone. *Patch Adams* is not just an entertaining movie with a curious alternative vision of medicine. Now the film can be viewed as a narrative that raises challenging moral questions about the relationship

---

33. *Meeting Jesus Again*, 15–16, 28–31.

(The real) Hunter "Patch" Adams with Kosovo refugee
camp children, Macedonia, 1999

between compassion and purity in contemporary culture. Like the Gospel of Mark, it presents its viewers with an alternative vision of life that challenges traditional cultural values: a subversive wisdom; a politics of compassion. On a theological level, viewing *Patch Adams* against the backdrop of *Meeting Jesus Again* and the Gospel of Mark raises crucial questions about the lack of political threat and danger in Borg's Jesus. Is it really possible for a person of compassion to challenge the politics of purity in any age or culture without getting hurt? *Patch Adams* and the Gospel of Mark seem to say no. Borg seems to equivocate.

Finally, reading the Gospel of Mark alongside *Patch Adams* can be a deeply enriching experience. The film's explicit juxtapositioning of four contemporary American institutions of purity gives viewers a new way to understand the political challenge of Mark's Jesus. It helps viewers to see the cost that compassion poses apart from any explicit ideological motif of "God's grand design" (e.g. Mark 8:31; 9:30–31; 10:32–34), and the ultimate joy one can find in following "the right path."

11. LEARNING FROM *THE LIFE OF BRIAN*
Saviors for Seminars[1]

Carl Dyke

Although religious establishment is formally prohibited and unbelievers are not systematically tortured, killed, forcibly converted, or segregated in ghettos, the United States remains saturated with a deeply, sometimes aggressively biblical culture. This characteristic, invisible like water to fish for most Christians, has been noted alike by thoughtful visitors[2] and bemused or outraged natives.[3] "Not only has biblical language continued to be a part of American public and political discourse, the churches have continuously exerted influence on public life right up to the present time."[4] As I write, the Kansas school board is engaged in a merely tactical retreat from its popular position that teaching all children articles of Christian belief about creation in the public schools is a perfectly reasonable thing to do. Attorney General John Ashcroft is holding daily staff prayer meetings in his offices at the Justice Department, the agency responsible for enforcing the establishment clause in the First

1. Thanks for thoughtful comments and helpful suggestions to Barbara R. Smith and Rachel Beaulieu, two critical intellectuals with little patience for the games I describe herein.
2. Examples include Alexis de Tocqueville, *Democracy in America*, ed. J. P. Mayer, trans. George Lawrence (Garden City: Anchor, 1969 [1850]), 287–301; and Max Weber, "The Protestant Sects and the Spirit of Capitalism," *From Max Weber: Essays in Sociology*, ed. and trans. H. H. Gerth and C. Wright Mills (New York: Oxford University Press, 1946 [1906]), 302–22.
3. An example is Richard Hofstadter, *Anti-Intellectualism in American Life* (New York: Vintage, 1972).
4. Robert N. Bellah et al., *Habits of the Heart: Individualism and Commitment in American Life* (Berkeley: University of California Press, 1985), 220.

Amendment.[5] My metropolitan daily newspaper reports with approval that the Principal of the Year in North Carolina public schools has a Christian motto taped to her work computer.[6] And the currency that I use informs me that in God we trust.

In short, Christianity is hegemonic in the United States—part of the commonsense grid that marks out the fields of normalcy and deviance on which all inhabitants of this country must play. From a critical perspective, resistances to this hegemony are automatically interesting, and outright counter-hegemonic gestures are a holy grail of critical social analysis. This essay's topic is one candidate for assessment as a counter-hegemonic gesture: Monty Python's movie *The Life of Brian* (1979).

In broad outline, the movie is an imaginative reconstruction of the historical life-world that produced the Christian Gospels. Brian, a nice but altogether ordinary Judean, finds himself drawn by a series of accidents into a void of meaning where his every word and action become deeply significant to a growing accumulation of unwanted disciples. As depicted by the Pythons, he is just one of many candidates for messiah as the people of Judea grasp chaotically after either spiritual or political relief from Roman domination. The plot obviously has some deep theological implications. In addition, because the movie is playful at various levels right down to the broadest slapstick and plays into the bourgeois Anglophilia that pays for PBS, it can be at least mildly entertaining to almost anyone uninvested in dogmatic religious and social conventions.

I am not interested in casual or formal bases for liking the movie so much as its importance for certain audiences and purposes. Ever since I first saw it as a teenager, I have thought the movie offers all sorts of useful lessons about the Gospels. This is why I rather unreflectively chose it as my topic for this essay and volume. Reflecting now on how I want to write this essay, I realize how everything I want to say about the movie is bound up in those first impressions. In particular, I realize that for me, the movie always has had important strategic values that have persisted and evolved under the layers of specialized knowledge and sophisticated interpretive operations I can now run it through. It is the movie's strategic values, only tangentially related to the Gospels, which will be the focus of this essay.

---

5. News item heard on National Public Radio, May 18, 2001.
6. Adrienne Lu, "In the Schools: Principal of the Year Uses Faith, Many Hands. Giving Credit, Taking Responsibility," *Raleigh News & Observer*, 14 May 2001, B1.

Since self-reflection got me to the point of looking at the movie in terms of strategies, I will start with a bit of autobiography. Knowing that the details of my adolescence are not of much interest to any reader, I have included only enough of the case to show how I developed an elementary strategic posture toward the movie and, using the movie, toward elements of my social milieu. This discussion will set the stage for more general reflections on the strategic values of the movie with respect to contrasting social positions (including contrasts over the meanings of the Gospels). Here, I will work with Antonio Gramsci's concepts of common sense and hegemony to illustrate one sort of strategic critical reception of the movie. I will then use Pierre Bourdieu's ideas about habitus and class to complicate strategic critical reception by looking at some of its conditions. My hypothesis is that *The Life of Brian* is likely to have special strategic values for the class fraction of critical intellectuals far beyond (or simply other than) its inherent resources of entertainment, edification, or even counter-hegemony.[7] I should say that I do not think there is a single correct strategic reception any more than God could be on the side of only one team in a basketball game. Accordingly, I start with strategic criticisms and end up strategically critical of strategic criticism.

THE GOSPELS, TANGENTIALLY

My upbringing, mostly insulated from hegemonic Christianity, was ideal to make me an audience for which *The Life of Brian* would be strategically important. I grew up just beyond the outer-commute fringe of Philadelphia in a relatively isolated semirural area, around which I frequently wandered alone. We did not socialize substantively with the locals. My parents were both educated and cosmopolitan, even more so after the family spent two years in Italy starting when I was ten. We were a PBS/NPR family. My dad, whose father was a carpet salesman and bartender, had worked a series of very odd jobs in order to afford a series of very right schools. He earned his doctorate in philosophy working on

---

7. There are several different ways I could have said this. I could have said that the movie supplies critical vocabulary in a "language game" (Wittgenstein), or discursive power in a "truth game" (Foucault). I could have joked that the movie is a big gun in the international arms race of ideas (Bourdieu, see below).

Camus, whose austere existentialist humanism probably attracted Dad as a rebellious a-theistic twist on the austere Protestantism of his own New England upbringing.

Needless to say, what for him was a statement was for me taken for granted (as a loved eldest son, I have felt no need to make my own rebellious statement[8]). Perhaps ironically, radical personal responsibility was the standard of my moral education. I was trusted to make independent judgments as long as I could give a reflective account of them in which care for others was prominently featured.[9] Critical thinking (I did not learn to call it that until much later) has been part of my unreflective worldview and habitual practice from my earliest memories. It is not something for which I can take credit, and I have gradually learned (by means of it, to be sure) to be suspicious of my reflex to think everyone should do it.

As a child I was dimly aware of organized religion, but in my early years it simply had no relevance to my life. Little friends would occasionally mention church as an ordinary activity, but there are many ordinary activities that may be shared or not shared (I also was not in Boy Scouts or Little League) and this one did not stand out. I do remember enjoying that I had my Sunday mornings free.

When *The Life of Brian* came out in 1979, I was in local public high school and locked in struggle with packs of born-again Christians. This was my first serious encounter with missionary Christianity. The pattern was always the same. Using one stratagem or another, they cut me from the herd and isolated me. That I was not fitting stably into any particular herd in high school must have made me look like easy prey. My faith credentials were examined and found to be in deplorable disorder. It usually took a while to convince the missionaries and their gently perplexed spokesman [*sic*] not only that I was not any variety of Christian, but that I had no religious affiliation whatever nor any sense of a void in my life in this respect. Finally persuaded of my innocence and/or ignorance, the spokesman delivered his joyous "good news."

I was dabbling in missionary skepticism in those days (I thought of it as open-mindedness) and was always in the mood for a good debate. I also thought I knew genuine good will when I saw it. So although I had

---

8. See Frank J. Sulloway, *Born to Rebel: Birth Order, Family Dynamics, & Creative Lives* (New York: Random House, 1996).

9. No doubt readers impatient with my autobiographical approach in this section will discover here the sources of my self-indulgence.

no interest whatever in getting someone else's religion, I generally expressed sincere thanks for the missionaries' care and inquired further as to the sources and outlines of their good news. At this point the conversation became a free-for-all about the content and meaning of both the Bible and Christian history. I knew a little about those things, and so did they. Sooner or later the record of bad behavior by Christians and the list of contradictions, ambiguities, and improbabilities in the Bible itself that I was able to list on demand produced a stalemate. I had no satisfactory answers for the big questions about "Life, the Universe, and the Meaning of It All" that religions have always answered best, but I saw no reason to cover my ignorance with metaphysical inventions. I was aware of religions other than Christianity, and they seemed no less (or more) plausible to me. We agreed that it was all a matter of faith; they exhorted me to look within my heart for mine (or to open my heart to Jesus, "assuming facts not in evidence," as the lawyers say); and we all parted friendly.

In these conversations and their outcomes I was smug. I thought I was a real intellectual and was certainly training for the part. Like many non-Christians raised among Christians, I thought I knew the holy texts better than the faithful. (This attitude had been especially easy to acquire during my two years in Italian public school, mumbling Hail Marys and Our Fathers every morning along with the rest of the class. Many Italian Catholics cheerfully do not bother to read the Bible directly, since that is what priests are for; and, like U.S. children with the pledge of allegiance, they may drone the prayers phonetically.) Further, like many non-Christians raised among Christians, I also thought I acted more in the spirit of Christian morals than many Christians, who seemed to me to be substituting ritual practices and attitudes for the hard work of living thoughtfully that Jesus recommended.

When *Life of Brian* showed up, I was just about sick of this little game of hunted-becomes-the-hunter. For one thing, I started to become aware that I was not at my most likable when picking at loose threads in other people's beliefs, even when they just darned me over or folded the holes under new wrinkles. For another, that phase in my construction as a critical intellectual was simply over. Demi-secular friends who had no real prospects of getting out of our backwater town kept playing the game with their equally localized religious counterparts in an ongoing cycle of mutually indispensable self-definition. They enjoyed the movie (as I did, and do) for its crude burlesque send-ups of the sorts of status-bearing religious sanctimony and bourgeois propriety they groused about every day over a beer or three, as well as for the patent of connoisseurship it conferred. I was tracked for college and looking for bigger fish to fry and a hotter stove to fry them on. Although I didn't know it yet, I had started to think counter-hegemonically about Christianity.

The Pythons' earlier movie, *Monty Python and the Holy Grail* (1975), was the lead-in. Its zany irreverence toward various conventions, including those of church religion (as reflected in the title and general plot of the Arthurian quest for the grail), had tickled me by offering legitimation and vocabulary for my own adolescent experiments with intellectual nonconformity. The local PBS station, knowing its audience well, showed the movie during every pledge break. I saw it a dozen or more times. "We are all conformists of some conformism or other," Gramsci says.[10] Indeed. I did not yet see the irony of the oppositional conformity that led me and my cognoscenti friends to memorize and perform long stretches of dialogue. "Strange women lying in ponds distributing swords is no basis for a system of government." Ha. As I headed toward the self-consciously more sophisticated university milieu, *The Life of Brian* became iconic to me as the model of how to rise above using an educated, serious, yet playful critique of the Christian pretentiousness I perceived all around me.

HEGEMONY AND COUNTER-HEGEMONY

> Note the problem of religion taken not in the confessional sense but in the secular sense of a unity of faith between a conception of the world and a corresponding norm of conduct. But why call this unity of faith "religion" and not "ideology," or even frankly "politics"?[11]

I gradually began to realize during college and graduate school that the story I just told makes sense only within a hegemonic Christian regime. The conversations were only apparently between Christians and a non-Christian. The entire ground of legitimate argumentation was Christian history and Christian doctrine; the only way for me to make any headway at all was to operate the tools of my interlocutors more ably than they did. More importantly, at that time I saw no dilemma in this situation—

---

10. Antonio Gramsci, *Selections from the Prison Notebooks*, ed. and trans Quintin Hoare and Geoffrey Nowell Smith (New York: International Publishers, 1971), 324.
11. Ibid., 326.

I fully accepted those grounds of debate and, in crucial respects, shared them. Although I found the Bible unconvincing and God/Jesus/Holy Spirit "unnecessary hypotheses," my own morals were (and are) secular derivatives of the ethical traditions of Christianity. In the terms of Gramsci's quote above, I unreflectively shared the norm of conduct while challenging the corresponding conception of the world; but by working with its texts and terms, I was inside the latter as well. *The Life of Brian* and I were a perfect fit.

Antonio Gramsci (1891–1937), a leading Marxist theorist and one of the founders of the Italian Communist Party, thought hard about the relationship between religion and politics because the revolution was not happening and he needed to figure out why. He moved beyond the vulgar, polemical Marxist position that religion is merely the opiate of the masses (roughly speaking, the position my friends and I held in high school) to understand the historical solidity and complexity of religion as part of the intricate intellectual and practical apparatus by which consent to relations of domination is created. Accordingly, he distinguished the extraordinary enforcement of domination by brute force from its more ordinary installation as legitimate order in people's conception of the world or worldview. Hegemony was his term for this ordinary form of domination in which force is generally hidden behind or replaced by commonsense conceptual and practical legitimacy.[12]

The key point to grasp about successful Gramscian hegemony is that it is permeating and preconscious. In fact, its elements are the foundations that consciousness is built upon. Hegemony is constitutive: there is no prehegemonic, preconsenting "self" that is then hegemonized. Hegemony is thus both the second nature of normalcy and the first nature of human nature. "One often hears that a certain habit has become a 'second nature'; but was the 'first nature' really the 'first'?"[13] For Gramsci, then, the first critique is always self-critique.

In modern societies, religion is only one mode of installation and function of this network of consent. The press in particular struck

---

12. Gramsci's "hegemony" and Weber's "legitimate domination" thus have much in common. A complete comparison is obviously beyond the scope of the present essay. Weber used the term "domination" in a value-neutral sense to describe any situation in which given orders are likely to be obeyed. Whether they should be given and should be obeyed is a different sort of analysis, one that Gramsci's concept of hegemony invites.

13. Antonio Gramsci, *Quaderni del carcere*, ed. Valentino Gerratana, vol. 2 (Torino: Einaudi, 1975), 1875. Translations from this source are my own.

Gramsci as an especially effective "material organization aimed at maintaining, defending and developing the theoretical or ideological 'front'" of a dominant class (whether ruling or in opposition). Yet,

> [t]he press is the most dynamic part of this ideological structure, but not the only one. Everything which influences or is able to influence public opinion, directly or indirectly, belongs to it: libraries, schools, associations and clubs of various kinds, even architecture and the layout and names of streets. It would be impossible to explain the position retained by the Church in modern society if one were unaware of the constant and patient efforts it makes to develop continuously its particular section of this material structure of ideology.[14]

The materiality of the fragmented public consciousness that issues from this multiplicity of sites of formation is perversely solidified by its uncoordinated multimodality. Without a monolithic target, opposition becomes intricately difficult and must be similarly multimodal.[15]

Hegemonic processes and practices support relations of domination without ever directly reflecting them. Therefore, counter-hegemonic processes and practices must also work subtly, using and twisting hegemonic forms to bring their status as nature/second nature into question.[16]

---

14. Antonio Gramsci, *Selections from Cultural Writings*, ed. David Forgacs and Geoffrey Nowell-Smith, trans. William Boelhower (Cambridge: Harvard University Press, 1985), 389. While Gramsci wrote before the full flowering of popular film, this statement on the special qualities of the press, and many others like it, provides suggestive material for those seeking to extend Gramsci's analysis into a world pervaded with a far greater variety of media such as film. See Stuart Hall et al., *Stuart Hall: Critical Dialogues in Cultural Studies*, ed. David Morley and Kuan-Hsing Chen (New York: Routledge, 1996); Marcia Landy, *Film, Politics, and Gramsci* (Minneapolis: University of Minnesota Press, 1994); and Raymond Williams, *The Sociology of Culture* (Chicago: University of Chicago Press, 1981), for various attempts to work this through. See also Gramsci, *Quaderni, vol. 2* (section 6 § 126), 795, for a very practical little note on providing little readers' guides as resources of critical interpretation for readers of the press in order to elevate their general cultural literacy.

15. This strikes me as an apt enough description of Michel Foucault's sense of the "microphysics of power." As he says (*Power/Knowledge: Selected Interviews and Other Writings 1972–1977*, ed. Colin Gordon, trans. Colin Gordon et al. [New York: Pantheon, 1980], 199), "But if power is in reality an open, more-or-less coordinated (in the event, no doubt, ill-coordinated) cluster of relations, then the only problem is to provide oneself with a grid of analysis which makes possible an analytic of relations of power."

16. In old-fashioned Hegelian terms this is an "immanent" critique. In more newfangled cultural-studies terms, this is an "inside/outside" critique. Since the original immanence was God (or Spirit), the advantage of the latter term is that it helps to clean out residues of (patriarchal) theology from the Hegelian philosophical system and its Marxian descendants.

Because of this need to work from inside the natural hegemonic order, there is always a certain functional ambiguity about whether the counter-hegemonic attack will be delivered or if the Trojan horse will remain sealed and become just another ornament on the public square. As a gesture perhaps countering hegemonic Christianity, this is the dilemma that *The Life of Brian* squarely faces.

Brian is not directly blasphemous.[17] Nor would it have a prayer of mainstream acceptance and effectiveness if it were. It is not a broadside or even a shot across the bows so much as a nudge in the ribs. With respect to Jesus, who makes three brief tangential appearances, the movie is downright orthodox. In each case, the message is not that Jesus is wrong, or even that worshipping Jesus is wrong, but that fallible humans find all sorts of creative ways to get worshipping Jesus wrong. As Python John Cleese remarks, reflecting the evolution of the movie's concept from the original *Jesus Christ: Lust for Glory* through *The Gospel According to St. Brian*, "I don't really know what we'd find funny about [Jesus]. I think you can only laugh at people if their behavior is basically inappropriate and I don't see that Christ's behavior was inappropriate. So I don't think you could probably be funny about him—only about the way that people subsequently tried to follow his teaching."[18] Small surprise that Jesus' behavior was appropriate when the Christian Jesus' behavior defines the ideal of appropriate behavior within Christian hegemony.

Even so, Cleese is too modest. The Pythons' Jesus is not just behaviorally appropriate: he is divine. This is shown in the opening scene, in which the three wise men initially mistake the baby Brian for the baby Jesus, bestowing their gifts lavishly and with much praise. But the heavenly glow issuing from the next manger down leaves no ultimate doubt about where or whether the divine presence is to be located. The unwise wise men show that men are fallible in their worship, but the object of that worship is left unquestioned.

Later, now-adult Jesus himself appears in a scene set during delivery of the Sermon on the Mount. A reverently performed, quietly charismatic Jesus is briefly audible, but as the camera draws back, focus quickly shifts to characters at the fringes of the audience straining to make out his words across great distance and accumulated crowd

---

17. For an extended discussion, and an illustration of the fine line between religious righteousness and dogmatic prudery, see Robert Hewison, *Irreverence, Scurrility, Profanity, Vilification and Licentious Abuse: Monty Python, the Case Against* (New York: Grove, 1981), 59–95.

18. From interview available on *The Life of Brian*, Criterion collection DVD.

sounds. Brian and his mother, Mandy, are party to an ordinary public squabble during which Jesus is reported to be saying "Blessed are the Cheesemakers." With a brawl about to break out, this blessing is questioned and glossed: "What's so special about the cheesemakers?" "It's not meant to be taken literally. Obviously it refers to any manufacturers of dairy products."[19] Further in, they learn that the Greek will inherit the earth. "Did anyone catch his name?"

Returning home, Brian is accosted by a healthy young man begging him to "spare a talent for an old ex-leper, sir." Conversation reveals that the fellow had been in fact a leper, miraculously cured by Jesus. "One minute I'm a leper with a trade, next moment me livelihood's gone. Not so much as a by your leave."[20]

While these episodes are certainly twists on the human reception of Jesus' saving words and miraculous works, those words, works, and their divine source are taken as givens. In terms of core Christian beliefs, the movie is reverent and unquestioning. This may be a strategic concession, but if so, it is one that leaves the premises from which the undesirable conclusions have been drawn intact. Accordingly, *Brian*'s directly hegemonic function is strong. So far, the Trojan horse is just a nice statue of a horse.

Academic religionists have had no trouble appreciating the hegemonic spirit and impact of the movie and appropriating it for their own strategic purposes. Biblical scholar Philip R. Davies remarks:

> I have long been of the conviction that Monty Python's *Life of Brian* is an indispensable foundation to any student's career in New Testament studies. In my view, it not only reflects a higher level of historical and biblical research than nearly all exemplars of the Hollywood genre which count among its targets, but also engages with a number of basic scholarly historical and theological issues.[21]

The authors of *Savior on the Silver Screen* identify the perspective of the movie as a non-Christian one, but then identify the target of the movie's satire not as Jesus' message but as institutional (church) authority and

---

19. Monty Python, *The Life of Brian* (New York: Grosset & Dunlap, 1979), 9.
20. Ibid., 13.
21. Philip R. Davies, "Life of Brian Research," *Biblical Studies/Cultural Studies: The Third Sheffield Colloquium*, ed. J. Cheryl Exum and Stephen Moore (Sheffield: Sheffield Academic Press, 1998), 400.

middle-class convention (I would add blind faith). "Thomas Merton has observed that we must become disillusioned, that is, we must get rid of our illusions if we are to make any progress in the life of Christ. In a sense, and from outside the Christian faith, *Life of Brian* urges the same."[22] It may be true that the movie is outside the Christian faith as formally defined, but only from inside Christian hegemony is it interesting or effort-worthy to urge anything of the sort.[23]

Indeed, critique of church institution and wealthy privilege could describe the positions of any of a series of monastic or Protestant sects within Christian history. The Cambridge-trained Pythons were way ahead of their academic interpreters on this one and sanctioned the movie's hegemonic appropriation by religious intellectuals. Python Terry Jones argues that the movie is "not blasphemous because it accepts the Christian story; in fact, the film doesn't make sense unless you take the Christian story, but it's heretical in terms of [being] very critical of the Church . . ." with John Cleese agreeing, "What we are is quite clearly making fun of the way people follow religion but not of religion itself. . . . I would defend *Life of Brian* as being a perfectly *religious* film."[24]

The Pythons make it clear that as long as the audience gets this about the movie, they are content. In fact, they understand their audience to be a small and sophisticated one. Jones points out that they "never had a mass audience. Python's always been [accepted by] sort of an intelligent, articulate minority, so our audiences would soon cop onto what the film was, really."[25]

They were rather less content with the dismissive or militant opposition *Life of Brian* received from some church officials and Christian communities when it was released, but this reaction too was strategically hegemonic.[26] Anathematizing the film offered easy opportunities for renewal of

---

22. Richard C. Stern, Clayton Jefford, and Guerric DeBona, O.S.B., *Savior on the Silver Screen* (Mahwah, N.J.: Paulist Press, 1999), 251.

23. "Urging" also seems like a suspiciously modernist thing to do—postmodernists tend to be more resolutely playful or ironic about their moral engagement. The authors seem to think the movie exhibits a postmodern sensibility, but this is at least questionable for the reason just mentioned, and also due to the notorious difficulty of pinning down a definition of postmodernism. The movie is often irreverent, unconventional, and anarchic, but does that make it postmodern?

24. David Morgan, *Monty Python Speaks!* (New York: Spike/Avon, 1999), 247–48.

25. Ibid., 248.

26. For details of media broadsides, picketing, petitions, boycotts, and threats of prosecution or violence, see Hewison, *Irreverence*.

church authorities' over-routinized charisma[27] and for exercises of community-affirming collective effervescence.[28] These were not serious receptions of the movie as such (often it was clear that the people in question had not seen it), but rather opportunistic potshots at a convenient target.

In turn, the Pythons' reaction is tellingly disingenuous—after all, if they were correct in their critical assessment of blind faith, church institutions, and bourgeois convention, they got exactly the responses they should have expected. Although many intellectuals are helplessly flummoxed when their sensible criticisms are not immediately and gratefully embraced by their targets, Jones's candid yet self-serving assessment of the Pythons' core audience shows that it is far more likely that the crafty Pythons too were preaching to their choir rather than naïvely attempting to convince the opposition.[29]

Overall, by accepting the common sense of Jesus' divinity and ethical authority, *The Life of Brian* locates itself squarely within the hegemonic network of Christianity. Like any Protestant enlightening, the movie is highly (sometimes savagely) critical of Christian practices and institutions, while leaving the core Christian worldview completely intact. At most, as *Savior on the Silver Screen* points out, the Pythons make an intellectual bid to transform the murky, unreflective, and self-contradictory morass of Christian common sense into a more thoughtful, systematic (disillusioned, or in Weber's terms disenchanted) ethic: that is, as Gramsci put it, to turn common sense into "good sense" or even "philosophy."[30] But since the audiences for the movie were preselected, as were its oppositions, the movie achieves at best a conventional anticonventional critical posture that easily fits within and may contribute to reproducing the relations it criticizes.

While I have focused on Christian hegemony, there are a variety of other ways that the movie is open to question as a counter-hegemonic gesture and may simply or functionally be hegemonic. From a feminist standpoint, for example, the movie is frustratingly uncritical. The

---

27. Max Weber, *Economy and Society: An Outline of Interpretive Sociology*, ed. Guenther Roth and Claus Wittich, 2 vols. (Berkeley: University of California Press, 1978), 1121ff.

28. Emile Durkheim, *The Elementary Forms of Religious Life*, trans. Karen E. Fields (New York: Free Press, 1995 [1912]), 424.

29. On persuasion, see Gramsci, *Prison Notebooks*, 338–39.

30. Ibid., 323–30.

Pythons are all men, and although they avoid most of the obvious sexisms and enjoy playing with gender by casting men as women (or even men as women as men, in the stoning scene), their characterizations of women are few, flat, and stereotyped. While there is some sympathy in the portrayal of the limited roles and opportunities available for women in biblical times, this theme is instrumentalized rather than scrutinized. The Pythons both depict and offer limited roles and opportunities.

From a postcolonial perspective, the movie also avoids the obvious orientalisms, but at the expense of erasing the Otherness of ancient society in the Holy Land altogether. Rather than playing on cultural exoticism, the movie uses exotic locales, costumes, and props as a setting for characters and scenarios that are culturally familiar, indeed, completely British. Even in the haggling scene over the fake beard and gourd where Brian, like any ignorant Western tourist, seeks to pay the asking price as though it is a ticket price and is completely baffled by the haggling ritual, Harry the merchant is played as a Cockney street vendor. The send-up is accordingly of class struggle, not ethnocentrism.

CLASS HABITUS AND THE CRITICAL FACULTY

There was a long time when I would have said that *The Life of Brian* is important because it is counter-hegemonic, placing it (from my perspective) on the side of the angels. As an established academic professional with a steady job, I now think this is much too simple. It is one thing to find hegemony dialectically embedded within counter-hegemony (the Trojan horse turned inside-out, so to speak). It is another to get beyond the kind of analysis that needs to see oppositions in terms of an ultimately binary array of forces, hegemonic and counter-hegemonic, dominant and subaltern. Gramsci has already granted that hegemony itself is multimodal. This is an insight worth exploring without leaping over-hastily to the conclusion that every opposition is a little bit of revolution. If *The Life of Brian* is not importantly counter-hegemonic, then how, and to whom, is it important in a more limited sense? For this sort of relational analysis, Pierre Bourdieu's work is especially helpful.

Bourdieu, now a fixture of French academic sociology, started his career as an anthropologist studying the Kabyles of Algeria. By breaking with the objective traditions of colonial anthropology and asking his informants why they acted as they did, he learned that the reasons for apparently identical actions "could vary considerably depending on the agents and also on the circumstances."[31] He concluded that cultural positions and processes, including, of course, receptions of movies, cannot be reduced to a single set of rules and hierarchical relations. Instead, he sees individuals and groups constructively deploying strategies within structured interactive fields.

Like Gramsci, but without the revolutionary agenda, Bourdieu is concerned with an ethnographic sociology of knowledge in which what we take for granted (our common sense) is brought into analytical focus. This is obviously a lot easier to do to other people than to do to ourselves. His concept of habitus calls attention to the same nature/second nature slide that Gramsci saw as a characteristic of hegemony. Habitus is the "sense of the possible" or "feel for the game" picked up as a set of dispositions through a lifetime of immersion in structured relations with others.[32] As an ordinary adaptation to our circumstances, we are habitually disposed to think and act in certain ways in situations and among other thinkers and actors that seem natural to us.

Again, like hegemony, habitus is constitutive—it is not something that is imposed on a preexisting self. "The schemes of the habitus, the primary forms of classification, owe their specific efficacy to the fact that they function below the level of consciousness and language, beyond the reach of introspective scrutiny or control by the will."[33] Nor, unlike the Marxist Gramsci, does Bourdieu think that this basic sense of who one is, what things are, and how things work within existing relations is the mere reflection in the last analysis of a massive system of class domination.[34] Classes, class fractions, and individuals do struggle for relative advantage, but they do so within fields or networks of positions rather than in simple top-down, bottom-up contests for ultimate power.

---

31. Pierre Bourdieu, *In Other Words: Essays Towards a Reflexive Sociology*, trans. Matthew Adamson (Stanford: Stanford University Press, 1990 [1982, 1987]), 20.

32. Compare this formulation to Ludwig Wittgenstein's "language games" (*Philosophical Investigations*, trans. G. E. M. Anscombe (Malden, Mass. and Oxford: Blackwell, 1997 [1953]), an inspiration Bourdieu acknowledges (e.g., *In Other Words*, 9); and to George Herbert Mead, who also discovered the genesis and operation of the self in "fields" of interactive differentiation and used the metaphor of game as illustration (e.g., *Selected Writings*, ed. Andrew J. Reck (Chicago: University of Chicago Press, 1964), 94–104, 267–93).

33. Pierre Bourdieu, *Distinction: A Social Critique of the Judgment of Taste*, trans. Richard Nice (Cambridge: Harvard University Press, 1984 [1979]), 466.

34. On this point, compare also to Stuart Hall et al., *Stuart Hall: Critical Dialogues*.

Bourdieu seeks to identify the practical logics that make class effective as a structure and practice. He argues that cultural fields, such as those containing movies and movie critiques, are sites of competition and domination in which practical oppositions of class distinction are played out. Within these fields, social actors position and identify themselves according to symbolic tastes and preferences that contain their practical assessment of the types and weights of capital—economic, political, cultural, intellectual, physical—that they are able to deploy or cash in for social advantage.

Bourdieu shows that classes are internally divided into class fractions by the dispersion of capitals. Once positioned, each class fraction has an interest in fortifying and normalizing its position with respect to other competing positions within differentiated fields, distinguishing itself from others by using them (and being used by them) to describe what it is not. Such distinguishing practices cannot be well understood in isolation, but only in relation to particular social-historical fields of possible positions.

This practical logic of distinction (or classification) with respect to competing positions produces habitus, a sense of the field and the positions in it. All social actors participate actively in their positioning, taking advantage of available space to distinguish themselves creatively. Thus, our selves and our conduct are structured and distinguished without being absolutely determined: we are both constrained and free, within limits.[35] Using the present case as an example, very few people have *The Life of Brian* rammed down their throats without some degree of active selection from a more or less varied menu of alternatives. But not everyone has access to the same menus. And there are some people for whom the movie, or one a lot like it, will make more sense and be more useful than others. This affinity may remain latent. The connection is enabled when the audience is fully equipped by histories and circumstances (habitus) with the correct ability to detect that sense and usefulness (taste). Then, the movie moves into a central cluster of likely choices and takes on a different level of meaning as part of a strategy of distinction.[36]

---

35. Accordingly, Bourdieu thinks that structure/agency debates are a (sometimes revealing) waste of time over a false dichotomy.

36. Max Weber called this dynamic of guided choice "elective affinity." For a powerful anthropological critique of materialism that avoids the obvious strategies of self-defense, see Marshall Sahlins, *Culture and Practical Reason* (Chicago: University of Chicago Press, 1976). Bourdieu meets Sahlins half way through his attention both to structure and construction, field and strategy.

Criticism is a strategy of distinction habitually deployed by a particular class fraction in modern industrial societies, the professional or quasi-professional critical intelligentsia. Plenty of critical thinking happens outside the walls of academe: as Gramsci noted, "all men [*sic*] are intellectuals . . . but not all men have in society the function of intellectuals."[37] However, such thinking has very little space to root and flower in the workaday world, and tends regularly to dissipate into grousing, periodic *charivaris*, or the third beer.[38] It is the professional, critical intellectuals who are by habitus and taste the core audience for which *The Life of Brian* has a chance of being strategically important rather than merely entertaining or momentarily offensive. Who are these people?

Although extravagantly educated and formally part of the upper bourgeoisie, the intelligentsia's dependence for their livelihood on service rather than on independent production deals them a serious and potentially dissonant status hit. They (we) are, as Bourdieu remarks, the "dominated fraction of the dominant class." While the intelligentsia's primary *function* in society is necessarily to help reproduce elites by ritually conferring educational capital on their children and progressively weeding out the "bad students" from the lower orders,[39] its *distinction* comes from knowing and understanding things at a higher level or more in depth, therefore perhaps more critically, than people whose lives are consumed with the everyday details of producing wealth.[40] The tension between function and distinction and the fact that neither is strictly necessary to the function or distinction of the wealth-generating elites who pay for it all mark off the primary grid within which members of this class fraction jockey for position.

---

37. *Prison Notebooks*, 9.

38. For a lengthy rebuttal of this offhand dismissal from, I think, the perspective of a highly intellectualized romantic populism (this may just be a mirror trap), see James Scott, *Domination and the Arts of Resistance: Hidden Transcripts* (New Haven: Yale University Press, 1990). For explanation of *charivari*, or carnival, see ibid.; or Robert Darnton, *The Great Cat Massacre and Other Episodes in French Cultural History* (New York: Vintage, 1985).

39. See Pierre Bourdieu and Jean-Claude Passeron, *Reproduction in Education, Society and Culture*, trans. Richard Nice, 2nd ed. (London: Sage, 1990); see also George W. Bush. For a caveat about "reproduction," see Williams, *The Sociology of Culture*, 181-205.

40. See Pierre Bourdieu, *Homo Academicus*, trans. Peter Collier (Stanford: Stanford University Press, 1994); *The State Nobility: Elite Schools in the Field of Power*, trans. Lauretta C. Clough (Stanford: Stanford University Press, 1998); and Bourdieu et al., *Academic Discourse: Linguistic Misunderstanding and Professorial Power*, trans. Richard Teese (Stanford: Stanford University Press, 1996), a series of books in which he has developed this analysis for the French case. For contrast, see Alvin W Gouldner, *The Future of Intellectuals and the Rise of the New Class* (New York: Continuum, 1979).

Within this agonistic field there are a variety of distinctive strategies that will work and reasons to choose among them. Of course, the primary threshold of competitive success is the institutional core of the schools. While there are plenty of successful professional intellectuals outside the schools—doctors, lawyers, engineers, managers, bureaucrats, and so forth—whose distinctions do depend on specialized knowledge and understanding, the technical demands and formal requirements of their functions virtually guarantee that they will not become critical intellectuals, properly speaking. People who are disposed to be bothered by this generally do not choose these fields, or strategically redefine critical thinking as "thinking outside the box" while taking the box for granted, as opposed to thinking about whether there ought to be boxes, where they came from, what shape they should be, who should own them, and so on. This is at most a casual audience for *The Life of Brian*, although they may think fondly of the movie from a time before their career paths fully coalesced.

The same is true of those intellectuals who successfully cross over professionally into the schools, but do so marginally as trainers in technical-vocational skills and knowledge. Since their strategy is to make a direct exchange of useful cultural capital for livelihood and status, and since the value of their capital tends to be immediately responsive to market selection and fluctuation,[41] they are unlikely to make any sort of posture critical of general social arrangements part of their professional identity. Indeed, such a posture would be foreign to their habitus and would likely never occur to them (it could be "in bad taste," "not for the likes of us," or, if they make virtue of necessity, even "immoral"). In the United States and particularly outside the cosmopolitan metropoles they are likely to be Christian, habitually and perhaps even sincerely. Their sect affiliations grant them entry to the legitimate networks in which right-thinking people do

---

41. As just one example, since golf is an expensive luxury activity subject to the availability of substantial marginal surpluses investable in leisure and optional status reinforcement, status-conferring college training of golf professionals is likely to be both highly attractive in flush times and highly vulnerable to market contraction in lean times. Presumably the contraction of such programs would move from outside in. Programs training members of social groups distinguished primarily by physical capital and moved by good times to just barely within the threshold of "golf culture" will find their market drying up before programs catering to social groups for which golf is not a luxury but an expected and primordial part of the class profile, that is, part of the habitus. Then again, those people do not need to go to college to learn the golf culture and are tracked for more prestigious careers than "club pro," which is why the really elite schools may have golf teams but never golf programs.

business with each other.[42] Such "cultural goodwill"[43] may characterize virtually the entire faculty at marginal schools. This can change quickly, however, for those whom the market does not favor and whose trajectory is accordingly downward (*Life of Brian* is fertile ground for sour grapes).

Historically, in fact, the term "intelligentsia" applies properly to the stratum of institutionally marginalized, surplus, socially functionless or under-functioned college-educated men in tsarist Russia.[44] This group included sundry anarchists, Bolsheviks, and Raskolnikovs. They were cranky and even dangerous because they had been trained for specialized higher-order thinking in a society that had limited need and appreciation for those intellectual skills.[45] No greater evidence of the extravagant wealth of our present society is needed than its ability not just to produce but also institutionally to incorporate and support such people. The ability to keep professional intellectuals whose entire manifest function and distinction is to think deep thoughts about this 'n' that is a luxury previously reserved for only the most wealthy and arrogant kings. The ability durably to institutionalize this arrangement was beyond even kings.

In Europe a few public intellectuals are supported by a residual historical reverence for the nobility of high culture and a nominally far broader and more differentiated political spectrum. Neither of these conditions exists in the United States where, therefore, public debate is handled by "pundits" and the critical intelligentsia is an exotic curiosity stashed in the inessential disciplines of the classical liberal arts and social sciences. Without a broad public audience, they can often be observed busily making a living biting the hands that feed them, temporarily muddling their students' certainties, publishing their findings in jargon-y specialized journals and edited volumes read only by each other, and performing useful symbolic functions of legitimation for the openness of the system by doing so.[46]

---

42. See Max Weber, "Protestant Sects"; Bellah et al., *Habits of the Heart*.

43. Bourdieu, *Distinction*, chap. 6.

44. Franco Venturi, *Roots of Revolution: A History of the Populist and Socialist Movements in Nineteenth-Century Russia*, trans. Isaiah Berlin and Francis Haskell (Chicago: University of Chicago Press, 1983), 220–31.

45. Calling themselves an "intellectual proletariat," they were caught in the middle of various tsars' more or less unsystematic efforts to modernize Russia from above without significantly changing traditional productive relations from below. So they were optimistically trained at state expense as the technical revolutionaries of a technical revolution that kept not happening. That some of them then shifted their revolutionary focus is small surprise.

46. See Russell Jacoby, *The Last Intellectuals: American Culture in the Age of Academe* (New York: Basic Books, 2000) for a discussion and illustration.

Despite strategic conservative drum beating and hand wringing in the U.S. culture wars, this is a relatively small group, and it is important not to use too broad a brush here.[47] Even in the liberal disciplines whose whole history can be told as a story of emergent critical thinking, solid institutionalization and social mobility have enabled a split between investors in political capital (committee work, program building, administration) and investors in intellectual capital. The former choose a profitable strategy for careerists with nominal investments in intellectual capital, but their functions and prospects also obviously bar them from much of a critical posture even when so disposed (the path from firebrand reformer to jaded administration lackey is notoriously well-beaten and strewn with good intentions). The latter are then further split between distinction strategies arranged around technical expertise and distinction strategies arranged around critical gestures.[48] Historians may stake their careers on knowing in great detail what happened and when, or they may earn their spurs in debates that seek to explain why. Philosophers may be logicians or metaphysicians, and as metaphysicians they may be historians. English professors may be grammarians, writers, new critics, or deconstructionists. Quantity/quality, theory/methodology (or theory/practice), fact/interpretation, art/science, rigor/intuition are some of the binaries that get tossed around to grid these fields. That these are false dichotomies (mirror traps) does not minimize their practical structuring effect or lessen their strategic usefulness. Myriad, specialized permutations along and across these general axes are possible, as any large academic department will show, while small departments ideally attract, and only happily keep, the strategists of breadth.[49]

Even distinguished from the academic technical intelligentsia, critical intellectuals are a motley crew. Again, just about the only thing they

---

47. On U.S. anti-intellectualism, see Hofstadter, *Anti-Intellectualism*; on the comparison of the U.S. to France in this regard, see Michèle Lamont, *Money, Morals, and Manners: The Culture of the French and the American Upper-Middle Class* (Chicago: University of Chicago Press, 1992).

48. Yet another familiar split that has little bearing on the present analysis can be seen between researchers and teachers, with their corresponding institutions, ideologies, and imperial claims.

49. Regarding the reception of *The Life of Brian* there is one further distinction to be made. As déclassé purveyors of vulgar popular culture, the Pythons are beneath public notice beyond, perhaps, an indulgent chuckle to the most privileged members of the intellectual elite (and to their more aggressive strategic emulators and groupies). In fact, the intrusion of popular-culture studies into the high academy is historically simultaneous with the intrusion and gradual entrenchment during the last forty to fifty years of middle- and even working-class students and faculty into what had been an upper-class reserve. My dad was the intruder; I am the entrencher. I show my class by this choice of topic, and I suspect I know who my audience is. "Honk if you're first or second generation."

share is criticism as their characteristic distinction strategy. So far, so obvious. The consequence of this for the (production and) reception of cultural artifacts like *The Life of Brian* has to do with their encoding or encodability as signs of mastery in the critical game. Not to put too fine a point on it, criticism would be useless as a strategy of distinction if just anyone could do it.[50] It requires a certain leisure, a room of one's own, and the acquisition of distinctive cognitive equipment, including specialized language, canonical expertise, ways of seeing, and habits of mind, through a lengthy and rigorous apprenticeship—which ideally must then be forgotten, so that the mastery of distinction appears graceful, natural, intuitive.[51] Reception or consumption and decoding of the encoded artifact (or active encoding of the artifact, for example in the cases of pop art or the ironic taste for kitsch) then becomes important as a form of communication, mutual recognition, and reciprocal validation among those in-the-know (connoisseurs, cognoscenti). While part of the pleasure is lamenting, perhaps sincerely, that the full meaning of the artifact is not more widely understood, mass acceptance takes the distinction out and is likely to cause loss of interest in all senses of the word.

The thrill of *The Life of Brian* for critical intellectuals like myself is that it is heavily encoded and encodable with messages and jokes about Christian theology and history (among other juicy subjects) that only I and a select few distinguished comrades can decode. Unlike the barbarous popular taste that seeks immediate comprehensibility, immediate pleasure, and immediate usefulness, the educated, critical taste takes chaste, dispassionate pleasure in painstakingly picking through the piece for its secret signs.[52] This is where critical intellectuals have an interest in disinterest and gain symbolic power by their legitimate monopoly of the means of analysis.[53] Where the movie was important for me and my friends in high school in a vulgar, immediately useful kind of way as a shared joke and an unspoken one-up in conversations

---

50. Note my earlier quick dismissal of barstool critics and my attempt to take criticism back from "thinking outside the box" vulgarizers.

51. Bourdieu, *Distinction*, 3. Failure to perceive this last step of the accomplishment and cover their tracks leads many new-class intruders into the high academy to commit the faux pas of treating their degrees and positions as the product of hard work.

52. Ibid., 30–35. This direct decoding is the pleasure I have partially foregone in electing to write the essay not primarily as a reception but as a critique of reception—thereby heightening the pleasure through self-denial and platonic transcendence to metacritique.

53. Bourdieu, *In Other Words*, 123–39.

with Christians about Jesus, as a professional intellectual I get a far more pure pleasure from the movie by being able to see it at many levels; for example, by recognizing how it is caught between hegemony and counter-hegemony.[54] It is now important as a sign of and playground for my distinctive critical sophistication.[55]

This play of class-fraction distinctions is rather less than a heroic counter-hegemonic assault and rather more than just playing with ideas. It is "deep play" because the stakes are much larger than anyone would wager if they were just playing.[56] What it means to be an intellectual, the spaces that intellectuals are able to occupy, and the status that they are able to enjoy there are the stakes. In short, intellectual identities and their "titles of cultural nobility"[57] are in play. The play is often especially deep, anxious, and aggressive for the new academics totally invested in intellectual capital, whose credentials do not have the distinguished weight of accumulated family cultural, economic, and political capital behind them.

This game can be described using the evaluative language of relative sophistication, culture, quality, and even morality. However, such judgments are no less positioning strategies than the training that enables them. The judgments that stick are the ones generated from privileged space. But then, every space offers a little privilege to its holder. *The Life of Brian* and its interpretation are tools of opposition, but not in any grand sense. They help generate distinctive identity and identifying judgments in a field of oppositions that are all about carving out elbow-room. Just as I have mapped my own shifting intellectual identity onto a series of strategic receptions of the movie, the Pythons' core audience

---

54. I am reminded of the nerdy scientist in *The Simpsons* who uses a toy to demonstrate physical principles to a class full of children, then refuses to let them play with it because they "can't enjoy it on as many levels" as he can.

55. There is nothing new in the insight that criticism is often functionally an exercise in strategic positioning or posturing rather than any kind of effective challenge to the structures it addresses. For example, Marx spent much of his early career criticizing critical critics like the Young Hegelians for thinking that once they had ruthlessly criticized something it was all taken care of. He tried to become more effective by attaching his critical posture to an active politics. His total critique of total critiques has certainly positioned him in a privileged place among critical intellectuals, but the lesser lights who have gamely tried to apply his ideas seem to keep missing the nuances (as any university professor who studies these things can explain in great detail), with devastating consequences to humanity.

56. Clifford Geertz, *The Interpretation of Cultures* (New York: Basic Books, 1973), 432–33.

57. Bourdieu, *Distinction*, 18.

(that "intelligent, articulate minority") could be charted as they use the movie to help justify and position themselves in conversations and careers. By their works you will know them.

CONCLUDING UNSCIENTIFIC PORCH SWING: APPRECIATING MOVIES AND GOSPELS

The original question I was given to write on was, roughly, what did this movie teach me about the Gospels? If I declined to say much about the Christian Gospels, it was in order to explore the ways in which *The Life of Brian* became important to me—and, I am postulating, a like-minded class fraction of critical intellectuals—as a chapter in a counter-gospel. That is, the movie and its interpretations function (in a small way, to be sure) as anchors for strategic claims to a privileged access to truth and, with it, social space, just as the Christian Gospels and their interpretations do for their faithful. In making this comparison and saying I have learned from it, I suppose I cannot help but seem to be demeaning the holy Word. On the contrary: I have just given it the highest praise I know.

12. THE CHARACTERIZATION OF MARTIN RIGGS IN *LETHAL WEAPON 1*
An Archetypal Hero

Fred Burnett

The *Lethal Weapon* (LW) movie franchise is one of the most successful in movie history. There have been four blockbuster installments, and there are rumors of a fifth; no action/hero movie in U. S. history has as many sequels. Reviewers overwhelming agree that the essence of the movie's appeal is the character of Detective Sergeant Martin Riggs (played by Mel Gibson) and his interaction with his partner Roger Murtaugh (played by Danny Glover). The movie has been billed as a "cop movie," an "action movie," and a "buddy movie." And, while the action sequences and the particular genre of cop/buddy movie are certainly relevant to the movie's appeal, the personal interaction brought by Gibson and Glover to the structural roles of "buddies and cops" is clearly what sets the LW series apart from all other movies of this type.[1] Utilizing a syncretistic mixture of comparative mythology, narrative criticism, and cultural studies, I will show how Riggs is a variant of archetypal hero mythology in terms of the absurd-nihilistic-warrior hero.

Reviewers agree that LW1 not only laid the foundation for Riggs's characterization in the sequels, but that it was different from his characterization in them. In LW1 Riggs is the archetypal hero whose driving

---

1. Throughout the essay I am assuming that you have seen the movie and, therefore, will not give an extensive summary of the plot or of individual scenes. For numerous reviews of LW1 that show the overwhelming appeal of the characters over plot or action, see the Internet Movie Database.

force is his so-called "death wish" (more on this below). Riggs's death wish is resolved in LW1 when he is accepted into Murtaugh's family as an adopted member. Once he is incorporated into Murtaugh's family, his poignant hero's quest for identity has ended; he becomes a new character after that. Every LW movie made after LW1 has a softer, gentler Martin Riggs, who still engages in lots of action but without the pathos of his lonely and tortured existence under the specter of a death wish. The profound appeal of Riggs in LW1 is his personal quest to find meaning for his existence in the face of overwhelming evil and death. His death wish is really his struggle to decide to stay alive one more day; his daily question, much like Hamlet's, is "to be or not to be."[2] Therefore, I will focus on Riggs's characterization in LW1 and lay bare the appeal and power of his character to audiences in the United States (though it was immensely popular elsewhere)[3] in terms of the American hero who struggles to find meaning in his or her existence.

Riggs's view of God, and by implication of religion, plays a central yet underlying role in his heroic quest for meaning; Riggs is a hero on a quest in a world in which God is dead, or at least practically and theoretically irrelevant. In a traditional theistic sense Riggs is a religionless hero who lives out his quest in the post-Nietzschean world of God's demise, and in the world of Albert Camus' absurd hero, Sisyphus, with all of the variations that those worlds require. Riggs falls within the larger structural themes of the traditional archetypal hero, but he greatly modifies and explodes them through his interaction with Murtaugh. When Murtaugh finally agrees that Riggs's mode of living and dealing with evil is the required way, it represents a cultural recognition that there is a major difference between the exemplar of the old hero (Murtaugh) and the new one (Riggs).[4] Since fictional heroes are reflective of surrounding culture, especially one as popular as Riggs, any secular or religious interpreter of postmodern American culture will find it useful to deal with the particular variations on hero mythology in Riggs's character.

---

2. Allegedly, Franco Zeffirelli, the director of *Hamlet* (1990), asked Mel Gibson to play Hamlet after he saw Gibson's portrayal of Riggs's constant struggle to answer the question of "why continue to 'be'?"

3. In 1987, LW1 was also released in Argentina, Finland, France, Sweden, and West Germany (Internet Movie Database).

4. See n. 10 below.

A STRUCTURAL COMPARISON OF RIGGS AND MURTAUGH

The portrayal of Riggs and Murtaugh in LW1 is a structuralist's paradise of binary oppositions. The opening scene in LW1 is a typical and idyllic garden of Eden shot of Murtaugh's suburban house. It is just before Christmas, and the house is shown as duly decorated with lights, while the musical background is supplied by the song "The Jingle Bell Rock." The opening shot of Murtaugh shows him in a nice bubble bath, and his three children and wife burst in to wish him a happy fiftieth birthday. In contrast to Murtaugh, the viewer first encounters Riggs as he awakens in his small, trashy trailer, walks naked to the refrigerator, drinks some beer, belches, and has a cigarette for breakfast. Riggs is completely alone, except for his dog, Sam.

It soon becomes clear that Murtaugh has regained Eden—a very nice house in the suburbs, a loving family, and he can enjoy it all in a tranquil retirement if he can make it a few more days on the job. With twenty years on the Los Angeles police force (LAPD), he has fought and survived all of the evils, has been duly rewarded (by attaining the rank of detective sergeant), and has fulfilled the hero's quest in American mythology by attaining a suburban Eden.

Riggs also has the rank of detective sergeant, but he has not attained an Eden. He apparently has not saved his money, or has lost it, because he lives in an inexpensive and trashy trailer. We learn quickly that his wife has recently been killed and that her death is the cause of Riggs's death wish.[5] In an early scene, viewers develop a deep empathy for Riggs as he sits in his lonely, trashy trailer, drinking heavily, and watches cartoons on TV. Bugs Bunny is wishing viewers a "Merrwy Christhmas" while Riggs puts his 9mm pistol into his mouth and comes very close to pulling the trigger. It is unclear at this point what stops him from killing himself, but he breaks down, clutches a picture of his wife, and, with tears running down his face, he says: "I miss you, Victoria Lynn!"[6] Murtaugh, therefore, has everything to live for, while Riggs's existence is a nihilistic one.

---

5. In the scene where Riggs is at her grave, the tombstone reads 1984 as her year of death. Her death was not as recent, therefore, as the story implies, since the movie was made in 1987. If three years have passed, then Riggs's mourning for her has an even more intense pathos.

6. There is no hint that Riggs's motive for killing himself is to go to some metaphysical place and be with his wife (*contra*, e.g., Charles Saint-Pierre, "Review of *Lethal Weapon 1*" [cited 7 August 2000]; available from Internet movie database, *imdb.com*). Quite to the contrary,

The plot and character development really begin when the two anti-
thetical characters are made partners. Murtaugh learns that his new
partner is "on loan from dope," burned-out, and probably suicidal. From
there, the contrasts between their characters continue to multiply. Riggs
is unattached and unconcerned about material goods; his only concern
is "doing the job." Murtaugh has a nice house, a large boat, and his main
concern is to stay alive and well until he can retire. Riggs smokes, drinks,
never exercises, and does not even purify himself with exercise and diet
before the final showdown with evil (Mr. Joshua, played by Gary Busey).
Murtaugh tells Riggs that he takes care of himself by exercising, eating
right, and keeping in shape. At one point Murtaugh remarks that the
LAPD might need to register Riggs as a "lethal weapon" because his special training in marksmanship and martial arts, coupled with his suicidal tendencies and destructive habits, make him a lethal threat to
himself and anyone who encounters him.[7] Murtaugh is an excellent cop
who follows the rules, values his family, and has fulfilled the dream of
making it to the good suburban life. As one tagline puts the contrast,
"Glover [Murtaugh] carries a weapon . . . Gibson [Riggs] is one."

In terms of hero mythology, Murtaugh represents the hero's quest
fulfilled, whereas Riggs is the hero who is questing for meaning in a

---

Riggs eschews all metaphysical comforts and explanations for her death. All that he says is that
he misses her (and obviously loved her), which makes his decision to continue to "be," even in
the face of existence without her, all the more filled with pathos. Still talking to her picture, he
says: "Hey, that's silly, isn't it? Well, I'll see you later; much later. Aaaah . . ." It is unclear what
is silly, but he seems to imply that talking to her picture is silly, and that he'll simply join her
later in experiencing death itself. He ends the whole monologue with an agonized "Aaaah . . ."
that now implies he's fully returned to his nihilistic reality. This reading is confirmed by one of
the final scenes just after Riggs's apocalyptic battle with the evil character (Mr. Joshua).
Standing in the rain at his wife's grave, all that he says is "Merry Christmas, Victoria Lynn. I
love you." There is a certain finality to his visit: he plants a small U.S. flag by the tombstone,
cleans off the stone, and then walks away. This seems to be Riggs's final goodbye to what he
now squarely realizes is his irretrievable family of the past (his wife). The final shot in this
scene is of her tombstone. Riggs is then shown going to Murtaugh's house, where he is incorporated into his new family. Significantly, Murtaugh's daughter answers the door, and Riggs
gives her a present for Murtaugh: the bullet that he had planned to use for his suicide. He tells
her: "Just tell him that I won't be needing it any more," and "he'll understand." Riggs's nihilistic existence has ended with the end of LW1; the existential struggle is over. Quotations from
the film are my own transcription.

7. Although many reviewers say that Riggs actually has been registered by the LAPD as a
lethal weapon, I find no evidence in LW1 to support that. Murtaugh only makes a semi-humorous
remark to that effect, which leads to a discussion that he does not want to work with Riggs. The
lethal weapon remark only functions as an indicator of Riggs's widespread reputation for rush-
ing into reckless and potentially lethal situations.

nihilistic world, a world not only without a meaningful relationship, but one in which death ends every relationship. Murtaugh has gained everything and is trying to keep it, but Riggs lives as if he has nothing else to lose. Much of the movie is spent with the two characters arguing about their different approaches to life and to police work. Many reviewers have said that the two characters have a "symbiotic" relationship; one balances the characteristics of the other. In the surface narrative, their gradual symbiosis into a partnership to fight evil is nicely portrayed in scenes where Murtaugh and Riggs literally seem to support each other after an explosion. For example, after the final fight scene Murtaugh does hold up an exhausted Riggs and says: "I got you partner; I got you!"[8] I agree that they have a symbiotic relationship, but their symbiosis is achieved because of a deeper structural fact: both fit the archetypal hero pattern, but Murtaugh represents an older variation that Riggs's nihilistic-warrior hero exposes as inadequate for fighting overwhelming evil in the postmodern world.[9]

THE ARCHETYPAL HERO

In spite of many differences among researchers on hero mythology, it is generally agreed that there is a common narrative structure. The center of the hero narrative pattern is that the hero is on a quest for something that he or she has lost. The myth is one of loss and recovery, particularly of the hero's identity. This narrative pattern of the hero's quest has been called the central myth of all Western literature, and indeed, of all literature, and the hero's quest is the archetypal plot.[10] Critics have traced the hero quest pattern to both the Hebrew Bible and the New Testament, with their archetypal stories of loss (the fall) and recovery (the establishment of God's rule), to Greek mythology (e.g., Jason and Perseus), and to Roman literature (e.g., Ovid's picture of the establishment of a utopian world). The narrative pattern of the hero's quest is so pervasive

---

8. Cf. Michael DeZubiria, "Review of *Lethal Weapon 1*" [cited 12 November 2000]; from Internet Movie Database at http://www.imdb.com. This site is no longer available.

9. A constant theme in the movie—usually in humorous scenes—is how old and out-of-date Murtaugh is. At the shooting range Riggs literally tells him to "step aside, old man"; the first time that they compare guns, Riggs says that "lots of old-timers carry those [Murtaugh's kind of gun]"; and, after their adventures, Murtaugh usually mumbles, "I'm too old for this shit!"

10. E.g., Northrop Frye, *Anatomy of Criticism: Four Essays* (Princeton: Princeton University Press, 1957), 192, 215.

and central to mythology and fiction that Joseph Campbell's designation of "monomyth" has been used again and again to describe it.[11] As Campbell puts it: "The standard path of the mythological adventure of the hero is a magnification of the formula represented in the rites of passage: *separation-initiation-return*: which might be named the nuclear unit of the monomyth."[12] Campbell's entire book focuses upon showing, "[W]hether presented in the vast, almost oceanic images of the Orient, in the vigorous narratives of the Greeks, or in the majestic legends of the Bible, the adventure of the hero normally follows the pattern of the nuclear unit above described: a separation from the world, a penetration to some source of power, and a life-enhancing return."[13] Indeed, Campbell can say: "Whether the hero be ridiculous or sublime, Greek or barbarian, gentile or Jew, his journey varies little in essential plan."[14]

The hero's quest is to find and recover someone or something that the hero or the hero's group has lost. The hero must overcome overwhelming forces in order to recover the loss, in the process discover his or her own identity, and then he or she must return to the familiar world and assume his or her proper and exemplary role. The hero's successful return restores life, energy, peace, or whatever benefit the hero's people need: "The effect of the successful adventure of the hero is the unlocking and release again of the flow of life into the body of the world."[15]

In analyzing Riggs in terms of the heroic monomyth, it is important to remember three things. First, there are seemingly an infinite number of variations on the basic myth.[16] Second, not all of the structural elements of the hero myth need to be explicit in any one story; they need only be implied.[17] Finally, the monomyth is changed and localized to fit the cultural landscape in which it lives. It might seem self-evident to say

---

11. Joseph Campbell, *The Hero with a Thousand Faces* (Princeton: Princeton University Press, 1972), 3–46; 245–46. Campbell says that he borrows the word "monomyth" from James Joyce (30). See also Frye, *Anatomy*, 316–26.

12. Campbell, *Hero*, 30.

13. Ibid., 35.

14. Ibid., 38.

15. Ibid., 40, cf. 35.

16. As Campbell puts it: "The changes rung on the simple scale of the monomyth defy description. Many tales isolate and greatly enlarge upon one or two of the typical elements of the full cycle (test motif, flight motif, abduction of the bride), others string a number of independent cycles into a single series (as in the Odyssey). Differing characters or episodes can become fused, or a single element can reduplicate itself and reappear under many changes" (ibid., 246).

17. As Campbell explains: "If one or another of the basic elements of the archetypal pattern is omitted . . . it is bound to be somehow or other implied." (ibid., 38).

that Martin Riggs bears little surface resemblance to an ancient Greek hero such as Perseus, but it is important to say so that the structural similarities might become all the more evident. Modern heroic quests will have neither the same metaphysical worldview as ancient narratives nor will heroic deeds from ancient times be the same as the ones that are needed now. Given these three caveats, however, the archetypal structure of the myth remains the same, and the hero performs her or his own contextual variant.

THE MONOMYTH IN THE UNITED STATES

A great deal of work has been done on the particular adaptations of the archetypal hero myth to culture in the United States. The monomyth undergirds such diverse surface presentations of heroes as Superman, Wonder Woman, gunfighters, and heroes in epic sci-fi adventures such as Star Trek. The hero's quest in the mythology of the United States is essentially to restore paradise and, in the process, discover or in some cases restore his own identity. Robert Jewett and John S. Lawrence, some of the first to analyze Campbell's understanding of the American monomyth in terms of its theological implications, rightly contend: "the American monomyth begins and ends in Eden. Stories in this genre typically begin with a small community of hard-working farmers and townspeople living in harmony. A disruption of harmony occurs, and must be eliminated by the superhero, before the Edenic condition can be re-established in a happy ending."[18]

> [The] *monomythic Eden* has distinctive features: It is neither the pure state of nature, the pastoral world of small farms and plantations, nor the urban metropolis. It is a small, well-organized community surrounded by a pastoral realm whose distinguishing trait is the absence of lethal internal conflict arising from its members. The citizens are law-abiding and co-operative, without those extremes of economic, political, or sexual desires that might provoke confrontations. . . . The majority's only failing is impotence in the face of the evil of others.[19]

---

18. Robert Jewett and John Shelton Lawrence, *The American Monomyth* (Garden City: Anchor, 1977), 169–70.
19. Ibid., 170.

To summarize: in the American monomyth: (1) evil always comes from outside to disrupt the Edenic community, which is always innocent and has done nothing to deserve the evil; (2) the ordinary institutions and means of the community cannot deal with the overwhelming evil; (3) a hero with a mysterious and unknown past emerges to help; the hero is unattached, selfless, and has the special skills that are necessary to (4) defeat the evil forces in a clear-cut victory that (5) restores the community to Edenic harmony; (6) the hero then usually leaves as mysteriously as he or she came in order to fight evil that will invade other Edens, or, as Campbell prefers, either the hero or the hero's life-force is incorporated into the community and continues to sustain it (e.g., Riggs and his energy are incorporated into Murtaugh's family).[20] The American monomyth is so prevalent and strong that Catherine Albanese can rightly say: "It surrounds Americans in public places and, through television and the print media, enters the privacy of their homes. *More strongly than the gospel of any church, which is heard perhaps once or twice a week, it shapes Americans from cradle to grave.*"[21] The monomythic Eden, therefore, is a metaphorical place that evokes harmony, innocence, justice, equity, or, in short, meaningfulness and the American yearning for millennial perfection.[22]

MURTAUGH'S FAMILY AS EDEN

The Edenic setting in LW1 is provided by the opening shots of Murtaugh's family life in suburbia. Murtaugh has an Edenic existence that he has attained by being a good cop. The opening shot of Riggs depicts a hellacious existence in which he, as the opposite of Murtaugh in Eden, is alone. What Murtaugh, as an implied hero himself, has gained in terms of family life, Riggs has lost, namely, his late wife. Riggs's place, modest though it is, has the *potential* to be an Eden—it is on the beach, and he still has "Sam," his affectionate dog—but Riggs needs someone to love. He needs the Eden of a family.[23] What was his

---

20. Ibid., xx. See also Catherine L Albanese, *America: Religions and Religion*, 2nd ed. (Belmont, Cailf.: Wadsworth, 1992), 469–70.

21. Ibid., 468–69, emphasis added.

22. Cf. ibid., chaps. 12–14.

23. This happens in LW2. He finds the perfect woman who, as with all American warrior heroes, is brutally murdered so that Riggs is left alone again. A hero simply can't be that "attached" to anyone or anything except fighting evil. If the hero does marry, then it usually involves a trap (see Dean A. Miller, *The Epic Hero* [Baltimore: The Johns Hopkins University

by everything that is legally and morally right, his loving wife, has been capriciously taken away.[24] The final scenes of LW1—after the apocalyptic battles against the overwhelming evil have been won—show a battered Riggs and Sam being incorporated into Murtaugh's family to enjoy an Edenic Christmas dinner. In the background the King (Elvis) is singing "I'll Be Home for Christmas." The only low-level disharmony that will bother them now in Eden is the future relationship of Sam the dog and the Murtaugh's cat, Burbank. The movie ends as it began: with an idyllic outside shot of Murtaugh's house, and we hear only a background screech from Burbank as Sam and Riggs enter Murtaugh's house. By the end of LW1, Riggs has fulfilled his twofold hero's quest of defeating evil in order to restore paradisiacal harmony, and he has conquered his own quest for meaning by being incorporated into a loving family. By using his heroic skills on the side of goodness, Riggs has regained his lost identity—a meaningful existence within the context of a loving and harmonious family.[25] In this case, the monomyth in LW1 truly "begins and ends in Eden."[26]

RIGGS AS THE MONOMYTHIC AMERICAN HERO

There is little doubt that Riggs fulfills the archetypal themes of the monomythic hero. However, unlike the paradigmatic American hero who is exemplary in innocence and purity (e.g., Superman), Riggs is the human—all too human—hero who drinks, curses, sleeps naked, hates God, and makes it clear that he is not afraid to push the legal envelope in order to kill or to die. Riggs represents a liminal monomythic nihilistic hero. In this section, therefore, I will first survey how Riggs fits the archetypal heroic themes, and then elaborate more fully on Riggs as a nihilistic hero.

Press, 2000], 115–20). That the hero must remain unattached was graphically illustrated in one of the Superman movies. Superman got married and time had to be rolled backward, quite literally, so that the marriage could be undone. In American mythology, if the hero falls in love, you can count on the loved one's contract being permanently canceled.

24. In LW2 we learn that she was killed by the evil designs of the South African mafioso, and the driving forces of Riggs's character in LW2 are justice and revenge. In LW1, however, all that we and Riggs know is that the capriciousness of existence, an automobile accident, has turned Riggs's meaningful existence into a nihilistic one.

25. Cf. n. 6.

26. E.g., by LW3 Riggs is offering intimate advice to Murtaugh's kids and wife, just as any other family member would do, and he even does mundane chores at Murtaugh's house such as his laundry.

Separation, Initiation, (Discovery), and Return

The first two archetypal themes of separation and initiation are only implied for Riggs's character in LW1. Separation for the archetypal hero is separation from what is familiar or comfortable into a realm that is different, or fantastical, or sublime.[27] Riggs's separation was from the familiar surroundings of his home in the United States and entry into the military service in Vietnam. We know almost nothing about Riggs's past, but we know enough: apparently, he was separated from his home and taken to a foreign place where he experienced a fantastical war.[28] Vietnam, then, begins Riggs's time of initiation.

We do not know if Riggs volunteered to go fight in Vietnam or if he was sent abroad by larger forces (the compulsory military draft): either option (voluntary or compulsory) fits hero mythology. What is clear is that Vietnam is the beginning of Riggs's "call to adventure," the first stage of his mythological journey, which "signifies that destiny has summoned the hero and transferred his spiritual center of gravity from within the pale of his society to a zone unknown."[29]

LW1 tells us only what we really need to know about the stages of separation and initiation for the hero: that he has not only survived severe tests in Vietnam but, most importantly, that he has gained the necessary skills that he needs to fight evil. Riggs made the Special Forces, the military's "elite of the elite" in Vietnam; there he apparently learned and honed his skills in martial arts and marksmanship, skills that will be his "helpers" in LW1 to defeat evil and restore paradise.[30]

Riggs's initiation does not end when he leaves Vietnam. His greatest trials really begin where the hero story of LW1 begins. Murtaugh is also a Vietnam veteran, and in the setting of Los Angeles both vets have exchanged one jungle and war (Vietnam) for the "concrete jungle" and the war against evil.[31] The difference of Riggs's initiation in the Los Angeles's setting is that it will also include the phase of "discovery," that is, the time when he journeys inward, fights inner demons, and emerges

---

27. Campbell, *Hero*, 30.

28. We know nothing about his home life, but he implies that he was never able to measure up in the past (to his mother? his father? his coach?) by saying, "It's [shooting] the only thing I was ever good at." He also tells the Murtaugh's at their first dinner that as a kid he went snorkeling and spear fishing.

29. Campbell, *Hero*, 58.

30. Cf. ibid., 97.

31. The film simply would not work if the setting had been Daleville, Indiana, instead of Los Angeles.

successfully. This part of the hero's initiation is what Campbell rightly calls "a favorite phase of the myth-adventure," and it constitutes the real hero story of LW1.[32]

It is here that Riggs's story and quest take on their own variations within the archetypal pattern of both ancient and modern heroes. Usually the yearning for the restoration of a lost Edenic state drives heroes on their quests. Riggs cannot restore the loss that he pines for, his lost wife, so his major quest-deed is an inward one: to find some meaning, some reason to continue his existence. His quest, therefore, is quintessentially one of the solitary individual in a nihilistic world.[33] As the archetypal hero, then, LW1 shows Riggs on a twofold quest. In the larger archetypal hero narrative, he overcomes all obstacles in order to restore Murtaugh's Edenic family with the rescue of Murtaugh's daughter. On the more fundamental archetypal level, Riggs fulfills his individual quest of facing his own nihilistic world and defiantly living within it.

Riggs fits the American monomythic hero pattern, but his variations on the pattern make his role as a nihilistic hero all the more apparent. We have already seen how Riggs differs from Murtaugh who, with his family values and clean living, represents the traditional hero more than does Riggs. When Riggs is compared with what is arguably the quintessential American hero, Superman, the nihilistic differences are even more apparent.[34]

Both Riggs and Superman share the archetypal quest of the hero, but the variations are significant. Superman comes from another world and has an exceptional birth; Riggs is clearly an ordinary human from this world. Superman is handsome but sexually unresponsive. He welcomes the regard and adoration of women (Lois Lane) for the selfless help that he gives them, but he does not want any kind of permanent relationship. Superman leads a double life as Clark Kent, a middle-class working man, in order to hide his identity and superhuman powers and to win Lois

---

32. Campbell, *Hero*, 97.

33. Campbell contends that no matter what the outward terrain, the passage of all mythological heroes fundamentally is "inward" (ibid., 29). But for the hero in the modern world—and certainly in the postmodern one—"no meaning is in the group—none in the world: all is in the individual." If any meaning is found, it is an unconscious, archetypal meaning that is raised to consciousness (ibid., 388). The hero's adventure boils down to a moment of "illumination," that is, "the nuclear moment when, while still alive, he found and opened the road to the light beyond the dark walls of our living death" (ibid., 259).

34. Not only is Superman a quintessential American hero, but I also pick him for his intertextual connections with Riggs: the director of LW1, Richard Donner, also directed the highly successful 1978 version of *Superman*.

Lane's affection. Clark Kent is unsuccessful with Lois Lane, and Superman remains aloof to her advances. In both his personas Superman remains selfless and sexually pure. In contrast to Superman, Riggs has already lost his sexual purity by having been married, or so one must presume, since he obviously won and accepted the affection of his late wife.[35] Superman never kills anyone; Riggs, of course, kills so many people that he's known as a "lethal weapon." Superman's character and values are simple—he is always on the side of good, and fights for truth, justice, and the American way. Unlike Riggs, one cannot imagine Superman—except in a spoof—cursing, chain-smoking, eating mostly junk food, and wantonly killing people. Unlike Superman, Riggs is a complex character in an ambiguous moral world, and he dispenses his own brand of justice, usually death, in proportion to the evil he encounters. Without superhuman powers and a different persona such as Clark Kent, all that Riggs has to rely upon is himself.

Riggs as Nihilistic Hero

One way to interpret the American monomyth is to say that the United States monomythic hero structurally replaces the biblical redemptive drama and Christ.[36] Catherine Albanese has one of the most accessible and extensive summaries of the history of the American monomyth in relation to the redemptive myth of the Bible.[37] She contends that the American monomythic plot "is related to the millennial Puritan and revolutionary background of American culture and, in fact, is a modified version of it."[38] In her view, and in mine, the millennial dominance of Puritan mythology laid the basic plank for American mythology and its developing monomyth:

---

35. Riggs remains sexually ascetic in LW1, though the director's cut has a scene of Riggs picking up a prostitute. We never see what happens (Riggs asked her if she wants to come home and watch TV with him), but the implication seems to be that Riggs did not stay sexually pure. The scene was cut from the version that was released to the general public so that Riggs could remain sexually pure.

36. For example, the overarching assumption of Jewett and Lawrence's work is "the American monomyth derives from tales of redemption. It secularizes the Judeo-Christian redemption dramas that have arisen on American soil, combining elements from the selfless servant who impassively gives his life for others and the zealous crusader who destroys evil. *The supersaviors in pop culture function as replacements for the Christ figure*, whose credibility was eroded by scientific rationalism. But their superhuman abilities reflect a hope of divine, redemptive powers that science has never eradicated from the popular mind" (*American Monomyth*, xx, emphasis added). On the biblical myth, also see Frye, *Anatomy*, 315–26.

37. Her entire book (*Religions and Religion*) is built around the many expressions of the "oneness" of American mythology, namely, the American monomyth, but see especially chaps. 12–14.

38. Ibid., 469.

One reason for the popular appeal of these dramas [the hero myths] . . . is that they tap mainstream Americans' fundamental understanding of themselves and their world . . . the one religion of Americans. For in the dramas are still visible the themes of millennial dominance and righteous innocence found in the Puritan and revolutionary visions. *The saving stranger*, though disguised by trappings of role and character, *is a transformed version of the messiah of the final battle*, the Word riding forth from Armageddon. Hence, the violent destruction of evil in the plot is portrayed as warranted and right. As the stranger fades into the distance, a millennium of peace and justice can reign in the plot's redeemed community.[39]

Riggs's character offers a particular variation on the redemptive monomyth. Riggs is a religionless hero, but he is also an ethical one; he values family, friendships, justice, and, above all, his duty to the job. Religion plays no explicit role in LW1—the Murtaugh family does not pray before it eats, there are no religious rituals of any kind, and there are no references to anyone as a "good religious person." Although the story takes place during the Christmas season, the only reference to it in the movie is when Riggs tells a suicidal guy on top of a building that it is "the silly season," when lots of people get depressed. Riggs has values that are not derived from an ostensible religious system. Riggs is a nihilistic hero. He is searching for meaning to his own existence. Although he has no overall redemptive plan or metanarrative about salvation, he does have values.[40]

The most important reference with respect to religion is when Riggs says that he hates God. The setting for the remark is just after Murtaugh and Riggs have met and are "stuck" with each other as partners:

> RIGGS: We both know why I was transferred. Everyone thinks I'm suicidal, in which case, I'm fucked and nobody wants to work with me; or they think I'm faking to draw a psycho pension, in which case, I'm fucked and nobody wants to work with me. Basically, I'm fucked.

---

39. Ibid., 470, emphasis added.
40. E.g., as the final apocalyptic battle (to regain Murtaugh's daughter Rianne) draws near, his only plan is to use his sniper's skills and go in and "shoot the motherfuckers." His only advice to Murtaugh is "just don't miss."

MURTAUGH: Guess what?
RIGGS: What?
MURTAUGH: I don't want to work with you!
RIGGS: Hey, don't.
MURTAUGH: Ain't got no choice! Looks like we both are fucked!
RIGGS: Terrific.
MURTAUGH: God hates me. That's what it is.
RIGGS: Hate him back; it works for me.

At first glance this does not sound like a hero in a secularized version of the biblical redemption myth. One would never expect heroes such as Superman to say that they hate God *and* advise others to imitate them in doing so. However, if Riggs even believes in God's existence, it is quite clear that God is irrelevant to the decisions that he makes every day (in that sense, Riggs is a practical atheist); if God exists, then Riggs's only relationship to God is one of scorn. More importantly, as a religionless hero, Riggs stands in a long tradition where the variant on the American monomythic hero is a religionless one. If one wants to compare Riggs with the heroes of the biblical drama, then the tradition of the religionless hero in the United States is where he fits.

Language for the religionless hero in America can be found right at the roots of the formation of the American monomyth. For example, out of his confrontation with church leaders, Thomas Jefferson created a new Bible entitled *The Life and Morals of Jesus of Nazareth*. Jefferson did not simply rewrite the Gospels, but he scissored and pasted sayings of Jesus so that he swept away inconsistencies from the church's Bible. Most importantly, Jefferson made Jesus into a rationalistic thinker. He eliminated "religion" and superstition from the archetypal hero of the biblical drama—Jesus himself. One could follow Jefferson's Jesus as a rational hero without being religious, and one could be a religionless hero without following the irrational and corrupt discourse of the church.[41]

There is much evidence to suggest that Jefferson hated many Christians, if not the church in general, and that Christians hated him. Jefferson embodied and helped form the American monomyth, but he felt that Jesus' teachings had been distorted from the beginning and that

---

41. Although Jefferson remained a member of the Anglican Church, his decision to publish *The Life and Morals of Jesus of Nazareth* showed where Jefferson really stood vis-à-vis institutional Christianity. Cf. A. Arnold Wettstein, "Religionless Religion in the Letters and Papers from Monticello," *Religion in Life* 45 (1976): 152–60.

Jesus' real enemies were institutional religious persons. The opposition that Jefferson received from Christians convinced him that "the Pharisees of old had not been destroyed by Jesus, but had merely changed dress and formed the Christian church itself."[42] Charles Mabee has cogently argued that Jefferson's influence on trying to have a moral Jesus who was free from institutional religion freed the American mythos from its Puritan origins so that Jefferson's view "was now moving into the mainstream of cultural consciousness and formation."[43]

Jefferson had helped begin a "civil religion," a variant of the monomyth that developed through the nineteenth and twentieth centuries, in which the hero's main monomythic role was to defend the "American way of life" (free speech, freedom from want and fear, and so forth). The American monomyth in its civil religious form not only became the dominant secular form of the myth, it "was a religious system that had sprung up in addition to the churches." One could be a member of a church or synagogue or whatever and still be part of the American civil religious monomyth, but *one could also be an atheist*, "since a good part of the symbolism of the civil religion could be used without reference to God."[44] As the monomythic hero, Riggs defends the American way of life in general (in Vietnam and on the streets of Los Angeles), and the American family in particular (by rescuing Murtaugh's daughter from the drug dealers and restoring Murtaugh's paradisiacal family).

There have been other calls for a religionless hero in American thought, particularly in theology. One of the most forceful is that of Dietrich Bonhoeffer who, facing his own impending death, called for the necessity of either living as if there were no God or, at least, as if God were helpless in the face of evil in the world: "God as a working hypothesis in morals, politics, or science, has been surmounted and abolished. . . . For the sake of intellectual honesty, that working hypothesis should be dropped, or as far as possible, eliminated." He concludes:

---

42. Charles Mabee, *Reimaging America: A Theological Critique of the American Mythos and Biblical Hermeneutics* (Macon, Ga.: Mercer University Press, 1985), 49; see also 48.

43. Mabee goes on to show the same kind of influence of Benjamin Franklin on the American mythos, and concludes: "Therefore, in Franklin, as well as in Jefferson, we witness the intellectual strivings for a new religious archetype in America. It represents essentially the same mentality as the traditional type-antitype structure of the Puritans, only now it is set in the broader context of the goals and aspirations of the Enlightenment. This dialectic between the scriptural Puritan thinkers and the natural philosophers of the Enlightenment established the interior dialectic of the American mythos" (ibid., 61–62).

44. Albanese, *Religions and Religion*, 460; see her complete summary in chap. 13.

[W]e cannot be honest unless we recognize that we have to live in the world *etsi deus non daretur* [even if there were no God]. And this is just what we do recognize—before God! God himself compels us to recognize it. . . . God would have us know that we must live as men who manage our lives without him. The God who is with us is the God who forsakes us (Mark 15:34). The God who lets us live in the world without the working hypothesis of God is the God before whom we stand continually.[45]

Bonhoeffer's view of life without God is much closer than Jefferson's to the view of Martin Riggs. Jefferson's God, as for most Deists, was simply inactive, or otiose, and thus Jefferson believed that people were called to live out of their own resources, particularly reason. Bonhoeffer's point is more that in modernity we have been *forsaken* by God and must live without a belief in God, that is, without believing in a God who dwells in a transcendent realm and who will fulfill human longings.

Riggs is the living embodiment of Bonhoeffer's person who has come of age. What Riggs knows and portrays is that any current solutions to evil in the world will not come from God but from humans, or more precisely, from Riggs himself.[46] However, Riggs's view of God's irrelevance, unlike Bonhoeffer's, does not presuppose the Christian faith, and there is no intersection of his language with theological assertions of any sort—about the cross, the weakness of God in the cross of Christ, and so forth. Riggs's nonreligious stance is not grounded in or to be viewed from any angle of the Christian faith; it is totally secular.[47]

To accept reality apart from God and to live squarely within the human situation is to accept the reality of one's own death. For

---

45. Dietrich Bonhoeffer, *Letters and Papers from Prison*, ed. Eberhard Bethge (New York: Touchstone, 1997), 360; cf. 359 for "*etsi deus non daretur.*" William Hamilton, writing in 1965, could say that "a strong case can be made that the most decisive theological influence on the younger generation of Protestants today is Dietrich Bonhoeffer," that is, more influential than Paul Tillich, Karl Barth, or Reinhold Niebuhr ("Dietrich Bonhoeffer," *Radical Theology and the Death of God*, ed. Thomas J. J. Altizer and William Hamilton [New York: Bobbs-Merrill, 1966], 113).

46. Cf. Hamilton, "Dietrich Bonhoeffer," 116.

47. Given Bonhoeffer's call for a secular existence, or one without reference to transcendence, it would be difficult, if not impossible, to distinguish Christians from non-Christians who live this way. Both postures would not appeal to metaphysical concepts, and especially to a transcendent God, as a means of explaining human affairs. Either stance is a religionless one that deals with reality apart from God, though what Bonhoeffer "says on 'non-religiousness' can be found only from the angle of his understanding of the Christian faith" (Gerhard Ebeling, "The 'Non-Religious Interpretation of Biblical Concepts,'" *Word and Faith* (Philadelphia: Fortress, 1963), 155).

Bonhoeffer, particularly in his writings shortly before his own death, Jesus was to be interpreted in terms of the freedom that comes from accepting one's death without fear. It was freedom from the fear of death, Bonhoeffer contended, that freed Jesus to give selfless help to others. Particularly in the pre-Easter Jesus, whom Bonhoeffer in effect argues had a "death wish" (like Riggs) in his last march towards Jerusalem, one sees the freedom to act selflessly for others. That freedom was the real significance of Jesus' life: "His [Jesus'] 'being there for others' is the experience of transcendence. It is only this 'being there for others', maintained till death, that is the ground of his omnipotence, omniscience and omnipresence."[48]

It is no great leap from Bonhoeffer's ideas to say that Riggs is the American monomythic religionless hero: he lives without reference to God and does not expect a God-hypothesis to explain anything; because he is unafraid of dying, he is free to go anywhere and fight for others against evil by any means he deems necessary. One could say, therefore, that Riggs is a secular Christ figure in Bonhoeffer's general sense, but Riggs would also have made Thomas Jefferson proud of the way he fights—without religion and in the face of an otiose God—for the "American way of life." Riggs has a view of God and religion that works hand in hand with his "death wish" to accomplish in a completely religionless fashion his own and others' redemption.

An American monomyth with a religionless hero has other variations that, unlike Jefferson's rationalistic Christ or Bonhoeffer's "being-for-others" Christ, hold up an absurd and/or nihilistic Christ as the exemplar of the hero. The variations are also part of the makeup of Riggs's character, and here the works of Albert Camus and Friedrich Nietzsche come immediately to mind.

RIGGS AS CAMUS' ABSURD HERO

Camus begins his famous essay on Sisyphus with the pronouncement "there is but one truly serious philosophical problem, and that is suicide. Judging whether life is or is not worth living amounts to answering the

---

48. Bonhoeffer, *Letters and Papers*, 381. It is accurate to say that Bonhoeffer's popularity in America was not just that he was "martyred" by the Nazis, but it was, as Hamilton says, that "he let us know what it is like when one gets ready to die. A martyr is not just a religious man who dies for a cause. He is a man—he could be religious or non-religious—who dies for others, and who has had the occasion to communicate somehow the experience of preparing for death" ("Dietrich Bonhoeffer," 113–14).

fundamental question of philosophy."[49] Everything else is secondary to this question. As we have seen, the driving force and pathos of Riggs's character, as well as the plot of LW1, is Riggs's "death wish": Will he commit suicide or not? If not, what is it that keeps him going in spite of his meaningless existence? Everything else in the movie is secondary to these questions.

The first thing to note is that Riggs is the only character in the movie who is not worried about his suicide; he has solved the "one truly philosophical problem" for himself. It is the other characters who are made nervous by being around Riggs—they're afraid that he'll kill both himself and them—and who are existentially unsettled by his zest for living fully in every situation. For example, Riggs handcuffs himself to a potential suicide victim and forces the man to jump off the building. The man is terrified at the possibility of dying, but Riggs is laughing as they emerge from the protective canvas onto which they've fallen; he not only did his job of bringing the man down from the building, but he *enjoyed* the way that he did it. In every dangerous situation, Riggs is admired by the other characters for the ways that he handles the problems, but he also disturbs them as a symbol of the absurd hero who could commit suicide, but doesn't, and who laughs at the threat of death. The reactions of the characters who live in the everyday world of the safe and the habitual are predictable: in one form or another, Riggs is again and again called "crazy."

What, then, is Riggs's "solution" to suicide? To put it differently, what is his reason for choosing to remain in an absurd existence? Just after Riggs has "controlled" the jump of the potential suicide victim, in one of the film's most poignant scenes, an extremely angry and shaken Murtaugh commands that Riggs come inside a building ("Get in here!!!"). He says:

Hey, okay clown, no bullshit! You wanna kill yourself?!
RIGG: Oh, for Christsake . . .
MURTAUGH [interrupting Riggs]: Shut up! Yes or no: you wanna die?! Yes or no?!!
RIGG: I got the job done! What the hell do you want?!
MURTAUGH [now yelling]: Just answer the question!!!
RIGGS: Well, what do you wanna hear, man?! Do you wanna hear

---

49. Albert Camus, *The Myth of Sisyphus and Other Essays*, trans. Justin O'Brien (New York: Vintage International, 1991), 3.

that sometimes I think about eatin' a bullet?! Huh? Well, I do! I do. I even got a special one for the occasion with a hollow point. Look . . . make sure it blows the back of my goddamned head out and do the job right! Every single day I wake up and I think of a reason not to do it, every single day! And, you know why I don't do it?! This is gonna make you laugh! You know why I don't do it?! The job! Doin' the job; now that's the reason.

Murtaugh, exasperated, wants to call Riggs's bluff and hands him a gun to see what Riggs will do. Riggs puts the gun to the side of his head, and Murtaugh tells him: "Put it in your mouth; bullet might go through your head, not kill you." Riggs is now totally caught up in the drama, thrusts the gun into his mouth, and slowly begins to pull the trigger. Riggs never flinches, and Murtaugh has to stick his finger between the hammer and gun just as the hammer is about to fire. Murtaugh realizes that if he had not done so, Riggs would be dead. This pivotal recognition scene closes with Murtaugh concluding: "You're not trying to draw a psycho pension. You really are crazy!"

Now even Riggs's closest partner is convinced that Riggs could kill himself and that he is even scornful of death. Immediately after the incident, Riggs's face relaxes with—well—a "crazy" look, and he announces that he's hungry and goes to get some hot dogs. Murtaugh, however, is terrified; he keeps repeating to himself that he's a dead man because he's Riggs's partner.[50] Riggs, as the hero who has resolutely faced the abyss of the absurd, has terrified Murtaugh to the core of his own fragile (and now absurd?) existence.

Riggs's solution to suicide is "doin' the job." It's a very mundane reason, and even he realizes that Murtaugh might laugh at such a mundane solution ("This is gonna make you laugh!") to the weightiest of all human questions. Who would have thought that the answer to an otherwise nihilistic existence (without his wife) was his mundane job as a policeman? Albert Camus would.

Riggs is Camus' perfect absurd hero. Riggs embodies Camus' conclusion that "even within the limits of nihilism it is possible to find the

---

50. As Dean Miller puts it, "[T]he warrior's epic tale often displays well-marked evidence that its hero is playing out a suicidal scenario, that he has devised or accepted a confrontation from which he cannot possibly escape alive. . . . but he will not go quietly, and most often he will not go alone; the hero is dangerous to be around at this moment, and not just to his enemies" (*Epic Hero*, 220, emphasis added).

means to proceed beyond nihilism."[51] Camus does not mean that a character such as Riggs has superseded nihilism by hoping in some future life, or in some hope of posthumous recognition (with streets named after him, for example), or in any other metaphysical or transcendent hope. Riggs is Camus' absurd man because he is the "conscious man" who knows that an absurd existence does not lead in any way tó God or to hope of any kind;[52] it leads directly to dealing one way or the other with the question of suicide.[53]

Not only that, but Riggs's decision to continue to live zestfully by "doin' the job" is a *daily* decision. Riggs has not made a once-for-all decision based on some metanarrative about a salvific hope, or even because he is serving others.[54] For Riggs it is difficult and exhilarating enough just to decide to live every day with scorn for both God and death. Riggs fits perfectly the paradigm of Camus' view of the absurd hero who deals forthrightly with the question of suicide.

Camus declares that Sisyphus is the absurd hero par excellence.[55] Sisyphus is not a god; he's a mortal who has been sentenced to live in hell—literally and metaphorically—and push a huge rock up a hill, only to have it roll back down so that the process can start all over again. Sisyphus does this work as a punishment from the gods, most likely for scorning them: "His scorn of the gods, his hatred of death, and his passion for life won him that unspeakable penalty in which the whole being is exerted toward accomplishing nothing." But Camus, astute reader that he is, does not focus his attention where the everyday, habitual reader does—on either Sisyphus pushing the rock up the hill or

---

51. Camus, *Myth of Sisyphus*, v.

52. Ibid., 40. For Camus the "absurd" arises out of the dialectic of our awareness of our longing to live on the one hand, and on the other, the "otherness" of the world and the naturalness of death. This is bedrock epistemology for Camus, and the absurd person tries neither to lose one side of the dialectic nor to posit a hope of any kind for finding a way out of the absurd (ibid., 21). Camus is fairly critical of thinkers who have thought their way through to the absurd, only to take an epistemological "leap" to some kind of hope. This amounts to "philosophical suicide" for Camus (ibid., 22–40).

53. Ibid., v.

54. There is no talk in the movie of his police work as "service to the community" and so forth.

55. Ibid., 120. It is interesting that Camus only spends five pages on Sisyphus (ibid., 119–23). Interpreters have perhaps overblown Sisyphus's importance for Camus. He is important as a paradigm of the absurd hero, but the paradigm is elaborated throughout the whole essay, not just in the section on Sisyphus. In applying the paradigm of Sisyphus to Riggs, therefore, my remarks will range far and wide throughout Camus' essay.

Sisyphus on top of the hill. Camus is interested in the space in which Sisyphus "goes back down to the plain." "It is during that return, that pause," Camus says, "that Sisyphus interests me." It is in that space of pause, his "hour of consciousness," that Sisyphus proves himself "superior to his [nihilistic] fate."[56]

For Camus, Sisyphus (and Riggs) faces an existence that is absurd and whose end is certain—death as annihilation.[57] What makes Sisyphus both a tragic and an absurd hero is his *consciousness* of his absurd condition. He "knows the whole extent of his wretched condition: it is what he thinks of during his descent." To "be" ("is-ness") for Camus is to be fully aware that one's existence is absurd. Sisyphus is because he is aware of his wretched existence, and that awareness is his "victory": "The lucidity that was to constitute his torture at the same time crowns his victory. *There is no fate that cannot be surmounted by scorn* [of the gods and one's fate]."[58]

But to leave the matter on the note of wretchedness would be misleading. Sisyphus's life of scorn also includes happiness and joy. For the absurd hero, who has dealt with meaninglessness and suicide and who is conscious of his or her fate (death), "Happiness and the absurd are two sons of the same earth. They are inseparable."[59] The descent of Sisyphus to return to his rock is surely "sometimes performed in sorrow, [but] it can also take place in joy."[60] Sisyphus's joy comes precisely from the fact that he is conscious that "[his] fate belongs to him. His rock is his thing. Likewise, the absurd man, when he contemplates his torment, silences all the idols."[61] Sisyphus, therefore, like all other absurd heroes "gives the recipe for the absurd victory."[62] All absurd heroes know that their end is death, but they also do not hope for anything after death. Remaining conscious of that fact and creating one's own life is the "is-ness" of authentic being:

---

56. Ibid., 121.

57. For Camus, it is the situation of us all: "The workman of today works every day in his life at the same tasks, and this fate is no less absurd [i.e., it will end in death and nothingness]. But it is tragic only at the rare moments when it becomes *conscious*" (ibid., emphasis added). There are several and contradictory variants of the myth of Sisyphus, but whatever his "end" was, Camus' point still stands.

58. Ibid., emphasis added.

59. Ibid., 122.

60. Ibid., 121.

61. Ibid., 123.

62. Ibid., 122.

If there is a personal fate, there is no higher destiny. . . . For the rest, he [Sisyphus and all absurd heroes] knows himself to be the master of his days. At that subtle moment when man glances backward over his life, Sisyphus returning toward his rock, in that slight pivoting he contemplates that series of unrelated actions which becomes his fate, *created by him*, combined under his memory's eye and soon sealed by his death.[63]

By being conscious of his fate, master of his days, and scorning the gods, Sisyphus, like all absurd heroes, is able to conclude "all is well."[64] For Camus, suicide is a *logical* solution to a meaningless existence, but he rejects suicide as a *legitimate* answer. In order to *be* authentically, one should, like the absurd hero, reject suicide in order to revolt against the absurd, one's inevitable death, and revolt passionately with the awareness of both the anxiety and the joy that daily living under the specter of the absurd brings.

It is not a superficial comparison to say that Riggs fulfills the paradigm of the absurd hero that Sisyphus portrays. Like Sisyphus, Riggs is acutely aware of his nihilistic existence; he makes a daily decision to "do the job" (police work of fighting incessant evil is surely as futile as pushing a rock up a hill); he enjoys "the myriad wondering little voices of the earth"[65] that rise up when one lives in absurd consciousness (for Riggs, his cigarettes, hot dogs, and petting his dog); and Riggs concludes, as does Sisyphus, "all is well," or at least as well as it's ever going to get. Riggs's scorn of God is not so much his explicit statement that hating God "works" for him as it is his revolt against the conditions, the structure, and the telos of life; at bottom, it is a revolt against death. This is what the other characters cannot see or understand about Riggs (or any other absurd hero) and who, out of their own habitual existence that is unaware of its absurdity, must pronounce Riggs crazy. Riggs is not driven by a "death wish," as they contend, but by a revolt against death, a revolt that he knows is ultimately futile. It is by embracing and dealing forthrightly with death that Riggs enjoys revolting against it; that is the ephemeral victory of the absurd hero.

Unlike Sisyphus, however, Riggs is not only an absurd hero; he is a "warrior" hero as well. He brings military training and trappings into his

---

63. Ibid., 123, emphasis added.
64. Ibid.
65. Ibid.

war against crime. Riggs fits the hero archetype well in the sense that heroes, especially warrior heroes, often act out a scenario that everyone knows is, in effect, a suicide. The hero usually puts himself or herself in a situation from which escaping alive is ultimately impossible, or, as classically portrayed, the hero has somehow been made aware of his or her fate, but acquires heroic status and admiration by resolutely facing the situation anyway. Like all warrior heroes, Riggs faces foes who will mercilessly kill him unless he overcomes them by his skills and craftiness. His extraordinary skills and cunning raise him to a level above the ordinary social fabric to which lesser persons succumb. In this sense, Riggs is, as are all warrior heroes, a liminal figure; that is, he "makes mincemeat of the normative pattern, and reshapes the social definition of the 'proper' end to fit his own death myth."[66]

One of the character traits that makes Riggs and warrior heroes so compelling is that he has chosen what his end will apparently be—death in combat against crime and evil. Although Riggs's death is not shown in LW1, most likely he will die in a horrendous fight and shootout with the bad guys. Death in combat is the heroic goal of the warrior hero. Very seldom does the hero commit suicide in the narrow sense of ending his or her own life as a "self-murder." If it does happen, it would be done in such a way as to be considered "heroic" and consonant with the hero's character.[67] The daily work life of Riggs—coupled with the implication of his impending heroic death—attracts people to heroes of his type. As Dean Miller puts it,

> Probably the greatest attraction of the hero as he acts for his society or social frame is also his great paradox: all the good things that human society openly provides or stands for are openly contradicted in him. As society demands a degree of routine, stability, and predictability, so the hero represents the dramatic interruption of continuity: a disturbingly antithetical *celeritas* versus the norms of social settlement and *gravitas*. . . . he is an uncompromising and unchanging figure of iconic *permanence*.[68]

The way that I have so far portrayed Riggs as the archetypal religionless and absurd hero does not necessarily rule out his appeal to religious

---

66. Dean Miller, *Epic Hero*, 327.
67. Ibid., 327–30.
68. Ibid., 330, Miller's emphases.

paradigms, especially to Christ as hero. Camus himself provides a bridge for us to such an interpretation: "It is possible to be Christian and absurd. There are examples of Christians who do not believe in a future life."[69] If one can imagine Jesus as a human, like all of the rest of us, and believe that Jesus was aware—in Camus' sense—that his death and torture had been useless, then Camus can say that "solely in this sense Jesus indeed personifies the whole human drama. He is the complete man, being the one who realized the most absurd condition. . . . And, like him, each of us can be crucified and victimized—and is to a certain degree."[70] But to lay out this final thread in the portrayal of Riggs and Jesus as archetypal heroes, we must go to the one to whom Camus alludes—Friedrich Nietzsche.

RIGGS AS THE *ÜBERMENSCH*

Riggs seems to be, at least from the other characters' viewpoints, obsessed with suicide, an obsession primarily spurred by his wife's accidental and senseless death. Her death seems to have been the moment at which Riggs became aware of the absurdity of existence, as Camus would put it. It is quite clear that Riggs's existence became meaningless without his wife, and it is clear that Riggs "hates" God. What is not clear is what it means for Riggs to hate God and how his hatred of God is related to his obsession with suicide. What suicide would mean for Riggs is never made clear: Would it be a revolt against God? A metaphysical reunion with his wife or, more likely, just "joining" his wife in the experience of dying? Would it be freedom from the tedium of human existence? Or what?

I have argued, with Camus, that Riggs squarely faced the question of suicide and the absurd and answered it daily with a scornful "yes." By doing so, he discovered the truth of his identity and daily existence, namely, "doin' the job." Riggs has joined with Nietzsche in this sense: embracing one's own death and the irrelevance of God is to embrace God's "death" (and the death of metaphysics).

---

69. *Myth of Sisyphus*, 112. One could certainly think of other paradigmatic figures out of other religious traditions, but the writers I am following, and indeed the American monomyth itself, stay consistently within a Christian mythological framework.

70. Ibid., 107.

For Nietzsche, God's irrelevance and Jesus' death were redemptive, because only by them could humans learn to depend upon themselves for solutions to their problems (the same theme as in Bonhoeffer). For Nietzsche, not only *could* humans live without God, they *should*. This also opens the possibility of hating any concept of God, particularly the Christian God. In this respect, both Nietzsche and Camus agree that by embracing nihilism, expressed metaphorically as the death of God, one can overcome the despair of a nihilistic existence by being fully aware of one's identity and fate. God, or more precisely the Christian idea of God, is what must be abandoned if lucidity about one's existence is to be gained. In his last work, *The Anti-Christ*, are some of Nietzsche's clearest statements on this point: "The thing that sets us apart is not that we are unable to find God, either in history, or in nature, or behind nature— but that we regard what has been honored as God, not as 'divine', but as pitiable, as absurd, as injurious; not as a mere error, but as a *crime against life*. . . . We deny that God is God. . . . If any one were to show us this Christian God, we'd be still less inclined to believe in him."[71] The death of God, or the denial of God, is the death of a certain kind of *meaning*; namely, that humans can find their identity and the truth of existence by positing metaphysical notions such as "god."

For Nietzsche, nihilism is relying upon metaphysical notions such as "god," since they force people to deny natural and life-affirming impulses such as the sexual drive and critical thinking itself. The Christian God is not only hostile to life but is the essence of "nihilism": "Christianity is called the religion of *pity*.—Pity stands in opposition to all the tonic passions that augment the energy of the feeling of aliveness: it is a depressant . . . by means of pity life is denied, and made *worthy of denial*—pity is the technic of nihilism."[72] "The Christian concept of God," he says, "is one of the most corrupt concepts that has ever been set up in the world: it probably touches low-water mark in the ebbing evolution of the god-type. God degenerated into *the contradiction of life*. . . . In him war is declared on life, on nature, on the will to live! . . . In him nothingness is deified, and the will to nothingness is made holy!"[73] In brief, nihilism,

---

71. Friedrich Nietzsche, *The Anti-Christ*, trans. H. L. Mencken (Tucson: See Sharp Press, 1999), 68, his emphases.

72. Ibid., 24, Nietzsche's emphases.

73. Ibid., 34; cf. 32, 39, 42–44.

or a belief in God or metaphysics of any kind, is the loss of the will to power, or what constitutes the highest values of humans—their dependence upon themselves and the drive to live fully.[74] For Nietzsche, therefore, atheism is the perfect form of a whole and healthy faith— faith in oneself as the source for solutions, and an affirmation of life. The denial of God is a healthy "will to power," since it affirms one's existence and dependence upon one's self.

Ironically enough, Jesus emerges as a hero, a "superman" (*Übermensch*) for Nietzsche. The quintessential characteristic of the Superman is the will to power to vanquish God. The Superman, in short, is a complete acceptance of an existence without dependence upon God or any metaphysical underpinnings. For Nietzsche, Jesus freely willed his own "suicide." By doing so, Jesus vanquished God. What Jesus did was kill the need for the Christian God, and indeed, opened the possibility for humans to become their own gods, or Superpeople.[75] For Nietzsche, Jesus chose his own kind of death (and he *stayed* dead). Christianity, particularly Paul, inverted Jesus' life by saying that God defeated death for Jesus, thus turning his death into a victory.[76] For Nietzsche Jesus' death, of course, did not "save" humanity, but it did show humans how to live. Jesus lived a life of compassion, and never talked of "sin" or created a gulf between God and humans. The church invented "sin," and this too was an inversion of Jesus' life and teaching.[77] Jesus lived and taught that there was no distance between God and humans:

> The life of the Savior was simply a carrying out of this way of life—and so was his death. . . . He no longer needed any formula

---

74. "When the center of gravity of life is placed, not in life itself, but in 'the beyond'—in *nothingness*—then one has taken away its center of gravity altogether. The vast lie of personal immortality destroys all reason, all natural instinct—henceforth, everything in the instincts that is beneficial, that fosters life and that safeguards the future is a cause of suspicion" (ibid., 61, Nietzsche's emphases).

75. Camus makes the same point, though he uses the term "man-god" (*Myth of Sisyphus*, 106–107).

76. As Nietzsche puts it: "I shall go back a bit, and tell you the authentic history of Christianity.—The very word 'Christianity' is a misunderstanding—at bottom there was only one Christian, and he died on the cross. The 'Gospels' died on the cross. What, from that moment onward, was called the 'Gospels' was the very reverse of what he had lived: 'bad tidings', a *Dysangelium*" (*Anti-Christ*, 56).

77. "I repeat that sin, man's self-desecration *par excellence*, was invented in order to make science, culture, and every elevation and ennobling of man impossible; the priest *rules* through the invention of sin" (ibid., 71, Nietzsche's emphases).

or ritual in his relations with God—not even prayer . . . he *knew* that it was only by a *way* of life that one could feel one's self 'divine,' 'blessed,' 'evangelical,' a 'child of God.' *Not* by 'repentance,' not by 'prayer and forgiveness' is the way to God: *only the Gospel way* [Jesus' way] leads to God—it is itself 'God'!"[78]

The person who overcomes the fear of pain and death and creates his or her own values is the *Übermensch*. Jesus was such a man. For Nietzsche, Jesus was a symbol of "suicide," of one who freely negated himself. As such, Jesus provided a model to imitate: the self-negation of one's metaphysical importance (no hope of an afterlife, or of a cosmic plan for one's existence, and so forth). In Jesus' kind of death, "God," or the need for any metaphysical underpinnings to one's existence, comes to an end. Jesus' "suicide" freed him from dependence upon God and metaphysical foundations. Nietzsche's vision and belief was that all humanity will someday embody the freedom of Jesus the Superman—to see that all of one's decisions, all of one's values, all of one's hopes and fears are within one's own self—and the realization of this "suicide" will transform all of human existence.

Nietzsche has been most influential with the so-called "death of God" thinkers in America. Whatever else the phrase the "death of God" might mean,[79] for Nietzsche one of the meanings of the phrase was the fact that "we" now recognize that the word "God" actually represents nothingness, or meaninglessness. This recognition leads one into an existence without dependence upon God, that is, (1) an existence without a transcendent or metaphysical meaning; and, (2) the possibility and necessity of creating one's own meaning, or of becoming Nietzsche's "Superhuman." In this sense, the "death of God" is the death of the understanding of the kind of existence that depends upon metaphysical speculations and metanarrative explanations; it is a "loss." The "loss," however, opens the possibility of a quest for a new existence—the possibility of a genuine "faith" in one's own existence. The Superman,

---

78. Ibid., 51, Nietzsche's emphases.

79. For a good summary of the possible meanings of the phrase the "death of God," see F. Thomas Trotter, "Variations on the 'Death of God' Theme in Recent Theology," *The Meaning of the Death of God. Protestant, Jewish and Catholic Scholars Explore Atheistic Theology*, ed. Bernard Murchland (New York: Vintage, 1967), 16–18; and Thomas J. J. Altizer and William Hamilton, *Radical Theology and the Death of God* (New York: Bobbs-Merrill, 1966), ix–xi.

the hero, is the person who courageously lives such a nihilistic existence and, in so doing, both wills and embraces the death of God.

Riggs is a nihilistic Superman in the mold of Nietzsche's Jesus. Riggs can be said to be one type of fulfillment of Nietzsche's nihilistic Jesus figure and, as Bonhoeffer, Camus, and Nietzsche all rightly foresaw, this kind of figure—who pulls intertextually in American mythology on absurdity, religionlessness, morality, and overcomes nihilism with nihilism—will always appeal to a segment of people who have "come of age" and to others who are on their way.

13. PARADOXICAL PROTAGONISTS
Sling Blade's Karl and Jesus Christ
Mark Roncace

Sling Blade opened in Chicago just before Thanksgiving in 1996. It was so unsuccessful in its first week that Miramax limited its showing to the East and West coasts. Despite its inauspicious debut, the film later received two Academy Award nominations, including Best Screenplay, which it won. Billy Bob Thornton wrote, directed, and starred in this slow-paced drama about a simpleton murderer released from a mental institution. The movie, which cost an infinitesimal $1 million to produce, has been called "one of the most unique and unsettling films in American cinema."[1] Its distinctive and disturbing qualities derive primarily from the portrayal of Karl Childers, a character that Thornton spent almost a decade developing as he performed his one-man stage shows. Karl, it will be argued, is a Christ-figure, whose complexities and ambiguities parallel in many ways the diverse images of Jesus found in the New Testament.[2] That is, both Karl and Christ are paradoxical protagonists who are at once weak and strong, gentle and violent, saviors and avengers.

THE STORY

Sling Blade, set in a small Arkansas town, tells the story of Karl Childers, a slightly humped-over, mildly mentally challenged man in his late thirties

---

1. Derek Germano, "Review of *Sling Blade*" [cited 24 April 2001]; available from http://thecinemalaser.com/dvd_reviews/sling-blade-dvd.
2. This essay uses "Jesus" and "Christ" interchangeably.

with a protruding lower lip; he speaks slowly, in a grunty voice that is punctuated frequently with "mmh-hmmm's." Karl has been living in a mental institution for the past twenty-five years, after murdering his mother and her teenage lover when he was twelve years old. As the film opens he is about to be released; in an interview with the local college newspaper, he recounts his personal history, including how the murders occurred. He tells how as a child he lived in a shed in his parents' back-yard because they did not want him in the house and how the neighbor-hood children often "made sport" of him. One day, he explains, while he was waiting for his mother to come out and give him his Bible lesson, he heard a commotion in the house. When he approached, he saw Jesse Dixon, who Karl knew had "takened advantage" of girls in the neigh-borhood, lying on top of his mother. Karl "just seen red" and picked up a sling blade that was nearby and killed Dixon. Then, when he realized that his mother was a willing participant, he struck and killed her too.

The simple plot begins to unfold after Karl is released from the men-tal hospital. Karl is reluctant to leave the institution, but having no choice, he returns to his small hometown and begins working at Bill Cox's small-engine repair shop. Karl soon befriends twelve-year-old Frank Wheatley (Lucas Black), who persuades his widowed mother, Linda (Natalie Canerday), to allow Karl to live in their garage. Frank is happy to have Karl as a friend because he misses his father, who com-mitted suicide, and Karl provides a calming presence and possible pro-tection from Doyle Hargraves (Dwight Yoakam), Linda's boyfriend, who drinks heavily, is abusive to both Linda and Frank, and does not like being around a "retard," as he calls Karl. Linda also has a close relation-ship with Vaughn Cunningham (John Ritter), a gay man who is the manager at the local grocery store where Linda works. Vaughn, who finds life dif-ficult in a small southern town, is very protective of Linda and Frank, fearing that Doyle will hurt them. After some initial hesitation, Vaughn accepts Karl and welcomes his living with Frank and Linda.

As the film progresses, Karl witnesses several instances of Doyle's destructive behavior, although, with one exception, he does not inter-vene. In one particularly disturbing scene, Doyle yells angrily at his friends to leave the Wheatley house, and when they are too slow in doing so, he shoves one of them, who is in a wheelchair, out the door. This vio-lent outburst causes Linda to demand that Doyle leave, but when he ini-tially refuses, Frank breaks into a rage, throwing empty beer cans at Doyle, who crouches against the door, too drunk to stand. Throughout the story, Karl has conversations with Frank in which the boy expresses his fear and hatred of Doyle. One also learns more details of Karl's tragic childhood, which included his father forcing him to bury alive his new-born baby brother. In one of the film's most poignant scenes, Karl returns to his father's house to confront him about the incident and to visit his brother's grave.

Although Doyle apologizes for his behavior and vows to change, the tension builds as Frank's and Linda's health and happiness are jeopardized by Doyle's presence. Finally, after Doyle decides to move in with the Wheatleys and to kick Karl out of the garage, Karl orchestrates a plan to be alone with Doyle and, after pausing to ask Doyle how one can contact the police, kills him with a freshly sharpened lawnmower blade. Karl then calmly reports the homicide to the authorities and sits down to await their arrival. In the last scene, Karl is back at the institution.

SLING BLADE AND THE WESTERN

The plot structure of *Sling Blade* reveals some basic similarities between Karl and Christ. Both are archetypal outsiders, strangers who enter a community and influence people's lives, save them from evil against which they are (or seem to be) powerless, and then depart. This, of course, is a popular device in myth, literature, and film. Many of the world's religions, for instance, have this kind of story in their narratives about the incarnation of the gods. The plot structure appears so frequently in American literature and film that it can be called the "American monomyth."[3] It is embodied clearly in Westerns, such as George Steven's *Shane* and Clint Eastwood's *Pale Rider* and *High Plains Drifter*. Accordingly, critics have long considered how the protagonist in the Western is a Christ-figure. *Sling Blade*, too, has almost all the classical elements of the Western: (1) the hero enters a community; (2) the hero is a stranger; (3) the community recognizes a difference between themselves and the hero; (4) there is conflict between the villains and the community; (5) the villains are stronger than the community; (6) the villains threaten the community; (7) the hero tries to avoid involvement in the conflict; (8) the antagonists endanger someone that the hero has

---

3. Robert Jewett and John Shelton Lawrence, *The American Monomyth* (Garden City: Anchor Press, 1977). Cf. also the essays by Walsh and Burnett in this volume.

befriended; (9) the hero fights the villains; (10) the hero defeats them; (11) the community is safe; and (12) the hero departs.[4]

The fact that *Sling Blade* bears more than a passing resemblance to the Western should not be surprising, for Thornton has indicated that he has been strongly influenced by this genre.[5] Thornton himself specifically compared Doyle, the abusive boyfriend, to the villain in Westerns: "If this was the Old West, somebody would kill that son-of-a-bitch."[6] Karl does, in fact, murder Doyle, thereby fulfilling the same plot function as the savior-hero of the Western. Yet it is important to observe that Karl differs from the classic Western hero in at least one crucial way. Karl is a simpleton, an odd-looking, marginalized figure, rather than a virile, handsome sharpshooter. As in the Western, the community does recognize a difference between themselves and Karl, but it is not because he has some exceptional ability (as is the case in the Western), but rather because he has a certain disability, namely his mental limitations. Karl, then, is not a triumphant hero who comes to rescue the poor and the oppressed; instead, he himself, by virtue of his condition, is among the disenfranchised and the alienated.

One, then, can compare the different ways that Karl and the Western hero are Christ-figures. The Western hero reflects primarily the image of Christ in Revelation. Here Christ is an exalted, powerful, militant figure who is a conquering warrior-judge and who violently destroys his enemies and inflicts wrathful punishment on them. This Jesus, like the Western hero, brings salvation through the destruction of others. Karl's depiction, however, is more complex because it has parallels with both this apocalyptic image of Christ and with the humble, earthly Jesus of the Gospels. In the Gospels, Jesus is a socially, economically, politically, and militarily powerless figure; and he associates with the poor, the lame, the blind, women, and sinners, that is, those on the margins of society. This Jesus' messiahship is gradually revealed through human weakness, suffering, and eventually crucifixion; thus salvation comes

---

4. Will Wright, *Six Guns and Society: A Structural Study of the Western* (Berkeley: University of California Press, 1975), 48–49; see also John Nelson, *Your God Is Alive and Well and Appearing in Popular Culture* (Philadelphia: Westminster, 1976); and Jewett and Lawrence, *American Monomyth*, xx.

5. Erik Bauer, "Southern Rebel: Interview with Billy Bob Thornton," *Creative Screenwriting* 4 (1997): 14; Nancy Hendrickson, "We Like the Way He Talks: The Dialogue of Billy Bob Thornton," *Creative Screenwriting* 5 (1998): 40. Thornton has said that *High Noon* is his favorite film.

6. Bauer, "Southern Rebel," 9.

through Jesus' own death. The power of *Sling Blade*, then, does not lie in its embodiment of the classic Western mythic structure. Rather, it is due to Thornton's complex portrayal of Karl, wherein are juxtaposed the New Testament's diverse images of Christ.[7]

To appreciate and understand Karl's complexity, it is important to recognize the Christ-likeness of both the violent, apocalyptic elements and the powerless, alienated qualities of Karl's portrayal. The former—the violent and the apocalyptic—are the ones Karl shares with the Western hero and with the Jesus of Revelation. Indeed, it has been recognized that the Book of Revelation, in part, has inspired and justified the militant and triumphalist ideology that characterizes the Western film and the American myth more generally.[8] Therefore, it is remarkable that the critics who discuss the Western hero as a Christ-figure focus on the Christ-likeness of the hero's sacrificial, salvific action and are reluctant to acknowledge the Christ-likeness of the protagonist's violence. For example, Michael Marsden argues that the West

> longed for a Christ who would ride in, deal effectively with evil, and dispense justice. . . . But this Western Savior must, of necessity, bring with him all the trappings of . . . a wrathful God, as in the Old Testament. He could not be the loving and forgiving and merciful Christ of the New Testament but must be, rather, a Christ who has been modified, changed by contact with the western experience.[9]

Marsden sets up a false dichotomy between the God of the Old Testament and of the New Testament, and then looks to the Old

---

7. Karl's parallels to Christ, discussed below, are drawn from all four Gospels (Matthew's image of Jesus as a teacher/mentor; Mark's suffering and dying Messiah; the particularly Lukan theme of open table fellowship; John's picture of a redeemer who enters the world and then returns to the heavenly realm), from Paul (the idea of the "foolishness" of Christ), and, of course, from Revelation. Drawing from a variety of biblical texts underscores the complexity and ambiguity in the depictions of both Karl and Christ.

8. Robert Jewett, for instance, observed: "Revelation provided the mythic framework" for this ideology, which he called the "Captain America Complex" (*The Captain America Complex*, 2nd ed. [Santa Fe: Bear, 1984], 24). See also Richard Slotkin, *Regeneration Through Violence: The Mythology of the American Frontier, 1600–1860* (Middletown, Conn.: Wesleyan University Press, 1973); and the essays in Lois Zamora, ed., *The Apocalyptic Vision in America: Interdisciplinary Essays on Myth and Culture* (Bowling Green, Ohio: Bowling Green University Popular Press, 1982).

9. Michael Marsden, "Savior in the Saddle: The Sagebrush Testament," *Shane: The Critical Edition*, ed. James Work (Omaha: University of Nebraska Press, 1984), 395.

Testament to find a parallel to the Western hero's violence. Yet it is the Christ of the New Testament, very much like the Western hero, who comes riding on a horse, deals with "evil," and dispenses justice through killing the opposition (cf. Revelation 19:11).

Similarly, in his article on *Shane*, Robert Banks observes that in the film, "ultimately restoration comes out of the barrel of his gun not the laying down of his life. Shane is therefore a variation on the Christ-figure." He then concludes, "Shane portrays a man who reflects characteristics of the judges in the Old Testament within a framework partly suggestive of Christ in the New Testament."[10] Thus, for Banks, Shane's taking of life instead of laying it down detracts from his being a Christ-figure. Like Marsden, Banks's reading results from a one-sided understanding of the Jesus of the New Testament—a reading that stops after the Gospels. The Jesus of Revelation, indeed, brings salvation through violence and the death of his enemies, much like Shane. Likewise, Bernard Brandon Scott argues, "With Jesus as movie producer, when Shane entered the saloon, instead of destroying his enemies, they would have put him to death."[11] Again, however, Shane's destroying his enemies is parallel to the action taken by the apocalyptic Jesus. Thus Scott, too, fails to consider the diversity of images of Jesus in the New Testament, and focuses instead only on the humble, suffering Jesus portrayed mainly in the Gospels.

Other critics come closer to acknowledging the Christlike qualities in the Western hero's violent actions, yet they do not quite get there. Conrad Ostwalt asserts that the Pale Rider (in the film by the same title) is a "complex messianic character" and observes that he is both "a demonic ghost who brings death with Hades on his heels," and at the same time a "human lover . . . hero . . . and defender of the righteous community."[12] Like the Jesus of the New Testament, the Pale Rider is a complex figure. But not only does Ostwalt refer to the protagonist's destructive behavior as "demonic," rather than Christlike, but he also concludes that it is "difficult to picture this Eastwood character as a representative from the kingdom of God." The Pale Rider, however, is very

---

10. Robert Banks, "The Drama of Salvation in George Stevens's *Shane*," *Explorations in Theology and Film*, ed. Clive Marsh and Gaye Ortiz (Oxford: Blackwell, 1997), 63, 70.

11. Bernard Brandon Scott, *Hollywood Dreams and Biblical Stories* (Minneapolis: Fortress, 1994), 66.

12. Conrad E. Ostwalt Jr., "Hollywood and Armageddon: Apocalyptic Themes in Recent Cinematic Presentation," *Screening the Sacred: Religion, Myth, and Ideology in Popular American Film*, ed. Joel W. Martin and Conrad E. Ostwalt Jr. (Boulder: Westview Press, 1995), 56–57.

much like Revelation's representative from the kingdom of God (Christ), whether or not one finds this difficult to imagine.

Akin to Ostwalt, Peter Malone recognizes the tension in Clint Eastwood's character in *High Plains Drifter*. He discusses the protagonist as a "Christ-figure" who is also an example of the "good/evil mysterious stranger." Concerning Eastwood's character, Malone observes: "One night he paints the town red, places a sign post at the edge of the lake beside which the town stands. The sign reads 'Hell.' He then sets the town alight and stands in the midst of the plains wielding his whip. It is obvious that a whip-lashing avenger in 'Hell' must be a demon. Yet this stranger has rescued and saved the poor."[13] Although Malone perceives the complexity of Eastwood's character—the one who wields the whip is the same one who rescued the helpless—he does not see that the image of Eastwood as a "whip-lashing avenger" parallels closely the apocalyptic, conquering Jesus. Rather, he states that it is "obvious" that the character is representative of a demon, not Christ.

Similarly, Lloyd Baugh writes concerning Shane, "The raw violence of the early fist-fight, and of the final gunfight in the saloon, adds a note of ambiguity to Shane, which does not however negate his being a Christ-figure."[14] Baugh's observation, here, is correct; but by saying that Shane's violence "does not negate" his being a Christ-figure, Baugh does not underscore sufficiently that Shane is a Christ-figure precisely because of, not in spite of, his "raw violence" and the ambiguity in his portrayal. Accordingly, Baugh highlights the sacrificial, rather than the violent, nature of Shane's final act: "The highest point of Shane's mission of liberation is his final sacrifice for love. Like Jesus, Shane conquers death . . . by dying to himself." While this may be a good comparison to the Gospel Jesus, Baugh, like the others, does not compare Shane to the apocalyptic Jesus, in which case he might have observed that Shane also conquers death by killing, not by being killed. Indeed, like the Jesus of Revelation, Shane inflicts violence rather than suffering violence, and he brings salvation through destruction—a biblical, Christlike feature of the Western hero's portrayal that many overlook.[15]

---

13. Peter Malone, *Movie Christs and Antichrists* (New York: Crossroad, 1990), 106.

14. Lloyd Baugh, *Imaging the Divine: Jesus and Christ-Figures in Film* (Kansas City: Sheed & Ward, 1997), 170.

15. Geoffrey Hill is an exception. Although he does not develop his discussion of Shane as a Christ-figure and employs a psychoanalytic approach rather than a theological one, Hill does refer to Shane as the "ambivalent, violent Prince of Peace." He observes that "like the Prince of

It is important, then, to recognize that the Western hero's violence is not only a reflection of the American myth, but also of the Christian myth. The Western protagonist's destructive qualities do not represent a cultural distortion of the Christ-figure because Christ too acts in a violent and vengeful manner. This, however, as has been demonstrated, is not readily acknowledged. One additional, exemplary quote emphasizes this: "Christ-figures in the movies should be interpreted through biblical criteria; they can be seen as redeemers, saviors, and liberators."[16] Conspicuously absent here is the image of Christ as a conqueror or destroyer, which falls well within "biblical criteria." These apocalyptic traits, to be sure, are characteristic of the hero's portrayal in both the Christian and the American myths.

SLING BLADE AND ITS CRITICS

Karl, like the protagonist of the Western, parallels the depiction of Christ as a warrior-judge when he brutally murders Doyle. The fact that Karl kills with a sling blade recalls that in Revelation, Jesus comes with "a sharp sickle in his hand" to execute divine judgment (Revelation 14:14–20).[17] However, just as critics have not adequately recognized the Christlike qualities of the Western hero's violence and have focused instead on his salvific presence and action, so too commentators on *Sling Blade* have not considered Karl's violence as reflective of one of the images of Christ in the New Testament and have highlighted instead the sacrificial nature of his actions.

In a recent article, Matthew McEver considers how the protagonist in four films—*Cool Hand Luke, One Flew Over the Cuckoo's Nest, Dead Poets Society*, and *Sling Blade*—can be viewed as a Christ-figure.[18] For McEver, these films are united by the notion that the "central character

---

Peace in the Christian Bible," Shane is "a man of ambiguity, recognizing the innate connection between violence and peace." See Hill, *Illuminating Shadows: The Mythic Power of Film* (Boston: Shambhala, 1992), 118, 124.

16. Peter Malone, "Edward Scissorhands: Christology from a Suburban Fairy-tale," *Explorations in Theology in Film*, ed. Clive Marsh and Gaye Ortiz (Oxford: Blackwell, 1997), 76; see also Malone's "Jesus on Our Screens," *New Image of Religious Film*, ed. John May (Kansas City: Sheed & Ward, 1997), 69–71.

17. All biblical quotations are from the New Revised Standard Version.

18. Matthew McEver, "The Messianic Figure in Film: Christology Beyond the Biblical Epic," *The Journal of Religion and Film* 2 (1998), [cited 24 April 2001]; available from http://www.uno maha.edu/~wwwjrf/McEverMessiah.htm.

is a non-conformist or unlikely redeemer who transforms lives and ultimately undergoes martyrdom." Accordingly, McEver writes, "*Sling Blade*
eventually does what any good christological film will do by making its
hero a martyr." Karl "sacrifices" his life in order to save the lives of Frank
and Linda, and in fact does "more than give his life for the happiness of
the child; he has sacrificed his soul." Thus Karl's murdering of Doyle is
an act of "atonement." McEver, therefore, concludes, "*Sling Blade*
enlarges our understanding of suffering on behalf of others." McEver's
reading, however, fails to give sufficient attention to the violent nature of
Karl's actions. Instead, he focuses on Karl's parallels to the Jesus of the
Gospels, or perhaps of Paul—a Jesus who lays down his life for others,
one whose love leads him to sacrifice for others. It seems clear enough,
however, that Karl is a rather strange representative of God's love and a
peculiar martyr, for in the end it is Doyle who is dead, not Karl. Like the
critics of the Western, McEver has overlooked the image of Karl as a violent, apocalyptic Christ.

Robert Johnston also discusses *Sling Blade* among a group of films
whose protagonist functions as a "Christ-figure," that is, "someone who
comes into society from the outside and through suffering love redeems
others."[19] Sara Anson Vaux advances a similar analysis of *Sling Blade*,
although she does not specifically discuss Karl as a Christ-figure.[20] She
writes that by killing Doyle, Karl is "deliberately taking the sin of murder on himself to spare Frank." She then concludes that Karl "gives up
his freedom to protect the ones he has learned to cherish." Likewise,
Maurice Yacowar underscores the loving nature of Karl's actions: "This
is not the familiar love—self-indulgence—but an alternative form of
honour—self-less love."[21] Akin to McEver's reading, Johnston, Anson
Vaux, and Yacowar highlight the salvific and sacrificial nature of Karl's
action, and exclude from their discussion the wrathful, vengeful Karl
who hacks Doyle to death.

---

19. Robert Johnston, *Reel Spirituality: Theology and Film in Dialogue* (Grand Rapids: Baker
Academic, 2000), 163.

20. Sara Anson Vaugh, "'Will You Ever Kill Anybody Again, Karl?'" *Christianity and the Arts*
5 (1998): 20–22. A condensed version of this article can be found in Vaux's recent book,
Finding Meaning at the Movies (Nashville: Abingdon, 1999). Here she places *Sling Blade* alongside *Forrest Gump* and *La Strada* in her chapter entitled "Purity of Heart," which again indicates her interpretation of Karl's portrayal.

21. Maurice Yacowar, "Love vs. Honour: *Donnie Brasco* and *Sling Blade*," *Queens Quarterly*
104 (spring 1997): 68.

At the opposite end of the interpretive spectrum are Harry Kiely's comments on *Sling Blade*. Similar to the critics' analyses of the Western hero, Kiely does not overlook Karl's destructive actions—in fact, he focuses exclusively on them—but he sees Karl's violence as utterly un-Christlike. Kiely contrasts the myth of "redemptive violence" with "the way of the cross" exemplified by Christ's death.[22] Karl, on Kiely's reading, is "a false savior" who "fosters a demonic illusion that the way of destruction is the way to life." For Kiely, then, Karl is not a Christ-figure, but rather an antichrist because he chooses the path of redemptive violence instead of the way of the cross. It is crucial to recognize, however, that the crucified Jesus of the Gospels is, in the end, the judging, avenging, conquering Christ. That is, the Jesus of the New Testament enacts both "the way of the cross" and "redemptive violence." In short, much like those who have studied the protagonist of the Western, the critics of *Sling Blade* have failed to perceive that part of Karl's Christ-likeness lies in his violent destruction of the enemy, Doyle.

KARL AS A CHRIST-FIGURE

Sling Blade is a film replete with religious themes, as Thornton intended.[23] In fact, not only did Thornton design the film to have a "strong religious sense," he has also specifically acknowledged that Karl is a Christ-figure: "There are a lot of Christ-like references. I was asked by a reporter one time, 'Now am I reading too much into this, or does the fact that Karl carried a book on carpentry, *A Christmas Carol*, and the Bible—?' No, you're not reading too much into it."[24] Of course, a writer or director need not intentionally incorporate religious themes for an interpreter to perceive them in a film, but the fact that Thornton purposefully integrated "Christ-like references" invites one to consider carefully those aspects of the film.

Sling Blade depicts Karl as a Christ-figure in a number of ways. In his speech, gait, and dress, Karl is a "fool" and thus a marginal figure. The outsider status of both Jesus and Karl is seen in their lowly beginnings,

---

22. Harry Kiely, "The False Promises of Violence: The Movie *Sling Blade* Fosters a Demonic Illusion that the Way of Destruction is the Way to Life," *Sojourners* 26 (November-December 1997): 37.

23. *The Mister Showbiz Interview: Billy Bob Thornton* [cited 24 April 2001]; from http://www.mrshowbiz.com/interviews/349. This page is no longer available.

24. Ibid.

literally on the outside—Karl in his parents' shed in the backyard and Jesus in a stable (at least according to Luke). Later in the film, Thornton shows the small indentation in the dirt floor of the shed where Karl used to sleep, conjuring images of the manger. Indeed, there was no room on the in(n)side for Jesus and Karl. Further, when he is first released from the hospital, Karl is shown standing outside places where normal life takes place—a barbershop, a police station, a store with an automated ape advertising its products,[25] and a fast-food restaurant. Also, Karl's outsider status is represented by his initially living in a back room of Bill Cox's repair shop and two scenes in which he simply stands outside the Wheatley house (without having knocked) waiting for someone to answer the door. While Karl is slowly integrated into a small community of those who accept him (Linda, Frank, Vaughn, his coworkers), he nonetheless always, to a certain extent, remains an outsider, symbolized by his living in the Wheatley garage, never in the house with the rest of the family. Similarly, Christ, as he is depicted in the Gospels, was an outsider, not part of the religious and social establishment. Rather, he, like Karl, was part of a small sub-community, and his special status kept him distinct from even them.

Further, Karl and his community, similar to Christ and his followers, are poor and ostracized. In one of their first conversations, Frank tells Karl how his love was spurned by Karen Cross (note the last name) because he and his mother were poor. Later in the conversation, Karl explains to Frank that his family, too, was poor and that his father had disowned him.[26] Both Karl and Frank, then, are economically oppressed and have experienced social alienation. Indeed, Karl, reminiscent of the earthly Jesus of the Gospels, is socially, politically, and economically powerless. Nevertheless, Karl changes the lives of those with whom he comes into contact. Like the Jesus presented in the Gospels, Karl's presence demands a response. Some accept him and offer him employment, food, housing, and their trust; others refuse to associate with him at all. Similarly, of course, some were drawn to Jesus, while others resisted him.

---

25. In many ways, *Sling Blade* is reminiscent of the novels of Flannery O'Connor (who Thornton acknowledges has influenced him), and one wonders if this gorilla is a gesture toward O'Connor's novel *Wise Blood* (also made into a film), which had a character who wore a similar gorilla suit.

26. One might draw a comparison between the Matthean theme of Christ's being accepted by those outside the Jewish community rather than by those within it, and Karl being accepted by marginalized strangers but not by his own father.

Reminiscent of the Jesus of the Gospels, Karl is a sage of sorts. Although he is a simpleton, he often comes up with strikingly wise solutions to problems. For instance, when no one else can fix a broken lawn tiller, Karl first checks the fuel tank and declares, "It ain't got no gas." His role as a teacher, however, is best seen as he develops into Frank's father figure. For example, after Karl overhears a conversation between Bill (his boss) and a father and son about how the local high school football team is shaping up and how the son is turning out to be a "chip off the ol' block," Karl (in the very next scene) goes to play football with Frank and his friends. After the game, Karl voices his pride in Frank, much as Frank's father had done before he died. More importantly, in their quiet conversations, Karl and Frank consider together a variety of difficult moral questions: Karl's murder of his mother and her lover; the murder of Karl's little brother; Frank's father's suicide; and how Frank should deal with Doyle. When Frank despairs, "Sometimes I think it'd been better if I wasn't even born," Karl responds with words of comfort and encouragement rather than with words of hate and rage toward Doyle, who is the cause of the boy's despair.

Karl also plays the role of teacher when he instructs Frank on certain matters—for instance, not to use bad language and to think good thoughts. Specifically, he tells Frank, "it ain't right to kill nobody." Here, then, Karl affirms the biblical injunction against murder. Of course he himself will later kill Doyle. Thus, his actions are not congruous with his message to Frank. This is similar to the portrayal of Jesus as a wise teacher who counseled his disciples to "turn the other cheek" and "to love your enemies and pray for those who persecute you," but who himself violently disrupts the moneychangers in the temple, not to mention his actions in Revelation. Here one can begin to see the paradoxical nature of the portrayals of Karl and Christ. Just as there is a tension between the Jesus of the Sermon on the Mount and the apocalyptic Jesus, so too there is a tension between Karl as a gentle and sage father figure to Frank and the violent, apocalyptic Karl who wields the blade of judgment.

There is also a prominent eating motif woven throughout the film that contributes to Karl's image as a Christ-figure. When Doyle is first told that Karl will be living in the Wheatley garage, his response is that he does not want to eat with Karl. "He'll make me sick," Doyle declares. Accordingly, a few scenes later Linda, Frank, and Doyle are eating dinner together (without Karl) and Doyle comments, "Who the hell could eat with him makin' all that goddamn racket with his throat?" Doyle, then, rejects table fellowship with Karl. By contrast, Bill and Karl's coworkers happily include Karl in their lunches at the local burger place; on another occasion Vaughn treats Karl to a meal; and Linda makes biscuits and mustard for Karl (his favorite food) in the middle of the night. Most notable, however, is Karl's participation in a meal in which Vaughn, his partner Paul, Linda, Frank, and Melinda (another mentally challenged person) are present. Like the Jesus of the Gospels (particularly in Luke's account), Karl eats with others whom traditional society ostracizes—two homosexuals, a single mother involved with a man, and another challenged individual. That this is a unique group of outcasts is brilliantly underscored by the camera angle in this scene, which, rather than placing viewers in the midst of the meal, keeps them at a distance, as if peering from around a corner. In the Gospels, of course, the religious leaders are depicted as declining table fellowship with certain people as a means to distinguish their establishment culture from those on the outside. Thus, in both *Sling Blade* and in the Gospels, table fellowship serves to define community boundaries; it is also a prominent theme that surfaces a number of times in both the film (see below) and Scripture.

Roughly the final quarter of the movie shows a series of scenes that all have pronounced biblical echoes and develop Karl's portrayal into a Christ-figure. First, Karl decides to go to see his father, who has disowned him. Just before this, Karl is shown praying by himself, reminiscent of Jesus, particularly in Luke. The fact that prayer is closely associated with Karl's encounter with his alienated father may recall Jesus' final plea to his father: "My God, my God, why have you forsaken me?" (Mark 15:34). Indeed, in a very real sense Karl's father's disowning of him had crucified his soul. While there may not be a direct Christlike parallel in Karl's confrontation with his father, the scene is permeated with biblical references. Karl tells his father that he has read the Bible and, although he cannot understand all of it, he has discovered that the stories he was told (perhaps about why he was mentally challenged) were not in there. Further, a picture of Jesus can be seen hanging on the wall as Karl enters the room; there is a cross-shaped image in the picture directly over his father's head; and after Karl walks out, a painting of the Last Supper becomes visible. Karl then stops in the backyard at his brother's grave, which is marked with a stone that has a cross on it. This "cross imagery" continues in the next brief scene, which shows Karl standing high on a wooden bridge. He is perched directly over one of the vertical pillars—which forms a T-shape with the horizontal planks—as the sun shines brightly in the sky. As this shot wonderfully suggests, Karl's portrayal has similarities both to the crucified Christ and to the

Son of Man who will come in the sky in glory, a reflection of the diverse images of Christ in the New Testament.[27]

Christlike parallels are also apparent in the next scene, as Karl enters the bedroom where Linda and Doyle are sleeping and declares that he wants to be baptized. Karl, strangely, carries a hammer in his hand, symbolic perhaps of the violence that is to come. Not only is this ritual cleansing symbolically linked with the horror of the murder, it is connected literally as well, because Karl's baptism occurs on the same day he kills Doyle. In the next scene Karl is baptized in a muddy river as the congregation sings "Softly and Tenderly Jesus Is Calling." The first part of the refrain to this song is notable, "Come home, come home, you who are weary, come home," because the baptism appears to be part of Karl's preparations before the murder that he knows will lead to his return home to the mental institution (see below). This notion is strengthened when Karl tells Frank in their final conversation that he is "real tired" (i.e., weary).

When Frank, Linda, and Karl return from the baptism, the eating theme reappears. Here Doyle again provides the contrast to open table fellowship. He actually twists the notion by ostensibly offering to treat Linda, Frank, and Karl to lunch, but in reality his ploy is to get Linda out of the house (to go pick up the food) so that he can talk to Karl and Frank alone. In this conversation with them, he asserts his authority as the "man of the house" and tells Karl that he is no longer permitted to live in the Wheatley garage because a "normal family" cannot have a "retard" staying with them. Consequently, when Linda returns with the food, Karl has left the house. He is not welcome at Doyle's table. Further, as it turns out, this is a "last supper" gone awry, for by the end of the day Doyle will be dead and Karl will be on his way back to the mental institution.

After Karl leaves the Wheatley house, the film climaxes with a series of scenes reminiscent of the passion narratives. It quickly becomes clear what Karl is intent on doing (killing Doyle), and, like Jesus in his final days, he prepares for the end. First he thanks Linda for her hospitality, and then goes to Frank's "secret place" where he knows he will find the boy. Frank, who is distraught at the prospect of Doyle moving in with them, suggests that Karl intervene: "You have to look out for me. You don't let that son-of-a-bitch run you off." After Karl instructs him not to talk that way, Frank continues: "Why don't you stop Doyle when he gets that a-way? You're older than him. You're stronger, too." Karl, however, similar to Jesus at his arrest, rejects the notion of using force to overcome

---

27. The image of Karl on a high place may also recall the transfiguration.

the enemy: "That feller's a whole sight meaner than me. He'd just whup the tar out of me." More importantly, Karl prepares for his departure by offering words of comfort to Frank: "If I ain't aroun' no more, it don't mean that I don't care for ya. I care for ya a good deal. I care for ya more than anybody they is. We made friends right off the bat." Like the disciples' response to Jesus predicting his death, Frank does not understand and resists the idea that Karl will be leaving: "I care for you too. But you'll be around; don't say that." Karl responds by reinforcing the bond between them: "It don't make no difference where I was to be. We'll always be friends. There ain't no way to stop that." Reminiscent of Jesus' words of comfort to his disciples in John 14 and 17, or perhaps of his last words in Matthew, "And remember, I am with you always, to the end of the age," Karl departs with words of encouragement and hope for those he leaves behind.

Further, Karl instructs Frank not to go home that night, but to stay with Vaughn. Like Jesus, who instructed his disciples to secure a donkey for him and to pray with him in the garden, Karl's plan involves the assistance of his friends. In addition, Karl gives Frank his stack of books (with the Bible on top), puts his arm around Frank, and tells him that he loves him (for the first time). This serves as a type of commissioning scene in which Frank is encouraged to continue in the love that they have developed.[28] Finally, in perhaps the clearest echo of the passion narratives, later that night Karl returns alone to the wooded secret place by the pond and meditates quietly. This recalls Gethsemane, as both Karl and Christ gather their thoughts before the end is upon them. In short, reminiscent of the Gospel passion narratives and of Jesus' last days on the earth, Karl demurs from the notion of using violence against the opponent; informs Frank that he is leaving (a message met with resistance); provides a word of comfort, saying that he will always be with him; instructs him what to do in the final hours; commissions him; and withdraws to a remote place before the climactic moments.

There are also some parallels in the denouement to the stories of Jesus and Karl. Not only do both arrive as archetypal outsiders, but after the climax—Christ's death and Karl's murder of Doyle—both return to the place from which they came, Christ to the heavenly realm (especially in

---

28. In her brief discussion of *Sling Blade*, Adele Reinhartz suggests that that Bible comes to symbolize Karl himself and will represent his own presence in Frank's life when he is gone. That is, "the gift of a Bible presages separation." See her article "Scripture on the Silver Screen," *The Journal of Religion and Film* 3 (1999), [cited 24 April 2001]; available from http://www.unomaha.edu/~wwwjrf/scripture.htm.

John) and Karl to the mental institution. Further, Karl and Jesus both sacrifice their lives but do not lose their lives; in fact, both return to a place that is better or more suitable for them. In this vein, it is important to see that Karl's return to the institution offers him a better life than the one he had in the "real world." Not only did he voluntarily return to the institution shortly after being released because he did not "care nothin' about bein' a free man," but also when he returned there after killing Doyle, he says of life out in the world: "It was too big." This suggests that he is more comfortable back in the institution. Karl, then, returns to live in a different world and he can no longer commune with Linda and Frank and others who had befriended him, because they must remain in the messy, complicated world that is "too big" (cf. the disciples). However, because Karl in some sense is not an ordinary human (i.e., he is mentally challenged), he does not die as might be expected of a person who committed Karl's act, but rather he remains alive. Thus, both Karl and Christ sacrifice their lives and are as a result no longer physically present with their close friends, but because neither are "normal" humans, they do not die but instead live on in another world. Finally, in the New Testament, salvation comes both through the sacrificial death of Christ (Gospels) and in Christ's ultimate conquering of the wicked forces (Revelation). Similarly, in *Sling Blade*, salvation for the community—Frank, Linda, and Vaughn—comes both through Karl's sacrificially giving up his life and through the murder of Doyle.

After killing Doyle and while waiting for the police to arrive, Karl eats his "last supper" as he finishes the biscuits (note the bread) that were to be eaten earlier in the day as part of the meal with Doyle. Thus, in an ironic twist, Karl does partake of the meal offered by Doyle, but only as Doyle lies dead on the floor. The reappearance of the eating motif at this juncture may be reminiscent not only of the Last Supper in the Gospels, but also of the messianic banquet in Revelation 19 in which the triumphant Christ celebrates victory over his enemies. Indeed, Doyle had been referred to as a "beast" and a "monster"—clear echoes of the imagery in Revelation—and his murder represents a defeat of the forces of evil.

Thus, both in Karl's function in the plot (i.e., structurally) and in the crafting of the details, Thornton has depicted a complex Christ-figure. Notably, the name Karl Childers resonates with "Christ-child."[29] This in itself points to the ambiguity in his portrayal; he has elements similar to

---

29. Other characters, too, have symbolic names. Doyle's last name, Hargraves, foreshadows his fate, and the last name of Karl's fellow inmate at the mental institution, Charles Bushman (J. T. Walsh), is also symbolic of his character, as his graphic and gruesome descriptions about his horrific crimes against women make clear.

both the powerful Christ and to the humble, simple child. Further, his tonsured haircut is that of a monk, but his gait, his seemingly oversized shoes, and mismatched body parts look more like that of a monster.[30] The monk is the monster. Moreover, as Bill observes, Karl is "mentally retarded" but is a "whiz with small engines" and is "strong as an ox." Indeed, he is a brilliant simpleton who is both weak and strong. As others have put it, Karl is a man who at once "enraptures and frightens"[31] and who is portrayed with both "gut-wrenching horror and heartbreaking greatness."[32] Encountering Karl, then, like experiencing the divine according to Rudolph Otto, evokes feelings of both *tremendum* and *fascinans*.[33] To elaborate and clarify the nature of Karl's complexity and ambiguity, it is helpful to return to the biblical depiction of Christ.

KARL AND THE MARGINALIZED SON OF MAN

Earlier attention was called to the diverse images of Jesus in the New Testament, pointing mainly to the differences between the humble, suffering Jesus of the Gospels and the apocalyptic, conquering Jesus of Revelation. This distinction, however, is not that sharp, for there are violent images of Jesus in the Gospels and images of a suffering Christ in Revelation. Specifically, for instance, in Revelation 5, the "Lion of the tribe of Judah" who "has conquered" is paradoxically also the "Lamb standing as if it had been slaughtered." Likewise, the Gospels depict a paradoxical Jesus who teaches a radical nonviolence—"If anyone strikes you on the right cheek, turn the other also" and "love your enemies and pray for those who persecute you" (Matthew 5:39, 44) and, at the same time, a Jesus who claims to bring violence—"I have not come to bring peace, but a sword. For I have come to set a man against his father, and a daughter against her mother, and a daughter-in-law against her mother-in-law" (Matthew 10:34–35). Moreover, the Gospels portray Christ both as a humble, suffering figure, one who is socially, politically, and militarily powerless, and as an all-powerful, apocalyptic judge and avenger.

---

30. Vaux makes the same observation ("'Will You Ever Kill Anybody Again, Karl?'" 20).

31. Carol Jenkins, "*Sling Blade*" [cited 26 April 2001]; available from http://netpad.com/movie/slingb.

32. Nicole Kasprzak, "*Sling Blade* Shines Above Post-Oscar Mediocrity" [cited 26 April 2001]; available from http://misc.vassar.edu/spring97/mar28/arts/slingblade.

33. Rudolph Otto, *The Idea of the Holy*, trans. John W. Harvey (New York: Oxford University Press, 1958).

One place in particular where these different images of Jesus are strikingly juxtaposed is the parable of the sheep and the goats in Matthew 25. In this text, the Son of Man, that is, the apocalyptic Jesus, separates the people from one another based on whether or not they provided for the Son of Man as they encountered him when he was hungry, thirsty, a stranger, naked, sick, and in prison. The righteous sheep had cared for the needy, and unwittingly for the Son of Man as well, who declared, "Just as you did it to one of the least of my brothers, you did it to me." Accordingly, the sheep inherit the kingdom and eternal life. The goats, by contrast, had not acted charitably toward the disenfranchised—the Son of Man—and thus are sent into eternal punishment.

In many ways, *Sling Blade* is a modern retelling of this parable. Karl, like the Son of Man, the Christ in the parable, is both weak and strong, an outcast and a powerful ruler. Similarly, the characters in the film are evaluated based on how they treat Karl, a person who needs food, clothing, and shelter, just as the sheep and goats are separated based on their actions toward the "least of these." That is, in the biblical text the Son of Man is at once "the least of these" and the judge who rewards and punishes. He is both the weak, disenfranchised sufferer and the powerful ruler. He is the marginalized one to whom acts of charity must be directed and he is the all-powerful king. Similarly, Karl is at once the marginalized figure to whom kindness must be shown and the almighty judge who saves some and condemns others. He is the fool who wields the sling blade, which he knows is properly called a Kaiser (king) blade. Indeed it is the simpleton outcast who acts as the king. The lamb is the lion.

Further, like the Jesus of the parable, Karl saves those who have been kind to him (Frank, Linda, and Vaughn) and destroys those who have not helped him (Doyle). In both the film and the parable, those who reject the protagonist in his weak and vulnerable form are ultimately subjected to his wrath and vengeance in his apocalyptic incarnation. In addition, those who helped "the least of these" in the parable and those who helped Karl could not have expected anything in return for their kindness, yet ironically it is the key to their salvation. Finally, if Matthew's audience was itself a relatively marginalized community, then, like the film, it is those on the edges of society who (are asked to) show kindness to those in need.

There is one particular feature of the film that draws attention to the similarity between Karl and Christ as simultaneously marginalized and powerful. Each of Karl's farewell conversations with Linda, Frank, and Vaughn conclude with Karl walking away as the other person calls out,

"Karl." Likewise, Doyle, when Karl lifts the lawnmower blade to strike him, cries out, "Karl!" Thus, just as both the sheep and the goats ask "Lord, when did we see you . . ." so each character in the film calls out to Karl, the judge, who is about to separate the sheep from the goats. Indeed, not everyone who says "Lord, Lord" will enter the kingdom. Some will be cast into the lake of fire.

PONDERING THE PARADOXICAL PROTAGONISTS

The juxtaposition and interplay of the different images of Jesus and Karl—as saviors and destroyers, as weak and strong, as advocates of peace and violent avengers—highlights the discontinuities, the paradoxes, of their portrayals. The Christ of the New Testament, on the one hand, is the epitome of foolishness and weakness, as Paul says: "But God chose what is foolish in the world to shame the wise; God chose what is weak in the world to shame the strong; God chose what is low and despised in the world, things that are not, to reduce to nothing things that are" (1 Corinthians 1:27–28). On the other hand, Christ is an all-powerful, apocalyptic, wrathful judge. Likewise, Karl is a powerless simpleton, and yet he brandishes the scythe of judgment. It is precisely in this paradox that Karl differs from the hero of the classic Western, for although both may be outsiders, the Western hero is not the weak fool, as are both Karl and Christ, in one sense at least. Thus, by bringing *Sling Blade* and the New Testament into dialogue, one is better able to recognize the paradoxical features of each protagonist's characterization. Film and Scripture elucidate one another.

This deeper understanding of the complexity of each protagonist's characterization relates to other aspects of the film and the New Testament that prove mutually enlightening. One of these is the conclusion to each work. *Sling Blade* has a morally ambiguous conclusion, which differs from that of the classic Western film. As Thornton himself observes: "It's not like he [Karl] walks away in the sunset."[34] This ending raises difficult questions. What, for instance, is one to think and feel about Karl's murder of Doyle? Would another solution have been better? These questions, in turn, can lead one to pose similar queries of Revelation, the conclusion to the New Testament. How, for example, is one to understand the violent acts of the apocalyptic Christ? Are death

---

34. *The Mister Showbiz Interview.*

and destruction necessary to institute the kingdom of God? *Sling Blade*'s complex conclusion, then, challenges, without rejecting per se, the "happy," neat ending of the traditional Western, the America monomyth, and the New Testament. Indeed, a sensitive viewing of *Sling Blade* leaves one to consider whether Karl is the hero or the villain. The film offers no easy answers. A sensitive reading of Revelation evokes similar questions concerning its protagonist to which, again, there are no facile answers.

Bringing *Sling Blade*'s portrayal of Karl and the New Testament's images of Christ into dialogue can also lead to reflection on matters of Christology. Karl's characterization invites consideration of the ambiguous nature of Jesus Christ as a figure of love and judgment, peace and violence, humility and power, kindness and vengeance, creativity and destruction. To be sure, the second element in these binary sets—the judging, violent, powerful, vengeful, and destructive—may for many be unpalatable features of Christ and Christ-figures. Yet they are undeniably present in Christ's portrayal and, therefore, can be integrated into a deeper christological understanding.

Rather than ignore or jettison these violent aspects of Christ and Christ-figures—and of the American and Christian myths—as (post)modern sensibilities might dictate, perhaps Mikhail Bakhtin's notions of "polyphony" and a "dialogic sense of truth" can help with this integration. Bakhtin developed these notions to describe what he perceived in the novels of Dostoevsky, but they can be fruitfully appropriated for biblical studies and theology, as others have done.[35] Briefly, unlike a monologic conception of truth, a dialogic sense "requires a plurality of consciousness" that "cannot be fitted within the bounds of a single consciousness."[36] Dialogic truth exists at the place where multiple consciousnesses—unmerged voices—intersect; that is, in conversation. Texts, of course, are not conversations, but according to Bakhtin, it is possible to produce in a literary work something that approximates an authentic dialogue. This mode of writing he called polyphonic. In a polyphonic work, unlike a monologic one, the author creates several

---

35. See, for example, Barbara Green, *Mikhail Bakhtin and Biblical Scholarship: An Introduction* (Atlanta: Society of Biblical Literature, 2000); and Carol Newsom, "Bakhtin, the Bible, and Dialogic Truth," *The Journal of Religion* 76 (1996): 290–306. The discussion of Bakhtin's concepts in the present paper is absurdly brief, but hopefully gestures in a helpful direction.

36. Mikhail Bakhtin, *Problems of Dostoevsky's Poetics*, trans. Carol Emerson (Minneapolis: University of Minnesota Press, 1984), 81.

consciousnesses that are genuinely independent of one another and of the author's perspective. In such a text, the dialogic play of these consciousnesses and their expressed ideas calls the reader to participate in the conversation. As a descriptive category, then, Bakhtin's idea of polyphony is useful for understanding the nature of the New Testament's diverse images of Jesus Christ. Indeed, one can easily identify a plurality of unmerged perspectives on matters of Christology within the New Testament. Following the Bakhtinian notion, then, it is in the intersection, in the dialoguing of these distinct consciousnesses, that truth may emerge. Viewed in this way, Revelation's depiction of Christ represents a distinct voice that participates in dialogue with each of the four Gospel writers' presentation of Jesus, with Paul's, with that of the author of Hebrews, and so on.[37] Seen in this light, each voice contributes important ideas and images that develop more fully—even if in enigmatic and contradictory ways—the portrayal of Jesus Christ. Thus, the harmonizing or silencing of voices detracts from the richness and depth of the christological conversation.

Finally, *Sling Blade*'s complex portrayal of Karl provokes us to ponder not only matters of New Testament Christologies, but also to reflect more generally on human experience as a constant struggle between charity and justice, peace and war, weakness and strength, compassion and wrath. That is, Jesus' and Karl's paradoxical features mirror the nature of human life lived, as it is, between these oppositions. Human history bears witness to this struggle, as Christians have been inspired by both the portrayal of Jesus as a gentle teacher of a selfless love and as a mighty warrior who destroys his foes. The same religion that has evoked loving and compassionate action toward other human beings is the same religion that produced the Crusades, the Inquisition, and the Salem witch trials. Although previous generations have not always successfully incarnated the various images of Christ, these various depictions need not be merged together or selectively eliminated because this reduces the number of dialogue participants. At times, perhaps, the polyphony sounds cacophonous and leaves one echoing Karl's sentiments: "I've read the Bible. I reckon I understand a good deal of it . . . but

---

37. Films, too, can lean in this dialogic direction. One thinks of Spike Lee's *Do the Right Thing* (1989), which places side by side the contrasting philosophies of Malcolm X and Martin Luther King Jr., or perhaps of Steven Soderbergh's *Traffic* (2000), which juxtaposes several different approaches to dealing with drugs in Mexico and the United States.

I can't understand all of it. . . . It wasn't what I expected in a lot of places." Nonetheless, it is precisely the polyphonic nature of the New Testament—its rich, mysterious tapestry of portrayals of Christ—that calls one into conversation with these multiple voices, a conversation from which dialogic truth may emerge. Indeed, dynamic, ambiguous, and paradoxical protagonists are much more engaging, memorable, and powerful mythic figures because they embody the complexities of human existence. *Sling Blade*'s Karl and Jesus Christ are two such protagonists.[38]

---

38. I am grateful to Deborah Whitehead for editing this paper and for offering several insightful observations that I have included in the essay. I also thank Amy Cottrill and Julie Sindler for their helpful comments on an earlier draft.

MOVIES CITED

Alice's Restaurant. Arthur Penn (director). 111 mins. United Artists, 1969.

Alien. Ridley Scott (director). 117 mins. Twentieth Century Fox, 1979.

Apt Pupil. Bryan Singer (director). 111 mins. Paramount Pictures, 1998.

The Beast from 20,000 Fathoms. Eugène Lourié (director). 80 mins. Warner Brothers, 1953.

Behemoth the Sea Monster. Eugène Lourié (director). 80 mins. London: Artistes Alliance, 1958.

The Bicycle Thief (Italian: *Ladri di Bicicletta*, 1948). Vittorio De Sica (director). 93 mins. Mayer-Burstyn, 1949.

Boys Don't Cry. Kimberly Pierce (director). 118 mins. Fox Searchlight Pictures, 1999.

Bram Stoker's Dracula. Frances Ford Coppola (director). 130 mins. Columbia Pictures, 1992.

The Brandon Teena Story (documentary). Susan Muska and Gréta Olafsdóttir (directors). 90 mins. Zeitgeist Films, 1998.

Conan the Barbarian. John Milius (director). 121 mins. Universal Pictures, 1982.

Cool Hand Luke. Stuart Rosenberg (director). 126 mins. Warner Brothers, 1967.

The Curse of Frankenstein. Terence Fisher (director). 82 mins. Hammer Film Productions, Ltd., 1957.

David and Bathsheba. Henry King (director). 116 mins. Twentieth Century Fox, 1951.

The Day the Earth Stood Still. Robert Wise (director). 92 mins. Twentieth Century Fox, 1951.

Dead Poets Society. Peter Weir (director). 128 mins. Buena Vista, 1989.

The Devil's Advocate. Taylor Hackford (director). 144 mins. Warner Brothers, 1997.

Do the Right Thing. Spike Lee (director). 120 mins. 40 Acres & a Mule Filmworks, 1989.

Dogma. Kevin Smith (director). 130 mins. View Askew, 1999.

Dr. Strangelove. Stanley Kubrick (director). 93 mins. Columbia Pictures, 1964.

Dracula. Tod Browning (director). 75 mins. Universal Pictures, 1931.

Easy Rider. Dennis Hopper (director). 94 mins. Columbia Pictures, 1969.

End of Days. Peter Hyams (director). 121 mins. Universal Pictures, 1999.

eXistenZ. David Cronenberg (director). 97 mins. Dimension Films, 1999.

The Exorcist. William Friedkin (director). 122 mins. Warner Brothers, 1973.

Falling Down. Joel Schumacher (director). 113 mins. Warner Brothers, 1993.

Fearless Vampire Killers, or *Pardon Me but Your Teeth Are in My Neck*. Roman Polanski (director). 124 mins. Metro-Goldwyn-Mayer, 1967.

Fellini Satyricon. Federico Fellini (director). 138 mins. United Artists, 1969.

Forrest Gump. Robert Zemeckis (director). 142 mins. Paramount Pictures, 1994.

Grand Canyon. Lawrence Kasdan (director). 134 mins. Twentieth Century Fox, 1991.

The Godfather. Francis Ford Coppola (director). 175 mins. Paramount Pictures, 1972.

The Greatest Story Ever Told. George Stevens (director). 260 mins. United Artists, 1965.

Hamlet. Franco Zeffirelli (director). 130 mins. Warner Brothers, 1990.

Heart of Darkness. Nicolas Roeg (director). 100 mins. Turner Pictures, 1994.

High Noon. Fred Zinnemann (director). 85 mins. United Artists, 1952.

High Plains Drifter. Clint Eastwood (director). 105 mins. Universal Pictures, 1972.

If . . . Lindsay Anderson (director). 111 mins. Paramount Pictures, 1968.

Indecent Proposal. Adrian Lyne (director). 117 mins. Paramount Pictures, 1993.

Independence Day. Roland Emmerich (director). 145 mins. Twentieth Century Fox, 1996.

The Iron Curtain. William A. Wellman (director). 87 mins. Twentieth Century Fox, 1948.

Jaws. Steven Spielberg (director). 124 mins. Universal Pictures, 1975.

The King of Kings. Cecil B. DeMille (director). 112 mins. Kino, 1927.

King of Kings. Nicholas Ray (director). 168 mins. Metro-Goldwyn-Mayer, 1961.

La Strada. Federico Fellini (director). 115 mins. USA Trans-Lux, 1954.

The Last Man on Earth (*L'ultimo uomo della Terra*). Sidney Salkow and Ulbaldo Ragona (directors). 86 mins. American International Pictures, 1964.

The Last Temptation of Christ. Martin Scorsese (director). 164 mins. Universal Pictures, 1988.

Left Behind: The Movie. Victor Sarin (director). 95 mins. Cloud Ten Pictures, 2000.

Lethal Weapon. Richard Donner (director). 112 mins. Warner Brothers, 1987.

Lethal Weapon 2. Richard Donner (director). 113 mins. Warner Brothers, 1989.

Lethal Weapon 3. Richard Donner (director). 118 mins. Warner Brothers, 1992.

Lifeforce. Tobe Hooper (director). 116 mins. TriStar Pictures, 1985.

The Lion King. Roger Allers and Rob Minkoff (directors). 89 mins. Walt Disney Productions, 1994.

Look Back in Anger. Tony Richardson (director). 115 mins. Warner Brothers, 1956.

The Mark of Lilith. Bruna Fionda, Polly Gladwin, and Isiling Mack-Nataf (directors). 32 mins. London College of Printing, 1986.

The Matrix. Andy Wachowski and Larry Wachowski (directors). 136 mins. Warner Brothers, 1999.

Mean Streets. Martin Scorsese (director). 110 mins. Warner Brothers, 1973.

The Medicinal Value of Laughter: An Alternative Look at Patch Adams. J. M. Kenny (director). 12 mins. Universal Pictures, 1999.

Michael. Nora Ephron (director). 105 mins. New Line Cinema, 1996.

Midnight Cowboy. John Schlessinger (director). 113 mins. United Artists, 1969.

Monty Python and the Holy Grail. Terry Gilliam and Terry Jones (directors). 90 mins. Columbia Pictures, 1975.

Monty Python's The Life of Brian. Terry Jones (director). 94 mins. Orion Pictures, 1979. DVD, Criterion, 1999.

The Mouse That Roared. Jack Arnold (director). 83 mins. Columbia Pictures, 1959.

Mr. Drake's Duck. Val Guest (director). 75 mins. United Artists, 1951.

Nosferatu, eine Symphonie des Grauens. F. W. Murnau (director). 75 mins. Kino, 1922.

Nosferatu, Phantom der Nacht. Werner Herzog (director). 107 mins. Twentieth Century Fox, 1979.

The Omen. Richard Donner (director). 111 mins. Twentieth Century Fox, 1976.

One Flew Over the Cuckoo's Nest. Milos Forman (director). 133 mins. United Artists, 1975.

Our Man in Havana. Carol Reed (director). 111 mins. Columbia Pictures, 1959.

Pale Rider. Clint Eastwood (director). 115 mins. Warner Brothers, 1985.

Patch Adams. Special Edition. Tom Shadyac (director). 116 mins. Universal Pictures, 1998.

Pleasantville. Gary Ross (director). 124 mins. New Line Cinema, 1998.

The Prime of Miss Jean Brodie. Ronald Neame (director). Twentieth Century Fox, 1969.

The Prince of Egypt. Brenda Chapman, Steve Hickner, and Simon Wells (directors). 90 mins. DreamWorks SKG, 1998.

Powder. Victor Salva (director). 111 mins. Buena Vista Pictures, 1995.

The Quatermass Xperiment. Val Guest (director). 82 mins. Hammer Film Productions Ltd., 1955.

The Rain People. Francis Ford Coppola (director). 101 mins. Warner-Seven Arts, 1969.

Red Menace. R. G. Springsteen (director). Republic Pictures Corporation, 1949.

The Return of the Jedi. Richard Marquand (director). 134 mins. Twentieth Century Fox, 1983.

Rosemary's Baby. Roman Polanski (director). 136 mins. Paramount Pictures, 1968.

Scarecrow. Jerry Schatzberg (director). 112 mins. Warner Brothers, 1973.

Seven (also *Se7en*). David Fincher (director). 123 mins. New Line Cinema, 1995.

Seven Days to Noon. John Boutling and Ray Boulting (directors). 94 mins. London Film Production, 1950.

The Seventh Sign. Carl Schultz (director). 97 mins. TriStar Pictures, 1988.

Shadow of the Vampire. E. Elias Merhige (director). 91 mins. Universal Studios, 2000.

Shampoo. Hal Ashby (director). 109 mins. Columbia Pictures, 1975.

Shane. George Stevens (director). 118 mins. Paramount Pictures, 1953.

A Simple Plan. Sam Raimi (director). 121 mins. Paramount Pictures, 1998.

Sling Blade. Billy Bob Thornton (director). 135 mins. The Shooting Gallery, 1996.

Star Wars. George Lucas (director). 121 mins. Twentieth Century Fox, 1977.

Stigmata. Rupert Wainwright (director). 103 mins. Metro-Goldwyn-Mayer, 1999.

Strategic Air Command. Anthony Mann (director). 112 mins. Paramount Pictures, 1955.

Superman. Richard Donner (director). 143 mins. Warner Brothers, 1978.

The Ten Commandments. Cecil B. DeMille (director). 220 mins. Paramount Pictures, 1956.

Terminator. James Cameron (director). 108 mins. Orion Pictures, 1984.

Them! Gordon Douglas (director). 94 mins. Warner Brothers, 1954.

The Thing from Another World. Christian Nyby (director). 87 mins. RKO Radio Pictures, 1951.

Things to Come. William Cameron Menzies (director). 100 mins. London Film Productions, 1936. Distributed by United Artists.

The Thirteenth Floor. Josef Rusnak (director). 100 mins. Columbia Pictures, 1999.

Total Recall. Paul Verhoeven (director). 113 mins. Twentieth Century Fox, 1989.

Traffic. Steven Soderbergh (director). 147 mins. USA Films, 2000.

True Grit. Henry Hathaway (director). 128 mins. Paramount Pictures, 1969.

True Lies. James Cameron (director). 144 mins. Twentieth Century Fox, 1994.

Vampires. John Carpenter (director). 108 mins. Columbia Pictures, 1998.

The Wild Bunch. Sam Peckinpah (director). 134 mins. Warner Brothers, 1969.

Wise Blood. John Huston (director). 108 mins. New Line Cinema, 1979.

Witness. Peter Weir (director). 112 mins. Paramount Pictures, 1985.

The Wizard of Oz. Victor Fleming (director). 112 mins. Metro-Goldwyn-Mayer, 1939.

Z. Costa-Gavras (director). 127 mins. Cinema V, 1969.

BIBLIOGRAPHY

Internet publications available at the time of writing may no longer be accessible.

Abraham, Nicolas. "Notes on the Phantom: A Complement to Freud's Metapsychology." Translated by Nicholas Rand. In *The Trial(s) of Psychoanalysis*, edited by Françoise Meltzer, 75–80. Chicago: University of Chicago Press, 1988 [1978].

Abraham, Nicolas, and Maria Torok. "Introjection—Incorporation: Mourning or Melancholia." In *Psychoanalysis in France*, edited by Serge Lebovici and Daniel Widlöcher, 3–16. New York: International Universities Press, 1980 [1972].

——. "A Poetics of Pyschoanalysis: 'The Lost Object—Me.'" Translated by Nicholas Rand. *SubStance* 43 (1984 [1978]): 3–18.

Aichele, George. *The Limits of Story*. Chico, Calif.: Scholars Press, 1985.

——. "Two Forms of Meta-Fantasy." *Journal for the Fantastic in the Arts* 1, no. 3 (1988): 55–67.

Aichele, George, and Gary A. Phillips. "Exegesis, Eisegesis, Intergesis." *Semeia* 69/70 (1995): 7–18.

Albanese, Catherine L. *America: Religions and Religion*. 2nd ed. Belmont, Calif.: Wadsworth Publishing Company, 1992.

Alford, Fred C. *What Evil Means to Us*. Ithaca, N.Y.: Cornell University Press, 1997.

Altizer, Thomas J. J., and William Hamilton. *Radical Theology and the Death of God*. New York: The Bobbs-Merrill Company, 1966.

Anderson, Melissa. "The Brandon Teena Story and *Boys Don't Cry*." *Cineaste* 25, no. 2 (2000): 54–56.

Apuleius. *The Golden Ass*. Translated by Jack Lindsay. Bloomington: Indiana University Press, 1960.

Arata, Stephen D. "The Occidental Tourist: *Dracula* and the Anxiety of Reverse Colonization." In *Dracula*, edited by Nina Auerbach and David J. Skal, 462–70. A Norton Critical Edition. New York: W. W. Norton & Company, 1997.

Arendt, Hannah. *Eichmann in Jerusalem: A Report on the Banality of Evil.* Rev. ed. New York: Penguin Books, 1965.

Ashley, Mike. "Revenants." In *The Encyclopedia of Fantasy*, edited by John Clute and John Grant, 810. New York: St. Martin's Griffin, 1997.

Atwood, Margaret. *Strange Things: The Malevolent North in Canadian Literature.* Oxford: Clarendon Press, 1995.

Auerbach, Erich. *Mimesis: The Representation of Reality in Western Literature.* Translated by Willard R. Trask. Princeton: Princeton University Press, 1968.

Auerbach, Nina. *Our Vampires, Our Selves.* Chicago: University of Chicago Press, 1995.

Augustine. *The Confessions of St. Augustine.* Translated by Rex Warner. New York: Penguin Putnam, 1963.

Babbington, Bruce, and Peter William Evans. *Biblical Epics: Sacred Narrative in Hollywood Cinema.* Manchester and New York: Manchester University Press, 1993.

Bach, Alice, ed. *Biblical Glamour and Hollywood Glitz.* Semeia 74. Atlanta: Scholars Press, 1996.

Bakhtin, Mikhail. *Problems of Dostoevsky's Poetics.* Translated by Carol Emerson. Minneapolis: University of Minnesota Press, 1984.

Banks, Robert. "The Drama of Salvation in George Stevens's *Shane.*" In *Explorations in Theology and Film*, edited by Clive Marsh and Gaye Ortiz, 59–71. Oxford: Blackwell, 1997.

Barber, Paul. "Forensic Pathology and the European Vampire." In *The Vampire: A Casebook*, edited by Alan Dundes, 109–42. Madison: University of Wisconsin Press, 1998.

Barthes, Roland. *Camera Lucida.* Translated by Richard Howard. New York: Hill and Wang, 1981.

——. *Mythologies.* Translated by Annette Lavers. New York: Hill & Wang, 1972.

Bataille, Georges. *Literature and Evil.* Translated by Alastair Hamilton. London/ New York: Marion Boyars, 1985.

Baudrillard, Jean. *Simulacra and Simulation.* Translated by Sheila Faria Glaser. Ann Arbor: University of Michigan Press, 1994.

——. *The Transparency of Evil: Essays on Extreme Phenomena.* Translated by James Benedict. London/New York: Verso, 1993.

Baudry, Jean-Louis. "Ideological Effects of the Basic Cinematographic Apparatus." In *Narrative, Apparatus, Ideology: A Film Theory Reader*, edited by Philip Rosen, 286–98. New York: Columbia University Press, 1986.

Bauer, Erik. "Southern Rebel: Interview with Billy Bob Thornton." *Creative Screenwriting* 4 (1997): 5–14.

Baugh, Lloyd. *Imaging the Divine: Jesus and Christ-Figures in Film.* Kansas City, Mo.: Sheed & Ward, 1997.

Bellah, Robert N., Richard Marsden, William M. Sullivan, Ann Swindler, and Stephen M. Tipton, *Habits of the Heart: Individualism and Commitment in American Life.* Berkeley: University of California Press, 1985.

Bellis, Alice Ogden. "Portrayal of Women in the Biblical Story of Moses and *The Prince of Egypt*. Paper presented at the Society of Biblical Literature Annual Meeting, Boston, Mass., 22 November 1999.

Benjamin, Walter. *Illuminations*. Translated by Harry Zohn. New York: Schocken Books, 1968.

Berardinelli, James. "*Patch Adams*: A Film Review." 1998. [cited 20 May 2001]. Available from http://movie-reviews.colossus.net/movies/p/patch.html.

Bloom, Harold. *American Religion: The Emergence of the Post-Christian Nation*. New York: Simon & Schuster, 1992.

Bodeen, DeWitt. "Midnight Cowboy." In *Magill's Survey of Cinema: English Language Films*, edited by Frank Magill, 3:1095–97. 1st series. Englewood Cliffs, N.J.: Salem Press, 1980.

Boer, Roland. "David Is a Thing." In *The Labour of Reading: Desire, Alienation, and Biblical Interpretation*, edited by Fiona C. Black, Roland Boer, and Erin Runions, 163–76. Atlanta: Society of Biblical Literature, 1999.

Bonhoeffer, Dietrich. *Letters and Papers from Prison*. Edited by Eberhard Bethge. Enlarged edition. New York: Touchstone, 1997.

Borg, Marcus. *Jesus: A New Vision*. San Francisco: Harper & Row, 1985.

——. *Meeting Jesus Again for the First Time: The Historical Jesus and the Heart of Contemporary Faith*. New York: HarperSanFrancisco, 1994.

Borges, Jorge Luis. *Dreamtigers*. Translated by Mildred Boyer and Harold Morland. Austin: University of Texas Press, 1964.

——. *Ficciones*. Edited by Anthony Kerrigan. New York: Grove Press, 1962.

——. *Selected Non-Fictions*. Edited by Eliot Weinberger. Translated by Esther Allen, Suzanne Jill Levine, and Eliot Weinberger. New York: Penguin Books, 1999.

Bourdieu, Pierre. *Distinction: A Social Critique of the Judgement of Taste.* Translated by Richard Nice. Cambridge: Harvard University Press, 1984 [1979].

——. *Homo Academicus*. Translated by Peter Collier. Stanford: Stanford University Press, 1994.

——. *In Other Words: Essays Towards a Reflexive Sociology*. Translated by Matthew Adamson. Stanford: Stanford University Press, 1990 [1982, 1987].

——. *The State Nobility: Elite Schools in the Field of Power*. Translated by Lauretta C. Clough. Stanford: Stanford University Press, 1998.

Bourdieu, Pierre, Jean-Claude Passeron, and Monique De Saint Martin, *Academic Discourse: Linguistic Misunderstanding and Professorial Power*. Translated by Richard Teese. Stanford: Stanford University Press, 1996.

Bourdieu, Pierre, and Jean-Claude Passeron. *Reproduction in Education, Society and Culture*. Translated by Richard Nice. 2nd ed. London: Sage Publications, 1990.

Broderick, Mick. *Nuclear Movies: A Critical Analysis and Filmography of International Feature Films Dealing with Experimentation, Aliens, Terrorism, Holocaust and Other Disaster Scenarios, 1914–1989*. Jefferson, N.C.: McFarland & Co., 1991.

Brooks, Xan. Review of *Boys Don't Cry*. *Sight and Sound* 10 (April 2000): 43–44.

Browne, David. "Film, Movies, Meanings." In *Explorations in Theology and Film*, edited by Clive Marsh and Gaye Ortiz, 21–34. Malden, Mass.: Blackwell, 1997.

Burrows, Elaine, Janet Moat, David Sharp, and Linda Wood. *The British Cinema Source Book*. London: British Film Institute, 1995.

Bush, Frederic. *Ruth, Esther*. Vol. 9. of *Word Biblical Commentary*. Dallas: Word Books, 1996.

Butler, Judith. *Bodies That Matter: On the Discursive Limits of "Sex."* London and New York: Routledge, 1993.

——. *Excitable Speech: A Politics of the Performative*. New York and London: Routledge, 1997.

——. *Gender Trouble: Feminism and the Subversion of Identity*. London and New York: Routledge, 1990.

——. *The Psychic Life of Power: Theories in Subjection*. Stanford: Stanford University Press, 1997.

Butler, Karen. "In *End of Days*, Satan Thwarted by Faith, Not Guns." [cited 13 November 2000]. Available from http://www.apbnews.com/media/celebnews/1999/11/24/end1124_01.html?s=daily.

Byars, Jackie. "Feminism, Psychoanalysis, and Female-Oriented Melodramas of the 1950s." In *Multiple Voices in Feminist Film Criticism*, edited by D. Carson, L. Dittmar, and J. R. Welsch, 93–108. Minneapolis: University of Minnesota Press, 1994.

Calvino, Italo. *The Uses of Literature*. Translated by Patrick Creagh. New York: Harcourt Brace Jovanovich, 1986.

Campbell, Joseph. *The Hero with a Thousand Faces*. Princeton: Princeton University Press, 1972.

Camus, Albert. *The Myth of Sisyphus and Other Essays*. Translated by Justin O'Brien. New York: Vintage International, 1991.

Caruth, Cathy, ed. *Trauma: Explorations in Memory*. Baltimore: Johns Hopkins University Press, 1995.

——. *Unclaimed Experience: Trauma, Narrative, and History*. Baltimore: Johns Hopkins University Press, 1996.

Caughie, John, and Kevin Rockett. *The Companion to British and Irish Cinema*. London: British Film Institute and Cassell, 1996.

Chatman, Seymour. *Story and Discourse: Narrative Structure in Fiction and Film*. Ithaca, N.Y.: Cornell University Press, 1978.

Clemens, Valdine. *The Return of the Repressed: Gothic Horror from The Castle of Otranto to Alien*. Albany, N.Y.: State University of New York Press, 1999.

Cohen, Stanley, and Laurie Taylor. *Escape Attempts: The Theory and Practice of Resistance to Everyday Life*. 2nd ed. London: Routledge, 1992.

Coover, Robert. *Pricksongs and Descants*. New York: Penguin Books, 1969.

Copjec, Joan. "The Orthopsychic Subject: Film Theory and the Reception of Lacan." *October* 49 (1989): 53–71.

Cotterell, Arthur. *A Dictionary of World Mythology*. New York: G. P. Putnam's Sons, 1979.

Craft, Christopher. "'Kiss Me with Those Red Lips': Gender and Inversion in Bram Stoker's *Dracula*." In *Dracula*, edited by Nina Auerbach and David J. Skal, 444–59. A Norton Critical Edition. New York: W. W. Norton & Company, 1997.

Crossan, John Dominic. "Felix Culpa and Foenix Culprit." *Semeia* 18 (1980): 107–11.

——. *The Historical Jesus: The Life of a Mediterranean Peasant*. San Francisco: HarperSanFrancisco, 1991.

Crossan, John F. "The Stake that Spoke: Vlad Dracula and a Medieval 'Gospel' of Violence." In *Dracula: The Shade and the Shadow*, edited by Elizabeth Miller, 180–90. Essex, U.K: Desert Island Books, 1998.

Crowley, John. "The Nightingale Sings at Night." In *Novelty, Four Stories*, 1–34. New York: Doubleday, 1989.

Cutts, John, and Penelope Houston. "Blacklisted." *Sight and Sound* 27 (1957): 15–19 and 53.

Darnton, Robert. *The Great Cat Massacre and Other Episodes in French Cultural History*. New York: Vintage, 1985.

Darr, Katheryn Pfisterer. "Ezekiel." In *The Women's Bible Commentary: Expanded Edition*, edited by Carol A. Newsom and Sharon H. Ringe, 183–90. Louisville: Westminster/John Knox, 1998.

Davenport-Hines, Richard. *Gothic: Four Hundred Years of Excess Horror, Evil and Ruin*. New York: North Point Press, 1998.

Davies, Philip R. "Life of Brian Research." In *Biblical Studies/Cultural Studies: The Third Sheffield Colloquium*, edited by J. Cheryl Exum and Stephen Moore, 400–14. Sheffield: Sheffield Academic Press, 1998.

Day, Linda. "Rhetoric and Domestic Violence in Ezekiel 16." *Biblical Interpretation* 8 (2000): 205–30.

Day, Peggy L. "The Bitch Had it Coming to Her: Rhetoric and Interpretation in Ezekiel 16." *Biblical Interpretation* 8 (2000): 231–55.

De Lauretis, Teresa. *Alice Doesn't: Feminism, Semiotics, Cinema*. Bloomington: Indiana University Press, 1984.

Dempsey, Carol J. "The 'Whore' of Ezekiel 16: The Impact and Ramifications of Gender-Specific Metaphors in Light of Biblical Law and Divine Judgment." In *Gender and Law in the Hebrew Bible and the Ancient Near East*, edited by Victor H. Matthews, Bernard M. Levinson, and Tikva Frymer-Kensky, 58–78. *Journal for the Study of the Old Testament Supplement* 262. Sheffield: Sheffield Academic Press, 1998.

Dennison, Michael J. *Vampirism: Literary Tropes of Decadence and Entropy*. New York: Peter Lang Publishing Group, 2001.

DeZubiria, Michael. Review of *Lethal Weapon 1*. [cited 12 November 2000]. Available from Internet Movie Database at http://www.imdb.com.

Dick, Philip K. "The Adjustment Team." In *The Turning Wheel and Other Stories*, 72–96. London: Coronet, 1977.

——. *Clans of the Alphane Moon*. London: Ace, 1975 [1964].

——. *The Cosmic Puppets*. London: Voyager, 1988 [1957].

——. *The Crack in Space*. London: Ace, 1966.

——. *The Divine Invasion*. New York: Timescape, 1991 [1981].

——. *Eye in the Sky*. London: Arrow, 1957.

——. *Flow My Tears*, the Policeman Said. New York: Vintage, 1993.

——. *The Man in the High Castle*. Harmondsworth, England: Penguin, 1965.

——. *The Martian Time Slip*. London: Gollancz, 1964.

——. *A Maze of Death*. London: Pan, 1970.

——. *A Scanner Darkly*. London: Gollancz, 1977.

——. "Schizophrenia and The Book of Changes." In *The Shifting Realities of Philip K. Dick*, edited by Lawrence Sutin, 175–82. New York: Vintage, 1995.

——. "Selection from *Exegesis* (c. 1975–80)." In *Philip K. Dick: Contemporary Critical Interpretations*, edited by Samuel J. Umland, 319–50. Westport, Conn.: Greenwood, 1995.

——. *The Three Stigmata of Palmer Eldritch*. Garden City, N.Y.: Doubleday, 1991 [1965].

——. *The Transmigration of Timothy Archer*. New York: Timescape, 1982.

——. *Ubik*. New York: Vintage, 1991.

——. *VALIS*. London: Corgi, 1981.

——. "We Can Remember It for You Wholesale." In *The SF Collection*, compiled by Edel Brosnan, 321–41. London: Chancellor, 1994.

Dickens, Charles. *David Copperfield*. New York: P. F. Collier & Son, 1911.

Dickinson, Thorold. "The Filmwright and the Audience." *Sight and Sound* 19 (1950): 20–25.

Dijkstra, Bram. *Evil Sisters: The Threat of Female Sexuality in Twentieth-Century Culture*. New York: Henry Holt & Company, 1996.

Doane, Mary Ann. *The Desire to Desire: The Woman's Film of the 1940s*. Bloomington: Indiana University Press, 1987.

——. *Femmes Fatales: Feminism, Film Theory, Psychoanalysis*. New York: Routledge, 1991.

Dobson, Alan P. "Anglo-American Relations and the Cold War." In *Deconstructing and Reconstructing the Cold War*, edited by Alan P. Dobson, 69–88. Aldershot, Hants, England: Ashgate, 1999.

Dodd, C. H. *The Parables of the Kingdom*. Rev. ed. New York: Charles Scribner's Sons, 1961.

Douglas, Mary. "Deciphering a Meal." In *Implicit Meanings: Essays in Anthropology*, edited by Mary Douglas, 249–75. London: Routledge & Kegan Paul, 1975.

Drosnin, Michael. *The Bible Code*. New York: Simon & Schuster, 1997.

Dundes, Alan. "The Vampire." In *The Vampire: A Casebook*, edited by Alan Dundes. Madison: University of Wisconsin Press, 1998.

Dunne, John Gregory. "A Report at Large: The Humboldt Murders." *The New Yorker*, 13 January 1997, 44–52.

Durkheim, Emile. *The Elementary Forms of Religious Life*. Translated by Karen E. Fields. New York: Free Press, 1995 [1912].

Ebeling, Gerhard. "The 'Non-Religious Interpretation of Biblical Concepts.'" In *Word and Faith*, 98–162. Philadelphia: Fortress, 1963.

Ebert, Roger. "*Nosferatu*." [cited 31 July 2001]. Available from http://www.suntimes.com/ebert/greatmovies/nosferatu.html.

——. "*Dracula*." [cited 31 July 2001]. Available from http://www.suntimes.com/ebert/greatmovies/dracul.html.

Eco, Umberto. *The Role of the Reader*. Bloomington: Indiana University Press, 1979.

Ehrenreich, Barbara. *Nickel and Dimed: On (Not) Getting by in America*. New York: Metropolitan Books, 2001.

Eliade, Mircea. *The Sacred and the Profane: The Nature of Religion*. Translated by Willard R. Trask. New York: Harcourt Brace & World, 1959.

Eliot, T. S. "Hamlet and His Problems." In *The Sacred Wood: Essays on Poetry and Criticism*, 95–103. London: Methuen, 1920.

Evans, Joyce A. *Celluloid Mushroom Clouds: Hollywood and the Atomic Bomb*. Boulder, Colo.: Westview Press, 1998.

Exum, J. Cheryl. *Plotted, Shot and Painted: Cultural Representations of Biblical Women*. Journal for the Study of the Old Testament Supplement 215. Gender, Culture, Theory 3. Sheffield: Sheffield Academic Press, 1996.

Fisher, David. "Two Premieres: Disney & U.P.A." *Sight and Sound* 23 (1953): 40–41.

Foucault, Michel. *Power/Knowledge: Selected Interviews and Other Writings 1972–1977*. Edited by Colin Gordon. Translated by Colin Gordon, Leo Marshall, John Mepham, and Kate Soper. New York: Pantheon, 1980.

Fox, Everett. "*The Prince of Egypt* from a Consultant's Point of View." Paper presented at the Society of Biblical Literature Annual Meeting, Boston, Mass., 22 November 1999.

Freedman, Carl. "Towards a Theory of Paranoia: The Science Fiction of Philip K. Dick." *Philip K. Dick: Contemporary Critical Interpretations*, edited by Samuel J. Umland, 7–17. Westport, Conn.: Greenwood, 1995.

Freeland, Cynthia A. *The Naked and the Undead: Evil and the Appeal of Horror*. Boulder, Colo.: Westview Press, 2000.

Freud, Sigmund. *Beyond the Pleasure Principle: The Standard Edition with a Biographical Introduction by Peter Gay*. Translated by James Strachey. New York: W. W. Norton, 1989 [1920].

———. *The Ego and the Id*. Vol. 19 of *The Standard Edition of the Complete Psychological Works of Sigmund Freud*. Translated by James Strachey. London: Hogarth, 1961 [1923].

———. *Inhibitions, Symptoms and Anxiety: The Standard Edition with a Biographical Introduction by Peter Gay*. Translated by James Strachey. New York: W. W. Norton, 1989 [1926].

———. "The Loss of Reality in Neurosis and Psychosis." In *On Psychopathology*, edited by Angela Richards and translated under the editorship of James Strachey, 10:219–26. The Pelican Freud Library. Harmondsworth, England: Penguin, 1979 [1924].

———. "Mourning and Melancholia." In *The Standard Edition of the Complete Psychological Works of Sigmund Freud*, vol. 14:239–58. Translated by James Strachey. London: Hogarth, 1957 [1917].

———. "Neurosis and Psychosis." In *On Psychopathology*, edited by Angela Richards and translated under the editorship of James Strachey, 10:209–18. The Pelican Freud Library. Harmondsworth, England: Penguin, 1979 [1924].

———. "Psychoanalytic Notes on an Autobiographical Account of a Case of Paranoia (Dementia Paranoides) (Schreber)." In *Case Histories II*, edited by Angela Richards and translated under the editorship of James Strachey, 9:131–223. The Pelican Freud Library. Harmondsworth, England: Penguin, 1979 [1911].

Frye, Northrop. *Anatomy of Criticism: Four Essays*. Princeton: Princeton University Press, 1957.

——. *The Great Code*. New York: Harcourt Brace Jovanovich, 1982.

Funk, Robert W. *Jesus as Precursor*. Philadelphia: Fortress Press, 1975.

Gaiman, Neil, and Terry Pratchett. *Good Omens*. New York: Ace Books, 1990.

Galambush, Julie. *Jerusalem in the Book of Ezekiel, the City as Yahweh's Wife*. Society of Biblical Literature Dissertation Series 130. Atlanta: Scholars Press, 1992.

Galbraith, Robert. "Salvation-Knowledge: Ironic Gnosticism in *Valis* and *The Flight to Lucifer*." In *Science Fiction Dialogues*, edited by Gary Wolfe, 115–32. Chicago: Academy Chicago Publishers, 1982.

Geertz, Clifford. *The Interpretation of Cultures*. New York: Basic Books. 1973.

Germano, Derek. Review of *Sling Blade*. [cited 24 April 2001]. Available from http://www.thecinemalaser.com/dvd_reviews/sling-blade-dvd.html.

Gesenius, Wilhelm. *Gesenius Hebrew Grammar*. Edited and enlarged by E. Kautzsch. Oxford: Clarendon, 1910.

The Gesundheit Institute. [cited 20 May 2001]. Available from http://www.patch adams.org/.

Giltz, Michael. "Hilary's Journey." *The Advocate* [cited 28 March 2000]. Available from http://www.advocate.com/html/ stories/808/808_cvr_hilary.asp.

Glover, David. *Vampires, Mummies, and Liberals: Bram Stoker and the Politics of Popular Fiction*. Durham, N.C.: Duke University Press, 1996.

Gouldner, Alvin W. *The Future of Intellectuals and the Rise of the New Class*. New York: Continuum, 1979.

Gramsci, Antonio. *Quaderni del carcere*. Edited by Valentino Gerratana. 4 vols. Torino: Einaudi, 1975.

——. *Selections from Cultural Writings*. Edited by David Forgacs and Geoffrey Nowell-Smith. Translated by William Boelhower. Cambridge: Harvard University Press, 1985.

——. *Selections from the Prison Notebooks*. Edited and translated by Quintin Hoare and Geoffrey Nowell Smith. New York: International Publishers, 1971.

Green, Barbara. *Mikhail Bakhtin and Biblical Scholarship: An Introduction*. Atlanta: Society of Biblical Literature, 2000.

Greenblatt, Stephen. *Renaissance Self-Fashioning*. Chicago: University of Chicago Press, 1980.

Greenwood, Sean. *Britain and the Cold War, 1945–1991*. Houndmills, Basingstoke: Macmillan Press, 2000.

Gunn, David. "Bathsheba Goes Bathing in Hollywood: Words, Images, and Social Locations." *Semeia* 74 (1996): 75–101.

Hall, Stuart, David Morley, and Kuan-Hsing Chen. *Stuart Hall: Critical Dialogues in Cultural Studies*. Edited by David Morley and Kuan-Hsing Chen. New York: Routledge, 1996.

Halliwell, Leslie. *The Filmgoers Companion*. 6th edition. New York: Hill & Wang, 1977.

Halperin, David J. *Seeking Ezekiel: Text and Psychology*. University Park: Pennsylvania State University Press, 1993.

Hamilton, William. "Dietrich Bonhoeffer." In Thomas J. J. Altizer and William Hamilton, *Radical Theology and the Death of God*, 113–20. New York: The Bobbs-Merrill Company, 1966.

Hanson, P. D. "Apocalypticism." In *The Interpreter's Dictionary of the Bible: Supplementary Volume*, edited by Keith Crim, Lloyd Richard Bailey, Sr., Victor Paul Furnish, and Emory Stevens Bucke, 28–34. Nashville: Abingdon, 1976.

Hendrickson, Nancy. "We Like the Way He Talks: The Dialogue of Billy Bob Thornton." *Creative Screenwriting* 5 (1998): 40–43.

Herlihy, James Leo. *Midnight Cowboy*. New York: Simon & Schuster, 1965.

Hewison, Robert. *Irreverence, Scurrility, Profanity, Vilification and Licentious Abuse: Monty Python, the Case Against*. New York: Grove, 1981.

Hill, Geoffrey. *Illuminating Shadows: The Mythic Power of Film*. Boston: Shambhala, 1992.

Hofstadter, Richard. *Anti-Intellectualism in American Life*. New York: Vintage, 1972.

Hollinger, Veronica. "Fantasies of Absences: The Postmodern Vampire." In *Blood Read*, edited by Joan Gordon and Veronica Hollinger, 199–212. Philadelphia: University of Pennsylvania Press, 1997.

——. "Introduction: The Shape of Vampires." In *Blood Read*, edited by Joan Gordon and Veronica Hollinger, 1–7. Philadelphia: University of Pennsylvania Press, 1997.

Houston, Penelope. "Glimpses of the Moon." *Sight and Sound* 23 (1953): 185–88.

Howard-Brook, Wes, and Anthony Gwyther. *Unveiling Empire: Reading Revelation Then and Now*. Maryknoll, N.Y.: Orbis Books, 1999.

Huxley, Aldous. *Ape and Essence*. London: Chatto & Windus, 1967.

Internet Movie Database. [cited 12 November 2000]. Available from http://www.imdb.com.

Jacoby, Russell. *The Last Intellectuals: American Culture in the Age of Academe*. New York: Basic Books, 2000.

Jakobson, Roman. *Language and Literature*. Edited by Krystyna Pomorska and Stephen Rudy. Cambridge, Mass.: Belknap Press of Harvard University, 1987.

Jameson, Fredric. "Imaginary and Symbolic in Lacan: Marxism, Psychoanalytic Criticism and the Problem of the Subject." In *The Ideologies of Theory*, 1:75–115. Minneapolis: University of Minnesota Press, 1988.

Jenkins, Carol. "*Sling Blade*." [cited 26 April 2001]. Available from http://www.net-pad.com/movie/slingb.html.

Jewett, Robert. *The Captain America Complex*. 2nd ed. Santa Fe, N. Mex.: Bear & Co, 1984.

Jewett, Robert, and John Shelton Lawrence. *The American Monomyth*. Garden City, N.Y.: Anchor Press, 1977.

Johnson, Basil. *The Manitous: The Spiritual World of the Ojibway*. New York: HarperCollinsPublishers, 1995.

Johnston, Robert. *Reel Spirituality: Theology and Film in Dialogue*. Grand Rapids: Baker Academic, 2000.

Kafka, Franz. *Parables and Paradoxes*. Translated by Willa and Edwin Muir, Clement Greenberg, Ernst Kaiser, Eithne Wilkens, and Tania and James Stern. New York: Schocken Books, 1958.

Kalmin, Richard. "Levirate Law." In *Anchor Bible Dictionary*, edited by David Noel Freedman, 4:296–97. New York: Doubleday, 1992.

Kasprzak, Nicole. "*Sling Blade* Shines Above Post-Oscar Mediocrity." [cited 26 April 2001]. Available from http://misc.vassar.edu/spring_97/mar28/arts/slingblade.html.

Keller, Catherine. *Apocalypse Now and Then: A Feminist Guide to the End of the World*. Boston: Beacon Press, 1996.

Kenny, Glen. "Extreme Cinema: The 25 Most Dangerous Movies Ever Made." *Premiere* 14 (February 2001): 92–97.

Kiely, Harry. "The False Promises of Violence: The Movie *Sling Blade* Fosters a Demonic Illusion that the Way of Destruction is the Way to Life." *Sojourners* 26 (November-December 1997): 34–37.

Klawans, Stuart. "Rough and Tumble: *Fight Club, Boys Don't Cry, The City*." *The Nation*, 8 November 1999, 32–36.

Köhler, Ludwig. *Old Testament Theology*. Translated by A. S. Todd. Philadelphia: The Westminster Press, 1957.

Köhler, Ludwig, and Walter Baumgartner. *The Hebrew and Aramaic Lexicon of the Old Testament*. Revised by Walter Baumgartner and Johann Jakob Stamm. Translated by M. E. J. Richardson. 5 vols. Leiden: E. J. Brill, 1994–2000.

Kreitzer, Larry. *Gospel Images in Fiction and Film: On Reversing the Hermeneutical Flow*. Sheffield: Sheffield Academic Press, 2002.

Kuhn, Annette. *Women's Pictures: Feminism and Cinema*. London: Verso, 1993.

Lacan, Jacques. *Écrits: A Selection*. Translated by Alan Sheridan. New York: W. W. Norton & Company, 1977.

——. *The Ethics of Psychoanalysis*. Edited by Jacques-Alain Miller. Translated with notes by Dennis Porter. London: Routledge, 1992.

——. *The Four Fundamental Concepts of Psychoanalysis*. Edited by Jacques-Alain Miller. Translated by Alan Sheridan. With an introduction by David Macey. London: Vintage, 1998.

——. *The Psychoses. The Seminar of Jacques Lacan: Book III, 1955–1956*. Translated by Russell Grigg. London: Routledge, 1993.

——. *The Seminar of Jacques Lacan: Book I: Freud's Papers on Technique*. Edited by Jacques-Alain Miller. Translated with notes by John Forrester. Cambridge: Cambridge University Press, 1988.

LaHaye, Tim, and Jerry B. Jenkins. *Left Behind: A Novel of the Earth's Last Days*. Wheaton, Ill.: Tyndale House, 1995.

Lamont, Michèle. *Money, Morals, and Manners: The Culture of the French and the American Upper-Middle Class*. Chicago: University of Chicago Press, 1992.

Landy, Marcia. *British Genres: Cinema and Society, 1930–1960*. Princeton: Princeton University Press, 1991.

——. *Film, Politics, and Gramsci*. Minneapolis: University of Minnesota Press, 1994.

Laplanche, J., and J.-B. Pontalis. *The Language of Psycho-analysis*. Translated by Donald Nicholson-Smith and with an introduction by Daniel Lagache. New York and London: W.W. Norton & Company, 1973 [1967].

Laurence, William L. *Dawn Over Zero: The Story of the Atomic Bomb*. New York: Alfred A. Knopf, 1956.

Leigh, Danny. "Boy Wonder." *Sight and Sound* 10 (March 2000): 18–20.

"Lethal Weapon." [cited 19 July 2001]. Available from http://us.imdb.com/ Title?0093409.

Lévi-Strauss, Claude. *The Naked Man*. Translated by John and Doreen Weightman. Vol. 4 of *Introduction to a Science of Mythology*. New York: Harper & Row, 1981.

Lincoln, Bruce. *Theorizing Myth: Narrative, Ideology, and Scholarship*. Chicago: University of Chicago Press, 1999.

Lindsey, Hal. *The Late Great Planet Earth*. Grand Rapids: Zondervan, 1970.

Lu, Adrienne. "In the Schools: Principal of the Year Uses Faith, Many Hands, Giving Credit, Taking Responsibility." *Raleigh News & Observer*, 14 May 2001, B1.

Mabee, Charles. *Reimaging America: A Theological Critique of the American Mythos and Biblical Hermeneutics*. Macon, Ga.: Mercer University Press, 1985.

Macalpine, Ida, and Richard A. Hunter. "Translators' Analysis of the Case." In Daniel Paul Schreber, *Memoirs of My Nervous Illness*, translated by Ida Macalpine and Richard Hunter with an introduction by Samuel M. Weber, 369–411. Cambridge, Mass.: Harvard University Press, 1988.

Mack, Burton L. *A Myth of Innocence: Mark and Christian Origins*. Philadelphia: Fortress Press, 1988.

——. *The Lost Gospel: The Book of Q and Christian Origins*. San Francisco: HarperSanFrancisco, 1993.

——. *Who Wrote the New Testament? The Making of the Christian Myth*. San Francisco: Polebridge Press, 1995.

Malone, Peter. "Edward Scissorhands: Christology from a Suburban Fairy-tale." In *Explorations in Theology in Film*, edited by Clive Marsh and Gaye Ortiz, 73–86. Oxford: Blackwell, 1997.

——. "Jesus on Our Screens." In *New Image of Religious Film*, edited by John May, 57–71. Kansas City, Mo.: Sheed & Ward, 1997.

——. *Movie Christs and Antichrists*. New York: Crossroad, 1990.

Marks, Herbert. "Biblical Naming and Poetic Etymology." *Journal of Biblical Literature* 114 (Spring 1995): 21–42.

Marsden, Michael. "Savior in the Saddle: The Sagebrush Testament." In *Shane: The Critical Edition*, edited by James Work, 393–404. Omaha: University of Nebraska Press, 1984.

May, John R. "The Demonic in American Cinema." In *Religion in Film*, edited by John R. May and Michael Bird, 79–100. Knoxville: University of Tennessee Press, 1981.

Mayer, Robert. "Hollywood Report." *Sight and Sound* 17 (1948): 32–34.

Mayne, Judith. "Feminist Film Theory and Criticism." In *Multiple Voices in Feminist Film Criticism*, edited by D. Carson, L. Dittmar, and J. R. Welsch, 48–64. Minneapolis: University of Minnesota Press, 1994.

McCrillis, Neal R. "British Comedy Films during the Cold War: Signs of Discord in the Anglo-American Special Relationship (1945–1960)." Paper presented at the Southern Conference of British Studies and Southern Historical Association, Louisville, Ky., 11 November 2000.

McEver, Matthew. "The Messianic Figure in Film: Christology Beyond the Biblical Epic." *The Journal of Religion and Film* 2 (1998). [cited 24 April 2001]. Available from http://www.unomaha.edu/~wwwjrf/McEverMessiah.htm.

McGinn, Bernard. *Anti-Christ: Two Thousand Years of the Human Fascination with Evil*. San Francisco: HarperSanFrancisco, 1994.

McVann, Mark. "Rituals of Status Transformation in Luke-Acts: The Case of Jesus the Prophet." In *The Social World of Luke-Acts: Models for Interpretation*, edited by Jerome H. Neyrey, 333–60. Peabody, Mass.: Hendrickson, 1991.

Mead, George Herbert. *Selected Writings*. Edited by Andrew J. Reck. Chicago: University of Chicago Press, 1964.

Medved, Michael. *Hollywood vs. America*. New York: HarperPerennial, 1991.

Metzger, Bruce M., and Roland E. Murphy, eds. *The New Oxford Annotated Bible: New Revised Standard Version*. New York: Oxford University Press, 1994.

Miller, Dean A. *The Epic Hero*. Baltimore: The Johns Hopkins University Press, 2000.

Miller, Elizabeth, ed. *Dracula's Homepage*. [cited 31 July 2001]. Available from http://www.ucs.mun.ca/~emiller/.

——, ed. *Dracula: The Shade and the Shadow*. Essex, U.K.: Desert Island Books, 1998.

Milton, John. *Paradise Lost and Paradise Regained*. New York: Signet Classic, 1982.

Mintz, Steven, and Randy Roberts, eds. *Hollywood's America: United States History Through Its Films*. St. James, N.Y.: Brandywine Press, 1993.

The Mister Showbiz Interview: Billy Bob Thornton. [cited 24 April 2001]. Available from http://mrshowbiz.com/interviews/349.

Modleski, Tania. *The Women Who Knew Too Much: Hitchcock and Feminist Theory*. New York: Methuen, 1988.

Moretti, Franco. "A Capital *Dracula*." In *Dracula*, edited by Nina Auerbach and David J. Skal, 431–44. A Norton Critical Edition. New York: W. W. Norton & Company, 1997.

Morgan, David. *Monty Python Speaks!* New York: Spike/Avon, 1999.

Moss, Donald and Lynne Zeavin. "Film Review Essay: The Real Thing? Some Thoughts on *Boys Don't Cry*." *International Journal of Psychoanalysis* 81 (2000): 1227–30.

Muhammad, Erika. "Independent Means." *Ms. Magazine*, February/March 2000, 75–77.

Mulvey, Laura. "Afterthoughts on 'Visual Pleasure and Narrative Cinema' inspired by *Duel in the Sun*." In *Feminism and Film Theory*, edited by Constance Penley, 69–79. New York: Routledge, 1988.

——. "Visual Pleasure and Narrative Cinema." In *Narrative, Apparatus, Ideology: A Film Theory Reader*, edited by Philip Rosen, 198–209. New York: Columbia University Press, 1986.

Nelson, John. *Your God Is Alive and Well and Appearing in Popular Culture*. Philadelphia: Westminster, 1976.

Neruda, Pablo. *100 Love Sonnets*. Translated by Stephen Tapscott. Texas Pan American Series. Austin: University of Texas Press, 1986.

Newman, Kim. *Anno Dracula*. New York: Carroll & Graf, 1983.

Newsom, Carol. "Bakhtin, the Bible, and Dialogic Truth," *The Journal of Religion* 76 (1996): 290–306.

Neyrey, Jerome H. "The Symbolic Universe of Luke-Acts: They Turn the World Upside Down." In *The Social World of Luke-Acts: Models for Interpretation*, edited by Jerome H. Neyrey, 271–304. Peabody, Mass.: Hendrickson, 1991.

Nietzsche, Friedrich. *The Anti-Christ*. Translated by H. L. Mencken. Tucson, Ariz.: See Sharp Press, 1999.

——. *Beyond Good and Evil: Prelude to a Philosophy of the Future*. Translated by Walter Kaufmann. New York: Vantage Books, 1966.

——. *Thus Spake Zarathustra: A Book for Everyone and No One*. Translated by R. J. Hollingdale. New York: Penguin Books, 1969.

Ostwalt, Conrad E., Jr. "Hollywood and Armageddon: Apocalyptic Themes in Recent Cinematic Presentation." In *Screening the Sacred: Religion, Myth, and Ideology in Popular American Film*, edited by Joel W. Martin and Conrad E. Ostwalt Jr., 55–63. Boulder, Colo.: Westview Press, 1995.

Otto, Rudolph. *The Idea of the Holy*. Translated by John W. Harvey. New York: Oxford University Press, 1958.

Peirce, Charles Sanders. *The Essential Peirce: Selected Philosophical Writings*, vol. 1 (1867–1893). Edited by Nathan Houser and Christian Kloesel. Bloomington: Indiana University Press, 1992.

Pharr, Mary. "Vampiric Appetite in *I Am Legend, Salem's Lot*, and *The Hunger*." In *The Blood Is the Life: Vampires in Literature*, edited by Leonard G. Heldreth and Mary Pharr, 93–103. Bowling Green, Ohio: Bowling Green State University Popular Press, 1999.

Pierce, Kimberly. "Brandon Goes to Hollywood." *The Advocate*. [cited 28 March 2000]. Available from http://www.advocate.com/html/stories/808/808_cvrpeirce.asp.

——. "Putting Teena Brandon's Story on Film: An Interview by Francesca Miller." *Gay and Lesbian Review Worldwide* 7 (fall 2000): 39-40.

Pippin, Tina. *Apocalyptic Bodies: The Biblical End of the World in Text and Image*. London and New York: Routledge, 1999.

Plato. *The Republic*. Translated with an introduction by Desmond Lee. 2nd rev. ed. London: Penguin Books, 1987.

"*The Prince of Egypt*: Production Notes." [cited 25 September 2000]. Available from http://moview.yahoo.com/shop?d=hv&id=1800019629&cfr=prod.

Prosser, Jay. *Second Skins: The Body Narratives of Transsexuality*. New York: Columbia University Press, 1998.

Python, Monty. *The Life of Brian*. New York: Grosset & Dunlap, 1979.

Rabkin, Eric, Martin H. Greenberg, and Joseph G. Olander, eds. *The End of the World*. Carbondale: Southern Illinois University Press, 1983.

Raible, Christopher Gist. "Dracula: Christian Heretic." In *Dracula: The Vampire and the Critics*, edited by Margaret L. Carter, 105–107. Ann Arbor, Mich.: UMI Research Press, 1988.

Reinhartz, Adele. "Scripture on the Silver Screen." *The Journal of Religion and Film* 3 (1999). [cited 24 April 2001]. Available from http://www.unomaha.edu/~wwwjrf/scripture.htm.

Reisz, Karel. "Hollywood's Anti-Red Boomerang." *Sight and Sound* 22 (1953): 132–37 and 148.

Robertson, James. *The Hidden Camera: British Film Censorship in Action, 1913–1972*. London: Routledge, 1989.

Robertson, James Oliver. *American Myth, American Reality*. New York: Hill & Wang, 1980.

Robinson, Kim Stanley. *The Novels of Philip K. Dick*. Studies in Speculative Science Fiction 9. Ann Arbor, Mich.: UMI Research Press, 1984.

Rosario, Vernon A. "Transgenderism Comes of Age." *Gay and Lesbian Review Worldwide* 7 (Fall 2000): 31–33.

Rowley, H. H. "The Marriage of Ruth." In *The Servant of the Lord and Other Essays on the Old Testament*, 161–86. London: Lutterworth Press, 1952.

Runions, Erin. "Called to Do Justice? A Bhabhian Reading of Micah 5 and 6:1–8." In *Postmodern Interpretations: A Reader*, edited by A. K. M. Adam, 153–64. St Louis: Chalice, 2001.

——. *Changing Subjects: Gender, Nation and Future in Micah*. Playing the Texts. Sheffield: Sheffield Academic Press, 2002.

——. "Violence and the Economy of Desire in Ezekiel 16.1–45." In *Prophets and Daniel*, edited by Athalya Brenner. *Feminist Companion to the Bible*. 2nd series. Sheffield: Sheffield Academic Press, 2001.

Sahlins, Marshall. *Culture and Practical Reason*. Chicago: University of Chicago Press, 1976.

Saint-Pierre, Charles. Review of *Lethal Weapon 1*. [cited 7 August 2000]. Available from Internet Movie Database at http://www.imdb.com.

Saul, David. "Children of the American Myth: David Koresh, the Branch Davidians, and the American Bible." In *The Bible and the American Myth: A Symposium on the Bible and Constructions of Meaning*, edited by Vincent L. Wimbush, 123–44. Studies in American Biblical Hermeneutics 16. Macon, Ga.: Mercer University Press, 1997.

Sayre, Nora. *Running Time: Films of the Cold War*. New York: The Dial Press, 1982.

Scheer, Steven C. "Patch Adams." [cited 20 May 2001]. Available from http://www.stevencscheer.com/patchadams.htm.

Schneider, Steve. "Full Devil Jackass." [cited 13 November 13, 2000]. Available from http://www.orlandoweekly.com/movies/review.asp?movie=521.

Schreber, Daniel Paul. *Memoirs of My Nervous Illness*. Translated by Ida Macalpine and Richard Hunter. With an introduction by Samuel M. Weber. Cambridge, Mass.: Harvard University Press, 1988.

Schwartz, Stephen. *Through Heaven's Eyes: The Prince of Egypt in Story and Song*. New York: Penguin Putnam Books, 1998.

Scott, Bernard Brandon. "Changing Genre and the Problem of Meaning: Moses and *The Prince of Egypt*. Paper presented at the Society of Biblical Literature Annual Meeting, Boston, Mass., 22 November 1999.

——. *Hollywood Dreams and Biblical Stories*. Minneapolis: Fortress Press, 1994.

Scott, James C. *Domination and the Arts of Resistance: Hidden Transcripts*. New Haven: Yale University Press, 1990.

Sedgwick, Eve Kosofsky. "Queer Performativity: Henry James's *The Art of the Novel*." *GLQ: A Journal of Lesbian and Gay Studies* 1 (1993): 1–16.

Senf, Carol A. "Daughters of Lilith: Women Vampires in Popular Literature." In *The Blood Is the Life: Vampires in Literature*, edited by Leonard G. Heldreth and Mary Pharr, 199–216. Bowling Green, Ohio: Bowling Green State University Popular Press, 1999.

Shields, Mary E. "Identity and Power/Gender and Violence in Ezekiel 23." In *Postmodern Interpretations: A Reader*, edited by A.K.M. Adam, 129–52. St Louis: Chalice, 2001.

——. "Multiple Exposures: Body Rhetoric and Gender Characterization in Ezekiel 16." *Journal of Feminist Studies in Religion* 14 (1998): 5–18.

Silverman, Kaja. *Male Subjectivity at the Margins*. New York: Routledge, 1992.

Sloan, Royal Daniel. "The Politics of Civil Defense: Great Britain and the United States." Ph.D. dissertation, University of Chicago, 1958.

Slotkin, Richard. *Regeneration Through Violence: The Mythology of the American Frontier, 1600–1860*. Middletown, Conn.: Wesleyan University Press, 1973.

Smith, Jonathan Z. *Drudgery Divine: On the Comparison of Early Christianities and the Religions of Late Antiquity*. Chicago: University of Chicago Press, 1990.

——. *Imagining Religion: From Babylon to Jonestown*. Chicago: University of Chicago Press, 1982.

——. *Map Is Not Territory: Studies in the History of Religion*. Leiden: E. J. Brill, 1978.

Solomon, Charles. *The Prince of Egypt: A New Vision in Animation*. New York: Harry N. Abrams, 1998.

Sontag, Susan. "The Imagination of Disaster." In *Against Interpretation and Other Essays*, 209–25. New York: Farrar, Straus & Giroux, 1966.

Stableford, Brian. "Lamias." In *The Encyclopedia of Fantasy*, edited by John Clute and John Grant, 557. New York: St. Martin's Griffin, 1997.

——. "Lilith." In *The Encyclopedia of Fantasy*, edited by John Clute and John Grant, 581. New York: St. Martin's Griffin, 1997.

——. "Man-Made Catastrophes." In *The End of the World*, edited by Eric Rabkin, Martin H. Greenberg, and Joseph G. Olander, 97–138. Carbondale: Southern Illinois University Press, 1983.

Staley, Jeffrey L. *Reading with a Passion: Rhetoric, Autobiography, and the American West in the Gospel of John*. New York: Continuum, 1995.

Stern, Richard C., Clayton Jefford, and Guerric DeBona, O.S.B. *Savior on the Silver Screen*. Mahwah, N.J.: Paulist Press, 1999.

Stiebert, Johanna. "Shame and Prophecy: Approaches Past and Present." *Biblical Interpretation* 8 (2000): 255–75.

Stoker, Bram. *Dracula*. Edited by Nina Auerbach and David J. Skal. A Norton Critical Edition. New York: W. W. Norton & Company, 1997.

Strada, Michael, and Harold Troper. *Friend or Foe? Russians in American Film and Foreign Policy, 1933–1991*. Lanham, Md.: Scarecrow, 1997.

Sulloway, Frank J. *Born to Rebel: Birth Order, Family Dynamics, & Creative Lives*. New York: Random House, 1996.

Sutin, Lawrence. *Divine Invasions: A Life of Philip K. Dick*. New York: Harmony Books, 1989.

——, ed. *The Shifting Realities of Philip K. Dick*. New York: Vintage, 1995.

Synder, William P. *The Politics of British Defense Policy*. N.p.: Ohio State University Press, 1964.

Tocqueville, Alexis de. *Democracy in America*. Edited by J. P. Mayer. Translated by George Lawrence. Garden City, N.Y.: Anchor, 1969 [1850].

Todorov, Tzvetan. *The Fantastic*. Translated by Richard Howard. Cleveland: Case Western Reserve University Press, 1973.

Tolkien, J. R. R. "On Fairy Stories." In *The Tolkien Reader*, 33–99. New York: Ballantine Books, 1966.

Trotter, F. Thomas. "Variations on the 'Death of God' Theme in Recent Theology." In *The Meaning of the Death of God. Protestant, Jewish and Catholic Scholars Explore Atheistic Theology*, edited by Bernard Murchland, 13–24. New York: Vintage, 1967.

Twitchell, James B. *Dreadful Pleasures: An Anatomy of Modern Horror*. New York: Oxford University Press, 1985.

van Gennep, Arnold. *The Rites of Passage*. Chicago: University of Chicago Press, 1960.

Vaux, Sara Anson. *Finding Meaning at the Movies*. Nashville: Abingdon Press, 1999.

——. "'Will You Ever Kill Anybody Again, Karl?'" *Christianity and the Arts* 5 (1998): 20–22.

Venturi, Franco. *Roots of Revolution: A History of the Populist and Socialist Movements in Nineteenth-Century Russia*. Translated by Isaiah Berlin and Francis Haskell. Chicago: University of Chicago Press, 1983.

von Rad, Gerhard. *Genesis*. Translated by John H. Marks. Philadelphia: The Westminster Press, 1961.

Wagar, W. Warren. "The Rebellion of Nature." In *The End of the World*. Edited by Eric Rabkin, Martin H. Greenberg, and Joseph G. Olander, 73–96. Carbondale: Southern Illinois University Press, 1983.

Waldman, Diane. "Film Theory and the Gendered Spectator: The Female or the Feminist Reader." *Camera Obscura* 18 (1988): 80–94.

Walker, Janet. "Psychoanalysis and Feminist Film Theory: The Problem of Sexual Difference and Identity." In *Multiple Voices in Feminist Film Criticism*, edited by D. Carson, L. Dittmar, and J. R. Welsch, 82–92. Minneapolis: University of Minnesota Press, 1994.

Walker, Michelle Boulos. *Philosophy and the Maternal Body: Reading Silence*. London: Routledge, 1998.

Walsh, Richard. *Reading the Bible: An Introduction*. Notre Dame, Ind.: Cross Cultural Publications, 1997.

Warrick, Patricia S. *Mind in Motion: The Fiction of Philip K. Dick*. Carbondale: Southern Illinois University Press, 1987.

Weart, Spencer R. *Nuclear Fear: A History of Images*. Cambridge, Mass.: Harvard University Press, 1988.

Weber, Max. *Economy and Society: An Outline of Interpretive Sociology*. Edited by Guenther Roth and Claus Wittich. 2 vols. Berkeley: University of California Press, 1978.

——. "The Protestant Sects and the Spirit of Capitalism." In *From Max Weber: Essays in Sociology*, edited and translated by H. H. Gerth and C. Wright Mills, 302–22. New York: Oxford University Press, 1946 [1906].

Weber, Samuel M. "Introduction to the 1988 Edition." In Daniel Paul Schreber, *Memoirs of My Nervous Illness*, translated by Ida Macalpine and Richard Hunter, vii–liv. Cambridge, Mass.: Harvard University Press, 1988.

Weems, Renita J. *Battered Love: Marriage, Sex and Violence in the Hebrew Prophets*. Minneapolis: Fortress, 1995.

Wettstein, A. Arnold. "Religionless Religion in the Letters and Papers from Monticello," *Religion in Life* 45 (1976): 152–60.

Wevers, John. W. *Ezekiel*. The Century Bible. London: Thomas Nelson & Sons, 1969.

Whitfield, Stephen. *The Culture of the Cold War*. Baltimore: John Hopkins University Press, 1996.

Williams, Raymond. *The Sociology of Culture*. Chicago: University of Chicago Press, 1981.

Wilson, Bryan. *Magic and the Millennium*. New York: Harper & Row, 1972.

Wilson, Katharina M. "The History of the Word *Vampire*." In *The Vampire: A Casebook*, edited by Alan Dundes, 3–11. Madison: University of Wisconsin Press, 1998.

Winnington, Richard. "Bicycle Thieves." *Sight and Sound* 19 (1950): 26.

Wittgenstein, Ludwig. *Philosophical Investigations*. Translated by G. E. M. Anscombe. Malden, Mass. and Oxford: Blackwell, 1997 [1953].

Worley, Lloyd. "Anne Rice's Protestant Vampires." In *The Blood Is the Life: Vampires in Literature*, edited by Leonard G. Heldreth and Mary Pharr, 79–92. Bowling Green, Ohio: Bowling Green State University Popular Press, 1999.

Wright, Basil. "Flesh, Fowl or . . . ?" *Sight and Sound* 19 (1950): 43 and 45.

Wright, Will. *Six Guns and Society: A Structural Study of the Western*. Berkeley: University of California Press, 1975.

Yacowar, Maurice. "Love vs. Honour: *Donnie Brasco* and *Sling Blade*," *Queens Quarterly* 104 (spring 1997): 57–69.

Yeats, W. B. "The Second Coming." [cited 11 June 2001]. Available from http://www.well.com/user/eob/poetry/The_Second_Coming.html.

Zamora, Lois, ed. *The Apocalyptic Vision in America: Interdisciplinary Essays on Myth and Culture*. Bowling Green, Ohio: Bowling Green University Popular Press, 1982.

Zanger, Jules. "Metaphor into Metonymy: The Vampire Next Door." In *Blood Read*, edited by Joan Gordon and Veronica Hollinger, 17–26. Philadelphia: University of Pennsylvania Press, 1997.

Zimmerli, Walther. *A Commentary on the Book of the Prophet Ezekiel. Vol. 1, Chapters 1–24*. Translated by Ronald E. Clements. Hermeneia. Philadelphia: Fortress, 1979 [1969].

Žižek, Slavoj. *For They Know Not What They Do: Enjoyment as a Political Factor*. London: Verso, 1991.

——. *The Sublime Object of Ideology*. London: Verso, 1989.

——. *The Ticklish Subject: The Absent Centre of Political Ontology*. London: Verso, 1999.

CONTRIBUTORS

George Aichele is professor of philosophy and religion at Adrian College, Adrian, Michigan. He is author of *The Control of Biblical Meaning: Canon as Semiotic Mechanism* (Trinity Press), editor of *Culture, Entertainment, and the Bible* (Sheffield Academic Press), and a coauthor of *The Postmodern Bible* (Yale University Press).

Roland Boer is Logan Research Fellow at Monash University, Melbourne, Australia. His research for the fellowship considers the implications of the tradition of Marxist literary criticism for biblical studies as well as the way Marxist theorists have engaged directly with the Bible. His most recent publications are *Knockin' on Heaven's Door* (Routledge) and *Last Stop Before Antarctica* (Sheffield Academic Press).

Ralph J Brabban received his Ph.D. in biblical studies from Baylor University in 1984. He is currently chair of the Department of Religion and Philosophy at Chowan College, and he resides in Murfreesboro, North Carolina.

Fred Burnett holds the Chora Chair of Christian Origins at the Universidad de Karen Elliott in Juarez, Mexico, where he also serves as interim president and provost. He has written *The Testament of Jesus-Sophia* (University Press of America) and articles for several major journals, and he was a coauthor of *The Postmodern Bible* (Yale University

Press). He is currently working on a book on postmodern historiography, and is a book review editor for *Religious Studies Review* in the area of Christian origins.

CARL DYKE is a historian at Methodist College, Fayetteville, North Carolina. He has also taught sociology, philosophy, and human development. His work covers theories of society, politics, and culture. He is currently revising a manuscript on the prehistory of postmodernism in which the main characters are Gramsci, Durkheim, and Weber.

JULIE KELSO is working on her doctoral thesis at the University of Queensland, Australia. In her thesis she considers the anomalies of female characters in the male dys/utopian text of Chronicles—Maacah, Athaliah, Huldah, and the Queen of Sheba—engaging with the work of Luce Irigaray. She has a background in visual theory and English literature.

NEAL R. McCRILLIS is the Mildred Miller Fort Foundation Distinguished Chair of International Education, director of the Center for International Education, and associate professor of history at Columbus State University in Columbus, Georgia. He is a specialist in British twentieth-century history and has published *The British Conservative Party in the Age of Universal Suffrage* (Ohio State University Press). He is now conducting research on British films during the Cold War and working on a multi-volume collection of Conservative Party documents.

TINA PIPPIN teaches religion and women's studies at Agnes Scott College, Decatur, Georgia. She is the author of *Apocalyptic Bodies: The End of the World in Text and Image* (Routledge), a coauthor of *The Postmodern Bible* (Yale University Press), and a coeditor of *The Postmodern Bible Reader* (Blackwell).

JENNIFER ROHRER-WALSH is an associate professor of English and co-director of the Methodist College honors program in Fayetteville, North Carolina. In addition to teaching literature for children, she has written three children's books. Her current work, a book of fables, focuses on national and state park regulations that differentiate humans from nature.

MARK RONCACE is a Ph.D. candidate in Hebrew Bible and an instructor at Emory University. His dissertation is a narratological and intertextual analysis of Jeremiah 37–40.

ERIN RUNIONS is a postdoctoral research associate at the Center for Research on Women at Barnard College, Columbia University, and (somewhat paradoxically) an anarchist anticapitalist, anti-neo-colonization activist. Her work seeks to bring together politics, culture, and the reading of biblical text, a task that she theorizes most extensively in her recent book, *Changing Subjects: Gender, Nation, and Future in Micah* (Sheffield Academic Press).

JEFFREY L. STALEY teaches New Testament part time in the Department of Theology and Religious Studies at Seattle University, Seattle, Washington. His interest in film goes back to his days as a doctoral student at the Graduate Theological Union in Berkeley, California, where Seymour Chatman, author of *Story and Discourse: Narrative Structure in Fiction and Film*, served on his dissertation committee.

RICHARD WALSH is assistant academic dean, co-director of the honors program, and professor of religion at Methodist College, Fayetteville, North Carolina. He is the author of *Reading the Bible: An Introduction* (Cross Cultural) and *Mapping Myths of Biblical Interpretation* (Sheffield Academic Press).

INDEX OF NAMES

327

INDEX OF TEXTS

NONCANONICAL SCRIPTURES